Status Communities in Modern Society

STATUS COMMUNITIES IN MODERN SOCIETY

Alternatives to Class Analysis

Editor
HOLGER R. STUB
Temple University

The Dryden Press Inc.
Hinsdale, Illinois

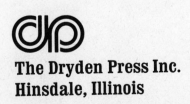

To Chresten and Anna Stub

Library of Congress Catalog Card Number: 70-187767
ISBN: 0-03-089146-9
Printed in the United States of America

PREFACE

This book is intended primarily for undergraduate or graduate students of social stratification. Though a book of readings, it can be used as a textbook and, as such, it allows for the use of additional monographs or studies for assigned reading pertinent to a course in social stratification.

The Weberian approach to stratification is followed, with special emphasis upon the importance of developing a new conception of middle strata in modern industrial society. The concept of *status community* is advanced as a possible alternative to the traditional rhetoric of social class. The articles emphasize the problems of using class analysis to describe and theorize about the middle levels of modern society. They provide theoretical and descriptive materials supporting the conception of status community. Hopefully, the consistency of perspective offered will present the reader with more than simply a collection of interesting readings.

Eight sections are provided, each with an introduction providing additional material for that section. These introductions also are to help the reader effectively interpret the readings that follow.

In addition to my intellectual debt to Max Weber, I am also deeply indebted to all the contributors of articles appearing in this work. I also wish to acknowledge a few of those who have influenced my thought and work in the area of social stratification; among my teachers were Don Martindale, F. S. Chapin,

Arnold Rose, and Roy Francis. The intellectual stimulation of Weber, Ossowski, Dahrendorf, Bensman, Riesman, Mills, Mayer, Wrong, Bottomore, and Lenski has been important in developing the perspective I hold on matters of inequality and stratification. I also wish to thank my friends and colleagues, Robert A. Kleiner and Jack V. Buerkle for the helpful criticism and the encouragement needed to carry out this project. Finally, I owe a great deal to the forebearance of an understanding family, Elin H. Stub, Lisa, and Peter.

CONTENTS

Status Communities in Modern Society

INTRODUCTION

"Some are more equal than others" may not be a very profound sociological generalization, but it does express social reality, even for men living in modern democratic societies. Inequality is a significant fact in human social life and, since the beginning of modern history, has led to a great deal of commentary. The study of inequality, called *social stratification*, has exhibited great vigor and growth in recent times. Despite the studies that began in 1929 with the Lynd's Middletown, and the large-scale research projects of the 1950's, especially the Yankee City series, the first textbook in social stratification was not published until the early 1950's.[1] Whatever else the production of textbooks may mean, it does signify someone believed that sufficient data, systematic thought, and academic interest was available to warrant textbook writing and publication.

Although eight to ten textbooks and several anthology editions have been published since the first, the field of social stratification continues to be characterized by a considerable amount of theoretical confusion. The purpose of this

[1] Joseph Kahl, *The American Class Structure* (New York: Holt, Rinehart and Winston, 1953); John F. Cuber and William F. Kenkel, *Social Stratification in the United States* (New York: Appleton-Century-Crofts, 1954); Kurt B. Mayer, *Class and Society* (New York: Random House, 1955). One of the first readers in sociology was Reinhard Bendix and Seymour M. Lipset, *Class, Status and Power* (New York: The Free Press, 1953).

collection of readings is threefold. First, a series of articles is included which highlight some of the problems centering around the use of the concept of social class for analysis of stratification in modern society. Second, readings are included to point the way to a more fruitful set of concepts and, hopefully, to illustrate the logic of incorporating the concept of status community, in addition to other concepts from Max Weber, into the body of accepted stratification theory. Finally, articles are included to introduce a unique set of descriptive materials concerning classes and status communities in American society. These articles also present the interrelated aspects of stratification, such as status symbols, prestige, life style, elites and status circles, and social mobility.

DEFINITIONS OF STRATIFICATION

The lack of a generally accepted theory of stratification has resulted in a number of competing concepts and definitions. It is apparent that the major concept in the field of stratification is *social class*. This term, however, encompasses a variety of bold conceptual and operational definitions. Unfortunately, the wide use of the concept of social class does not imply any great theoretical development or consistency. On the whole, the field of stratification in American sociology has lacked systematic theoretical guidelines. Definitions of social class have varied from the use of rough income levels; vague and subjectively defined prestige categories (such as scales for determining family prestige level from the contents of living rooms); to composite measures based upon such characteristics as income, education, occupation, house type, dwelling area, or ethnic identity. Arnold Rose has stated: "Specification as to the ingredients and procedures used in formulating a measure of class are almost as numerous as the researchers who use the concept. The result is that nearly anything can be shown to be related or not related to class in the United States."[2]

American sociologists, in contrast to their European colleagues, have used a wide variety of non-Marxist definitions of social class. Despite the fact that Marx gave the concept of class a prominent place in the literature of stratification, Americans generally have ignored him, other than paying him homage as the first important stratification theorist.

In attempting to devise specific ways of measuring social class, various *operational* definitions have emerged. One of these is W. Lloyd Warner's *Index of Status Characteristics*, which is formed by combining measures of (1) source of income (inherited wealth, salary, wages, and so on), (2) occupation, (3) dwelling area (section of the town or city in which the person lives), and (4) house type. Each of these four status characteristics are rated by the interviewer on a seven point scale. Generally, each characteristic is given a different weight. For example, occupation may receive a weight of 4, source of income and house type each a weight of 3, and dwelling area a weight of 2. The values found on the 7

[2] Arnold M. Rose, "The Concept of Class in American Sociology," Chapter 24 in this volume.

point scale are then multiplied by the appropriate weight. Any person or family rated thus could receive a weighted total ranging from 12 (highest status) to 84 (lowest status).

In research, indices constructed along the lines of the I.S.C. have been widely used to determine the relationships between social class and a variety of other phenomena, such as delinquency, separation and divorce, child-rearing practices, political behavior, mental disorder, and success in school. These research attempts often show interesting results. However, the measuring and validity of such scales is open to criticism. One such criticism, for example, is that there is no adequate system of "sociological arithmetic" available to add such basically different social characteristics as source of income, occupation, dwelling area, and house type. These four have no common basis for making comparisons. When we add up the numerical values assigned to each of the four characteristics by our seven point weighted rating technique, what kind of a sum do we get? One scholar has likened this bit of arithmetic to the adding of apples and oranges.[3] The result is simply a sum of *both* apples and oranges.

The *conceptual* definitions of social class used in a good deal of empirical research are seldom clear. They might refer to class, for example, in terms of Schumpeter's definition, given below, or they may refer to the kind of aggregates resulting from measures such as the I.S.C. or the Edwards scale of the U.S. Bureau of Census. This latter scale divides populations into six hierarchical groups called "social-economic classes." They are ranked in descending order; (1) professional persons, (2) proprietors, managers, and officials, (3) clerks and kindred workers, (4) skilled workers and foremen, (5) semiskilled workers and unskilled workers.

Part of the definitional confusion in both theory and method stems from a failure to distinguish between two conceptions of social stratification; one conception is based on the classic definition of social class, and the other utilizes various conceptions of social rank. An analysis of social classes implies a hierarchy of groupings, established over time, membership in which is self-consciously restricted to those deemed worthy by the possession of valued characteristics or symbols. As Schumpeter wrote:

> Class is something more than an aggregation of class members . . . a class is aware of its identity as a whole, sublimates itself to such, has its own peculiar life and characteristic "spirit." Yet one essential peculiarity . . . of the class phenomenon lies in the fact that class members behave toward one another in a fashion characteristically different from their conduct toward members of other classes. They are in closer association with one another; they understand one another better; they work more readily in concert.[4]

[3] Stanislaw Ossowski, *Class Structure in the Social Consciousness* (New York: The Free Press, 1963), chap. 3.

[4] Joseph Schumpeter, *Imperialism and Social Class* (New York: Meridian Books, 1951), p. 181.

Social ranking, by contrast, refers to gradations made on the basis of one or more relevant social characteristics. A population can be ranked by wealth, occupational prestige, education, and so on. But the aggregates of people resulting from any ranking based on one or more of these variables may or may not share a life style, common ideology, or consciousness of belonging together. They might not possess enough of an identity to warrant the possibility of such a collectivity passing on a set of common norms, values, and identifying behaviors to the next generation. Most research considering social inequality as a factor involves the use of *social ranking* rather than *social class* analysis.[5]

This collection includes some material expressing and illustrating the utility of Max Weber's perspective, relative to stratification, along with those showing the influence of that perspective. Essentially, Weber directed the emphasis from an overriding reliance on economic factors to a close scrutiny of factors such as status, prestige, and political power. The most relevant writings of Rose, Mayer, Wrong, and Wilensky are included among the theoretical statements included in Chapter 3. Much of this commentary is critical of current concepts and theoretical formulations. Several critics direct their aim at the concept of class. In general, they attempt to show its inadequacies as a conceptual tool for analyzing modern society.

An increased awareness of the variety of life styles at the middle income level has helped to aggravate the mounting criticism. The major contribution to the variety of life styles is the increase in social differentiation throughout the middle strata of modern society. In the field of stratification, social differentiation refers to certain kinds of heterogeneity present within the social structure. In this instance, the important elements of social differentiation are the (1) range of income levels, (2) variety of occupational groups, (3) range of prestige and deference, (4) differences in educational background, and (5) variety of political power groups in society. The increased heterogeneity in modern society does not, however, prevent the development of pervasive norms relating to consumer orientation.

David Riesman has argued that the middle class American is generally motivated to expect and work toward the acquisition of a "standard package" of consumer goods[6]—a phenomenon closely related to the development of mass advertising. However, even though such a characterization of the middle class may be true, it does not follow that, therefore, all middle level people share similar life styles. Adherence to the consumption norms implied by the "standard package" do not preclude the development of important differences in political attitudes, educational standards, intellectual norms, sociopolitical participation, family relationships, and other factors that distinguish life styles.

The great variety of life styles seriously threatens a conceptualization of the

[5] Ossowski, *Class Structure*, chap. 3.

[6] David Riesman, *Abundance for What? and Other Essays* (New York: Doubleday, 1964), pp. 111-146.

stratification structure in terms of broad classes. This would apply whether one is considering the simplified 2 to 3 class system of Marx or the 6 to 9 class system of Warner: the capitalist and proletariat classes of Marx; the upper upper, lower upper, upper middle, lower middle, upper lower, and lower lower classes of Warner. The particular economic opportunities, ideologies, and constraints that come to characterize the life styles emerging from the new occupations pose a number of questions for the student of stratification.

STATUS COMMUNITY: AN ALTERNATIVE

The problems outlined above argue for the utility of the concept of status community as an alternative to the concept of social class. The concept is Weber's, and its utility is dependent on the development and use of Weber's two other major stratification concepts—class (wealth, or economic power) and party (political influence).

Most of the readings do not explicitly follow Weber's approach. They are, however, chosen to present illustrative material tending to support Weber or to provide comprehensive descriptive data on modern life pertinent to the development of Weberian conceptions. Weber's basic concepts of class, status, and party (the latter often expressed as power) refer to three analytically distinct dimensions of stratification. By *class*, Weber refers to the specific economic component of individual and family life manifested by "the possession of goods and the opportunities for income."[7] *Status* refers to "status groups," or communities of an amorphous type consisting generally of those sharing the same honor and deference. Status honor is "expressed by the fact that . . . a specific *style of life* can be expected from all those who wish to belong to the circle."[8] Weber's third stratification variable is *party*, which pertains to collectivities that function for the purpose of exercising power in the sphere of communal action, for example, the area of politics.

Although the three stratification dimensions advanced by Weber are highly interrelated in social life, they can be analytically distinguished. As previously mentioned, this set of readings is presented in the interest of advancing the theoretical and methodological development of these three dimensions, with particular emphasis on the concept of status and status community.

In Chapter 1, "Theoretical Perspectives of Stratification," two readings deal primarily with the history of inequality and some of the forms it has taken as well as some of the major attempts at explaining these forms. Weber's classic work on "Class, Status, and Party," along with a selection from Schumpeter's work are included in this section.

Chapter 2, "Contemporary Theoretical Conceptions of Stratification," in-

[7] Hans H. Gerth and C. Wright Mills (eds.), *From Max Weber: Essays in Sociology* (New York: Oxford, 1946), p. 181.

[8] Gerth and Mills, ibid., p. 187.

cludes works from Rose, Mayer, Wrong, and Wilensky. This section focuses on inadequacies in the concept of social class for analyzing the modern industrial state. The concluding article draws on the arguments set forth in the preceding articles, among others, and illustrates the possible utility of adopting the concept of status community to describe and ultimately analyze stratification in modern society. In a sense it is an attempt to present a slightly different way of looking at the so-called "middle mass" phenomenon. This phenomenon is seen as characterizing the bulk of the population falling between the more clearly delineated strata at the top and bottom of contemporary social structure. On closer inspection, this middle mass seems to be much less homogeneous than the concept "mass" suggests. It demands new, more precise conceptions. The blurred perspective offered by concepts incorporating the idea of *mass* in dealing with parts of the social structure obscures the differences in life style, consumption behavior, and other social realities as much, if not more, than the concept of class.

Chapters 3, 4, and 5 include articles illustrating basic theoretical propositions or describing characteristics of existent social strata and status communities in the United States. Bensman's basic article on the "Musical Community," not only develops a theory of status communities, but illustrates the degree to which occupational specialization can lead to the formation of a status community. Articles ranging from Cohen and Hodges' "The Characteristics of the Lower Blue-Collar Class," to Freedgood's discussion of "Life in Bloomfield Hills," show the diversity of life styles that exist. The paper by Miller, "The American Lower Class: A Typological Approach," along with Lasswell's "Intellectual Status," indicate that some of our everyday generalizations in the area of stratification are very dubious, especially as they pertain to the middle levels of the social structure.

Chapter 6, "Status Symbols, Prestige, and Life Styles," focuses more precisely on the major indicators of life style and on status symbols of various types.

Chapter 7, "Elites and Status Circles," presents a number of articles dealing with the question of elites in modern society. The number and importance of the various established and emerging elites, strategic and otherwise, is further evidence of the incredible heterogeneity in the modern industrial state. New concepts dealing with the wide variety of stratification collectivities, status and ethnic communities, strata, and classes that appear to constitute contemporary social structure are sorely needed.

Chapter 8, "Social Mobility," includes a broad based discussion by Smelser and Lipset as well as works that indicate some of the personal and social psychological aspects of mobility.

CHAPTER 1

THEORETICAL PERSPECTIVES OF STRATIFICATION

Concern over inequality, power and privilege goes back to the origin of human society. The lead article in this section places the beginning of stratification at the dawn of civilization, 5000 years ago. While forms of social differentiation and social ranking are found in most societies, unstratified societies do exist. In East Africa, for example, a number of societies are organized by age-sets. Age-mates are social equals, and each age-set controls its members. At certain intervals new-sets, younger persons, are brought into the system, and all of the older age-sets move up one notch to the next age-grade. "Rights to marry, to beget children, to establish a homestead, to participate in civil and judicial councils, to officiate at rituals, to go on raids, are all variably integrated with this age-stratification."[1] Since the system operates on seniority, whatever inequalities are associated with a given age-determined position are always temporary. Smith asserts, that despite the distinctness and homogeneity of these age groupings, "it is patently ridiculous to designate these cohorts by the same term used for castes, estates, slavery, or social classes."[2]

[1] M. G. Smith, "Pre-Industrial Stratification Systems," in Neil J. Smelser and Seymour M. Lipset (eds.), *Social Structure and Mobility in Economic Development* (Chicago: Aldine, 1966), p. 150.

[2] Smith, ibid., p. 150.

Smith further identifies a number of primitive societies wherein the level of role differentiation is so slight that stratification apparently does not occur. When only a few social, economic, and political roles exist in a society, the likelihood of evaluation and invidious comparison seems to diminish. As Lenski has pointed out, a low level of differentiation and division of labor is associated with a minimum of economic surplus above the subsistence level. A society functioning at the subsistence level is likely to have relatively little inequality in the distribution of such basic needs as food, shelter, and clothing.[3]

Two elements in the history of most human societies that are prerequisite to stratification are *differentiation* of function or activities and their social *evaluation*. The vast increase in the number of social roles, jobs, and activities that characterized the change from primitive to modern society has made possible the development of many new life styles. The variety of human activities, along with an evaluation, has stimulated great variation in systems of authority and reward. These are important features in the types of social organization that emerge with a high level of differentiation.

The conscious evaluation of differences among men has become a feature of most societies. With evaluation, invidious comparison becomes tempting and, in fact, has become an integral aspect of the interpersonal relations of many men—status and prestige. The social effects of differentiation and evaluation present us with an interesting paradox. The increase in social differentiation has led not only to the making of invidious comparisons and their social and psychological consequences, but also to a new order of interdependence among men and their social organization. Moreover, increased differentiation has provided a wide set of optional jobs and functions that have, in turn, promoted great variety in the life styles open to modern man. Human choice, without which freedom is somewhat pointless, has been vastly expanded by these basic features in modern society. Yet, at the same time, the social distance between the richest and the poorest reveals much greater extremes than ever before in man's history. Thus, although inequality has increased, so has the opportunity for choice as well as the freedom so necessary for making choices.

There is little doubt that modern industrial societies have experienced social changes decidedly altering their stratification systems. In spite of the apparent increase in social differentiation, dichotomous conceptions of class structure have persisted in modern social thought. Ossowski[4] points to the long history of the dichotomic notion in the popular conceptions of stratification, as well as its being a long lasting academic classification. The assumption that the social structure forms a dichotomy of an upper and a lower class has been used in semi-conscious and conscious ways as guides for social action and political and social propaganda. The conception of society structured as a polarized, two-level status

[3] Gerhard Lenski, *Power and Privilege* (New York: McGraw-Hill, 1966), Chapters 4 and 5.

[4] Stanislaw Ossowski, *Class Structure in the Social Consciousness* (New York: The Free Press, 1963), chap. 2.

system, has shown remarkable persistence, despite the fact that it has seemed to be an oversimplification for a long time. Even during Marx's lifetime, the extent of differentiation manifested by the existence of numerous status groupings was clearly evident. In his own time, a dichotomic conception of class structure came into conflict with social reality.

Although Marx discussed classes other than the capitalistic and proletarian varieties, he did not give them a solid place in his scheme of social stratification. The class struggle, which he believed inevitable, was only possible when the capitalist society became fully polarized into two classes. Marx argued that some kind of two-class system had been characteristic of human society since early civilization. He saw societies throughout history as consisting of a series of dichotomous structures beginning with freeman and slave, proceeding to patrician and plebian, lord and serf, guildmaster and journeyman, and, finally, to capitalist and proletarian.

A considerable portion of Max Weber's work was devoted to an analysis of Marxian theories. He borrowed from Marx's rich sociological insights and fashioned a more comprehensive approach to stratification. His conceptualization fell between the somewhat "objective" approach of Marx and a "subjective" interpretation. Marx saw the content and quality of a man's life as determined by the objective facts of his relation to economic and other related social forces. Weber, though by no means downgrading economic factors, gave more room to some of the social, psychological and political aspects of stratification. By adding the dimensions of status and party to that of class, he provided, not only a theoretical recognition of the subjective features of prestige, honor, and status groups, but also the important element of political power.

Weber distinguished between property classes and acquisition classes. The latter constituted a class of persons who possessed highly salable personal attributes or expertise. The modern day professional manager, financial expert, and system consultants would be considered members of the acquisition class. Weber's elaboration on Marx and the resultant increase in the level of conceptual precision, brought him to recognize the importance of the middle levels, although he did not specifically give the middle class a prominent place in his scheme. During Weber's life, the heterogeneity of status groupings in modern society was such that a precise delineation of a middle class was all but impossible. The social changes wrought by urbanization and industrialization had brought about a degree of heterogeneity in social organization that defied easy definition or generalization. In fact, Weber's major emphasis in his discussion of stratification was on the dimension of status; itself directly related to the concept of status community.

1 *Harold M. Hodges*

STRATIFICATION THEN AND NOW

Bone fragments, rudimentary weapons, crude stone implements, occasional paintings and carvings: from such meager evidence archeologists have tentatively reconstructed some three-fifths of mankind's one-million-year span on earth. Ingenious as this detective work has been, our knowledge of early man is still flimsy. We can only speculate what his social life was like; and if we know little of his family and economic life, we know even less about who wielded the power and enjoyed the prestige, who was top dog and who was underdog. It is not, in fact, until the end of *pre*history—the more than 99 percent of the human era which pre-dates written records—that we can chart with any certainty the ways in which our ancestors *stratified* their societies.

PREHISTORY AND ANCIENT HISTORY

The Near East: The dawn of stratification

It was some 5000 years ago that the first "civilizations" emerged in the area which we identify today as Iran, Iraq, Egypt, and Israel. It was then and there, too, that the first truly stratified societies are thought to have evolved. In the nomadic and incipient agricultural stages which preceded the three earliest civilizations—in Mesopotamia, Egypt, and the Indus Valley—man apparently lacked the complex economic organization and the massing of population which must exist before permanent systems of stratification can take root. Until the people of this area settled in the great river valleys of the "fertile crescent" and forged economies based on domesticated herd animals and the cultivation of cereal, they were apparently roving bands of food gatherers, fishermen, and hunters. But once the encroaching deserts drove them into the rich valleys and encouraged them to form their first truly permanent settlements, they swiftly attained pinnacles of political, economic, esthetic, and social refinement.[1]

Although many of these ancient societies were to be short-lived in the face of barbarian invasions and wars with covetous neighbors, their patterns of

[1] See Gideon Sjoberg, *The Preindustrial City* (New York: The Free Press of Glencoe, 1960), Ch. 2, or two articles in *Scientific American*, 203 (September, 1963): Robert J. Braidwood, "The Agricultural Revolution," pp. 88-148, and Robert M. Adams, "The Origin of Cities," pp. 153-68; for concise yet scholarly accounts of the socio-economic structures of the earliest civilizations, see Graham Clark's *World Prehistory, An Outline* (Cambridge: University of Cambridge Press, 1962), Chs. 4 and 5, and Henri Frankfort, *The Rise of Civilization in the Near East* (Garden City, N. Y.: Doubleday Anchor Books, 1963) Chs. III and IV.

growth were strikingly similar: each gradually accumulated sufficient agricultural surpluses to allow for trade and manufacturing, and it was trade and manufacturing which supplied the main impetus for more accelerated growth and expansion. Villages located along trade routes grew into towns and then cities; urban growth in turn saw further specialization of labor, new industries, and the appearance of middlemen who sold the commodities contributed by farmers, artisans, and traders.

Rank hierarchies: Their emergence and their shapes

As these civilizations along the Euphrates, Tigris, Nile, and Indus rivers expanded and flourished, lasting *rank hierarchies* began to take hold. Most such Near Eastern societies were theocracies; their focal points were sacred cities, and they were governed by "divine" rulers–priest-kings and priestly followers–who gained increasing ascendance. Only later did secular nobles appear to challenge the dominion of the religious elite.[2] Some of these newer nobles had been bureaucrats and servants to kings; but most were ennobled warriors who achieved prominence when their societies were either threatened by conquest or when they sought forcibly to expand their own boundaries. The more affluent of the priests and warriors, then, were at the apex of the first civilizations.

The features of these civilizations, as we shall see, varied somewhat from society to society, but in most a small core of artisans and city-dwellers enjoyed intermediate status between the nobility and the mass of farmers, serfs, and slaves at the bottom.[3] Thus each of the early cities in Sumer and Akkad had its *patesi*–its hereditary civil and religious ruler. Yet the middle-ranking commoners fared unusally well because from the beginning they were committed to trade and industry. The basic economy was always agricultural in the rich deltas of the rivers, but commerce and industry, especially cloth-making, saw the growth of large-scale business operations. In Egypt of the First Dynasty, too, a middle class of professionals, scribes, artists, and artists [sic] prospered.

The plight of the masses

But in most of these earliest civilizations the preponderance of people enjoyed little freedom. Subservient to the land and to their rulers, they inherited their lowly social positions in a caste-like arrangement which effectively impeded upward mobility. They were peasants, and it was their lot to replenish the bins of the priest and warrior nobles.

Nor, typically, did these herdsmen and tillers of the soil profit from the

[2] It seems probable that the priests were generally the first to achieve power because of the belief of the masses that they inhabited a world of the supernatural; only the priesthood had the power to deal with the gods; for elaborations of this question, see the many works of Clark, Braidwood, and J. H. Breasted.

[3] Sjoberg, op. cit., Ch. 5; for vivid and well documented descriptions of such civilizations, see *The Horizon Book of New Worlds* (New York: American Heritage Publishing Co., Inc., 1962).

growing complexity and cultural richness of their homelands. Instead, the gap between top and bottom widened. The peasants became more and more subordinate to the dictates of the ruling elite; the latter, as its power expanded, increasingly consolidated its gains and ruled ever more harshly. Conquests of new territories only accelerated this exploitation of the masses. As markets became larger, agricultural productivity became all the more important; but instead of gaining additional freedom and rewards for their efforts, those who worked the soil drifted into serf-like status. Such, with variations here and there, was the basic drift as each of these earliest civilizations became more complex.

The birth of the middle class

In the meanwhile, as the "have-not" populace at the bottom was becoming both poorer and more numerous, the city-dwellers were solidifying their middle-class status. Proportionately miniscule as they were in numbers, craftsmen, artisans, traders, merchants, and professionals enjoyed an esteem which derived from their functional importance to the economy. The ascendance of the entrepreneur, in particular, was notably marked in the later, mercantile-oriented phases of Babylonian history, and among the sea-faring, trade-minded Phoenicians. Though they enjoyed somewhat less freedom and power, the artisan and craftsmen in these societies also won a measure of autonomy by organizing tightly knit guilds and marketing their scarce talents in a supply-and-demand context. At the nadir of these urban social structures were unskilled and semi-skilled working men; their lot was often as grim as that of the herdsmen and peasants. Yet as much as commerce and the artisan crafts flourished, the socio-economic systems in each of these countries tended to remain patriarchal, under the management of monarchs or their bureaucratic minions. And the worst, for the average inhabitant of these kingdoms, was still to come.

Logic would appear to dictate that serfdom and slavery would mark the earlier, not the later phases of the histories of civilizations. But this, as Hobhouse, Wheeler, and Ginsberg have demonstrated, has not been the case.[4] Instead, slavery *grew* with the advance of most civilizations. In the main a consequence of the capture of prisoners in the wars, enslavement was particularly marked in the Imperial phase of Egyptian history; and most of these slaves, as with the Sumerians and Semites so frequently captured by the Babylonians, were foreigners. Agricultural serfs, in the interim, although not slaves, did little better. They were, on the whole, miserably housed and poorly fed, despised and exploited by the middle and upper classes, and doomed to eke out a drab life under stern discipline.

It is humbling to recall that fully half of recorded history had passed before any of our ancestors in Europe could read or write. While Babylonia's King

[4] L. Hobhouse, G. Wheeler, and M. Ginsberg, *The Material Culture and Social Institutions of the Simpler Peoples* (London: Chapman and Hall, Ltd., 1915), Vol. II, p. 236.

Hammurabi was evolving his intricate written code, and at the time of the first pyramid building in Egypt, Europeans were constructing nothing more complex than kitchen middens–an anthropological nicety for garbage dumps. The most advanced of the continentals, the Swiss lake dwellers, were still enmeshed in the "New Stone Age"; the Near Eastern peoples, simultaneously, had advanced well into the Bronze Age.

Eastern superiority was not to last, however. One by one, the great kingdoms declined or collapsed. The Egyptian dynasties were to remain intact the longest; but successive invasions by Assyrians, Persians, Greeks, and Romans finally reduced the nation to second-rate status. Other civilizations–Assyrian, Chaldean, Persian–waxed and waned; but it remained for the Greeks to establish the most advanced civilization of all.

Greece: The golden age

Between 2000 and 1000 B.C., waves of Indo-European barbarians found their way down the mountainous Greek peninsula. They encountered the highly developed Minoan culture; but instead of laying it to waste, they adopted it and added to it. The drama of this invasion, capped by the fall of Troy, is chronicled in Homer's *Iliad* and *Odyssey*. In the four or five centuries following the Achaean and then the Dorian invasions, until 800 B.C., the Balkan peninsula suffered a "dark age" of stagnation. But in the half-millenium to follow, Greek culture was to soar to new heights. The accomplishments of Classical Greece, particularly during the Age of Pericles, are far too vast and complex to allow for comment here. It is the Greek social-class structure, instead, which is our concern.

From the beginning, the class system of Greece was less rigid than the class systems which had prevailed in the Near East. But its features evolved slowly. During the dark ages the Greek city-states had each been dominated by clan chieftains; a noble class appeared next, only to be challenged by a new moneyed class which drew its wealth from industry and trade. The blue-blooded aristocracy compromised with reality, as they have so often since, by marrying into these emergent *nouveaux riches* ranks; thus a new governing oligarchy, wealthier and more powerful than before, held sway in such city-states as Athens, Sparta, and Corinth. The state of flux, however, continued; impoverished artisans and peasants threatened revolt, and their numbers were large enough so that their demands for democracy often proved effectual. In other cases "tyrants," sometimes of noble birth, championed the cause of the "common man," led him in revolt, and then became his often-enlightened rulers.

Each of the city-states varied. Sparta, for example, was rigorously hard-living, simple, and military, and Athens more devoted to a harmonious balance of body, mind, and spirit. In each, democracy alternated with despotism, oligarchy, aristocracy, and tyranny. But ultimately the "golden mean"–the ideal of moderation–and the classical emphasis upon the nobility of man led to the rule of the *demos*: the people. Even in Greece, however, democracy for *all* was more a myth than a reality.[5] Reigning supreme were the politically powerful citizens; below them, free but lacking the right to vote, were the members of the larger business community; at the bottom was the unfree class–slaves and agricultural serfs. Nor did slavery apall the Greeks, even the freedom-loving Athenians. Most slaves were captured "barbarians," and their labor was believed necessary in order to assure citizens the free time needed to cultivate the arts and to pursue civic duties. Some slaves, who in Athens comprised almost one-third of the population, worked as laborers and miners; others were employed as servants and entertainers. Many were well-treated and some were even emancipated; but most were at the mercy of their masters.

Hellenistic Greece emerged after the conquest of the city-states by Philip II of Macedon in 356-337 B.C. It was an age of extremes in wealth and poverty. Affluent bourgeoisie came to dominate the social scene, and the lot of the proletarian masses worsened. Indebtedness and unrest among the urban masses alternated with periods of enlightened largesse on the part of many of the wealthy. Slaves were badly treated on the one hand, yet often granted freedom and even citizenship on the other. It was an era of flux and shifting, confused values: Greek civilization was on the decline. The end came with the Roman conquest of Greece in 146 B.C.

The Roman empire: Legal democracy

The Romans quickly absorbed much of the artistic and intellectual culture of the Greeks, and within three centuries they had amassed an empire whose boundaries included the whole world of ancient civilization west of Persia: *pax Romana* ruled in what is now England, Belgium, Switzerland, France, Spain, Portugal, Morocco, Algeria, and Tunisia.

Democracy, especially in the political and legal sense, fared relatively well in the Roman empire. The earlier rule of the noble patricians gradually gave way to that of the plebeians; the latter won power because they contributed the main manpower to the Roman armies. But their victories were largely legal, not social and economic. The common man, it is true, could and did win a seat in the Plebeian Assembly, but only the wealthier commoners secured admittance to the Senate; and it was the politically potent Senatorial class which gained socio-economic dominance.

Thus the breach between rich and poor remained. Probably never before had the rank and file of a nation enjoyed such political freedom; neither, however, had urban tenements and slums ever been so common. Slavery, too, still prevailed (more than one Italian in four was a slave in the first century B.C.)–but, with the end of the foreign wars during the Augustan age, it gradually declined. Although the slaves' place was taken slowly by free tenant-farmers, the latter's economic lot was equally precarious. Agriculture, in fact, remained the basis of Roman wealth and occupied the energies of most of the population

[5] None elaborated the Greek ideals more cogently than Aristotle and Plato. . . .

even though trade had become the life-blood of the empire. Unhappy as the plight of the average Roman was, however, the social order was not altogether closed. Even the most humbly born could occasionally clamber to a position of economic abundance, in particular through the ranks of the army or bureaucracy.

After the death of Emperor Marcus Aurelius in 180 A.D. the Roman empire began its final decline. Amidst political disintegration and economic decay, artisans began to abandon their trades and city life rapidly deteriorated. Conditions were no better in the rural regions. As independent farmers fled before the invading streams of barbarians or simply abandoned their holdings because of economic failure, many returned to virtual serfdom under the aegis of the few large estates that could offer military and economic protection. Shortly, the pendulum of power and prestige had swung to the great Byzantine empire erected by Constantine. Continental Europe had entered the "Dark Ages"; it was to be virtually without a civilization for four centuries. Other systems of stratification emerged in the Byzantine and Islamic empires; but they differed only in degree from those which had prevailed throughout ancient history.

CASTE IN INDIA

The vast alluvial plains of the Indus Valley housed one of the three very earliest civilizations. Yet we know less of its history or character than we do of the complex societies which flourished at the same time in Mesopotamia and Egypt. Although short and dark-skinned men of a Stone Age culture were earlier inhabitants of the great Indian subcontinent, it was apparently the Aryans who forged India's true civilization. A light-skinned, fair-haired people of the same basic stock which peopled Greece in the second millennium B.C., they gradually pushed the original Dravidian natives southward and built a stable and intricate society upon the cultural base established by their predecessors.

Few written records survive to tell us about these people. We must instead rely upon evidence excavated by archeologists and upon a semi-mythical literature of hymns, rituals, religious writings, and philosophical treatises; above all we must depend upon the vast sacred lore known as the *Vedas*. And it is to the *Vedas* that we must turn for an idealized–not factual–description of India's system of social stratification.

Hinduism: The four Varnas

India's basic religion, Hinduism, apparently resulted from a merger of several earlier religions. Its spiritual core inheres in the belief in Brahman: a single, eternal, unchanging essence or soul which is embodied in each individual. But though each is invested with Brahman, Hindu adherents are not deemed quite equal. For each is born into a distinct *Varna* (or caste)–either the *Brahman, Kshatriya, Vaisya,* or *Sudra*. The *Brahmans* are priests and, as such, official purveyors of sacred lore. Their status is unsurpassed. Below them are the warriors and princely rulers of the *Kshatriya* caste. The third-ranking *Vaisyas*, far larger in numbers, include herdsmen, peasants, traders, craftsmen, and merchants. Occupying the very bottom niche are the *Sudras*; many are industrial workers and it is their lot to perform the most menial of tasks. There are others, however, whose lots are even lowlier and less enviable than the *Sudras'*: the outcastes. Variously known as *Pariahs, Chandalas,* and *Harijans*, and now as the Scheduled Castes, they are outside and below the four castes, beyond the pale of Hinduism. Members, for the most part, of isolated tribes, they are regarded as "scum."

This is the *ideal* Indian social order, a ". . . mythological rationalization developed by the dominant priests which has served to keep the other castes in their assigned places."[6] The reality is more complex: it consists of a vast mosaic of castes and subcastes, some defined sharply and some vaguely. There are perhaps 5000 of them and they are constantly forming and reforming; the four official categories comprise, in fact, hardly one-tenth of India's total population.

Castes in mid-century

Nonetheless, though not so rigid as religious theory would claim, castes are still a stark reality. Their features are so deeply embedded in India's mores, in fact, that even the government of the new democratically oriented India has not been able to breach their barriers effectively. Even though intercaste marriages are now legal and caste restrictions on education and public employment illegal, the system still continues. Industrialization and urbanization, it is true, have weakened its force; outcastes and *Sudras* can change their status identities in the impersonal *milieus* of such cities as Bombay and Calcutta; public schooling has lessened caste prejudices; consciousness of national identity and democratic ideals have altered caste-toned values, and members of diverse castes have been thrown together in the process of travel and migration. But the system, especially in rural areas and in urban slums, remains a dominant feature of the Indian social scene.

How did so inflexible a social system evolve? Only conjecture can supply the answers. Castes were apparently unknown in the early days of the Aryan invasion, although legend indicates that in the Persian society from which these Indo-Europeans came there were four caste-like groupings: priests, warriors, agriculturalists, and artificers. In the Aryan's new Indian home, nevertheless, warriors and priests, although accorded greater prestige, were not sharply differentiated from the peasants below them. Eventually, however, the invaders may have developed caste-type arrangements to serve as buffers from the darker-skinned individuals they encountered as they moved southward.[7] The growing complexity of religion, too, might have enacted a role: as in other early societies,

[6] Kurt B. Mayer, *Class and Society* (Garden City, N. Y.: Doubleday & Company, Inc., 1955), p. 15.

[7] Credence is lent this theory by the word *varna*; it is the Hindu word for "color."

prestige and power were probably granted the priests who were endowed with the ability to propitiate the gods. Hindu tradition, at any rate, relates that the major four-fold caste divisions were firmly established by 600 B.C.

Ritual purity: Taboos

If urbanites and the better educated are less committed to caste distinctions in today's India, the majority are still restrained by its intricate dictates in their everyday social intercourse.[8] For most, membership in castes and outcastes is hereditary and fixed for life; only rebirth might promise upward mobility. Ritual-laden taboos still prescribe that marriages are to be endogamous: that none may marry above or below his inherited rank; "ritual purity" deems that certain occupations–garbage disposal, for example–are unclean and fit for only certain castes; mere contact with such "untouchables" is thought contaminating, and there is a taboo against receiving food and drink from low-caste persons. Even water, if contaminated by the touch of a person of an inferior caste, may not be drunk. And in some areas of India, not simply touching, but passing near or even seeing a low-caste person is believed to be defiling. "Avoidance rites" decree that higher-ranking barbers must not shave the members of lower castes; others are forbidden to travel in public conveyances which carry inferior caste members. For the person who would violate such norms, punishment is swift and severe: caste expulsion. And, once expelled, he cannot be visited by his closest friends and even members of his family; he has become a pariah.[9] Such is the hold, even today, of the caste tradition. Its hold may be weakening in the larger cities, but for the rank and file of India's population, it is a stratification system which continues virtually unabated.[9a]

THE FEUDAL ORDER: MEDIEVAL EUROPE AND CONTEMPORARY SURVIVALS

It is perhaps ironic that no sooner had Christianity taken firm root in Rome than encroaching "barbarians"–Goths, Angles, Franks, Saxons, Vandals, and Huns–succeeded in splintering the once vast and compact empire. For if the precepts of Christ had introduced new, humanitarian values–the universal brotherhood of

[8] See B. Shiva Rao, *The Industrial Worker in India* (London: George Allen & Unwin, 1939), or Taya Zinkin, *Caste Today* (London: Oxford University Press, 1962).

[9] See E. A. H. Blunt, *The Caste System of Northern India* (London: Oxford University Press, 1931), Ch. 1.

[9a] For a readable analysis of the current status of India's caste system, see Subhash Chandra Mehta, "Persistence of the Caste System," *Atlas* 6 (November, 1963), pp. 268-273. Although admitting that "urbanism and industrialism will sound the death knell of the caste system, for modern factory organization cannot be efficiently geared to caste," Mehta adds that regardless of the many factors which are supposed to be disrupting the caste system, "it has withstood all onslaughts and is still a strong and tenacious force."

man and the equality of all, whatever their station, in the eyes of God–these were soon to be forgotten in practice.

A degree of order was restored on the European continent during the reign of Charlemagne; yet the period between his death in the year 814 and the Norman conquest of Britain in 1066 witnessed continuous warfare and political disorder. These were the Dark Ages at their ugliest. It was not, however, an era of total stagnation: what men did, even before 300 and continuing on throughout the Carolingian period to about 1000, William Carroll Bark has observed, "was to strike out in a new direction in search of new solutions to problems found unsolvable in the Graeco-Roman West of ancient times." It amounted, he adds, to the discovery of a "new, more traversable route through the maze of history."[10]

By the year 1100, Europe had begun to emerge as a solid socio-political entity. The classical inheritance was still confined to isolated monasteries, but the emergent kingdoms of France, England, Scotland, and the Scandinavian countries had gradually begun to supplant chaos with order. Although less "civilized" than the societies of Byzantium and Baghdad, these new European nations did encourage an inchoate renascence which was eventually to forge the continental Europe which we know today. The "Middle Ages" and their most characteristic feature–feudalism–had commenced.[11]

Feudalism: The Carolingian mold

The "feudal regime" flourished in many places–in certain of the Christian kingdoms of Spain, the Latin principalities of the Near East, in England, in virtually all of western Europe–but its main outlines took form in its original home: in the Franco-German regions lying between the Loire and the Rhine, the heart of the Carolingian state during the tenth, eleventh, and twelfth centuries. Although it assumed somewhat variant forms in different places,[12] wherever it flourished feudalism was essentially a means of carrying on some kind of government on a local basis where no organized state existed.

The status of townsmen and merchants, which had become so solidified and well-defined during the previous centuries, had been splintered during the precedent-shattering tumult of the Dark Ages. And, with fuedalism, a new socio-economic order emerged: *land*, rather than capital and marketable goods, became the only source of subsistence for virtually every man, woman, and

[10] William Carroll Bark, *Origins of the Medieval World* (Garden City, N. Y.; Doubleday & Company, Inc., Anchor books, 1959), p 343.

[11] For the reader who would seek highly readable accounts of this era, few sources are more commendable than George Holmes' *The Later Middle Ages, 1272-1485* (Edinburgh: Thomas Nelson and Sons, Ltd., 1962) and Friedrich Heer's *The Medieval World* (New York: The World Publishing Co., Mentor edition, 1963).

[12] Writing about feudalism in England, Holmes warns that the ". . . historian must acknowledge wide regional variations, stemming from geographical differences and distinctions of custom going back to the first English settlements, and perhaps beyond," when peoples from different social systems settled in different places. Ibid., p. 15.

child. "Everyone," Joseph A. Kahl notes, "from king to humblest peasant, lived directly or indirectly off the land, whether he personally cultivated the soil or confined himself to collecting and consuming the products."[13] Prestige and power in this new social complex came to depend, he adds, on the individual's hereditary relationship to the land. "Those who possessed land were free and powerful, while others were dependent both economically and politically."[14]

Feudalism, in the strictest sense of the term, involved only those of noble status; at first, before the system engulfed virtually the whole of continental Europe and Britain, the local count reigned supreme over his hundred-odd square miles of holdings. Lesser land-owning lords, caught between hostile or warring counts, aligned themselves with one count or another and became their vassals. Gradually, however, the counts themselves became the fiefs of dukes and even kings. In the end, virtually every feudal lord owed allegiance to a more powerful overlord or *suzerain*. Such relationships, often contractual, became reciprocal, two-way affairs. The *suzerain* on the one hand could offer his vassal protection, justice, and continuing ownership of his land. The knightly vassal, in turn, would be liable to service in his overlord's army and would owe him certain yearly fees.

Le peuple: The Third Estate

Feudalism was just as real for the rank-and-file peasant: he, like fully nine in every ten, was a serf. He lived in a village which, with its encompassing farmlands, constituted a "manor." Although it is probable that he seldom wanted to escape—for the outside world was certainly as perilous as it was unknown—he could only leave his manor with the permission of his "lord." Unlike a slave, however, he was more than a mere chattel with whom the lord could do as he pleased; he enjoyed a legal status which not only prescribed his duties to the lord, but the lord's to him. His status, in short, was essentially one of limited bondage. He was generally called upon to till so many yearly strips of cultivated land, to pay certain annual or sporadic tributes (for example, *tallage*: a kind of specious poll tax levied by lords when they needed funds or foodstuff), and to serve, when called, in the lord's military forces. And when he died, an inheritance tax was usually levied before his heir could take over his cottage and belongings. The lord, in turn, was obliged to give his serfs physical protection and to assure them a measure of justice (the celebrated *droit de seigneur*, for example, was rarely practised).

This, then, was the essential outline of manorial life for the peasant—a life which varied only in detail from one manor to the next.[15] Some of his masters

[13] Joseph Kahl, *The American Class Structure* (New York: Holt, Rinehart and Winston, 1953), p. 16.

[14] Kahl, ibid., p. 16; in fact, one writer observes, feudal society was ". . . the quintessence of hereditary aristocracy, privilege by birth instead of proved merit." Herbert J. Muller, *Freedom in the Modern World* (New York: Harper & Row, 1963), p. 67.

[15] See N. Nielson, *Medieval Agrarian Economy* (New York: Holt, Rinehart and Winston, 1936), Ch. II and Heer, op. cit., Ch. 2.

were harsh and others were gentle and paternalistic; but life, for most peasants, consisted of unremitting drudgery, crude but adequate living quarters, and simple pleasures. Theirs, in the official feudal structure, was the *Third Estate*. Above this socio-politico-economic unit–the estate of *le peuple*–were the two other recognized strata: the *First* (nobility) and the *Second* (clergy).[16]

Variations on the feudal theme

The three feudal estates were always less a social reality than a legal fiction. *Le peuple* were certainly at the bottom, but there were others, also technically members of this estate rank, who enjoyed a freer and more affluent life. These were the *villeins* or free and semi-free tenants whose station was roughly equivalent to today's sharecroppers on the Mississippi delta. Many such free peasants actually enjoyed a higher standard of living–and even a somewhat higher social esteem–than those parish priests of the Second Estate who lived and worked among the serfs. Aristocrats, too, commanded varying degrees of status. Some of the lowlier, with minimal land holdings, were no more than coequals with the more affluent *villeins*; still others–royal fiefs of princely rank or owners of vast agricultural possessions–consorted with bishops and archbishops.[17] The middling nobility, simultaneously, often possessed an actual social rank which was equivalent to that of prelates and *abbes*.[18] The discrepancies between estate level and status level were, then, a prominent feature of the feudal system.

Status, economic, and power inequalities occurred within the Third Estate as well. In general, the more rural and isolated a Feudal system, the more depressed and homogeneous was the lot of the peasant, and the more servile and serf-like his status. But in those areas situated along trade routes, and blessed with prolonged periods of peace and growing agricultural surpluses, a new element–the *bourgeoisie*–emerged. Its evolution was gradual but inexorable.

The rise of the bourgeoisie

With the decay of ancient cities which followed the breakup of the Roman empire, commercial centers and the merchants who populated them disappeared.

[16] This and the following descriptions of feudalism were drawn in the main from four sources: Henri Pirenne, *Economic and Social History of Europe* (London, 1936), Ch. 1; Edward P. Cheyney, *The Dawn of a New Era, 1250-1453* (New York and Evanston: Harper & Row, Publishers, Torchback edition, 1962); Marc Bloch, *La Societe Feudale* (Paris: Editions Albin Michel, 1940); and F. L. Ganshof, *Feudalism* (New York and Evanston: Harper & Row, Publishers, 1961).

[17] The nobility had much in common–their dependence on landed property and their initiation into the warlike arts of knighthood, for example–but there were obviously wide differences between the country knight, ". . . absorbed in the management of a small estate, hunting, and the politics of the shire, and the great earl who was a power in the court and kingdom" (Holmes, op. cit., p. 26).

[18] Within the ecclesiastical organization, a hierarchy of ranks and titles evolved which closely paralleled the ranks and titles of the nobility; but the priesthood was–officially–a celibate order and titles were thus non-inheritable. Yet, though entrance into the clergy was theoretically open to all, a disproportionate ratio of its initiates were drawn from the noble ranks (Heer, op. cit., p. 29).

As an agrarian economy supplanted the commercial, such basic crafts as metal working and weaving became confined to local manors. Gradually, however, pack-peddling itinerant traders appeared on the scene. Exhorbitant local tax levies, unpredictable transportation, and banditry made the plight of such traders a hazardous one. But as money came back into circulation and excess population saw craftsmen leave the manor for trade centers, a new cycle commenced.[19] In snowballing fashion, the more people moved to cities the more they needed a complex economic system which could provide them with food, clothing, and eventually, luxury items.[20]

It was the twelfth century, in particular, which saw the burgeoning of nascent towns and the consequent evolution of the *bourgeoisie* as a distinct social stratum. New towns sprang up throughout Latin Christendom, but they grew most rapidly along such natural trade arteries as rivers and sea coasts. Northern Italy, especially, but also the Baltic coast, the upper Danube, Rhine, Seine, and Thames rivers, and Flanders proved to be attractive environments for such independent city-states as Genoa, Venice, and Milan, and such free cities as Hamburg, Frankfort, and Nuremburg. As their power increased, the burgesses evolved all sorts of devices to protect and promote their interests; foremost among these was the *"gild,"* or guild, system. The latter, founded by butchers, bakers, stonemasons, hatters, goldsmiths, furriers and representatives of the scores of other trades which took hold with ever-increasing specialization, helped guarantee reliable products by establishing an intricate system of vocational training. Only after years as an apprentice and journeyman could a craftsman win his master's spurs; and those who achieved this status frequently became affluent business magnates with a considerable voice in their town's affairs.

There were professional men, too, in these medieval towns; lawyers and physicians were paramount among them. Yet they rarely enjoyed the status that they do today. The surgeon, for example, was typically a member of the low-status guild of barbers, and lawyers were often little more than civil servants with a smattering of formal schooling. The status of the *burgher*—the town dweller—was also ill-defined; neither churchman, noble nor free agricultural tenant, he only slowly acquired legal recognition. But, though never large in proportionate numbers, the townsmen had a profound effect upon the medieval social structure. They ushered in the commercial revolution—the necessary predecessor to the later industrial convulsion which would re-make the western world, they blurred class lines more than ever before, and the new social hierarchy which they created was the forerunner of the social class system which we know today.[21]

[19] John W. McConnell, *The Evolution of Social Classes* (Washington, D. C.: American Council on Public Affairs, 1942), p. 54.

[20] Pirenne, op. cit., p. 96.

[21] See Elinor G. Barber, *The Bourgeoisie of 18th Century France* (Princeton: Princeton University Press, 1955) for an account of the bourgeoisie of earlier centuries, see Herbert J. Muller, op. cit., pp. 72-80.

Serfdom did not die out immediately. It lingered in much of Germany until the revolutions of 1848, and it persisted in Russia until more recently. Nor did a significant segment of the population of Europe move to the cities until the nineteenth century. The urbanization of Europe had nonetheless commenced; the country-to-city flow, a mere trickle in its incipient phases, was eventually to become a torrent which would re-structure the socio-economic map of the Occidental world.[22]

THE CLASS ORDER: THE TWENTIETH CENTURY

Historical "epochs" are little more than convenient pigeonholes; such glib categories as the "Renaissance" or the "Age of Charlemagne," however deftly they summarize the complexity of the past, obscure a fundamental fact: the continuous, ever-flowing character of all history. And so it is with the "Industrial Revolution" which ushered in the "modern world." The best we can say is that *sometime* between A.D. 1700 and 1850, the western world underwent a quickened pace of evolution which, if not cataclysmic, profoundly altered the course of history. Trace the revolution to what we will–the opening of the North American continent, the breakthrough of science, the emergence of democratic governments, the advent of harnessed steam–its "causes" were exceedingly complex. They did not take place "overnight," nor could they have occurred at all without a milleniums-long cultural base on which to build.

The response to industrialism

Despite the re-birth of town life during feudalism's declining years, Europe's social and economic structure remained agrarian in character almost up to the American and French revolutions. But, particularly in the northwestern corner of Europe–in England, northern France, and the Lowlands–the "Commercial Revolution" laid the grounds for what was to follow. Commercial capitalism, together with its correlative economic philosophy, mercantilism, had paralleled the emergence of the national state. Capitalism, a system of production featuring the *entrepreneur*–a middle-man who bought the raw materials and hired the piecework employees who were to transform them into finished products–represented a critical advance. So did the growth of the first factories and their rudimentary production lines. Keyed by such inventions as the power loom and the spinning jenny, England's textile industry was the advance guard of a movement which would soon engulf the whole world of manufacturing. Then, in

[22] The preceding discussion, for purposes of clarity and economy, has been limited to the evolution of social classes in the ancient Near East and medieval Europe; for a detailed discourse on stratification in nonliterate societies, see Gunnar Landtman, *The Origin of the Inequality of the Social Classes* (Chicago: The University of Chicago Press, 1938). For an account of the social structure of post-feudal Europe, see Sir George Clark's *Early Modern Europe, from about 1450 to about 1720* (New York: Oxford University Press, Galaxy Edition, 1960).

quick succession, came the steam engine and the age of iron. New and more efficient means of transportation–canals and railroads–stepped up the process further. England, relatively unscathed by the generation-long Napoleonic wars, led the way; its Manchester-Liverpool industrial complex was the world's first. Belgium and the bordering fringes of northern France were industrialized next. Momentarily checkmated by political disunity, the areas of the Ruhr and Silesia, northern Italy, and the northeastern United States followed suit a bit later. Although belated too, the pace of industrialization in Japan and Soviet Russia proved even swifter. Today Communist China and India are undergoing similar transformations. In time, Latin America, Indonesia and the fledgling African states are certain to join the chase.

It is hardly surprising that the web of social stratification in these newly industrialized nations is undergoing radical re-alignment; the distribution of economic, status, and power rewards in any society is and must be delicately attuned to the prevailing socio-political conformation.

Class in industrial society: The growth of a new order

Historically, at least in the ancient Near Eastern, classical, and feudal eras, the social strata had been rather clearly demarcated. Boundaries, to be sure, were always in some degree permeable and fuzzy; but they were never again to be quite so sharply disjointed, nor were those who exercised the greatest power to be the selfsame people who enjoyed the greatest prestige and material abundance. Prior to the coming of the Industrial Revolution, those of top and bottom rank, and to a lesser extent those of middling rank, had each been characterized by distinctive styles of life: dress, speech, manners, education, recreation, and leisure-time pursuits varied sharply from level to level. One could tell at a glance who "belonged" where.

Industrialization and its diverse complex of corrolaries was to alter this picture. Not only was the number and alignment of class levels to be recast, but class-typed differences, so sharply defined through the ages, were to diminish. Even more dramatically, the *shape* of the industrial stratification system, previously pryamid-like–with the affluent few at the top and the indigent many at the base–was due for a revolutionary transformation.[23] A new level–the middle class–was to achieve a numerical and substantive dominance which many observers interpret as the most significant social change of our time.[24]

Viewed against the snail's-pace perspective of historical change, this divorce from tradition seems so cataclysmic that it amounts to a mutation. Yet the shift, as fundamental as it has been, is linked to a centuries-long drift which commenced with the last gasps of feudalism. The extremes, the upper class and the

[23] See Arnold Toynbee, *The Industrial Revolution* (Boston: Beacon Press, 1962).

[24] The intricate relationships between technological changes and the class structure of western Europe are discussed by G. D. H. Cole in *Studies in Class Structure* (London: Routledge and Kegan Paul, 1955), Ch. II.

lower, are of course not dead; and there are many who contend that one or the other will ultimately become dominant. But power alignments aside, it is apparent that the most industrially advanced peoples—the British and the Americans for example—are above all middle-class peoples.

The evolution of the middle class

The middle class, as we have seen, did not take hold overnight; but when capital supplanted land as the dominant key to power and status, the ascent of the middle class became inevitable. It was at first an inchoate level intermediate between the landed aristocracy and the proletariat. Its ranks were composed of an ill-defined grouping of professionals, independent enterprisers, craftsmen, and artisans. Shortly, however, the more imaginative, daring, and providential attained dominance. The reigns of many such men were to prove short-lived, but others, as population explosions provided unceasing manpower, were always on hand to take their places. These were the successful ones; some of them established merchant and manufacturing dynasties which prevail to this day. Beneath them in the power and economic hierarchy and larger in numbers were the slightly less prosperous entrepreneurs and professionals. Beneath them in turn, and numerically the most dominant, were successive layers of semi-professionals, small and salaried businessmen, salesmen, and clerks.

Colonial and Revolutionary America

The evolution of the middle classes took varying forms in each society. But no matter what their *millieu*, they were characterized almost from the start by an *open*-class value system: ideally, if not always in fact, admission to their ranks was based on talent rather than heredity. This was especially true in such fledgling nations as the United States and Australia; for in these societies there was no tradition of an entrenched aristocracy or peasantry. In the early colonial days, one writer admits, a certain measure of class distinction was evident. "Something resembling the caste (sic) system of England was transplanted to the American colonies. But the opportunities for middle class individualism were too great for caste monopoly and restriction to long endure."[25] There were, in fact, overtones of a middle-class revolt against upper-class privilege in the War of Independence. Although such an assertion seems somewhat bold in light of the complex ideological and economic pressures which precipitated the revolution, it is not altogether lacking in substance.

If the wealthier bourgeoisie were generally more loyal to the empire than the smaller merchants, the policy of economic repression instituted by the British in the 1760's rallied colonial opposition at all levels so effectively that the revolutionary die was inevitably cast. Yet in emphasizing the democratizing

[25] Henry Grayson, *The Crisis of the Middle Class* (New York: Holt, Rinehart and Winston, 1955), p. 85; see, too, Richard B. Morris, *The American Revolution* (Princeton: D. Van Nostrand Co., Inc., 1955), Ch. 1.

effects of the colonial revolution, we are liable to exaggerate. There were some leavening outcomes, it is true: the "all men are created equal" passage of the Declaration of Independence was to prove of lasting ideological consequence; many quasi-feudal survivals were swept away, the states north of Maryland abolished slavery, and the political principle of proportional representation—unknown in the parliamentary bodies of the old world—was adopted. Though on the whole the philosophy of natural rights and the humanitarian doctrines of the Age of Enlightenment promoted practicing democracy in America, the "common man" who enjoyed less than successful bourgeois status was to play an underdog role until the Age of Jackson some 30 years later. The upper reaches of the American middle class, on the other hand, had attained new highs in the realms of power and status.

The denouement of feudalism: The French Revolution

It remained, however, for the French Revolution to elevate the masses whom Edmund Burke characterized as the "swinish multitude." Until 1789 the Old Regime in France was still legally aristocratic and even feudal; French citizens still belonged by law to one of the three Estates. But popular conceptions to the contrary, it was not the impoverished masses who launched the French revolution. There was unrest among the urban proletariate and the rural peasantry, to be sure; but as in the Bolshevik uprising in Russia 128 years later, the mainspring of the rebellion was both intellectual and middle-class. It was above all the relatively prosperous landed peasantry and urban bourgeoisie, resentful because their economic power was not consonant with a like degree of political power and social prestige, and the writings of Voltaire, Rousseau and Jefferson, which truly ignited what amounted to the "revolt of the Third Estate." The French bourgeois, in fact, supported the revolution because, in part, *they favored the caste norms inherent in the Estate ideology.*[26] They rarely wished to overthrow privilege; they simply wanted part of it. They had achieved economic abundance, but were balked in their efforts to win the status and political power which attached to nobility.

The causes of the French Revolution were of course more subtle and multifold, but the ascendance of the middle class from the ranks of the peasantry was certainly one of its catalysts. When in the later phases of the revolution the urban proletarians took over the reins from the essentially bourgeois Robespierre, the "have-nots" seemed for a while to have won the day; yet it was not until the early part of the nineteenth century that the truly underprivileged gained any effective measure of bargaining strength. The French revolution,

[26] Cf. Bernard Barber, *Social Stratification, A Comparative Analysis of Structure and Process* (New York: Harcourt Brace Jovanovich, 1957), pp. 481-488; for a classical analysis of the causes and consequences of the revolution, see Alexis de Tocqueville's *The Old Regime and the French Revolution* (Garden City, N. Y.: Doubleday Anchor Books, 1955); see, also, Crane Brinton, *A Decade of Revolution* (New York: Harper & Row, 1963).

nonetheless—and to a lesser extent the Latin American revolts which followed—witnessed the final denouement of feudalism. The middle classes had finally broken the barrier. And an altogether *new* system of stratification had emerged triumphant.[27]

Modern social classes, unlike the feudal, are neither legal entities nor organized, self-conscious groups, "There are no official, rigid criteria of class position. Upper and middle class status symbols are in principle accessible to anyone with the necessary wealth to purchase them."[28] Of even greater consequence, the boundaries which separate the class levels are more "open" than ever before. They are no longer hermetically sealed in fact or in principle. This is not to say that feudal survivals are altogether absent: in agrarian nations in general—and in Latin America and Southeast Asia in particular—class lines are still hard, noble blood still begets disproportionate esteem, power, and economic wherewithal, and the bulk of the populations remain rural-dwelling, impoverished, and often without effective political representation. It is in the more industrialized nations, and above all in the urban nuclei of these nations, that the more fluid class norms and practices most dramatically prevail.

To stress the relative numerical and ideological dominance of the middle class in the industrial society is not to deny the staying power of social classes or the continuity of the upper class and the lower class. "Open-class" societies are still stratified societies; and there remain privileged and underprivileged strata wherever man has gathered in large and lasting social groups.

The upper classes in industrial societies

Except in many non-industrial societies, the definition of the term "upper class" is more troublesome than ever before. The confusion arises not so much from this level's changing membership as it does from the changing qualities which admission to its ranks entails. In ancient and medieval yesteryears, to be upper class meant that one simultaneously enjoyed superior power, social prestige, and economic abundance. But except for rare instances, to be "upper class" in America today means possession of one or at best two of these ingredients. As a result, it is less clear than ever just who is "upper" and who not. Are the "uppers" those listed in the exclusive pages of the *Social Register*? Are they the insiders in the political, military, or corporate power elite? Are they those who make up New York's flamboyant "Cafe Society"? Are they the sprinkling of nobility and entertainment-world celebrities who are perennially present at lavish "society" parties? Each is variously and in some degree legitimately labeled "upper"; yet despite some overlap here and there, the members of each group would probably exclude those in the remaining groups from their own

[27] For a richly documented description of the several social classes in "feudal" or pre-industrial societies in India, the Orient, the Near East, and Mexico as well as in feudal Europe, see Gideon Sjoberg, op. cit., Ch. V.

[28] Kahl, op. cit., p. 22.

inner circles. To complicate matters the more, none of these groups can claim disproportionate social esteem, power, or monetary plenty.[29]

The matter is only slightly clearer in Europe. For "society" there generally connotes "nobility": a distinguishable social unit whose membership is not only explicit, but also graded into clear-cut levels. Rare is the native of Britain who is unaware, for example, that an earl "outranks" a viscount; and if he is in doubt, he can readily turn to the authoritative pages of *Burke's Peerage*. Britain's House of Lords, too, is a highly visible seat of aristocracy. Yet being "born to the purple" in today's Europe means something altogether different from what it meant 500 or even 100 years ago. For the wealth, property, and power which formerly attached to noble status has been gradually dissipated by the inroads of commercialism and industrialism. A handful of noble families have managed to maintain their affluence; but most long ago abandoned their "stately homes" to the newly rich. The dissolute, shallow young blue-bloods caricatured by such authors as Charles Dickens and P. G. Wodehouse are largely a phenomenon of the past; the once-aristocratic doors of Oxford and Cambridge are increasingly open to the bright sons of manual laborers, and the sons of hereditary lords enter the once-demeaning ranks of commerce as readily today as they formerly did the army and the Church of England. Not only have a British king and a British princess married commoners, but commoners now freely consort in England's highest social circles.[30]

The scene is similar in other European countries. In France in particular, the gilded nobility has never regained the status and power it enjoyed before the Napoleonic wars; in other nations the ex-royalty and near-royalty have often fled to such last outposts as Portugal's Estoril coast. Except where "marriages of convenience" have kept the linkage between aristocracy and wealth intact, a new nobility of talent and money now reigns supreme in the cities of Europe.[31]

The underdog

Lower classes still endure in Europe and America. But in contrast to that of the nobility, their social and economic status has generally improved more than it has deteriorated. Particularly in highly industrialized Germany, Britain, France, Belgium, and the United States, and especially in the post-World-War-II years, the economic gap between the bottom and the top has narrowed. Class-consciousness and advocacy of the Marxian doctrine of class warfare is more dominant in Europe than in America. But even in France and Italy, where close

[29] This muddled picture is well described by Cleveland Amory in *Who Killed Society?* (New York: Harper & Row 1960); nor is the question of "elite" status altogether clear in England; see, for example, G. D. H. Cole, *Studies in Class Structure*, op. cit., pp. 68-69 and 101-107.

[30] For an account of "elites" in British society, see ibid., Ch. V.

[31] See A. Goodwin (ed.), *The European Nobility in the Eighteenth Century* (London: Adam and Charles Black, 1953).

to 50 percent of the laborers have on occasion aligned themselves with the Communist party, the underprivileged have increasingly identified more with their nations' destinies than with fellow-laborers in other lands. Pockets of poverty and sub-marginal subsistence still exist,[32] and economic recessions still hurt the unskilled and semi-skilled more than the white collarite; but the standard of living in industrial nations has gradually risen, and none have benefitted more concretely and dramatically than the least skilled segments of labor.

Though industrialism has supplanted feudalism, people are still "unequal"; but new *sources* of inequality have taken the place of traditional sources. Social position is no longer so intimately dependent upon heredity, nor is high or low status inevitably a corollary of high or low power and income. Marketable talent and occupational skill are more and more the basic determinants of class placement. More than ever before, one's full-time occupational role, and the skill with which he performs that role, determine a man's place in the socio-economic spectrum. Further, the occupant of an "inferior" social position has increasing access to "superior" symbols of status. Although lower class in fact, he can frequently "play the role" attaching to middle-class status so adroitly that many will take him to be middle class.

In short, the boundaries which once so sharply and clearly defined class position are becoming ever-fuzzier and ill-defined; mass communications and mass education have afforded the necessary clues and mass production the necessary means to breach the gaps. This is not to claim that inter-class mobility has continually speeded up or that social classes will eventually cease to exist. It is merely that the more visible and tangible components of class position have been weakened. This is true in Europe and in America, too.

Our equalitarian ideology notwithstanding, social classes and social-class differences continue to differentiate American from American in important ways. The Soviet Union too, despite official denials and the promise of the Marxian dialectic, is stratified in a manner markedly similar to our own society.[33] Those agrarian and semi-urbanized societies which have inherited a semi-"feudal" tradition are obviously stratified.[34]

32 . . . Among the more persuasive indictments of John K. Galbraith's popular notion that poverty in this country is no longer "a massive affliction [but] more nearly an afterthought" are Dwight Macdonald and Michael Harrington. See Macdonald, "Our Invisible Poor," *The New Yorker* (January 19, 1963) and Harrington, *The Other America, Poverty in the United States* (Baltimore: Penguin Books Inc., 1963).

33 Alex Inkeles, "Social Stratification and Mobility in the Soviet Union: 1940-1950," *American Sociological Review*, 1950, 15: 465-479.

34 Hsiao-Tung Fei, "Peasantry and Gentry: An Interpretation of Chinese Social Structure and Its Changes," *American Journal of Sociology* (July, 1946), pp. 1-17. Strictly speaking, F. L. Ganshof advises, "true feudalism was confined to France, Germany, the Kingdom of Burgundy, Arles and Italy during the Middle Ages (op. cit., p. xx). Marc Bloch's term, "feudal society," is perhaps closer to the semi-feudalism of other peoples and other times.

2 *Joseph Schumpeter*

THE PROBLEM OF CLASSES

1. We here mean by classes those social phenomena with which we are all familiar—social entities which we observe but which are not of our making. In this sense every social class is a special social organism, living, acting, and suffering as such and in need of being understood as such.[1] Yet the concept of class occurs in the social sciences in still another meaning—a meaning shared with many other sciences. In this sense it still corresponds to a set of facts, but not to any specific phenomenon of reality. Here it becomes a matter of classifying different things according to certain chosen characteristics. Viewed in this sense, class is a creation of the researcher, owes its existence to his organizing touch. These two meanings are often annoyingly mixed up in our social-science thinking, and we therefore emphasize what should be self-evident, namely, that there is not the slightest connection between them as a matter of necessity. Whenever there is any actual coincidence of their contents, this is either a matter of chance, or—if it is really more than that—must be demonstrated, generally or specifically, by means of pertinent rules of evidence. It can never be assumed as a matter of course. This word of caution applies especially to the field in which theoretical economics operates. In theoretical economics, a landlord—the very term implies the confusion we oppose—is anyone who is in possession of the services of land. But not only do such people not form a social class. They are divided by one of the most conspicuous class cleavages of all. And the working class, in the sense of economic theory, includes the prosperous lawyer as well as the ditch-digger. These classes are classes only in the sense that they result from the scholar's classification of economic subjects. Yet they are often thought and spoken of as though they *were* classes in the sense of the social phenomenon we here seek to investigate. The two reasons that explain this situation actually make it more troublesome than it would otherwise be. There is, first, the fact that the characteristic by which the economist classifies does have some connection with the real phenomenon. Then there is the fact that the economic theorist finds it exceedingly difficult to confine himself strictly to his problems, to resist the temptation to enliven his presentation with something that fascinates most of his readers—in other words, to stoke his sputtering engine with the potent fuel of the class struggle. Hence the amusing circumstance that some people view any

[1] We also mean to imply that a class is no mere "resultant phenomenon" [*Resultatenerscheinung*], such as a market, for example (for the same viewpoint, from another theoretical orientation, see Spann, loc. cit. [sic]). We are not concerned with this here, however. What does matter is the distinction between the real social phenomenon and the scientific construct.

distinction between economic theory and the facts of social class as evidence of the most abysmal failure to grasp the point at issue; while others see any fusion of the two as the most abysmal analytical blundering. Hence, too, the fact that the very term class struggle, let alone the idea behind it, has fallen into discredit among the best minds in science and politics alike—in much the same way that the overpowering impression of the Palazzo Strozzi loses so much by its inescapable juxtaposition with the frightful pseudo-architecture of modern apartment houses.

2. Of the many sociological problems which beset the field of class theory—the scientific rather than the philosophical theory, the sociological rather than the immediately economic—four emerge distinctly. First, there is the problem of the *nature* of class (which is perhaps, and even probably, different for each individual scientific discipline, and for each purpose pursued within such a discipline)—and, as part of this problem, the function of class in the vital processes of the social whole. Fundamentally different, at least theoretically, is the problem of class *cohesion*—the factors that make of every social class, as we put it, a special living social organism, that prevent the group from scattering like a heap of billiard balls. Again fundamentally distinct is the problem of class *formation*—the question of why the social whole, as far as our eye can reach, has never been homogeneous, always revealing this particular, obviously organic stratification. Finally, we must realize—and we shall presently revert to this point—that this problem is again wholly different from the series of problems that are concerned with the *concrete causes and conditions* of an individually determined, historically given class structure—a distinction that is analogous to that between the problem of the theory of prices in general and the problems such as the explanation of the level of milk prices in the year 1919.

We are not, at this point, seeking a definition that would anticipate the solution of our problem. What we need, rather, is a characteristic that will enable us, in each case, to recognize a social class and to distinguish it from other social classes—a characteristic that will show on the surface and, if possible, on the surface alone; that will be as clear or as fuzzy as the situation itself is at first glance. Class is something more than an aggregation of class members. It is something else, and this something cannot be recognized in the behavior of the individual class member. A class is aware of its identity as a whole, sublimates itself as such, has its own peculiar life and characteristic "spirit." Yet one essential peculiarity—possibly a consequence, possibly an intermediate cause—of the class phenomenon lies in the fact that class members behave toward one another in a fashion characteristically different from their conduct toward members of other classes. They are in closer association with one another; they understand one another better; they work more readily in concert; they close ranks and erect barriers against the outside; they look out into the same segment of the world, with the same eyes, from the same viewpoint, in the same direction. These are familiar observations, and among explanations which are traditionally adduced are the similarity of the class situation and the basic class type.

To this extent the behavior of people toward one another is a very dependable and useful *symptom* of the presence or absence of class cohesion among them–although it does not, of course, go very deeply, let alone constitute a cause. Even more on the surface–a symptom of a symptom, so to speak, though it hints at a far-reaching basic orientation–is the specific way in which people engage in social intercourse. These ways are decisively influenced by the degree of "shared social *a priori*," as we might say with Simmel. Social intercourse within class barriers is promoted by the similarity of manners and habits of life, of things that are evaluated in a positive or negative sense, that arouse interest. In intercourse across class borders, differences on all these points repel and inhibit sympathy. There are always a number of delicate matters that must be avoided, things that seem strange and even absurd to the other class. The participants in social intercourse between different classes are always on their best behavior, so to speak, making their conduct forced and unnatural. The difference between intercourse within the class and outside the class is the same as the difference between swimming with and against the tide. The most important symptom of this situation is the ease or difficulty with which members of different classes contract legally and socially recognized marriages. Hence we find a suitable definition of the class–one that makes it outwardly recognizable and involves no class theory–in the fact that intermarriage prevails among its members, socially rather than legally.[2] This criterion is especially useful for our purposes, because we limit our study to the class phenomenon in a racially homogeneous environment, thus eliminating the most important additional impediment to intermarriage.[3]

3. Our study applies to the third of the four questions we have distinguished–to the others only to the extent that it is unavoidable. Let us begin by briefly discussing three difficulties in our way–a consideration of each of them already constituting an objective step toward our goal.

First: We seek to interpret the class phenomenon in the same sense in which we understand social phenomena generally, that is, *as adaptations* to existing needs, grasped by the observer–ourselves–as such. We shall pass over the logical difficulties inherent in even this simple statement, such as whether it is admissible to apply our own conceptual modes to cultures remote from us. There is also the question of the extent to which the condition of culturally primitive peoples in our own time may be taken as a clue to the past state of modern civilized peoples, and the even more important question of the extent to which historical data are at all valid for theoretical purposes. One difficulty, however,

[2] In support of this criterion we may now also invoke the authority of Max Weber, who mentions it in his sociology, though only in passing.

[3] We do not use the term "estate" since we have no need of it. Technically it has fixed meaning only in the sense of status and in connection with the constitution of the feudal state. For the rest, it is equated, sometimes with "profession," and sometimes with "class." Caste is merely a special elaboration of the class phenomenon, its peculiarity [is] of no essential importance to us.

we must face. Unless specifically proven, it is an erroneous assumption that social phenomena to which the same name has been applied over thousands of years are always the same things, merely in different form. This is best seen in the history of social institutions. Anyone will realize that common ownership of land in the ancient Germanic village community—supposing, for the moment, that its existence had been proven—is something altogether different from common land ownership in present-day Germany. Yet the term ownership is used as though it always implied the same basic concept. Obviously this can be true only in a very special sense, to be carefully delimited in each case. When taken for granted, it becomes a source of one-sided and invalid constructions. The fact that there may occur in the language of law and life of a given period expressions that we regard as equivalent to our chosen concept, proves nothing, even when those expressions were actually used in an equivalent sense. Similarly, the actuality of the institution we call marriage has changed so greatly in the course of time that it is quite inadmissible to regard that institution always as the same phenomenon, from a general sociological viewpoint and without reference to a specific research purpose. This does not mean that we renounce the habit, indispensable in analysis, of seeking, wherever possible, the same essential character in the most diverse forms. But the existence of that character must be a fact, its establishment the result of study, not a mere postulate. This applies to our problem as well. When we speak of "the" class phenomenon and take it to mean that group differences in social values, found everywhere, though under varying conditions, are everywhere explained by the same theory, that is not even a working hypothesis, but merely a method of presentation in which the result is anticipated—a result that has meaning only from the viewpoint of the particular theory in question. "Master classes," for example, do not exist everywhere—if, indeed, the concept of "master" has a precise content at all.

Second: The class membership of an individual is a primary fact, originally quite independent of his will. But he does not always confirm that allegiance by his conduct. As is well known, it is common for nonmembers of a class to work with and on behalf of that class, especially in a political sense, while members of a class may actually work against it. Such cases are familiar from everyday life—they are called fellow travelers, renegades, and the like. This phenomenon must be distinguished, on the one hand, from a situation in which an entire class, or at least its leadership, behaves differently from what might be expected from its class orientation; and, on the other hand, from a situation in which the individual, by virtue of his own functional position, comes into conflict with his class. There is room for differences of opinion on these points. For example, one may see in them aberrations from the normal pattern that hold no particular interest, that have no special significance to an understanding of society, that are often exceptions to the rule more apparent than real. Those who view the class struggle as the core of all historical explanation will generally incline to such opinions and seek to explain away conflicting evidence. From another viewpoint, however, these phenomena become the key to an understanding of political history—one without which its actual course and in particular its class evolution become altogether incomprehensible. To whatever class theory one may adhere, there is always the necessity of choosing between these viewpoints. The phenomena alluded to, of course, complicate not only the realities of social life but also its intellectual perception. We think that our line of reasoning will fully answer this question, and we shall not revert to it.

Third: Every social situation is the heritage of preceding situations and takes over from them not only their cultures, their dispositions, and their "spirit," but also elements of their social structure and concentrations of power. This fact is of itself interesting. The social pyramid is never made of a single substance, is never seamless. There is no single *Zeitgeist*, except in the sense of a construct. This means that in explaining any historical course or situation, account must be taken of the fact that much in it can be explained only by the survival of elements that are actually alien to its own trends. This is, of course self-evident, but it does become a source of practical difficulties and diagnostic problems. Another implication is that the coexistence of essentially different mentalities and objective sets of facts must form part of any general theory. Thus the economic interpretation of history, for example, would at once become untenable and unrealistic—indeed, some easily demolished objections to it are explained from this fact—if its formulation failed to consider that the manner in which production methods shape social life is essentially influenced by the fact that the human protagonists have always been shaped by past situations. When applied to our problem, this means, first, that any theory of class structure, in dealing with a given historical period, must include prior class structures among its data; and then, that any general theory of classes and class formation must explain the fact that classes coexisting at any given time bear the marks of different centuries on their brow, so to speak—that they stem from varying conditions. This is in the essential nature of the matter, an aspect of the nature of the class phenomenon. Classes, once they have come into being, harden in their mold and perpetuate themselves, even when the social conditions that created them have disappeared.

In this connection it becomes apparent that in the field of our own problem this difficulty bears an aspect lacking in many other problems. When one seeks to render modern banking comprehensible, for example, one can trace its historical origins, since doubtless there were economic situations in which there was no banking, and others in which the beginnings of banking can be observed. But this is impossible in the case of class, for there are no amorphous societies in this sense—societies, that is, in which the absence of our phenomenon can be demonstrated beyond doubt. Its presence may be more or less strongly marked, a distinction of great importance for our solution of the class problem. But neither historically nor ethnologically has its utter absence been demonstrated in even a single case, although there has been no dearth either of attempts in that direction (in eighteenth-century theories of culture) or of an inclination to assume the existence of classless situations.[4] We must therefore forego any aid from this side, whatever it may be worth,[5] though the ethnological material nevertheless retains fundamental significance for us. If we wanted to start from a classless society, the only cases we could draw upon would be those in which societies are formed accidentally, in which whatever class orientations the participants may have either count for nothing or lack the time to assert themselves—cases, in other words, like that of a ship in danger, a burning theater, and so on. We do not completely discount the value of such cases, but quite apparently we cannot do very much with them. Any study of classes and class situations therefore leads, in unending regression, to other classes and class situations, just as any explanation of the circular flow of the economic process always leads back, without any logical stopping point, to the preceding circular flow that furnishes the data for the one to follow. Similarly—though less closely so—analysis of the economic value of goods always leads back from a use value to a cost value and back again to a use value, so that it seems to turn in a circle. Yet this very analogy points to the logical way out. The general and mutual interdependence of values and prices in an economic situation does not prevent us from finding an all-encompassing explanatory principle; and the fact of regression in our own case does not mean the nonexistence of a principle that will explain the formation, nature, and basic laws of classes—though this fact naturally does not necessarily furnish us with such a principle. If we cannot derive the sought-for principle from the genesis of classes in a classless state, it may yet emerge from a study of how classes function and what happens to them, especially from actual observation of the changes in the relationship of existing classes to one another and of individuals within the class structure—*provided* it can be shown that the elements explaining such changes also include the reason why classes exist at all.

[4] The theory of the "original" classless society is probably headed for a fate similar to that which has already overtaken the theory of primitive communism and primitive promiscuity. It will prove to be purely speculative, along the line of "natural law." Yet all such conceptions do receive apparent confirmation in the conditions of the "primitive horde." Where a group is very small and its existence precarious, the situation necessarily has the aspects of classlessness, communism, and promiscuity. But this no more constitutes an organizational principle than the fact that an otherwise carnivorous species will become vegetarian when no meat is available constitutes a vegetarian principle.

[5] The explanatory value of historically observable genesis must not be overrated. It does not always lead to an explanation and never offers an explanation ipso facto, not even when a phenomenon appears immediately in its "pure" form, which is neither inevitable nor even frequent.

3 *Robert A. Nisbet*

THE TRIUMPH OF STATUS: TOCQUEVILLE

Tocqueville is the first and, throughout the nineteenth century, the major exponent of the view that the modern regime is characterized not by the solidification but by the fragmentation of social class, with the key elements dispersed: power to the masses and to centralized bureaucracy, wealth to an ever-enlarging middle class, and status to the varied and shifting sectors of society which, in the absence of true class, become the theaters of the unending and agonizing competition among individuals for the attainment of the marks of status.

The clue to the modern order lies for Tocqueville in the relentless leveling of classes that has characterized the history of the West since the end of the Middle Ages. "In running over the pages of our history, we shall scarcely find a single great event of the last seven hundred years that has not promoted equality of condition."[1] Given this formidable background of history, is it likely, he asks, that capitalism or any other feature of modern society will arrest a tendency now so deeply embedded in historical reality?

"The gradual development of the principle of equality is a providential fact. It has all the chief characteristics of such a fact: it is universal, it is durable, it constantly eludes all human interference, and all events as well as all men contribute to its progress. Would it be wise to imagine that a social movement, the causes of which lie so far back, can be checked by the efforts of one generation? Can it be believed that the democracy which has overthrown the feudal system and vanquished kings will retreat before tradesmen and capitalists? Will it stop now that it has grown so strong and its adversaries so weak?[2]

Tocqueville's answer to these questions forms the theme of his sociology of stratification. The dissolution of social class that began in the late Middle Ages under the twin impacts of political centralization and social individualism can only complete itself in the modern order. The dispersion of power among the democratic mass, the ever more prominent place occupied by political bureaucracy, the virtual enshrinement of the norm of equality, the incessant competition for wealth in the fluid forms that capitalism has brought, and the profound urge to status achievement in a society where each man regards himself as the equal of all—these and other forces make true social class impossible. There are,

[1] *Democracy in America*, [Philip Bradley, ed. (New York: Alfred Knopf, 1945)], I, 5. The central thesis of Tocqueville's later work, *The Old Regime and the French Revolution* is substantially an expansion of this proposition plus his related demonstration of the roots of administrative centralization in the old order.

[2] Ibid., 6.

of course, economic strata, even extremes of wealth. But these do not promote a sense belonging to a class.

"I am aware that among a great democratic people there will always be some members of the community in great poverty and others in great opulence; but the poor, instead of forming the great majority of the nation, as is always the case in aristocratic communities, are comparatively few in number, and the laws do not bind them together by ties of irremediable and hereditary penury .... As there is no longer a race of poor men, so there is no longer a race of rich men; the latter spring up daily from the multitude and relapse into it again. Hence, they do not form a distinct class which may be easily marked out and plundered; and, moreover, as they are connected with the mass of their fellow citizens by a thousand secret ties, the people cannot assail them without inflicting an injury upon themselves.

"Between these two extremes of democratic communities stands an innumerable multitude of men almost alike, who, without being exactly either rich or poor, possess sufficient property to desire the maintenance of order, yet not enough to excite envy."[3]

It is in these terms exactly that Tocqueville's view of class, class consciousness, and class conflict may be seen as the obverse of Marx's. The tensions of democratic-commercial society, far from promoting revolution, constantly diminish the possibility of revolution. "Such men," Tocqueville writes of the great democratic middle, "are the natural enemies of violent commotions; their lack of agitation keeps all beneath them and above them still and secures the balance of the fabric of society. Not, indeed, that even these men are contented with what they have got or that they feel a natural abhorrence for a revolution in which they might share the spoil without sharing the calamity; on the contrary, they desire, with unexampled ardor, to get rich, but the difficulty is to know from whom riches can be taken. The same state of society that constantly prompts desires, restrains these desires within necessary limits; it gives men more liberty of changing, and less interest in change."[4]

Such class lines as do persist are waning evidences of the mild influence that the landed class once held in such places as New York and the stronger influences that the planters held in the South before the American Revolution. "In most of the states situated to the southwest of the Hudson some great English proprietors had settled who had imported with them aristocratic principles and the English law of inheritance . . . They constituted a superior class having ideas and tastes of its own and forming the center of political action. This kind of aristocracy sympathized with the body of the people, whose passions and interests it easily embraced; but it was too weak and too shortlived to excite either love or hatred. This was the class which headed the insurrection in the South and furnished the best leaders of the American Revolution."[5]

[3] Ibid., II, 252.

[4] Ibid., 252 f.

[5] Ibid., I, 47. See also his *Journey to America,* 19 and passim.

But the gathering tides of democracy after the American Revolution sterilized the role of the quasi-aristocracy, and there are left, Tocqueville emphasizes, only the shifting categories of rich and poor, categories not likely to produce classes in the true sense; and so far as political power is concerned, it is more likely, in a democracy, Tocqueville argues, to lie with the masses of the poor than with the rich. "Among civilized nations, only those who have nothing to lose ever revolt," and while "the natural anxiety of the rich may produce a secret dissatisfaction," their sheer devotion to wealth and property will ensure almost any degree of political compliance.[6]

The character of wealth in a democracy tends to make true class impossible. It is typically commercial, trading, and manufacturing wealth, not landed. Democracy not only "swells the number of working-men, but leads men to prefer one kind of labor to another; and while it diverts them from agriculture, it encourages their taste for commerce and manufactures."[7] Commerce does not stimulate the democratic passion for well-being; the reverse is true. "All the causes that make the love of worldly welfare predominate in the heart of man are favorable to the growth of commerce and manufactures. Equality of conditions is one of those causes; it encourages trade, not directly, by giving men a taste for business, but indirectly, by strengthening and expanding in their minds a taste for well-being."[8]

It is, in short, a political interpretation of capitalism that Tocqueville gives us and, characteristically, he places the interpretation in the context of democracy's difference from aristocracy. Under aristocracy, the rich are at the same time the governing power; they do not have time for the responsibilities of trade and commerce, and where an aristocrat does attempt, now and then, to enter trade, the counteractive opinion of his peers is sudden and compelling.

In democratic countries, on the other hand, "where money does not lead those who possess it to political power, but often removes them from it, the rich do not know how to spend their leisure. They are driven into active life by the disquietude and the greatness of their desires, by the extent of their resources, and by the taste for what is extraordinary, which is always felt by those who rise, by whatever means, above the crowd. Trade is the only road open to them."[9]

In one respect only does Tocqueville see the outlines—though only the outlines—of a class, a new mode of aristocracy forming within capitalism. This is the manufacturing class. Tocqueville did not regard the system of division of labor in the optimistic light of his liberal contemporaries. It is one of the marks of his alienated view of modern society that he sees, not improvement, but degradation in the specialization of the worker. Such degradation he thought a permanent aspect of the system and one that would only heighten the superior-

[6] *Democracy in America,* I, 248.

[7] Ibid., II, 154.

[8] Ibid., II, 154.

[9] Ibid., II, 155.

ity and influence of the manufacturing class in democracy. The latter becomes more powerful and, as a *category*, more intrenched, as the working class becomes more degraded. "Men grow more alike in the one, more different in the other; and inequality increases in the less numerous class in the same ratio in which it decreases in the community. Hence it would appear, on searching to the bottom, that aristocracy would naturally spring out of the bosom of democracy."[10]

So it might seem. But what Tocqueville sees as the perpetual mobility of commercial democracy makes such an aristocracy impossible, in fact. There is too much circulation of the members of the classes—especially of the rich class, which is constantly losing its members, to be replaced by others. Thus, and here is the essence of Tocqueville's view of class in capitalism, the very converse of Marx's: "though there are rich men, the class of rich men does not exist; for these rich individuals have no feeling or purposes, no traditions or hopes, in common; there are individuals, therefore, but no definite class.

"Not only are the rich not compactly united among themselves, but there is no real bond between them and the poor. Their relative position is not a permanent one; they are constantly drawn together or separated by their interests. . . . The one contracts no obligation to protect nor the other to defend, and they are not permanently connected either by habit or by duty. . . . An aristocracy thus constituted can have no great hold upon those whom it employs, and even if it succeeds in retaining them at one moment, they escape the next; it knows not how to will, and it cannot act."[11]

The differences here between Marx and Tocqueville are engaging. It is precisely *because* of the lack of reciprocal obligation between the manufacturers and workers, *because* of the dissolution of uniting bonds of protection and defense, that Marx sees the two classes becoming ever more distinct, each ever more inclusive of habits, ideas, and beliefs. But for Tocqueville true class can exist *only* in the presence of reciprocality, co-operation, and mutual dependence, and where these are gone, there can remain only levels, abstract strata, not true classes.

It is love of money and of the well-being associated with money that Tocqueville finds the single most important factor in establishing the status system of democracies. This is indeed the major difference between democracy and aristocracy. In the latter, men enjoy physical comforts without really caring for them. "The heart of man is not so much caught by the undisturbed possession of anything valuable as by the desire, as yet imperfectly satisfied, of possessing it and by the incessant dread of losing it."[12]

"When . . . the distinctions of ranks are obliterated and privileges are destroyed, when hereditary property is subdivided and education and freedom

[10] Ibid., II, 160.

[11] Ibid., II, 160.

[12] Ibid., II, 128.

are widely diffused, the desire of securing the comforts of the world haunts the imagination of the poor, and the dread of losing them that of the rich. Many scanty fortunes spring up; those who possess them have a sufficient share of physical gratifications to conceive a taste for these pleasures, not enough to satisfy it. They never procure them without exertion, and they never indulge in them without apprehension. They are therefore always straining to pursue or to retain gratifications so delightful, so imperfect, so fugitive."[13]

Not even Marx could exceed the emphasis Tocqueville places upon the role of money in democratic society and its determinative influence in matters of status. "Men living in democratic times have many passions, but most of their passions either end in the love of riches or proceed from it. The cause of this is not that their souls are narrower, but that the impotence of money is really greater at such times. When all the members of a community are independent of or indifferent to each other, the co-operation of each of them can be obtained only by paying for it: this infinitely multiplies the purposes to which wealth may be applied and increases its value. When the reverence that belonged to what is old has vanished, birth, condition, and profession no longer distinguish men, or scarcely distinguish them; hardly anything but money remains to create strongly marked differences between them and to raise some of them above the common level. The distinction originating in wealth is increased by the disappearance or diminution of all other distinctions. Among aristocratic nations, money reaches only to a few points on the vast circle of man's desire; in democracies, it seems to lead to all."[14]

Hence the incessant preoccupation with individual achievement, with social superiority and inferiority, with prestige, in democracy. The fateful combination of recession of social class and dissemination of political and moral equality leads to gnawing concern with status. Equality is, by its nature, a mercurial and elusive goal. It is possible to imagine a degree of freedom, Tocqueville writes, that would satisfy all men, but men will never establish any equality with which they can be contented. No matter how completely they equalize political, legal, and even economic conditions, the remaining differences and inequalities among them–intellectual, cultural, social–will only be magnified. "When inequalities do not strike the eye; when everything is nearly on the same level, the slightest are marked enough to hurt it. Hence the desire for equality always becomes more insatiable in proportion as equality is more complete."[15] Men become the more anxious about their own status and more apprehensive of that of others in proportion as the fixed lines of class dissolve and the ethos of democratic equality spreads. The role of money heightens this.

"Since in such communities nothing is stable, each man is haunted by a fear of sinking to a lower social level and by a restless urge to better his condition.

[13] Ibid., II, 129.

[14] Ibid., II, 228. See *Journey to America,* 69 f.

[15] *Democracy in America,* II, 138.

And since money has not only become the sole criterion of a man's social status but has also acquired an extreme mobility–that is to say it changes hands incessantly, raising or lowering the prestige of individuals and families–everybody is feverishly intent on making money or, if already rich, on keeping his wealth intact."[16]

Quite apart from status anxiety, there is a built-in indecisiveness about one's status in the minds of those who live in times when aristocracy is fading. "When it is birth alone, independent of wealth, that classes men in society, everyone knows exactly what his own position is in the social scale; he does not seek to rise, he does not fear to sink. In a community thus organized, men of different castes communicate very little with one another; but if accident brings them together, they are ready to converse without hoping or fearing to lose their own position. Their intercourse is not on a footing of equality, but it is not constrained."[17]

But where a moneyed aristocracy succeeds to an aristocracy of birth, the reverse occurs. "As the social importance of men is no longer ostensibly and permanently fixed by blood and is infinitely varied by wealth, ranks still exist, but it is not easy to distinguish at a glance those who respectively belong to them. Secret hostilities then arise in the community; one set of men endeavor by innumerable artifices to penetrate, or to appear to penetrate, among those who are above them; another set are constantly in arms against these usurpers of their rights; or, rather, the same individual does both at once, and while he seeks to raise himself into a higher circle, he is always on the defensive against the intrusion of those below him."[18] Particularly in England, Tocqueville notes, are these phenomena of status invasion and status rejection notable.

In the United States, where a genuine aristocracy of birth was never more than faint and where money has become the controlling medium of everyone's social status, social intercourse is easier and freer of hostilities. The reserve that characterizes the Englishman's wary protection of status is lost to the American for whom failure to respond quickly and enthusiastically to any overture is cause for suspicion of snobbery. The American is slow to take insult in the easy idiom of democratic equality. "Despising no one on account of his station, he does not imagine that anyone can despise him for that cause, and until he has clearly perceived an insult, he does not suppose that an affront was intended."[19] Distinctions of rank in civil society being negligible and in political society nonexistent, the American does not feel compelled to either pay or require special attention from others.

It is different, however, when the American goes to Europe. There, for the first time, status, beginning with his own, becomes a perplexing problem. He becomes sensitive and captious, Tocqueville observes. Traces of rank persist, the

[16] *The Old Regime,* xiii.

[17] *Democracy in America,* II, 168.

[18] Ibid., II, 169.

[19] Ibid., II, 172.

privileges of birth and wealth cannot be overlooked, but they are not easily defined. "He is, therefore, profoundly ignorant of the place that he ought to occupy in this half-ruined scale of classes, which are sufficiently distinct to hate and despise each other, yet sufficiently alike for him to be always confounding them. He is afraid of ranking himself too high; still more is he afraid of being ranked too low. This twofold peril keeps his mind constantly on the stretch and embarrasses all he says and does."[20]

For such a man, society is not a recreation but a serious toil, Tocqueville writes. "He is like a man surrounded by traps. . . . He weighs your least actions, interrogates your looks, and scrutinizes all you say lest there should be some hidden allusion to affront him. I doubt whether there was ever a provincial man of quality so punctilious in breeding as he is: he endeavors to attend to the slightest rules of etiquette and does not allow one of them to be waived towards himself; he is full of scruples and at the same time of pretensions; he wishes to do enough, but fears to do too much, and as he does not very well know the limits of the one or of the other, he keeps up a haughty and embarrassed reserve."[21]

Americans, Tocqueville notes, are forever talking, when abroad, of the absolute equality that prevails in the United States. All praise it openly, yet it is as though each of them privately aspires to show that, for his part, he is an exception to the general equality of birth that he boasts of. Hardly an American exists "who does not claim some remote kindred with the first founders of the colonies; and as for the scions of the noble families of England, America seems to be covered with them." When an American of wealth reaches Europe, his first care is to surround himself with luxuries; "he is so afraid of being taken for the plain citizen of a democracy that he adopts a hundred distorted ways of bringing some new instance of his wealth before you every day. His house will be in the most fashionable part of the town; he will always be surrounded by a host of servants . . ."[22]

Reading the foregoing words, one cannot conquer the feeling that their chief relevance, as well as charm of insight, is to the status system in the United States itself—though not perhaps until a generation or two after Tocqueville's visit. Like so much in Tocqueville, his words have a value to the empirical realities of an American society that became manifest only in the 1880's. Tocqueville consistently underplays the role of the quasi-aristocracy in the United States formed by the great families of wealth and breeding that could trace their ancestry and holdings back to early colonial days. His words on the American in the presence of European aristocracy have in fact as much point when directed to the *new* American rich in the presence of these older strains of American wealth found in New York, Boston, and Charleston. His notebooks show that he was well aware of this.

[20] Ibid., II, 173.
[21] Ibid., II, 173.
[22] Ibid., II, 173 f.

Tocqueville was profoundly impressed by the master-servant relation in modern democratic-commercial society. His chapter on this subject is a kind of paradigm of the impact of democracy on the status structure of traditional society and is among the most important in the book.[23]

Under an aristocracy, Tocqueville notes, such as that in England, servants form a distinct class. Gradations of status within this class are as deeply textured as within the master class. Generations of servants may succeed one another without any change of position. Masters and servants form two communities and "are superposed one above the other, always distinct, but regulated by analogous principles. This aristocratic constitution does not exert a less powerful influence on the motions and manners of servants than on those of masters; and although the effects are different, the same cause may be traced." In such a servant class, notions of honor, service, virtue, and fame can take root, *mutatis mutandis,* even as they do among the masters. There is indeed a sort of "servile honor," and it is still possible in England to find men of noble and vigorous minds in the service of the great. Once, of course, this was common, and there were many "who did not feel the servitude they bore and who submitted to the will of their masters without any fear of their displeasure."[24]

But, lower down, are the menials, those for whom the term *lackey* was invented by the French in the old regime. "This word *lackey* served as the strongest expression, when all others were exhausted, to designate human meanness."[25] Permanent inequality of conditions inevitably creates a class whose very essence is willing and constant obedience; whose own norms of achievement are bounded by unflagging obedience and even anticipation of command. "In aristocracies the master often exercises, even without being aware of it, an amazing sway over the opinions, the habits, and the manners of those who obey him, and his influence extends even further than his authority.

"In aristocratic communities not only are there hereditary families of servants as well as of masters, but the same families of servants adhere for several generations to the same families of masters (like two parallel lines, which neither meet nor separate); and this considerably modifies the mutual relations of these two classes of persons. Thus, although in aristocratic society the master and servant have no natural resemblance, although, on the contrary, they are placed at an immense distance on the scale of human beings by their fortune, education and opinions, yet time ultimately binds them together. They are connected by a long series of common reminiscences, and however different they may be, they grow alike; while in democracies, where they are naturally almost alike, they always remain strangers to one another."[26] In the same way that masters, in an

23 Ibid., II, Ch. 5. As I point out below, both Weber and Simmel were to continue Tocqueville's special interest in the relations of masters and servants.

24 Ibid., II, 178.

25 Ibid., II, 178 f.

26 Ibid., II, 179.

aristocracy, come to regard their servants as secondary and inferior extensions of themselves, servants regard themselves in the same light, and feel their own moods, fancies, pride, and despair fluctuate with those of their masters.

But consider now the effects of the democratic revolution on this relationship. "The laws and, partially public opinion, already declare that no natural or permanent inferiority exists between the servant and the master. But this new belief has not yet reached the innermost convictions of the latter, or rather his heart rejects it; in the secret persuasion of his mind the master thinks that he belongs to a peculiar and superior race; he dares not say so, but he shudders at allowing himself to be dragged to the same level. His authority over his servants becomes timid and at the same time harsh; he has already ceased to entertain for them the feelings of patronizing kindness which long uncontested power always produces, and he is surprised that, being changed himself, his servant changes also. He wants his attendants to form regular and permanent habits, in a condition of domestic service that is only temporary; he requires that they should appear contented with a pride of a servile condition which they will one day shake off, that they should sacrifice themselves to a man who can neither protect nor ruin them, and, in short, that they should contract an indissoluble engagement to a being like themselves and one who will last no longer than they will."[27]

And the servants? What Tocqueville calls a "confused and imperfect phantom of inequality" haunts their minds. They rebel in their hearts against a subordination that they have nominally chosen. "They consent to serve and they blush to obey; they like the advantages of service, but not the master; or, rather, they are not sure that they ought not themselves to be masters, and they are inclined to consider him who orders them as an unjust usurper of their own rights."[28]

"Then it is that the dwelling of every citizen offers a spectacle somewhat analogous to the gloomy aspect of political society. A secret and internal warfare is going on there between powers ever rivals and suspicious of one another . . . The lines that divide authority from oppression, liberty from license, and right from might are to their eyes so jumbled together and confused that no one knows exactly what he is or what he may be or what he ought to be. Such a condition is not democracy, but revolution."[29] Such a condition, in Tocqueville's mind, characterized France after the Revolution.

American society Tocqueville finds somewhere in between the two extremes of master-servant relations. The Americans, he writes, not only are unacquainted with the kind of man who forms the fixed servant class of aristocratic nations, they cannot believe that he ever existed. There is, to be sure, a class of menials and a class of masters, but like all other classes in democracy, "these classes are

[27] Ibid., II, 183 f.

[28] Ibid., II, 184 f.

[29] Ibid., II, 185.

not always composed of the same individuals, still less of the same families; and those in command are not more secure of perpetuity than those who obey."[30]

In a fully developed democracy like the United States, servants are not only equal among themselves, "but it may be said that they are, in some sort, the equals of their masters." Within the terms of the covenant of domestic service, one is superior, the other inferior, but "beyond it they are two citizens of the commonwealth, two men." The American master-servant relation is comparable to the officer-soldier relation in democratic armies. Within the contract, subordination; out of it, equality.

The money contract of service will produce able and willing service within democracy's households, but there is not, cannot be, the kind of mutual devotion, the "warm and deep-seated affections which are sometimes kindled in the domestic service of aristocracy," nor will there be comparable instances of self-sacrifice. "In aristocracies masters and servants live apart, and frequently their only intercourse is through a third person; yet they commonly stand firmly by one another. In democratic countries, the master and the servant are close together; they are in daily personal contact, but their minds do not intermingle; they have common occupations, hardly ever common interests."[31]

4 *Max Weber*

CLASS, STATUS, PARTY

1: ECONOMICALLY DETERMINED POWER AND THE SOCIAL ORDER

Law exists when there is a probability that an order will be upheld by a specific staff of men who will use physical or psychical compulsion with the intention of obtaining conformity with the order, or of inflicting sanctions for infringement of it.[1] The structure of every legal order directly influences the distribution of

[30] Ibid., II, 181.

[31] Ibid., II, 182.

From *From Max Weber: Essays in Sociology*, edited and translated by H. H. Gerth and C. Wright Mills.

[1] *Wirtschaft und Gesellschaft* (Tubinger, 1922 ed.), part III, chap. 4, pp. 631-640. The first sentence in paragraph one and the several definitions in this chapter which are in brackets do not appear in the original text. They have been taken from other contexts of *Wirtschaft und Gesellschaft*.

power, economic or otherwise, within its respective community. This is true of all legal orders and not only that of the state. In general, we understand by 'power' the chance of a man or of a number of men to realize their own will in a communal action even against the resistance of others who are participating in the action.

'Economically conditioned' power is not, of course, identical with 'power' as such. On the contrary, the emergence of economic power may be the consequence of power existing on other grounds. Man does not strive for power only in order to enrich himself economically. Power, including economic power, may be valued 'for its own sake.' Very frequently the striving for power is also conditioned by the social 'honor' it entails. Not all power, however, entails social honor: The typial American Boss, as well as the typical big speculator, deliberately relinquishes social honor. Quite generally, 'mere economic' power, and especially 'naked' money power, is by no means a recognized basis of social honor. Nor is power the only basis of social honor. Indeed, social honor, or prestige, may even be the basis of political or economic power, and very frequently has been. Power, as well as honor, may be guaranteed by the legal order, but, at least normally, it is not their primary source. The legal order is rather an additional factor that enhances the chance to hold power or honor; but it cannot always secure them.

The way in which social honor is distributed in a community between typical groups participating in this distribution we may call the 'social order.' The social order and the economic order are, of course, similarly related to the 'legal order.' However, the social and the economic order are not identical. The economic order is for us merely the way in which economic goods and services are distributed and used. The social order is of course conditioned by the economic order to a high degree, and in its turn reacts upon it.

Now: 'classes,' 'status groups,' and 'parties' are phenomena of the distribution of power within a community.

2: DETERMINATION OF CLASS-SITUATION BY MARKET-SITUATION

In our terminology, 'classes' are not communities; they merely represent possible, and frequent, bases for communal action. We may speak of a 'class' when (1) a number of people have in common a specific causal component of their life chances, in so far as (2) this component is represented exclusively by economic interests in the possession of goods and opportunities for income, and (3) is represented under the conditions of the commodity or labor markets. [These points refer to 'class situation,' which we may express more briefly as the typical chance for a supply of goods, external living conditions, and personal life experiences, in so far as this chance is determined by the amount and kind of power, or lack of such, to dispose of goods or skills for the sake of income in a given economic order. The term 'class' refers to any group of people that is found in the same class situation.]

It is the most elemental economic fact that the way in which the disposition over material property is distributed among a plurality of people, meeting competitively in the market for the purpose of exchange, in itself creates specific life chances. According to the law of marginal utility this mode of distribution excludes the non-owners from competing for highly valued goods; it favors the owners and, in fact, gives to them a monopoly to acquire such goods. Other things being equal, this mode of distribution monopolizes the opportunities for profitable deals for all those who, provided with goods, do not necessarily have to exchange them. It increases, at least generally, their power in price wars with those who, being propertyless, have nothing to offer but their services in native form or goods in a form constituted through their own labor, and who above all are compelled to get rid of these products in order barely to subsist. This mode of distribution gives to the propertied a monopoly on the possibility of transferring property from the sphere of use as a 'fortune.' to the sphere of 'capital goods'; that is, it gives them the entrepreneurial function and all chances to share directly or indirectly in returns on capital. All this holds true within the area in which pure market conditions prevail. 'Property' and 'lack of property' are, therefore, the basic categories of all class situations. It does not matter whether these two categories become effective in price wars or in competitive struggles.

Within these categories, however, class situations are further differentiated: on the one hand, according to the kind of property that is usable for returns; and, on the other hand, according to the kind of services that can be offered in the market. Ownership of domestic buildings; productive establishments; warehouses; stores; agriculturally usable land, large and small holdings–quantitative differences with possibly qualitative consequences–; ownership of mines; cattle; men (slaves); disposition over mobile instruments of production, or capital goods of all sorts, especially money or objects that can be exchanged for money easily and at any time; disposition over products of one's own labor or of others' labor differing according to their various distances from consumability; disposition over transferable monopolies of any kind–all these distinctions differentiate the class situations of the propertied just as does the 'meaning' which they can and do give to the utilization of property, especially to property which has money equivalence. Accordingly, the propertied, for instance, may belong to the class of rentiers or to the class of entrepreneurs.

Those who have no property but who offer services are differentiated just as much according to their kinds of services as according to the way in which they make use of these services, in a continuous or discontinuous relation to a recipient. But always this is the generic connotation of the concept of class: that the kind of chance in the *market* is the decisive moment which presents a common condition for the individual's fate. 'Class situation' is, in this sense, ultimately 'market situation.' The effect of naked possession per se, which among cattle breeders gives the non-owning slave or serf into the power of the cattle owner, is only a forerunner of real 'class' formation. However, in the cattle loan and in the naked severity of the law of debts in such communities, for the first time mere 'possession' as such emerges as decisive for the fate of the individual. This is very much in contrast to the agricultural communities based on labor. The creditor-debtor relation becomes the basis of 'class situations' only in those cities where a 'credit market.' however primitive, with rates of interest increasing according to the extent of dearth and a factual monopolization of credits, is developed by a plutocracy. Therewith 'class struggles' begin.

Those men whose fate is not determined by the chance of using goods or services for themselves on the market, e.g. slaves, are not, however, a 'class' in the technical sense of the term. They are, rather, a 'status group.'

3: COMMUNAL ACTION FLOWING FROM CLASS INTEREST

According to our terminology, the factor that creates 'class' is unambiguously economic interest, and indeed, only those interests involved in the existence of the 'market.' Nevertheless, the concept of 'class-interest' is an ambiguous one: even as an empirical concept it is ambiguous as soon as one understands by it something other than the factual direction of interests following with a certain probability from the class situation for a certain 'average' of those people subjected to the class situation. The class situation and other circumstances remaining the same, the direction in which the individual worker, for instance, is likely to pursue his interests may vary widely, according to whether he is constitutionally qualified for the task at hand to a high, to an average, or to a low degree. In the same way, the direction of interests may vary according to whether or not a *communal* action of a larger or smaller portion of those commonly affected by the 'class situation,' or even an association among them, e.g. a 'trade union,' has grown out of the class situation from which the individual may or may not expect promising results. [Communal action refers to that action which is oriented to the feeling of the actors that they belong together. Societal action, on the other hand, is oriented to a rationally motivated adjustment of interests.] The rise of societal or even of communal action from a common class situation is by no means a universal phenomenon.

The class situation may be restricted in its effects to the generation of essentially *similar* reactions, that is to say, within our terminology, of 'mass actions.' However, it may not have even this result. Furthermore, often merely an amorphous communal action emerges. For example, the 'murmuring' of the workers known in ancient oriental ethics: the moral disapproval of the work-master's conduct, which in its practical significance was probably equivalent to an increasingly typical phenomenon of precisely the latest industrial development, namely, the 'slow down' (the deliberate limiting of work effort) of laborers by virtue of tacit agreement. The degree in which 'communal action' and possible 'societal action,' emerges from the 'mass actions' of the members of a class is linked to general cultural conditions, especially to those of an intellectual sort. It is also linked to the extent of the contrasts that have already evolved, and is especially linked to the *transparency* of the connections between the causes and the consequences of the 'class situation.' For however different life chances may be, this fact in itself, according to all experience, by no means gives birth to 'class action' (communal action by the members of a class). The fact of being conditioned and the results of the class situation must be distinctly recognizable. For only then the contrast of life chances can be felt not as an absolutely given fact to be accepted, but as a resultant from either (1) the given distribution of property, or (2) the structure of the concrete economic order. It is only then that people may react against the class structure not only through acts of an intermittent and irrational protest, but in the form of rational association. There have been 'class situations' of the first category (1), of a specifically naked and transparent sort, in the urban centers of Antiquity and during the Middle Ages; especially then, when great fortunes were accumulated by factually monopolized trading in industrial products of these localities or in foodstuffs. Furthermore, under certain circumstances, in the rural economy of the most diverse periods, when agriculture was increasingly exploited in a profit-making manner. The most important historical example of the second category (2) is the class situation of the modern 'proletariat.'

4: TYPES OF 'CLASS STRUGGLE'

Thus every class may be the carrier of any one of the possibly innumerable forms of 'class action.' but this is not necessarily so. In any case, a class does not in itself constitute a community. To treat 'class' conceptually as having the same value as 'community' leads to distortion. That men in the same class situation regularly react in mass actions to such tangible situations as economic ones in the direction of those interests that are most adequate to their average number is an important and after all simple fact for the understanding of historical events. Above all, this fact must not lead to that kind of pseudo-scientific operation with the concepts of 'class' and 'class interests' so frequently found these days, and which has found its most classic expression in the statement of a talented author, that the individual may be in error concerning his interests but that the 'class' is 'infallible' about its interests. Yet, if classes as such are not communities, nevertheless class situations emerge only on the basis of communalization. The communal action that brings forth class situations, however, is not basically action between members of the identical class; it is an action between members of different classes. Communal actions that directly determine the class situation of the worker and the entrepreneur are: the labor market, the commodities market, and the capitalistic enterprise. But, in its turn, the existence of a capitalistic enterprise presupposes that a very specific communal action exists and that it is specifically structured to protect the possession of goods per se, and especially the power of individuals to dispose, in principle freely, over the means of production. The existence of a capitalistic enterprise is preconditioned by a specific kind of 'legal order.' Each kind of class situation, and above all when it rests upon the power of property per se, will become most clearly efficacious when all other determinants of reciprocal relations are, as far as possible, eliminated in their significance. It is in this way that the utilization of the power of property in the market obtains its most sovereign importance.

Now 'status groups' hinder the strict carrying through of the sheer market principle. In the present context they are of interest to us only from this one point of view. Before we briefly consider them, note that not much of a general nature can be said about the more specific kinds of antagonism between 'classes' (in our meaning of the term). The great shift, which has been going on continuously in the past, and up to our times, may be summarized, although at the cost of some precision: the struggle in which class situations are effective has progressively shifted from consumption credit toward, first, competitive struggles in the commodity market and, then, toward price wars on the labor market. The 'class struggles' of antiquity–to the extent that they were genuine class struggles and not struggles between status groups–were initially carried on by indebted peasants, and perhaps also by artisans threatened by debt bondage and struggling against urban creditors. For debt bondage is the normal result of the differentiation of wealth in commercial cities, especially in seaport cities. A similar situation has existed among cattle breeders. Debt relationships as such produced class action up to the time of Cataline. Along with this, and with an increase in provision of grain for the city by transporting it from the outside, the struggle over the means of sustenance emerged. It centered in the first place around the provision of bread and the determination of the price of bread. It lasted throughout antiquity and the entire Middle Ages. The propertyless as such flocked together against those who actually and supposedly were interested in the dearth of bread. This fight spread until it involved all those commodities essential to the way of life and to handicraft production. There were only incipient discussions of wage disputes in antiquity and in the Middle Ages. But they have been slowly increasing up into modern times. In the earlier periods they were completely secondary to slave rebellions as well as to fights in the commodity market.

The propertyless of antiquity and of the Middle Ages protested against monopolies, pre-emption, forestalling, and the withholding of goods from the market in order to raise prices. Today the central issue is the determination of the price of labor.

This transition is represented by the fight for access to the market and for the determination of the price of products. Such fights went on between merchants and workers in the putting-out system of domestic handicraft during the transition to modern times. Since it is quite a general phenomenon we must mention here that the class antagonisms that are conditioned through the market situation are usually most bitter between those who actually and directly participate as opponents in price wars. It is not the rentier, the share-holder, and the banker who suffer the ill will of the worker, but almost exclusively the manufacturer and the business executives who are the direct opponents of workers in price wars. This is so in spite of the fact that it is precisely the cash boxes of the rentier, the share-holder, and the banker into which the more or less 'unearned' gains flow, rather than into the pockets of the manufacturers or of the business executives. This simple state of affairs has very frequently been decisive for the role the class situation has played in the formation of political parties. For example, it has made possible the varieties of patriarchal socialism and the frequent attempts–formerly, at least–of threatened status groups to form alliances with the proletariat against the 'bourgeoisie.'

5: STATUS HONOR

In contrast to classes, *status groups* are normally communities. They are, however, often of an amorphous kind. In contrast to the purely economically determined 'class situation' we wish to designate as 'status situation' every typical component of the life fate of men that is determined by a specific, positive or negative, social estimation of *honor.* This honor may be connected with any quality shared by a plurality, and, of course, it can be knit to a class situation: class distinctions are linked in the most varied ways with status distinctions. Property as such is not always recognized as a status qualification, but in the long run it is, and with extraordinary regularity. In the subsistence economy of the organized neighborhood, very often the richest man is simply the chieftain. However, this often means only an honorific preference. For example, in the so-called pure modern 'democracy,' that is, one devoid of any expressly ordered status privileges for individuals, it may be that only the families coming under approximately the same tax class dance with one another. This example is reported of certain smaller Swiss cities. But status honor need not necessarily be linked with a 'class situation.' On the contrary, it normally stands in sharp opposition to the pretensions of sheer property.

Both propertied and propertyless people can belong to the same status group, and frequently they do with very tangible consequences. This 'equality' of social esteem may, however, in the long run become quite precarious. The 'equality' of status among the American 'gentlemen,' for instance, is expressed by the fact that outside the subordination determined by the different functions of 'business,' it would be considered strictly repugnant–wherever the old tradition still prevails–if even the richest 'chief,' while playing billiards or cards in his club in the evening, would not treat his 'clerk' as in every sense fully his equal in birthright. It would be repugnant if the American 'chief' would bestow upon his 'clerk' the condescending 'benevolence' marking a distinction of 'position,' which the German chief can never dissever from his attitude. This is one of the most important reasons why in America the German 'clubby-ness' has never been able to attain the attraction that the American clubs have.

6: GUARANTEES OF STATUS STRATIFICATION

In content, status honor is normally expressed by the fact that above all else a specific *style of life* can be expected from all those who wish to belong to the circle. Linked with this expectation are restrictions on 'social' intercourse (that is, intercourse which is not subservient to economic or any other of business's 'functional' purposes). These restrictions may confine normal marriages to within the status circle and may lead to complete endogamous closure. As soon as there is not a mere individual and socially irrelevant imitation of another style of life, but an agreed-upon communal action of this closing character, the 'status' development is under way.

In its characteristic form, stratification by 'status groups' on the basis of conventional styles of life evolves at the present time in the United States out of the traditional democracy. For example, only the resident of a certain street ('the street') is considered as belonging to 'society,' is qualified for social intercourse, and is visited and invited. Above all, this differentiation evolves in such a way as to make for strict submission to the fashion that is dominant at a given time in society. This submission to fashion also exists among men in America to a degree unknown in Germany. Such submission is considered to be an indication of the fact that a given man *pretends* to qualify as a gentleman. This submission decides, at least *prima facie*, that he will be treated as such. And this recognition becomes just as important for his employment chances in 'swank' establishments, and above all, for social intercourse and marriage with 'esteemed' families, as the qualification for dueling among Germans in the Kaiser's day. As for the rest: certain families resident for a long time, and, of course, correspondingly wealthy, e.g. 'F. F. V., i.e. First Families of Virginia,' or the actual or alleged descendants of the 'Indian Princess' Pocahontas, of the Pilgrim fathers, or of the Knickerbockers, the members of almost inaccessible sects and all sorts of circles setting themselves apart by means of any other characteristics and badges . . . all these elements usurp 'status' honor. The development of status is essentially a question of stratification resting upon usurpation. Such usurpation is the normal origin of almost all status honor. But the road from this purely conventional situation to legal privilege, positive or negative, is easily traveled as soon as a certain stratification of the social order has in fact been 'lived in' and has achieved stability by virtue of a stable distribution of economic power.

7: 'ETHNIC' SEGREGATION AND 'CASTE'

Where the consequences have been realized to their full extent, the status group evolves into a closed 'caste.' Status distinctions are then guaranteed not merely by conventions and laws, but also by *rituals*. This occurs in such a way that every physical contact with a member of any caste that is considered to be 'lower' by the members of a 'higher' caste is considered as making for a ritualistic impurity and to be a stigma which must be expiated by a religious act. Individual castes develop quite distinct cults and gods.

In general, however, the status structure reaches such extreme consequences only where there are underlying differences which are held to be 'ethnic.' The 'caste' is, indeed, the normal form in which ethnic communities usually live side by side in a 'societalized' manner. These ethnic communities believe in blood relationship and exclude exogamous marriage and social intercourse. Such a caste situation is part of the phenomenon of 'pariah' peoples and is found all over the world. These people form communities, acquire specific occupational traditions of handicrafts or of other arts, and cultivate a belief in their ethnic community. They live in a 'diaspora' strictly segregated from all personal intercourse, except that of an unavoidable sort, and their situation is legally precarious. Yet, by virtue of their economic indispensability, they are tolerated, indeed, frequently privileged, and they live in interspersed political communities. The Jews are the most impressive historical example.

A 'status' segregation grown into a 'caste' differs in its structure from a mere 'ethnic' segregation: the caste structure transforms the horizontal and unconnected coexistences of ethnically segregated groups into a vertical social system of super- and subordination. Correctly formulated: a comprehensive societalization integrates the ethnically divided communities into specific political and communal action. In their consequences they differ precisely in this way: ethnic coexistences condition a mutual repulsion and disdain but allow each ethnic community to consider its own honor as the highest one; the caste structure brings about a social subordination and an acknowledgment of 'more honor' in favor of the privileged caste and status groups. This is due to the fact that in the caste structure ethnic distinctions as such have become 'functional' distinctions within the political societalization (warriors, priests, artisans that are politically important for war and for building, and so on). But even pariah people who are most despised are usually apt to continue cultivating in some manner that which is equally peculiar to ethnic and to status communities: the belief in their own specific 'honor.' This is the case with the Jews.

Only with the negatively privileged status groups does the 'sense of dignity' take a specific deviation. A sense of dignity is the precipitation in individuals of social honor and of conventional demands which a positively privileged status group raises for the deportment of its members. The sense of dignity that characterizes positively privileged status groups is naturally related to their 'being' which does not transcend itself, that is, it is to their 'beauty and excellence' (χαλο-χαγαϑια). Their kingdom is 'of this world.' They live for the present and by exploiting their great past. The sense of dignity of the negatively privileged strata naturally refers to a future lying beyond the present, whether it is of this life or of another. In other words, it must be nurtured by the belief in a providential 'mission' and by a belief in a specific honor before God. The 'chosen people's' dignity is nurtured by a belief either that in the beyond 'the last will be the first,' or that in this life a Messiah will appear to bring forth into the light of the world which has cast them out the hidden honor of the pariah people. This simple state of affairs, and not the 'resentment' which is so strongly emphasized in Nietzsche's much admired construction in the *Genealogy of Morals*, is the source of the religiosity cultivated by pariah status groups. In passing, we may note that resentment may be accurately applied only to a limited extent; for one of Nietzsch's main examples, Buddhism, it is not at all applicable.

Incidentally, the development of status groups from ethnic segregations is by no means the normal phenomenon. On the contrary, since objective 'racial differences' are by no means basic to every subjective sentiment of an ethnic community, the ultimately racial foundation of status structure is rightly and absolutely a question of the concrete individual case. Very frequently a status group is instrumental in the production of a thoroughbred anthropological type. Certainly a status group is to a high degree effective in producing extreme types, for they select personally qualified individuals (e.g. the Knighthood selects those who are fit for warfare, physically and psychically). But selection is far from being the only, or the predominant, way in which status groups are formed: Political membership or class situation has at all times been at least as frequently decisive. And today the class situation is by far the predominant factor, for of course the possibility of a style of life expected for members of a status group is usually conditioned economically.

8: STATUS PRIVILEGES

For all practical purposes, stratification by status goes hand in hand with a monopolization of ideal and material goods or opportunities, in a manner we have come to know as typical. Besides the specific status honor, which always rests upon distance and exclusiveness, we find all sorts of material monopolies. Such honorific preferences may consist of the privilege of wearing special costumes, of eating special dishes taboo to others, of carrying arms—which is most obvious in its consequences—the right to pursue certain non-professional dilettante artistic practices, e.g. to play certain musical instruments. Of course, material monopolies provide the most effective motives for the exclusiveness of a status group; although, in themselves, they are rarely sufficient, almost always they come into play to some extent. Within a status circle there is the question of intermarriage: the interest of the families in the monopolization of potential bridegrooms is at least of equal importance and is parallel to the interest in the monopolization of daughters. The daughters of the circle must be provided for. With an increased inclosure of the status group, the conventional preferential opportunities for special employment grow into a legal monopoly of special offices for the members. Certain goods become objects for monopolization by status groups. In the typical fashion these include 'entailed estates' and frequently also the possessions of serfs or bondsmen and, finally, special trades. This monopolization occurs positively when the status group is exclusively entitled to own and to manage them; and negatively when, in order to maintain its specific way of life, the status group must *not* own and manage them.

The decisive role of a 'style of life' in status 'honor' means that status groups are the specific bearers of all 'conventions.' In whatever way it may be manifest, all 'stylization' of life either originates in status groups or is at least conserved by them. Even if the principles of status conventions differ greatly, they reveal certain typical traits, especially among those strata which are most privileged. Quite generally, among privileged status groups there is a status disqualification that operates against the performance of common physical labor. This disqualification is now 'setting in' in America against the old tradition of esteem for labor. Very frequently every rational economic pursuit, and especially 'entrepreneurial activity,' is looked upon as a disqualification of status. Artistic and literary activity is also considered as degrading work as soon as it is exploited for income, or at least when it is connected with hard physical exertion. An example is the sculptor working like a mason in his dusty smock as over against the painter in his salon-like 'studio' and those forms of musical practice that are acceptable to the status group.

9: ECONOMIC CONDITIONS AND EFFECTS OF STATUS STRATIFICATION

The frequent disqualification of the gainfully employed as such is a direct result of the principle of status stratification peculiar to the social order, and of course, of this principle's opposition to a distribution of power which is regulated exclusively through the market. These two factors operate along with various individual ones, which will be touched upon below.

We have seen above that the market and its processes 'knows no personal distinctions': 'functional' interests dominate it. It knows nothing of 'honor.' The status order means precisely the reverse, viz.: stratification in terms of 'honor' and of styles of life peculiar to status groups as such. If mere economic acquisition and naked economic power still bearing the stigma of its extra-status origin could bestow upon anyone who has won it the same honor as those who are interested in status by virtue of style of life claim for themselves, the status order would be threatened at its very root. This is the more so as, given equality of status honor, property per se represents an addition even if it is not overtly acknowledged to be such. Yet if such economic acquisition and power gave the agent any honor at all, his wealth would result in his attaining more honor than those who successfully claim honor by virtue of style of life. Therefore all groups having interests in the status order react with special sharpness precisely against the pretensions of purely economic acquisition. In most cases they react the more vigorously the more they feel themselves threatened. Calderon's respectful treatment of the peasant, for instance, as opposed to Shakespeare's simultaneous and ostensible disdain of the *canaille* illustrates the different way in which a firmly structured status order reacts as compared with a status order that has become economically precarious. This is an example of a state of affairs that recurs everywhere. Precisely because of the rigorous reactions against the claims of property per se, the 'parvenu' is never accepted, personally and without reservation, by the privileged status groups, no matter how completely his style of life has been adjusted to theirs. They will only accept his descendants who have been educated in the conventions of their status group and who have never besmirched its honor by their own economic labor.

As to the general *effect* of the status order, only one consequence can be stated, but it is a very important one: the hindrance of the free development of the market occurs first for those goods which status groups directly withheld from free exchange by monopolization. This monopolization may be effected either legally or conventionally. For example, in many Hellenic cities during the epoch of status groups, and also originally in Rome, the inherited estate (as is shown by the old formula for indiction against spendthrifts) was monopolized just as were the estates of knights, peasants, priests, and especially the clientele of the craft and merchant guilds. The market is restricted, and the power of naked property per se, which gives its stamp to 'class formation,' is pushed into the background. The results of this process can be most varied. Of course, they do not necessarily weaken the contrasts in the economic situation. Frequently they strengthen these contrasts, and in any case, where stratification by status permeates a community as strongly as was the case in all political communities of antiquity and of the Middle Ages, one can never speak of a genuinely free market competition as we understand it today. There are wider effects than this direct exclusion of special goods from the market. From the contrariety between the status order and the purely economic order mentioned above, it follows that in most instances the notion of honor peculiar to status absolutely abhors that which is essential to the market: higgling. Honor abhors higgling among peers and occasionally it taboos higgling for the members of a status group in general. Therefore, everywhere some status groups, and usually the most influential, consider almost any kind of overt participation in economic acquisition as absolutely stigmatizing.

With some over-simplification, one might thus say that 'classes' are stratified according to their relations to the production and acquisition of goods; whereas 'status groups' are stratified according to the principles of their *consumption* of goods as represented by special 'styles of life.'

An 'occupational group' is also a status group. For normally, it successfully claims social honor only by virtue of the special style of life which may be determined by it. The differences between classes and status groups frequently overlap. It is precisely those status communities most strictly segregated in terms of honor (viz. the Indian castes) who today show, although within very rigid limits, a relatively high degree of indifference to pecuniary income. However, the Brahmins seek such income in many different ways.

As to the general economic conditions making for the predominance of stratification by 'status,' only very little can be said. When the bases of the acquisition and distribution of goods are relatively stable, stratification by status is favored. Every technological repercussion and economic transformation threatens stratification by status and pushes the class situation into the foreground. Epochs and countries in which the naked class situation is of predominant significance are regularly the periods of technical and economic transformations. And every slowing down of the shifting of economic stratifications leads, in due course, to the growth of status structures and makes for a resuscitation of the important role of social honor.

10: PARTIES

Whereas the genuine place of 'classes' is within the economic order, the place of 'status groups' is within the social order, that is, within the sphere of the distribution of 'honor.' From within these spheres, classes and status groups influence one another and they influence the legal order and are in turn influenced by it. But 'parties' live in a house of 'power.'

Their action is oriented toward the acquisition of social 'power,' that is to say, toward influencing a communal action no matter what its content may be. In principle, parties may exist in a social 'club' as well as in a 'state.' As over against the actions of classes and status groups, for which this is not necessarily the case, the communal actions of 'parties' always mean a societalization. For party actions are always directed toward a goal which is striven for in a planned manner. This goal may be a 'cause' (the party may aim at realizing a program for ideal or material purposes), or the goal may be 'personal' (sinecures, power, and from these, honor for the leader and the followers of the party). Usually the party action aims at all these simultaneously. Parties are, therefore, only possible within communities that are societalized, that is, which have some rational order and a staff of persons available who are ready to enforce it. For parties aim precisely at influencing this staff, and if possible, to recruit it from party followers.

In any individual case, parties may represent interests determined through 'class situation' or 'status situation,' and they may recruit their following respectively from one or the other. But they need be neither purely 'class' nor purely 'status' parties. In most cases they are partly class parties and partly status parties, but sometimes they are neither. They may represent ephemeral or enduring structures. Their means of attaining power may be quite varied, ranging from naked violence of any sort to canvassing for votes with coarse or subtle means: money, social influence, the force of speech, suggestion, clumsy hoax, and so on to the rougher or more artful tactics of obstruction in parliamentary bodies.

The sociological structure of parties differs in a basic way according to the kind of communal action which they struggle to influence. Parties also differ according to whether or not the community is stratified by status or by classes. Above all else, they vary according to the structure of domination within the community. For their leaders normally deal with the conquest of a community. They are, in the general concept which is maintained here, not only products of specially modern forms of domination. We shall also designate as parties the ancient and medieval 'parties,' despite the fact that their structure differs basically from the structure of modern parties. By virtue of these structural differences of domination it is impossible to say anything about the structure of parties without discussing the structural forms of social domination per se. Parties, which are always structures struggling for domination, are very frequently organized in a very strict 'authoritarian' fashion. . . .

Concerning 'classes,' 'status groups,' and 'parties,' it must be said in general that they necessarily presuppose a comprehensive societalization, and especially a political framework of communal action, within which they operate. This does not mean that parties would be confined by the frontiers of any individual political community. On the contrary, at all times it has been the order of the day that the societalization (even when it aims at the use of military force in common) reaches beyond the frontiers of politics. This has been the case in the solidarity of interests among the oligarchs and among the democrats in Hellas, among the Guelfs and among Ghibellines in the Middle Ages, and within the Calvinist party during the period of religious struggles. It has been the case up to the solidarity of the landlords (international congress of agrarian landlords), and has continued among princes (holy alliance, Karlsbad decrees), socialist workers, conservatives (the longing of Prussian conservatives for Russian intervention in 1850). But their aim is not necessarily the establishment of new international political, i.e. *territorial*, dominion. In the main they aim to influence the existing dominion.[2]

[2] The posthumously published text breaks off here. We omit an incomplete sketch of types of 'warrior estates.'

CHAPTER 2

CONTEMPORARY CONCEPTIONS OF STRATIFICATION

The following readings either emphasize a problem relating to the utility of the concept of social class or present a particular theoretical perspective. Although the two aims are somewhat interrelated they can be analytically distinguished. The problem involving the concept of social class was referred to in the "Introduction" and is elaborated by the articles in this section. The theoretical perspective emphasized, although to a considerable extent indirectly, is that of Max Weber.

Weber did not elaborate a theory of stratification. His efforts were primarily confined to creating an empirically supported conceptual scheme for the analysis of certain aspects of stratification in modern society. Although his scheme followed from that of Marx, it challenged a number of critical points of Marxian theory. Weber belongs among the so-called conflict theorists; his work in stratification served most to provide an improved set of conceptual tools with which to move beyond Marxian theory.

There are currently *two* dominant theoretical perspectives guiding most of the theorizing in American sociology. These have been labeled as *conflict* theory, and *functionalist* theory. Gerhard Lenski has done a concise job of describing the conflict and functionalist perspectives. He writes that "conflict theorists approach the problem of social inequality from the standpoint of the various individuals and subgroups within Society. Their needs and desires, rather than the needs of society as a whole, provide the basic postulates for this school of theorists."[1]

Weber's elaboration of some of Marx's theories helped to bring forth the perspective of stratification as a consequence of a multitude of groups and individuals in conflict over scarce goods.

The three dimensions of stratification posited by Weber are: *class, status,* and *party*. Those concepts facilitate a major modification of Marx's formulation. Marx conceived of stratification as ultimately consisting of two large classes determined on the basis of the organization of production in society. The owners and controllers of the production system were at the top, in the *capitalist* class, and the nonowning, controlled members of society were at the bottom, in the *proletariat*. These large economically determined classes were considered major elements in the dynamics of social change, primarily because conflict would inevitably occur between them. This class conflict provided the dynamics of history; to Marx, conflict was the key to social change.

To Weber, conflict was also a fundamental aspect of social organization. But rather than being polarized between two dominant classes, it occured at many points in the social structure. Weber's recognition of the importance of status and political power led away from the Marxian reliance on economic organization and the motives and restraints related to it. The three dimensions introduced by Weber facilitate the analysis of multiple sets of factors in describing and explaining inequality and stratification. Included in this multiple dimensional approach is the recognition that conflict also occurs in and among the various class, status, and political power groupings that emerge in highly differentiated industrial societies. As will be pointed out in the article concluding this section, the focus on status community flows from the need to look more closely at that part of society, namely, the middle levels, within which a great variety of different combinations of class, status, and political power occur.

The second dominant theoretical approach in stratification is functionalism, which has also been called the "integrative" or "consensual" approach. The most important contributions in this theoretical perspective were made by Kingsley Davis, Wilbert Moore, and Talcott Parsons.[2] The functionalists consider social inequality a necessary aspect of all societies. In order for societies to have the most crucial positions filled by the most able members of the population, some kind of system of unequal rewards must occur. The particular system of rewards is ultimately determined by the central value system of that society. Thus stratification is not a feature of society that can be eliminated, nor will it go away by itself.

[1] Gerhard Lenski, *Power and Privilege*, (New York: McGraw-Hill, 1966), p. 16.

[2] Kingsley Davis and Wilbert Moore, "Some Principles of Stratification," *American Sociological Review*, 5 (1945), pp. 242-249; Talcott Parsons, "A Revised Analytical Approach to the Theory of Social Stratification," in Talcott Parsons (ed.), *Essays in Sociological Theory*, (New York: The Free Press, 1954), pp. 386-439.

Lenski summarizes the essential difference between the conflict theorists and the functionalists.

> Conflict theorists, as their name suggests, see social inequality as arising out of the struggle for valued goods and services in short supply. Where the functionalists emphasize the common interests shared by the members of a society, conflict theorists emphasize the interests which divide. Where functionalists stress the common advantages which accrue from social relationships, conflict theorists emphasize the element of domination and exploitation. Where functionalists emphasize consensus as the basis of social unity, conflict theorists emphasize coercion. Where functionalists see human societies as social systems, conflict theorists see them as stages on which struggle for power and privilege take place.[3]

In the past few years, a few major works have attempted to facilitate a synthesis of the conflict and functional perspectives in stratification. The most notable example is contained in Lenski's work. He begins by pointing out that the process is already underway. He asserts that the two older theories were essentially *normative* systems of explanation, whereas the new synthesis, to which he contributes, is essentially analytic in emphasis. He relates this new movement toward a more analytical theory to the increased use of scientific methods in the study of inequality.

The readings in this section should make the student aware of the difficulties in coming to grips with the social realities surrounding the issues of inequality and stratification in modern society, and the attendant problem of conceptualizing these realities. That we possess a potent rhetoric of social class makes our task even more difficult. In stratification, the history of ideas and their verbal presentations, in both popular and scholarly writing, create issues that contribute to the murkiness surrounding most of the major questions in the field.

[3] Lenski, *Power and Privilege*, p. 16-17.

5 *Kurt B. Mayer*

THE CHANGING SHAPE OF THE AMERICAN CLASS STRUCTURE

The subject of social stratification is currently in a truly paradoxical state. On the one hand social class or socio-economic status, as the more cautious sociologists often prefer to call it, has become the most widely used variable in empirical sociological research. Moreover, the sociologist's fascination with class or status also has carried over into the popular non-fiction literature, as evidenced by the remarkable success of Vance Packard's *The Status Seekers* on the best seller list. Stratification concepts are now part and parcel of the intellectual baggage, and indeed, of the everyday vocabulary of the educated laymen. This is surely a handsome tribute to the efficiency of sociological teaching and research.

Yet at the same time, and this is the paradox, the conceptual confusion which has long characterized this field shows no signs of abating. At the very time that voluminous textbooks on social stratification are published and the term is copiously employed in all manner of empirical investigations, a running debate is carried on in the professional journals about the meaning of the very concepts employed. Indeed, sociologists find it increasingly necessary to devote entire sessions at their national and international professional meetings not only to the presentation of findings from stratification research but to the clarification of basic theoretical and conceptual issues. Such a session was held at the 1958 annual meeting in Seattle, where Rudolf Heberle entitled his paper "Recovery of Class Theory" while Robert Nisbet called his contribution "The Decline and Fall of Social Class," arguing that "the term social class is by now useful in historical sociology, in comparative or folk sociology, but that it is nearly valueless for the clarification of the data of wealth, power, and social status in the contemporary United States and much of Western society in general."[1] In 1963, only five years later, another such session was organized by the author of a recent book, *Class in American Society*,[2] who sent out a clarion call to his colleagues: "It is time that we took a broad critical look at the subject.... We need some challenging ideas on the functions of class in the affluent society, its characteristics, its likely future, and the role of social mobility as well."

What accounts for this curious situation? The renowned English sociologist, Professor T. H. Marshall, put his finger on it rather neatly when he told the

From *Social Research*, 30 (Winter, 1963), pp. 458-468. Reprinted with permission of the author and publisher.

[1] Both of these papers have been published in the *Pacific Sociological Review*, 2 (Spring, 1959), pp. 18-24 and 11-17, respectively.

[2] Leonard Reissman, *Class in American Society* (New York: The Free Press, 1959).

Third World Congress of Sociology some years ago: "It is both remarkable and slightly ludicrous that it should prove necessary to carry out the most elaborate research in order to discover what the shape of the class structure is in modern societies. To past generations it constituted the 'social order' by which their lives were, and should be, governed, and they had no doubts about its nature. It is reasonable to suppose that our modern difficulties arise from the gradual replacement of a simple, clear and institutionalized structure by a complex, nebulous, and informal one."[3] The need for continuous conceptual clarification and theoretical reassessment arises in large part from the increasing complexity of modern social structures and their rapid changes. By the time we have fashioned some conceptual tools to analyze our stratification system and tested them in empirical research, the underlying social reality has already changed and the image they present has become distorted. Nevertheless, with a properly focused apparatus a picture of the changing stratification system which is not too wide of the mark can be obtained.

The concepts necessary to discern the current shape of the class structure and its probable future changes are not new but it seems to this writer that they are sometimes inadequately handled if not needlessly confused. Certain conceptual distinctions are *not* merely terminological questions and matters of arbitrary definition but are essential for a useful analysis of contemporary social reality.

The first of these distinctions is that between social differentiation and social stratification.[4] Social differentiation refers to the hierarchical ordering of *social positions*. Evidently this is a universal characteristic of all societies since a division of specialized functions and roles is essential for their survival. Inherent in this functional differentiation of roles is a process of evaluation and ranking. Every society not only develops a division of labor but also judges and evaluates the importance of different functions and thereby ranks the positions in its social structure in importance.

Social stratification, on the other hand, refers to the fact that in many, though *not* in all, societies certain *collectivities of people* continue to occupy the same positions through several generations. In other words, *if* societies are stratified there exist groupings of people, social strata, who manage to monopolize access to certain positions on an *hereditary, permanent* basis. Now, some of the conceptual confusion in the field of social stratification arises from the fact that certain theorists of the structural-functional persuasion do not make this distinction but instead define social stratification as "a structure of regularized inequality in which men are ranked higher or lower according to the value

[3] T. H. Marshall, "General Survey of Changes in Social Stratification in the Twentieth Century," *Transactions of the Third World Congress of Sociology*, III (London: International Sociological Association, 1956), pp. 3-4.

[4] Cf. the lucid treatment of this point by Walter Buckley, "Social Stratification and Social Differentiation," *American Sociological Review*, 23 (August, 1958), pp. 369-375. See also Dennis H. Wrong, "The Functional Theory of Stratification: Some Neglected Considerations," *American Sociological Review*, 24 (December, 1959), pp. 777-782.

accorded to their various *roles and activities*."[5] Note that this definition refers to stratification as a hierarchy of social *positions*, whereas this writer holds that social strata are collectivities of people who occupy hierarchical positions hereditarily.

To be sure, definitions depend upon one's purpose, but if one uses the functionalist definition of stratification one cannot investigate the relationship between the existence of hierarchies of differentiated positions and the existence—or the absence—of groupings of people who monopolize access to such positions for several generations. This is unfortunate, for the fact is that there do exist societies which are socially differentiated, that is, one finds a division of labor and of functions and roles, with corresponding rank differences and prestige differentials, but where the incumbency of such roles and positions is not hereditary. These are classless societies.

It is true that such classless societies are found only among relatively small, non-literate societies which live close to the level of subsistence and in a few types of agricultural communities, such as the Israeli kibbutzim. This poses the fascinating question whether a classless society would be possible in a complex, highly developed industrial society. We shall argue that the answer is yes, and indeed that American society is currently travelling along this road at least part of the way, but we will defer this discussion until later since we must first be concerned with some further conceptual distinctions before the point can be made.

If we want to apprehend the nature of modern societies we cannot perceive their hierarchies of positions as unidimensional. Instead, we must follow the lead of Max Weber and distinguish at least three different rank orders: an economic hierarchy, a prestige hierarchy, and a power hierarchy. Note that these are hierarchies of positions, not of people. But they are interrelated because individuals who hold positions in one order can often, though by no means always, employ this as a basis for also holding corresponding positions in one or both of the other hierarchies. For example, a high position in the economic hierarchy may also support a high position in the prestige hierarchy and in the power hierarchy—but not automatically so, and here lies an important difference between modern industrial societies and earlier social structures.

Certainly, when one looks at the history of Western societies one is impressed with the fact that pre-industrial social structures were all characterized by clearcut, highly visible and relatively unambiguous divisions not only of social positions but also of social strata. Despite many concrete differences in time and place, the various classes of people were then clearly demarcated and sharply set off from each other because they occupied congruent positions in each of the separate rank orders and because their positions were also hereditary. In feudal society, for example, a man's estate was not only hereditary and legally fixed but also generally implied well-matched positions in the economic, prestige, and

[5] Bernard Barber, *Social Stratification* (New York: Harcourt, Brace, 1957), p. 7. Italics mine.

power hierarchies. Differing sharply in wealth, honor, prestige, and political power, each class was characterized by distinctive patterns of conduct, by a sharp sense of social distance, and by outward symbols of a distinct way of life which placed narrow limits on inter-marriage and social intercourse. At the same time, the prevailing ideologies and religious creeds explained and justified the existing hierarchical arrangements.

The situation is quite different, however, in modern industrial societies where social classes are no longer set apart by tangible, legal boundaries. Of course, the three rank orders of positions exist here, too, and if anything they have become considerably more differentiated and more complex. But in the absence of legal restrictions, dynamic economic, technological and demographic forces have greatly increased the social mobility of individuals and families and of entire groups. This has been accompanied by a democratization of behavior patterns and a change in ideology toward equalitarianism. The result of these massive changes has been two-fold: many individuals now move up or down the separate rank orders at different rates of speed, thereby creating sizeable proportions of the total population who find themselves at noticeably different levels of the three hierarchies of social position at any given time, a fact which bedevils all unidimensional conceptual schemes of social stratification. At the same time, the increased mobility has also greatly weakened the inheritance of positions, particularly in the middle ranges of the economic, prestige, and power orders. In modern, industrial societies, therefore, social classes still clearly inhabit both the top and the bottom of the rank hierarchies, but they are now beginning to dissolve in the middle. Moreover, since the middle ranges have been greatly expanding, this portends major changes in the shape of the social structure.

If we now focus specifically on American society, we note that impressive changes have taken place during the last quarter century in the positional hierarchies. The most obvious transformation has occurred in the economic hierarchy which no longer represents a pyramid with a broad base, a smaller middle and a narrow top. The pyramid diagram was indeed applicable before World War II, but during the past two decades major shifts have occurred in the occupational structure and in the distribution of incomes. The unskilled occupations and the farm jobs have contracted sharply while the proportion of the labor force working in white collar jobs and in the skilled manual categories has expanded. Well over half of the labor force today is employed in white collar and skilled manual jobs.

The shifts in the distribution of income which have accompanied these changes in the occupational structure have been even more dramatic. In terms of constant (1959) dollars, median family incomes rose 50 percent during the 1950's alone.[6] Underlying this increase in median family incomes has been a major shift of families upward along the entire income scale. The proportion of families with incomes of less than $5,000 declined from 80 percent in 1949 to

6 U.S. Bureau of the Census, *U.S. Census of Population: 1960, General and Economic Characteristics, United States Summary*. Final Report PC (1)–1C. (Washington, D.C.: U.S. Government Printing Office, 1962), p. xxix.

42 percent in 1959, while the proportion receiving incomes between $5,000 and $10,000 increased from 17 percent to 43 percent during the decade, and families with incomes of $10,000 and over rose from 3 percent to 15 percent. Note, however, that despite the remarkable overall rise in income, somewhat more than one-fifth of all American families still had incomes of less than $3,000 in 1959. Despite this very significant lag, to which we shall return later, it is no exaggeration to conclude that the economic rank order of American society has changed its shape from the traditional pyramid to a diamond bulging at the middle and somewhat flat at the bottom.

The transformation of the economic structure has also significantly affected the shape of the prestige hierarchy. The time-honored invidious distinctions between the style of life of white collar employees and of manual workers have become blurred to a considerable extent. The rising standard of living has made many elements of a middle class style of life, such as home ownership, suburban living, paid vacations, and highly valued consumer goods, available not only to white collar employees but also to large numbers of manual wage earners. Nor has this trend been confined to material status symbols. The economic leveling has been accompanied by a visible "democratization" of behavior patterns. The gap in formal education which has traditionally set the wage worker sharply apart from the white collar employee has been reduced considerably as the median number of school years completed by the American population twenty-five years of age and over rose from 8.6 in 1940 to 10.6 in 1960.[7] The rise in educational achievements, combined with the increasing exposure to the mass media of communication, has induced large numbers of people at the lower social levels to adopt behavior patterns which differ little from those of the higher status circles who, quite significantly, seem to have relaxed stiff etiquette and elaborate social rituals in favor of greater informality, partly because domestic servants have become a vanishing breed.

Most visible, perhaps, has been the diminishing difference in wearing apparel: as the factories have installed lockers and cafeterias, the traditional blue shirts and lunch boxes of the workers have largely disappeared. The sports shirts and slacks they now wear to and from work resemble the increasingly informal attire of the supervisory personnel. Indeed, in growing numbers workers now wear the sports shirts on the job, as automation reduces the number of "dirty" jobs. Similarly, "correct speech" patterns are being diffused more widely by schools and mass media at the same time that standards of English usage are constantly becoming more lax among the well-educated.

To be sure, this assimilation of life styles has not obliterated all status differentials. There remain important differences in food habits, reading tastes, leisure time pursuits, participation in formal and informal associations, church attendance, and so forth, which all serve as badges of belonging to separate status groups. In fact, there is reason to believe that emphasis on subtle prestige

[7] U.S. Bureau of the Census, ibid., p. xxi.

differences is increasing precisely because crude and highly visible status differences have become blurred. But the heightening emphasis on symbolic minutiae counts little as compared to the growing proportion of Americans whose style of life is becoming steadily more similar.

Unfortunately, we have much less information about what is happening in the power dimension. This is an area where empirical research has barely begun to penetrate the surface, especially at the national level. Until we get the urgently needed information, it would appear that this hierarchy still retains its pyramid shape. The great mass of the population is apathetic and participates little in the decision-making process. This leaves the field to the relatively small minorities of policy makers and the somewhat larger groups who execute the policies. At the present time it is far from clear whether the national structure of power is monolithic or pluralistic, but there is no doubt that both access to and exercise of power remain more concentrated than the distribution of positions in the economic and prestige rank orders.

Finally, the crucial question of the effects which structural changes in the various hierarchies of roles and positions have had on the collectivities of people who occupy these roles must be raised. How have these changes affected the intergenerational transmission of positions, or the opportunities to attain them? It would appear that we still find rather clearly delimited classes both at the top and the bottom of the positional hierarchies. Here there are segments of the population whose position in all three rank orders is congruent and continues to be transmitted by ascription.

At the top is a numerically small but influential upper class of big businessmen, top corporation officials, independently wealthy men and women, and some professionals who originate from this class or are associated with it. It is difficult to estimate their numbers but one may hazard a guess that they comprise about one half of one percent of the total population. These people are our economic elite, and most though not all of them move in top prestige circles. Many of them also belong to the power elite, although not all of them avail themselves of the opportunities to exercise power, nor are all men in top power positions necessarily members of the upper class. It is true that this class is not really homogeneous; there are status differences between old upper class families who have been wealthy for generations and whose hallmark is inconspicuousness, and the newer, flashy cafe society circles and Texas billionaires. Still, their way of life, their attitudes, values and tastes differ from those of the rest in many respects and they successfully endeavor to pass on their positions on a hereditary basis.

At the other end of the scale there is a lower class of impoverished people. It comes as something of a shock that in our affluent society there is still a great mass of people who are literally poor and underprivileged in every respect. Who are they? They are the unskilled workers, migrant farm workers, unemployed workers who have been displaced by automation, and many of the non-whites. How many of them are there? This depends upon the statistical standards used, but even the most conservative yardstick indicates well over thirty million people. This is "the other America" as Michael Harrington has so poignantly described it in a recent book,[8] a submerged fifth of our total population, literally forgotten and invisible to the rest of society. For them poverty is a permanent way of life. Here, too, the three dimensions coincide and the positions at the bottom are also transmitted from father to son. Particularly dismaying is the fact that the prospects for improving their lot and reducing their numbers are not at all bright.

Who is in between these two classes? There are first of all the skilled and semi-skilled urban manual workers, the core of what has been traditionally the working class. They account for about a third of the population, but the traditional dividing line between manual workers and white collar employees no longer holds, because large segments of the working class now share a "white collar" style of life and many also accept middle class values and beliefs. To be sure, we still have a sizeable segment of workers who are not socially mobile, who live in a separate working class culture, emphasizing a philosophy of "getting by" rather than "getting ahead." They, too, form a stable class with congruent, hereditary positions. But one of the great gaps in our current knowledge in the field of social stratification is that we have no reliable information about the size of this group as compared to those manual workers who are mobile or are at least encouraging and urging, successfully for the most part, their children to move out of the working class. These latter form an important segment of the population, of indeterminate size, which is quite literally in transition, with positions no longer congruent and no longer hereditary.

Immediately beyond them is the white collar world, a truly heterogeneous aggregate of salaried employees, independent enterprisers, and professionals. They comprise well over two-fifths of the population. It has been customary to call them middle class and to distinguish between an upper and lower middle class. It seems to this writer, however, that these designations are losing their validity. Here we have so much mobility that many people hold different positions in the various rank orders and the situation is becoming so fluid that one can no longer truly speak of classes in the middle ranges of positional hierarchies. We therefore boldly conclude that what we have been accustomed to calling the middle class or middle classes is well on the way to losing its class character altogether. What is emerging here is social differentiation without stratification. More and more the bulk of white collar positions are opened up to competition through achievement and ability. They are less and less passed on from generation to generation on the basis of monopolistic pre-emption. Increasingly, there is free upward and downward mobility all the way up and down the widening middle ranges of the economic and prestige hierarchies.

To sum it up, America's social structure today and in the proximate future

[8] Michael Harrington, *The Other America: Poverty in the United States* (New York: Macmillan, 1962).

can be perceived as a diamond where the top and bottom are still pretty rigidly fixed, inhabited by upper and lower classes. A working class of the traditional sort also persists but comprises nowadays only a part of the manual workers. Between the extremes, however, classes are disappearing. To be sure, prestige, power and economic differentials persist here too, of course, and prestige differentials tend even to become accentuated as crude economic differences diminish and lose their visibility. But these differentials are no longer the hallmarks of social classes. In the middle ranges of the various rank orders we are witnessing the beginnings of a classless society in a modern industrial economy. It already involves roughly one-half of our population and may well involve more than that in the future although there are no signs that the top and bottom classes are likely to disappear altogether. This is a somewhat different classless society from that envisaged by Marx a century ago, but it is at least a partially classless society nevertheless.

6 *Dennis H. Wrong*

SOCIAL INEQUALITY WITHOUT SOCIAL STRATIFICATION

Recently, several sociologists have, notwithstanding the increased preoccupation of their colleagues with the subject of class, argued that the concept of social class is becoming more and more irrelevant to the understanding of advanced industrial societies.[1] They have largely confined their remarks to the United States. Several European writers, however, have made similar suggestions with respect to the major countries of Western Europe, though rather more tentatively since much that has already become a reality in America remains a trend on the other side of the Atlantic.[2] On the whole, the claim that social classes have disappeared or are disappearing has been rejected by the majority of Ameri-

Reprinted from *The Canadian Review of Sociology and Anthropology*, 1:1 (1964), by permission of the publisher.

[1] Arnold M. Rose, "The Concept of Class and American Sociology," *Social Research*, 25 (Spring, 1958), 53-69; Robert A. Nisbet, "The Decline and Fall of Social Class," *Pacific Sociological Review,* 2 (Spring, 1959), 11-17; Wilbert E. Moore, "But Some Are More Equal Than Others," *American Sociological Review,* 28 (February, 1963), 14-15.

[2] T. H. Marshall, "General Survey of Changes in Social Stratification in the Twentieth Century," *Transactions of the Third World Congress of Sociology*, 3 (International Sociological Association, 1956), 1-17; George Lichtheim, *The New Europe: Today and Tomorrow* (New York, 1963), 198-215.

can sociologists. For the most part their rejection has been based on little more than a preference for different definitions of class and has been offered good-humouredly as if the matter were merely a trivial issue of terminology. Yet, as so often in sociology, definitions defended on pragmatic or operational grounds turn out on closer examination to obscure full recognition of the contrast between past and present and of the new possibilities latent in contemporary social reality.

Those writers who maintain that social class is no longer a useful concept take what has been called a "realist" position regarding the existence of classes. They are committed, that is, to the view that social classes, in the words of one of them, "are groups possessed both of real and vital common economic interests and of a group-consciousness of their general position in the social scale."[3] From such a standpoint, neither the existence of a scale of income distribution, nor of a rank-order of occupations with respect to status or prestige, nor of functional hierarchies of power and authority, necessarily implies the presence of clearly demarcated *groups*, as distinct from differentiated individuals or social roles, which are identifiable as social classes.

The so-called "realist versus nominalist" dispute over the kind of objective reality that should be ascribed to social classes has long been a standard theoretical and methodological issue in discussions of social stratification. Yet it has not always been acknowledged that all of the major nineteenth- and twentieth-century theorists of class were unmistakably on the "realist" side, regardless of whether they thought classes were based on economic interests, shared values, or common access to social power.

To Marx, a class was not fully formed until it had ceased to be merely a potential membership-group (class *an sich*) and had achieved a solidarity based on awareness of the common interests of its members in opposition to those of another class (class *fur sich*).

Joseph Schumpeter wrote: "Class is something more than an aggregation of class members . . . A class is aware of its identity as a whole, sublimates itself as such, has its own peculiar life and characteristic 'spirit'."[4]

Max Weber is frequently cited by American sociologists in support of the contention that stratification in modern societies involves at least three partially independent hierarchies. He is also often invoked to justify the treatment of status rankings of occupations as synonymous with "class structure." Weber is the source of the "class-status-power" triad so favoured by contemporary sociologists, but he was clearly concerned with identifying relatively cohesive groups differentiated with respect to these three bases of stratification and did not consider each as forming a continuous scale on which individuals or positions could be located. Thus, defining "class," like Marx, in strictly economic terms, he saw classes as "possible, and frequent, bases for communal action," although he was less certain than Marx that aggregates of people sharing like interests

[3] Marshall, "General Survey of Changes in Social Stratification," 15.

[4] Joseph A. Schumpeter, *Imperialism and Social Classes* (New York, 1955), 107.

would become aware of their common interests and resort to "communal action" to advance them. Commonly regarded as the first modern social theorist to stress the importance of status, Weber was chiefly concerned to describe "status groups" or *Stande*—a term that clearly designates Self-conscious collectivities. With reference to power, he used the less fortunate term "party," which nevertheless is unambiguous in connoting a collective entity rather than an attribute with respect to which individuals or roles vary continuously.

Finally, W. Lloyd Warner has always insisted that the six social classes he discovered in Newburyport were ultimately derived from "the way in which people in American communities actually classify themselves," although his critics have repeatedly challenged the validity of this claim after re-analysing Warner's own data.

I doubt that any of these men would have devoted so much time and effort to the study of class had they thought it a matter of indifference whether classes "really" existed in the experience of their members or were no more than artifacts constructed by the sociologist as a means of ordering and summarizing his observations. The grouping together by the sociologist of individuals sharing a common position with respect to several distinct variables is a thoroughly legitimate and useful procedure in certain kinds of empirical research. But to call the resultant groupings "social classes" is to risk confusion with the quite different meaning of class in the writings of the leading theorists of stratification. Those researchers who use such terms as "socioeconomic group" or "level" at least implicitly recognize the distinction. But there are others who persist in referring to combined measures of occupation, income, or education as "indexes" of social class, although the entity these measures allegedly indicate appears to have no independent reality and "class" becomes no more than a shorthand expression for the ensemble of the very variables that have been combined to form the index.[5]

Critics of the realist conception of social classes have attributed to it the necessary implication that members of a society must be fully aware of the class system and its nature can therefore be determined by a simple opinion poll.[6] Surely, this is a specious argument. To assert that social controls and expectancies are present in the minds and sentiments of the people whose conduct they influence is not to maintain that these people can readily put them into words. Even in the case of social norms in primary groups, which are clearly operative influences on behaviour, those who conform to them are not always able to provide a coherent account of the codes that guide and restrain them in their

[5] Marshall, "General Survey of Changes in Social Stratification," 5-6. Rose, "The Concept of Class," 65-69.

[6] See, for example, Bernard Barber, *Social Stratification* (New York, 1957), 76-77; Nelson N. Foote, Walter Goldschmidt, Richard Morris, Melvin Seeman, and Joseph Shister, "Alternative Assumptions in Stratification Research," *Transactions of the Second World Congress of Sociology*, 2 (International Sociological Association, 1953), 386-387.

day-to-day interactions with [others].[7] The kind of awareness-in-behaviour that frequently characterizes social class relations may involve still less self-consciousness since classes (except in small isolated local communities) are not even potential primary groups; hence the frequent use of the term "quasi-group" to describe them.

The existence of classes, then, is a matter of degree depending upon the extent to which their members are conscious of their unity and of the boundaries separating them from other classes.[8] But recognition of this does not invalidate the realist position. All the theorists previously mentioned, with the exception of the ahistorical Warner, dealt at length with what Schumpeter called *class formation* and saw it as a process frequently falling short of the eventual emergenc[e] of fully developed classes. All of them attempted to specify the conditions under which aggregates of similarly situated individuals acquire cohesion and begin to behave as if they constitute at least a fictive membership-group. Nor does the existence of individuals or families whose position is marginal within the class structure pose special theoretical difficulties for this is an inevitable result of inter-class mobility, which is also a temporal process of uncertain outcome.

Finally, if the existence of a class system implies *some* stratification, it is also possible for particular classes–most frequently new and rising classes–to exist which do not fit into an orderly hierarchical system.[9] Thus if we regard social stratification as a stratification of groups, classes may be formed in partial independence of stratification. But, more important, inequalities in the distribution of income, prestige, and power may exist in complete independence of it.

So far, my emphasis has been primarily definitional and I have done no more than insist on a number of distinctions that are widely recognized in theory, although often ignored in research practice. Applied to contemporary

[7] William F. Whyte reports that his main informant, Doc, remarked to him: "Now when I do something, I have to think what Bill Whyte would want to know about it and how I can explain it . . . Before I used to do these things by instinct." *Street Corner Society* (Chicago, 1943), 10.

Many of the simplifications to which sociologists are prone in discussing the question of the degree to which people are aware of the determinants of their own behaviour result from a failure to take into account Ryle's distinction between "knowing how" and "knowing that." See Gilbert Ryle, *The Concept of Mind* (New York, 1949), 25-61.

[8] As Andreas Miller has written: "A social class is a real group, set aside from its social environment by natural boundaries . . . In a classless society one can speak of differences in social status. It would, however, be of no value to look for a class-system in a society without differences in social status . . . An adequate conception of the class-system can only be reached by answering the question whether the community investigated is divided into strata by clear boundaries, what is their number, location, and strength." "The Problem of Class Boundaries and Its Significance for Research into Class Structure," *Transactions of the Second World Congress of Sociology*, 2 (1953), 343, 348-49.

[9] Stanislaw Ossowski, "Old Notions and New Problems: Interpretations of Social Structure in Modern Society," *Transactions of the Third World Congress of Sociology*, 3 (1956), 18-25.

industrial societies, however, these distinctions are acquiring new relevance, for modern societies are unmistakably moving in the direction of maintaining considerable institutionalized inequity in the absence of a class system, a condition that the Polish sociologist, Stanislaw Ossowski, has characterized as "non-egalitarian classlessness."[10] This condition has not yet been fully achieved even in the United States, much less in Western Europe. But the steady approach toward it increasingly transforms social classes into "ghost" communities preserving a fitful and wavering identity rooted in historical memories, similar to that ascribed by Nathan Glazer to the "ghost nations" of third-generation American immigrants which continue to play a minor role in American politics.[11]

Since so many American sociologists have failed to see any significance in the disappearance of social classes in view of the survival of pronounced status inequalities, I shall briefly suggest several differences between societies where classes to some degree are present and societies where social inequality is relatively detached from stratification.

1. Income, educational, and status mobility are experienced differently in the two societies. The person who moves upward (or downward) in a classless society does not encounter a class boundary in addition to the career obstacles he has to overcome in order to rise. Surely, it is the relative absence of classes in American society, whatever the historical causes for this absence, that accounts for the general belief that mobility is greater in the United States than in Europe, a belief that Lipset and Bendix have shown to be unfounded.[12] Quite minor improvements in status or income are more readily perceived as mobility where no class boundary has to be crossed or confronted. There have been no real counterparts in the United States to the British "angry young men:" persons of provincial and working-class origin who rise through educational or occupational attainment but become embittered on experiencing real or imagined exclusion when they try to cross a class line. The closest American equivalent is the experience of upwardly mobile Negroes and members of ethnic or religious minorities. The fact that occupational status rankings are similar in America and Britain, and indeed in all advanced industrial societies,[13] merely underlines the difference between these rankings and a social class system.

2. More important, the distinction between stratification and social inequality aids us in understanding the political sociology of modern industrial societies.

[10] Stanislaw Ossowski, *Class Structure in the Social Consciousness* (New York, 1963), 100-118.

[11] Nathan Glazer, "Ethnic Groups in America: From National Culture to Ideology," in Morroe Berger, Charles H. Page and Theodore Abel, editors, *Freedom and Control in Modern Society* (New York, 1954), 172-173.

[12] Seymour Martin Lipset and Reinhard Bendix, *Social Mobility in Industrial Society* (Berkeley, 1959), 11-75.

[13] Alex Inkeles and Peter H. Rossi, "National Comparisons of Occupational Prestige," *American Journal of Sociology*, 61 (January, 1956), 329-339.

The distinction holds, it should be noted, regardless of whether economic interest or style-of-life is considered the essential basis of class. The latter—the "Marx vs. Warner" issue—is a separate definitional problem. However, last-ditch defenders of the relevance of the class concept, such as Rudolph Heberle in a recent paper,[14] fall back on the Marxist view of classes as interest-groups divided by ownership or non-ownership of the means of production. They plausibly argue that, although classes separated by sharp status and associational boundaries have been largely supplanted by a continuous hierarchy of status, conflicts of interest have by no means disappeared and the major opposing groups continue to think and act in concert politically, at the very least in their voting behaviour. The prediction of American Marxists in the 1930's that national cleavages of economic interest would increasingly supersede regional and ethnic divisions as the main basis of political alignment has on the whole been borne out.

But a second part of the prediction was that more tightly drawn class lines would result in an intensification of the political class struggle between Left and Right. The opposite has occurred: "class" has become a more important determinant of voting at the same time that the bitterness of class struggle has unmistakably abated.[15] While it may, therefore, be formally correct to insist that the term "class" in the Marxist sense is still applicable where society-wide conflicts of interest find political expression, it is surely more relevant to the understanding of modern politics to recognize that today economic interest-groups and the political associations based on them do not, in T. H. Marshall's words, "permeate the whole lives of their members, as social classes do, nor are they always in action, and at times the constituent sub-groups may be more important than the largest aggregates."[16]

Ralf Dahrendorf attributes the obsolescence of the Marxist two-class system to what he aptly calls the "institutional isolation of industry" in modern society. But he tries to preserve the emphasis on conflict and change in Marxist class theory by re-defining classes as the result of tension between power-holders and their subordinates, arguing that the division between owners and non-owners of property, and even conflicts of economic interest in general, are merely special cases of this more fundamental phenomenon.[17] Dahrendorf does not hesitate to conclude that there are as many class systems in a modern society as there are functional hierarchies of power and that a single individual may therefore simultaneously be a member of several different classes if he belongs to several associ-

[14] Rudolph Heberle, "Recovery of Class Theory," *Pacific Sociological Review*, 2 (Spring, 1959), 18-28.

[15] Seymour Martin Lipset, *Political Man* (New York, 1960), especially chapters 9 and 13.

[16] Marshall, "General Survey of Changes in Social Stratification," 13.

[17] Ralf Dahrendorf, *Class and Class Conflict in Industrial Society* (Stanford, Calif., 1959), especially part two.

ations each with its own structure of authority. In effect, Dahrendorf makes three main contentions: that social conflict is generated by differences in power; that classes are conflict-groups; and that all conflict-groups are classes. He may be right on the first two points (I am inclined to think that he is), but the third assertion surely represents the most quixotic effort to uphold the continuing usefulness of the concept of class in recent sociological writing.[18] Moreover, it would seem to be of no use at all in understanding the major political divisions in modern societies, although this has been precisely the most valuable feature of class theories which take their point of departure from Marx. Yet notwithstanding the inadequacies of his own class theory, Dahrendorf shows a far more acute grasp of the many differences between stratified and non-egalitarian classless societies than most American sociologists.

3. The absence of classes also helps account for the invisibility of poverty in the United States to which several writers have recently called attention. The poor are composed of a number of categories of persons with particular demographic characteristics whose economic plight is no longer clearly linked to what Marx or Weber would consider a "class situation."[19] Both in status and in economic terms, only the American Negroes come close to constituting a definable and cohesive deprived group, with the possible exception of tenant farmers and labourers in certain sectors of the agricultural economy. There is indeed some justification for calling Negroes *the* American lower class.[20]

The emerging social structure of post-bourgeois industrial society can best be understood if, except for secondary purposes and for historical analysis, we abandon the concept of social class and re-define much of the work done under this label as a contribution to the sociology of equality and inequlity. . . .

American sociologists have failed to see that the absence of classes may both in ideology and in social fact *more* effectively conceal existing inequalities than a social structure clearly divided into recognizable classes. The invisibility of poverty in the United States already referred to, suggests such a conclusion, as

[18] Both Kurt B. Mayer and Lewis A. Coser have similarly criticized Dahrendorf's thesis in reviews of his book. See Mayer's review of the German edition, *American Sociological Review*, 23 (October, 1958), 592-593, and of the English edition, ibid., 25 (April, 1960), 288; and Coser, *American Journal of Sociology*, 65 (March, 1960), 520-521.

[19] . . . [A] study of poverty in the United States by Oscar Ornati indicates that the following were "poverty-linked characteristics" in 1960: Nonwhite, Female head of household, Age 65 and over, Age 14-24 head of household, Rural Farm, Residence in South, Nonwage earner, Part-time wage earner, More than Six Children under 18, Education less than 8 years. None of the groups defined by these characteristics, with the possible exception of Rural Farm, represents a socioeconomic class. Ornati, "Poverty in an Affluent Society," preliminary draft, New York: The New School for Social Research and the Twentieth Century Fund (mimeographed), chapter 5. For a discussion of the nonclass nature of contemporary American poverty see Henry M. Pachter, "The Income Revolution," *Dissent*, 4 (Summer, 1957), 315-318.

[20] Rose, "The Concept of Class," 64.

does the fact that income distribution has become more unequal in the past decade,[21] the very decade of the "affluent society," which has witnessed so much individual and collective mobility, the mass diffusion of formerly restricted status symbols, and the breakdown of long-standing ethnic, religious, and even racial barriers to opportunity.

In distinguishing conceptually between stratification and inequality and noting some of the consequences of their increasing factual separation in contemporary society, I have avoided direct discussion of mobility and equality of opportunity. Many writers who have insisted as I have that stratification involves a hierarchy of groups rather than of positions or of individuals possessing unequal amounts of income, prestige, and power, have gone on to argue that stratified groups, or social classes, must necessarily be hereditary.[22] By transmitting the unequal privileges of one generation to the next through the family, classes thus inevitably prevent the full institutionalization of equality of opportunity.

The class systems of the past have undeniably been hereditary, though permitting sufficient mobility to justify distinguishing them from *caste* systems. But need this be so in the future? Historically, biological continuity has been the major means of preserving the internal solidarity and the distinctive ethos of classes from generation to generation, but is it necessarily the only possible means? George Orwell wrote: "The essence of oligarchical rule is not father-to-son inheritance, but the persistence of a certain world-view and a certain way of life imposed by the dead upon the living. A ruling group is a ruling group so long as it can nominate its successors. Who wields power is not important, provided that the hierarchical structure remains always the same."[23] Orwell was writing of political elites, but his point that permanence of structure need not depend on biological continuity may well have a broader relevance. Hereditary social classes may not be succeeded by non-egalitarian classlessness but by new classes whose members are not recruited by the inter-generational transmission of privileges through the family and whose cohesion does not depend on familial socialization.

Equality of opportunity could literally be achieved in full only by a method of allocating individuals to social positions that was strictly random, such as drawing lots. In contrasting equal opportunity with the inheritance of social position, however, sociologists obviously mean by the former the allocation of individuals to positions according to the single criterion of demonstrated ability to carry out the position's requirements. They have usually assumed that

[21] I am indebted to Oscar Ornati for having shown me the data from a later section of his study, "Poverty in an Affluent Society," indicating this to be unmistakably the case.

[22] See especially Walter Buckley, "Social Stratification and the Functional Theory of Social Differentiation," *American Sociological Review*, 23 (August, 1958), 369-375; and Kurt B. Mayer, "The Changing Shape of the American Class Structure," *Social Research*, 30 (Winter, 1963), 458-468.

[23] *Nineteen Eighty-Four* (New York, 1949), 370-371.

equality of opportunity thus defined is not only morally superior to any hereditary principle but would also prove to be more humanly tolerable, eliminating the social gulf that has existed between hereditary social classes and removing the envy and sense of injustice of low-status individuals who feel deprived of social rewards only by the accident of birth.

There is some evidence that the absence of clear-cut class lines in the United States and the prevailing "democracy of manners" make it easier for low-status individuals to tolerate hereditary inequalities provided they continue to believe that at least *some* opportunity to rise is available to them and their children.[24] But the most devastating attack on the belief that an inegalitarian order combined with full equal opportunity would reduce social conflict has been made by the English sociologist, Michael Young, in his brilliant sociological satire *The Rise of the Meritocracy: 1870-2033.*[25] This book has been completely ignored by American sociologists (with the exception of myself[26]), failing even to receive reviews in the journals, although it contributes vastly more to our theoretical understanding of class and inequality than the innumerable continuing studies of community class structures or of correlations between "class affiliation" and various kinds of behaviour.

Young's book is cast in the form of an historical interpretation written by a sociologist in the year 2033. His meritocratic social order is located in England, rather than "nowhere," and its evolution under the pressure of social forces powerfully at work in today's world is fully described. Although like other anti-Utopian writers Young's purpose is to warn rather than to prophesy, the form he has chosen gives his book a sociological relevance greater than that of many similar efforts which do not succeed in becoming more than a kind of sociological science-fiction or satiric caricatures of contemporary society.

The meritocracy is the result of three forces: the attack by socialists on all hereditary privileges, the pace of international economic competition requiring Britain to maintain high rates of economic growth,[27] and improvements in intelligence testing which have made it possible to reorganize the school system so that students can be segregated by intelligence at progressively earlier ages and trained for their eventual positions in the social order. The testing centers and the school system thus have become the vehicles for selecting the ruling elite of meritocrats. Possessing a monopoly of ability, the meritocracy easily prevails in

[24] Robert E. Lane, *Political Ideology: Why the American Common Man Believes What He Does* (New York, 1962), 57-81.

[25] Michael Young, *The Rise of Meritocracy* (London, 1958), passim.

[26] See Dennis H. Wrong, "The Functional Theory of Stratification: Some Neglected Considerations," *American Sociological Review*, 24 (December, 1959), 778-782; and "All Men Are Equal But Some . . . ," *Dissent*, 7 (Spring, 1960), 207-210.

[27] Several writers have recently argued that the maintenance of high rates of economic growth sets severe limits to the achievement of greater equality of condition as distinct from equality of opportunity. See Lichtheim, *The New Europe*, 188-189; also C. A. R. Crosland, *The Conservative Enemy* (New York, 1962), 29-34.

conflicts of interest with the lower strata, who are completely bereft of leadership since all their potential leaders have been elevated into the meritocracy, and who must live with the knowledge that they have been scientifically proven to be inferior in ability to their rulers. The family, however, has survived in its present form and, echoing the functional theory of inequality, Young sees this as the Achilles heel of the regime. The meritocratic parents of inferior children and women, whose occupational skills suffer as a result of their withdrawal to bear and raise children, become infected with a discontent that eventually leads to revolution.

In Young's account the meritocracy clearly constitutes a unified ruling group, sharing common interests and a similar style of life, even though it is not recruited by heredity. And the same is true to a lesser degree of the "technicians"–the regime's euphemism for the industrial working class. Rather than defining class and stratification by the hereditary principle and calling the meritocracy a "classless" or unstratified society, it is surely more reasonable to see it as a new form of class society.

Yet one must raise some doubts about the general relevance of Young's meritocracy to contemporary trends in advanced industrial societies. One might question, to begin with, his assumption that the family will remain cohesive and unchanged when so much else has been transformed. More important, the very plausibility of Young's account depends heavily on the roots of the meritocracy in English history with its characteristic "inevitability of gradualness." Thus Young sees the sharpness of class lines and the steepness of the status hierarchy that have existed in English society from feudalism to the present day as surviving even when birth has been entirely supplanted by merit as the basis of status. While the independence of stratification in general from the particular form of stratification by hereditary social classes is thus brilliantly suggested, one is forced to wonder whether a meritocracy would have the same consequences in an industrial society that lacked the pervasive continuities of English history–in, say, the United States.

I know of only one even sketchy account of a possible American meritocracy. It is provided, not by a sociologist, but by a lawyer and unsuccessful politician, Stimson Bullitt, in his perceptive little book *To Be a Politician*.[28] Bullitt envisages an American meritocratic order as being far more stable and less riven by class conflict than Young's Britain. He writes:

> The free flow up and down and the narrow range of variations in revealed ability among members of the great majority will make class differences less sharp. Also, the classes will be equally well fed and in most ways equally free; people on different levels of talent will be closer in many ways than were the social classes of the past. All people will have greater understanding, and therefore sympathy, for persons on other levels of talent than used to be the case between classes whose members lived like different species (pp. 177-178).

[28] (New York, 1961), 162-193.

While Bullitt attributes the absence of class tensions in a meritocratic United States in part to general prosperity and a high degree of material equality–conditions which are absent in Young's less economically self-sufficient England–the traditional classlessness of American society clearly leads him to anticipate an American meritocracy that would resemble a continuous hierarchy of unequal positions rather than Young's more stratified order.

Will the decline of hereditary social classes and the trend toward meritocracy eventuate in non-egalitarian classlessness or in a new class society allocating individuals by specialized abilities rather than by birth? What will be the peculiar discontents of each order? What form will the ancient dream of an egalitarian society, equally frustrated by both, take under these conditions? These are likely to be the questions, only dimly adumbrated in our present imperfectly affluent society, with which future sociologists of inequality will concern themselves. We are not likely to make much progress in answering them if we cling to a conceptual apparatus that does not distinguish between stratification and inequality or between stratification in general and the particular form it has taken in the hereditary class societies of the past.

7 *Harold L. Wilensky*

WORK, CAREERS, AND SOCIAL INTEGRATION

The aim of the study is to link specific attributes of work situation and career to styles of life, and more broadly to variations in the strength and kinds of ties that bind persons and groups to community and society. The study should yield a typology of life styles which will permit assessment of (a) theories of the 'mass society' and (b) current portraits of stratification in the urban-industrial community.

'Style of life' is used to designate consumption patterns (the way people spend their money), and patterns of participation and media exposure (the way they spend their leisure time). Participation, consumption and media exposure

From *The International Social Science Journal*, Vol. XII, No. 4, 1960. Reproduced with the permission of UNESCO.

Note: Paper read in part at the American Sociological Society meetings, Chicago, September 1959. Based on a program of research made possible by grants from the National Institute of Mental Health (M-2209), 1958-1960, and a fellowship at the Center for Advanced Study in the Behavioral Sciences, 1956-1957. I am indebted to G. E. Swanson and M. Janowitz for many helpful suggestions.

are each examined for their status significance and for their function as major sources of social integration. Put crudely, the person can be tied to the system as well as placed in it by social interaction (attachments to kin, friends and formal association), by a package of 'goodies' (possessions and a schedule of purchases) and by mass entertainments which, while they trivialize meaning, vulgarize taste, deaden reflection, and distract attention, also accent shared values, provide information, and broaden horizons.[1] That various types of social relations, consumption habits, and media exposure have differential effect in linking persons to larger communal ends is clear. That each pattern of behaviour may be shaped in some degree by work situation and career seems likely. That together these patterns sufficiently cohere to be called 'styles of leisure' seems possible.[2]

Guiding propositions

Three generalizations represent a guiding orientation for the labour-leisure study.

In societies at a high level of economic development much social behaviour still varies by class (in a Marxian economic sense). Engels' observations about English millworkers of 1844 surely still apply to several groups in the working class—to many unskilled labourers (whose work is likely to be heavy, dirty and despised) and to semi-skilled operatives on old-fashioned mechanical conveyor belts (whose sense of oppression is well described in Walker and Guest, *Man on the Assembly Line*). In their attitudes, these workers not only approximate the alienated machine slaves of the classic indictment, but, in their objective life chances, they also face more unemployment and insecurity, more obstacles to the upward escape and in every way receive fewer of the rewards to be had. Such

[1] For analysis of the mass media's 'narcoticizing dysfunction' as well as their functions of status conferral and norm reaffirmation, see P. Lazarsfeld and R. K. Merton, "Mass communication, popular taste and organized social action," in B. Rosenberg and D. M. White (eds.), *Mass Culture* (New York: The Free Press, 1957), pp. 457-473; E. Van den Haag, "Of happiness and despair we have no measure," in B. Rosenberg and D. M. White (eds.), op. cit., pp. 504-536, for a cogent critique of popular culture. Both essays display a precision usually absent in polemics in this area. Edward Shils, "Mass society and its culture," Daedalus-Tamiment Institute Seminar, June 1959 (mimeographed), presents a most thorough defence of popular culture, based on a sound historical sense; cf. J. Dumazedier, "Realites du Loisir et Ideologies," *Esprit* 6 (Juin 1959), pp. 3-20.

[2] There is no real evidence that among large populations these areas of off-work behaviour—the activities and orientations people evidence in their social participation, consumption and media exposure—comprise 'styles' in any usual meaning of that term. Style implies a form (as against substance) which is consistent through time, and coheres enough to cross-cut diverse spheres of life. For a lucid discussion of this concept and a review of ethnological data, see A. L. Kroeber, *Style and Civilization* (Ithaca, New York, Cornell University Press, 1957). The cross-cutting dimensions of leisure we are using are: solo versus group (and within group, the range of values, interests and status levels represented by the pattern of behaviour—from family localism through ever-widening circles and networks of involvement), deviant versus conforming, fluid versus habitual, and committed versus alienated or apathetic. Our data will permit correlation among items of behaviour and attitude within and between various areas along each of these dimensions; if there are 'styles' we hope to be able to specify them.

men probably comprise no less than a fifth or sixth of the labour force in America–more elsewhere. Accordingly our study includes two small samples of deprived workers. Our aim is to locate and explain the two most common patterns of 'underdog' response:

Individuation (a pattern of life which is deviant, solo, alienated, fluid). Impoverished primary group relations and no secondary contacts other than those at work. Two variants: (a) Apathetic retreat from work and life–privatized leisure (more napping, eating and drinking alone, passive spectatorship, etc.); (b) explosive compensation for tensions of both work and leisure (more tavern brawls, 'blowing top,' law violation, etc.). Over time the same person may alternate between these two individuated patterns, extreme apathy and extreme activism.

Family-home localism (less deviant, less solo, less alienated, more habitual). This represents a retreat of a different kind–a withdrawal to the narrow circle of kin and friends; a primary group life without strong links to the larger community.

In short, I am aware that class still tells, that a large slice of the labour force behaves the way it does mainly because of low and unstable income, low status, and their psychological correlates.[3] But we speak here of the backwash of economic development.

With advancing industrialism and urbanism, traditional indices of class–present income and occupational category–no longer serve to distinguish between styles of life and degrees of social integration for a growing middle mass. Much behaviour, whether group structured or not, cross-cuts all or several social-economic strata. This is especially true with respect to the media of mass communication, consumption and some aspects of politics and social participation.[4] We need not belabour this point, for the stratification literature abounds

[3] See two thorough reviews of the relevant literature: Genevieve Knupfer, "Portrait of the underdog," in R. Bendix and S. M. Lipset (eds.), *Class, Status and Power*, (New York: The Free Press, 1953), pp. 255-263; and S. M. Lipset, "Working-class authoritarianism," *American Sociological Review*, 24 (August, 1959), pp. 482-501.

[4] For instance, if we ask 'What behaviour and attitudes show least and most relationship to income bracket?,' we find that attitudes regarding equality (e.g. Welfare State issues) show a strong link to income, but attitudes regarding freedom (e.g. civil rights) as well as world affairs show much weaker relationship and on some issues none at all. Education, and perhaps ethnic origin and father's social-economic status–indicators of preadult, preoccupational socialization–may provide a better means of distinction than present class position. Lipset (op. cit., p. 489) shows that level of education affects tolerance on Stouffer's civil liberties scale much more than does occupational stratum (although one wonders whether education would be related to tolerance in the Soviet Union, or whether in America a high-school or college education would not be requisite to leadership positions in both safely-integrating organizations and extremist political movements). Education, however, may join income and occupational stratum as a weak predictor of life style and integration, since inequalities in education are likely to be reduced more rapidly than the other inequalities (colleges and high schools level down while opportunity opens the way up). Meanwhile, many old differences have already diminished. For example, the time spent reading magazines and books is closely related to income and education; but the time spent

in discussion of 'blurring class lines'—the worker going 'middle class' or the 'status proletarianization of white-collar strata'—of the ascendency of 'popular culture' and the emergence of a 'consumer-oriented society'—and there is impressive support for these ideas.

If social class no longer predicts much behaviour in the middle mass, what attributes of social structure do serve as indicators? The labour and leisure study looks to two major clusters of variables linked to economic development: (a) Specific variations in work situation (tasks, social relations, dimensions of career, if any, and related career contingencies); (b) the individual's mobility experience, aspirations and expectations (including his work commitments).

The general argument is this: if we consider people on the same social-economic level, and at the same stage of the life cycle, the variations in behaviour among groups differently situated with respect to these work situation variables will be greater than the variation among social-economic strata. In their ties to the larger community, factory maintenance men, traffic clerks, printers, professors, and solo lawyers will resemble one another more than they resemble their status counterparts among main assembly-line workers, accountants, dentists, house counsel, or bureaucratic engineers.

reading newspapers is not (A. Campbell and C. A. Metzner, 'Books, libraries, and other media of communication', in: D. Katz, et. al., *Public Opinion and Propaganda* [Hinsdale, Ill., The Dryden Press, 1954]), pp. 235-242).

Television habits, of course, are the best case in point: although the TV set may have vastly varied impact on the lives of families differently situated, the actual number of hours it grips us is only slightly related to social class. Average hours among TV-owners with incomes below $4,000 is 24 hours a week, above $4,000, 22 hours a week (NBC Television, *TV Today, Report II*, 1952, p. 18). In the 1952 election campaign, neither education nor income and occupational level made a difference in media exposure or involvement (M. Janowitz and D. Marvick, *Competitive Pressure and Democratic Consent* [Ann Arbor, Michigan, Bureau of Government, Institute of Public Administration, 1956], pp. 57-71; cf. R. E. Lane, *Political Life* (New York, Ill., The Free Press, 1959), pp. 80-6). Rich or poor, educated or not, Mr. Nixon's dog 'Checkers' entered your living room one way or another.

Finally, consider the shifting role of class in political attitudes and behaviour. Philip Converse offers one of the rare studies which analyse the behaviour of comparable national samples over time. He shows a marked decline in the relationship between social class and political-economic attitudes from 1945 to 1956—whether 'class' is indicated by occupational category or by subjective identification. The same is true of voting behaviour. True, the relationship between low status and Democratic voting was greater in Truman's 1948 triumph than in the war-time election of 1944. But the elections of 1952 and 1956 show a big decline in the class vote (Philip E. Converse, 'The shifting role of class in political attitudes and behavior', in: E. E. Maccoby, et al. [eds.], *Readings in Social Psychology*, 2nd ed. [New York, Holt, Rinehart and Winston, 1958], pp. 388-399). From these data, there is no reason to believe that 'candidate' appeals as opposed to 'issue' and 'party' appeals are a temporary aberration reflecting the Eisenhower personality. So long as the Cold War continues, and recessions are short, the class vote is likely to go the way of the ethnic vote of the old urban machines. (See also data on the social composition of mass movements in many countries cited in W. Kornhauser, *The Politics of Mass Society* New York, The Free Press, 1959], Part III.)

Careers, life style and social integration

Now we want to link work situation to leisure style and at the same time view both in the context of changes over the life cycle. Consideration of 'careers,' with special attention to the 'other-directed' Organization Man, can illustrate an approach to the problem.

The volume of writing about careers is large. There is uncommon agreement that types and rates of mobility are crucial to an understanding of modern society. And there are hints that work-life mobility may be more fateful than intergeneration mobility.[5] It is therefore remarkable that detailed work histories which cover a decade or more have been reported in only about a dozen studies, and have been related to other sociological variables in still fewer.[6] Limited as

[5] H. L. Wilensky and H. Edwards, "The skidder: ideological adjustments of downward mobile workers," *American Sociological Review*, 24 (April, 1959), pp. 215-231. Cf. W. Read, "Some factors affecting upward communication at middle-management levels in industrial organizations," unpublished Ph.D. thesis, University of Michigan, 1959, which reports a correlation of +0.41 ($p < 0.01$) between upward work-life mobility and holding back 'problem' information from the boss among 52 middle-level executives (mean age 37), but no correlation for intergeneration mobility.

[6] The studies include: P. E. Davidson and H. D. Anderson, *Occupational Mobility in an American Community* (Stanford, Stanford University Press, 1937)–based on a cross-section sample of 1,242 men (7 percent of the San Jose, California, labour force). W. H. Form and D. C. Miller, "Occupational career pattern as a sociological instrument," *American Journal of Sociology*, 54 (January, 1949), pp. 217-329–the most detailed analysis of 'career patterns," based on 276 job histories (sample stratified to match the Ohio labour force). S. M. Lipset and R. Bendix, "Social mobility and occupational career patterns," *American Journal of Sociology*, 57 (January and March 1952), pp. 336-374, 494-504–which analyses life-time work histories of 935 male heads of families in Oakland, California, a probability sample of segments of blocks (17 highest and lowest SES tracts were omitted, non-completion rate for the remaining 55 was about 18 percent). W. L. Warner and J. C. Abegglen, *Occupational Mobility in American Business and Industry* (Minneapolis, University of Minnesota Press, 1955)–based on a 48 percent return from 17,546 top executives (questionnaire mailed in two waves). *The Mobility of Tool and Die Makers, 1940-51*, Bulletin No. 1120 (United States Department of Labor, November 1952); *Occupational Mobility of Scientists* (1,000 Ph.D.s in chemistry, physics, biology), Bulletin No. 1121 (1953); *The Mobility of Electronics Technicians, 1940-1952*, Bulletin No. 1150, (1953); *Mobility of Molders and Core Makers, 1940-1952*, Bulletin No. 1162 (June 1954)–the United States Bureau of Labor Statistics series on work histories of skilled populations. G. L. Palmer, "Interpreting patterns of labor mobility," in E. W. Bakke, et al., *Labor Mobility and Economic Opportunity* (New York, Wiley & Sons, 1954)–summary of four publications of the WPA National Research Project, 1938-39, based on life-time work histories of 2,500 Philadelphia radio workers, weavers and loom fixers, machinists, and hosiery workers. L. G. Reynolds, *The Structure of Labor Markets* (New York, Harper & Row, 1951)–complete work histories of 450 male manual workers in New Haven. Parnes' study of the 17-year work experience of more than a thousand government clerical employees in Columbus in 1948 cited in H. S. Parnes, *Research on Labor Mobility* (New York, Social Science Research Council Bulletin 65, 1954), pp. 37, III, 123–a good critical assessment of research in this entire area. Finally, the Six City Survey of Occupational Mobility, reported in Gladys Palmer, *Labor Mobility in Six Cities* (New York Social Science Research Council, 1954); C. A. Myers, "Patterns of labor

the few systematic studies of job histories are, they leave no doubt that modern adult life imposes frequent shifts between jobs, occupations, employers, and work-places, and that these moves often involve status passage which is momentous for both the person and the social structure.

Let us look at career patterns and related career contingencies as a special case in the analysis of work-life mobility. Just as the concept of 'profession' loses its precision when we speak of the 'professionalization of auto-workers in Detroit'[7] so the concept of 'career' loses utility when we speak of the 'career of the ditch-digger.' In dealing with the organization of work it is better to take a more restricted view of career.

A career, viewed structurally, is a succession of related jobs, arranged in a hierarchy of prestige, through which persons move in an ordered, predictable sequence. Corollaries are that the job pattern is instituted (socially recognized and sanctioned within some social unit) and has some stability (the system is maintained over more than one generation of recruits).

The proportion of the labour force in careers, so conceived, may be increasing, but it is doubtful whether it is as yet more than a quarter or a third. For there is a good deal of chaos in modern labour markets, as in the lives of both buyers and sellers—chaos intrinsic to urban-industrial society. Rapid technological change dilutes old skills, renders others obsolete and creates demand for new ones; a related decentralization of industry displaces millions, creating the paradox of depressed areas in prosperous economies; metropolitan deconcentration shifts the clientele of service establishments, sometimes smashing or re-structuring careers; and recurrent crises such as wars, depressions, recessions, coupled with the acceleration of fad and fashion in consumption add to the general unpredictability.

Our interviews with 108 blue-collar workers and 39 lower white-collar work-

mobility," in W. Haber, et al. (eds.), *Manpower in the United States* (New York, Harper & Row, 1954), pp. 154-165; Albert Reiss, Jr., "Occupational Mobility of Professional Workers," *American Sociological Review*, 20 (December 1955); A. J. Jaffe and R. O. Carleton, *Occupational Mobility in the United States*, 1930-1960 (New York, King's Crown Press, 1954); and individual city reports, e.g. M. S. Gordon, *The Mobility of San Francisco Worker 1940-1949* (Institute of Industrial Relations, University of California, Berkeley, 1951). The six city study, although based on only one decade, contains the most adequate data and most extensive and representative sample. From it we can say that in most cases changing jobs means changing *both* occupation and industry, and projecting the data, the average worker will hold 12 jobs in a 46-year work-life and only one man in five will remain at the same occupation level throughout his work-life—*if* the decade 1940-1950 is typical, *if* the census categories are meaningful, etc.

[7] N. N. Foote, "The professionalization of labor in Detroit," *American Journal of Sociology*, 58 (January 1953), pp. 371-380. Theodore Caplow in another worthy effort at comparative analysis succumbs to the common tendency to label as 'professionalization' what is happening to real estate dealers (realtors), junk dealers (salvage consultants), and laboratory technicians (medical technologists). Personal service functionaries like barbers, bellboys, bootblacks, taxi drivers, it appears, are also 'easily professionalized' (*The Sociology of Work* [Minneapolis, University of Minnesota Press, 1954]), pp. 48, 139).

ers in a large parts-supplying factory (spring and summer, 1959), underscore the point.[8] These men are relatively secure; most live in 'middle-class' neighbourhoods. Despite the fact that 93 percent have at least 14 years with one employer, their 'careers' show extraordinary disorder.

For both groups, median number of full-time jobs held since completion of education is six (21 cases held 10 or more), median number of occupations, three (32 cases, at least five). How about ordered progression? One-fifth of the white-collar workers and almost one-third of the blue-collar workers have gone nowhere in an unordered way. A typical case: Helped on father's farm until 1932; 1932-34, part-time clerk in a grocery store; 1934-37, plating work in a factory; 1937-39, father's farm; 1939-59, machine work, 2 years; brick-layer's helper, 2 years; window repair, 2 years; assembler, 5 years; tool attendant, 8 years; truck driver, 1 year; drill machine operator, 8 months; all jobs in the same factory.

Seven in ten of the white-collar workers and six in ten of the blue-collar workers have experienced some movement across occupational strata.[9] By no stretch of the imagination could more than 45 percent of the total sample be said to have given evidence of an ordered progression in function or status (predictable by either the worker or an expert). Mobility patterns of another 45 percent (43 percent of the white-collar movers and 47 percent of the blue-collar movers) must be viewed as more or less chaotic. A typical case: 1918-22, silk dyer in factory; 1922-30, jigg tender for coal company; 1930-41, self-employed painter; 1941-57, an inspector in factory; 1957-59, trucker, then labourer (bumped). Furthermore, even when a man is coded as holding one position for a long time, the stability is often deceiving, for rights and duties of job classes continually change.

Careers, though they grip only a minority of the labour force, are a major source of stability for modern society, as Weber, Mannheim, and many others have noted. Every group must recruit and maintain its personnel and motivate role performance. Careers serve these functions for organizations, occupational groups and societies. At the same time they give continuity to the personal experience of the most able and skilled segments of the population—men who otherwise would produce a level of rebellion or withdrawal which would threaten the maintenance of the system. By holding out the prospect of continuous, predictable rewards, careers foster a willingness to train and achieve, to adopt a long view and defer immediate gratifications for the later pay-off. In

[8] All are white, high-seniority union members in Detroit. Medium family income: about $7,000. Three in four are between 45 and 65 years of age. Among blue-collar workers the more skilled are over-represented.

[9] The patterns: (a) much up or down (e. g. between manual and non-manual, clerk and college-educated engineer); (b) medium up or down (e. g. semi-skilled operative and skilled maintenance, clerk and non-college accountant); (c) fluctuating (one move up and one down); (d) unstable (two or more moves up and two or more down); (e) stable on one level.

Mannheim's phrase, they lead to the gradual creation of a 'life plan.'[10] It becomes important to ask, 'What is happening to careers?'

It is likely that with continuing industrialization careers are becoming on average more discrete and are characterized by more numerous stages, longer training periods, less fluctuation in the curve of rewards (amount, timing, duration), a more bureaucratic setting and more institutionalization, but are less widely visible (fewer, smaller publics recognize them).

Each of these dimensions of career is related to life style and thus to the types and levels of integration of persons and groups into community and society. The point can be illustrated with references to the 'other-directed' Organization Man celebrated in recent American literature. If we are specific in defining work role and career, we are able to view much of popular sociology in clearer perspective. Consider three dimensions of careers–number of ranks, career curve, organizational setting. Giving Riesman and Whyte[11] a sympathetic reading and putting their observations in this context, we may state the Organization Man theme as follows: Certain attributes of a class of large, complex organizations and of one type of career shape the work behaviour and life style of middle managers and technicians.

At work, these men play it safe, seek security, cultivate smooth human relations. In the community they put down many but shallow roots; they pick up and drop friends the way they buy and trade cars and homes–speeding up the obsolescence of both.

This is a life style which is active, group-centred, conforming and fluid–a pseudo-community pattern, unguided by stable values. Behaviour both at work and off work is characterized by expedient conformity ('if I don't do this, I'll get into trouble') and by other-direction, or conformity as a way of life whatever the content of values and norms conformed to ('A man should get along with the gang').

Now, the aspects of work organizations which permit us to call this fellow an organization man are those which necessitate residential mobility and provide stable careers with opportunity for climbing through many ranks. The following structural attributes of organizations and occupations seem to be at the root of this mobility and its accompanying way of life:

1. Organizations with tall hierarchies; careers with many stages, affording quick and steady climb. Mobility consequences: much career opportunity.
2. Organizations with a high ratio of managers to managed. Careers with administrative posts at the end. Mobility consequences: much career opportunity.
3. Organizations with history and prospect of continued growth. For example, organization or occupational group produces wide variety of products and services (diversification is a cushion against fluctuating demand), or an indis-

[10] Karl Mannheim, *Man and Society in an Age of Reconstruction*, trans. by E. A. Shils (New York: Harcourt Brace Jovanovich, 1940), pp. 56, 104-106, 181.

[11] D. Riesman, et al., *The Lonely Crowd* (New Haven, Yale University Press, 1950); W. H. Whyte, Jr., *The Organization Man* (New York, Simon & Shuster, 1956).

pensable service in continuous demand (e.g. education, breakfast cereal). Mobility consequences: stable career opportunity and expectations.

4. Long, prescribed training, e.g. executive development and/or rotation programmes, professional schools. Mobility consequences: stable career opportunity and expectations.
5. Multiple units, geographically scattered. Mobility consequences: career climb associated with residential mobility.

Long exposure to this type of work situation may indeed produce a pseudo-community style of life. The mobility–the cycle of arrival and departure–fosters shallow roots. The opportunity for stable careers both attracts and shapes men who value security and play it safe.

To test this idea, we are comparing middle-level executives or engineers in two large work-places with contrasting structure and growth potential.[12] It is my guess that the organization man flourishes only in the middle ranks of those organizations and occupational groups which approximate to the above description.[13]

It is obvious that only a tiny fraction of the population works in such organizations, and has such well-ordered work lives. There are millions, even among the work-commited, who will never experience the joys of a life plan

[12] A study of about 600 Detroit mothers illustrates how differences in work environment can be reflected in such matters as child-rearing philosophies and practices. Miller and Swanson [D. Miller and G. E. Swanson, *The Changing American Parent* (New York: Wiley and Sons, 1958)] found sharp contrasts between the child training of families whose heads work in large bureaucratic organizations and those whose heads were more free-enterprising or less used to urban living (self-employed, born on a farm or abroad, and so on). In general, parents exposed to low-risk work situations–wage-workers or salaried employees in big hierarchical organizations–put less accent on an active, independent approach to the world in their child training; they were also less concerned with 'internalization,' with development of strong 'built-in' self-control. These 'bureaucratic' parents encourage an accommodating, adjustive way of life. They were more concerned that their children learn to be 'nice guys'–able to make numerous friends easily. While this study does not permit specific links between child training 'styles' and such attributes of organizational structure as those listed above, it is consistent with my hypotheses.

One can argue that the stable career in the growing, complex multi-unit organization produces the organization man; the style of life he develops is expressed in his child-rearing practices and in his demands upon the school system; the revamped family and school in turn shape college life in the appropriate mould. The colleges then produce a supply of young men on the make, who, through self-selection and recruitment, are distributed among jobs appropriate to their pre-disposition, reinforcing the pseudo-community pattern.

[13] Why in the middle ranks? (a) Men at the bottom are too close to the task and what it takes to get it done to become enamoured of procedure, or over-committed to sociability. Top executives have an overview of the whole enterprise. They also have to relate it and justify it to the community in terms of organizational purposes. Contrast the middle ranks: they are most insulated from both the day-to-day task and the overview of both enterprise and community. They are therefore more vulnerable to technicism, less likely to show initiative (encourage innovations that fit the organization's mission). (b) Jobs in the middle are less clearly defined, and the criteria of success are often vague. The top men are

provided by a secure and growing organization of the right characteristics. Most men do not have careers; among those who do, career curves vary.

One can hold, with Riesman and Whyte, that these men of regular career, however few, provide a model for a life style which will diffuse throughout the population. But there are other counteracting tendencies that may carry the day.

For it is these very organizations (hierarchical, administration-heavy, multi-unit, steadily growing) and these very jobs and careers (middle management and staff) that will undergo the most drastic changes in coming years.

As with technological change in the past, white-collar automation means both upgrading and downgrading. The insurance adjuster finds himself attending only to troublesome, challenging cases; office mechanization takes care of the routine semi-clerical tasks which once burdened him. On the other hand, the office manager with 30 subordinates in a payroll department confronts an electronic brain programmed and run by others and has only two girls working under him. This is only the beginning. The high-speed computer takes over routine clerical work, but it also makes it possible to restructure and in effect downgrade a great many administrative and technical jobs.

If we combine the rapid handling of information by computers, the application of mathematics and statistics to administrative problems (mathematical programming and operations research), and the recruitment and training of better-educated managers who are smart enough to use the staff to put these methods to work, then we have a formula for revolution in the middle bureaucracy. As several observers suggest,[14] the new 'information technology' can routinize tasks once done in conference and committee by men skilled in human relations and the workings of the organizational machinery. It can allow the top to control the middle, as scientific management in the past allowed supervisors to control the workers.

In short, middle management may become highly structured and controlled. Innovation and planning would be centralized. Top executives, surrounded by programmers, research and development men, and other staff experts, would be

responsible for profit, survival and growth in the long run, but how much responsibility for enterprise success or failure can be assigned to anyone in the middle? Similarly, men at the bottom are more clearly accountable (with process prescribed and product inspected, quality-controlled, etc.). Yet, competition among the 'comers' in the middle is keen. Strong competition for vaguely-defined jobs breeds insecurity. Insecurity breeds both over-conformity and underconformity and encourages 'politicking'. The insecure fear change and seek safety in fixed rules (whether they fit organizational needs or not), or if sticking to useful rules makes the boss unhappy, they under-conform. Cf. H. L. Wilensky and C. N. Lebeaux, *Industrial Society and Social Welfare* (New York, Russell Sage Foundation, 1958), pp. 243ff; R. G. Francis and R. C. Stone, *Service and Procedure in Bureaucracy* (Minneapolis, University of Minnesota Press, 1956), pp. 162ff; P. M. Blau, *The Dynamics of Bureaucracy* (Chicago, University of Chicago Press, 1955).

14 H. J. Leavitt and T. L. Whisler, "Management in the 1980s," *Harvard Business Review, 36* (November-December 1958), pp. 41-48. Cf. C. E. Weber, "Change in managerial manpower with mechanization of data-processing," *Journal of Business*, 32 (April 1959), pp. 151-163.

more sharply separated from everybody else. The line between those who decide 'What is to be done and how' and those who do it—that dividing line would move up. The men who once applied Taylor to the proletariat would themselves be Taylorized.

The implications seem plain enough: the execution of controllable routine acts does not require great job enthusiasm, sociable conformity, or any other character trait beyond reliability and disciplined work habits. The model of Organization Man, which I concede to be the vanguard model of mid-century America may, like our cars, be far from the model of the eighties.

IMPLICATIONS FOR THE URBAN–INDUSTRIAL FUTURE

It seems likely that we are headed toward an organization of work in which a small group of executives, merchants, professional experts, and politicians labour

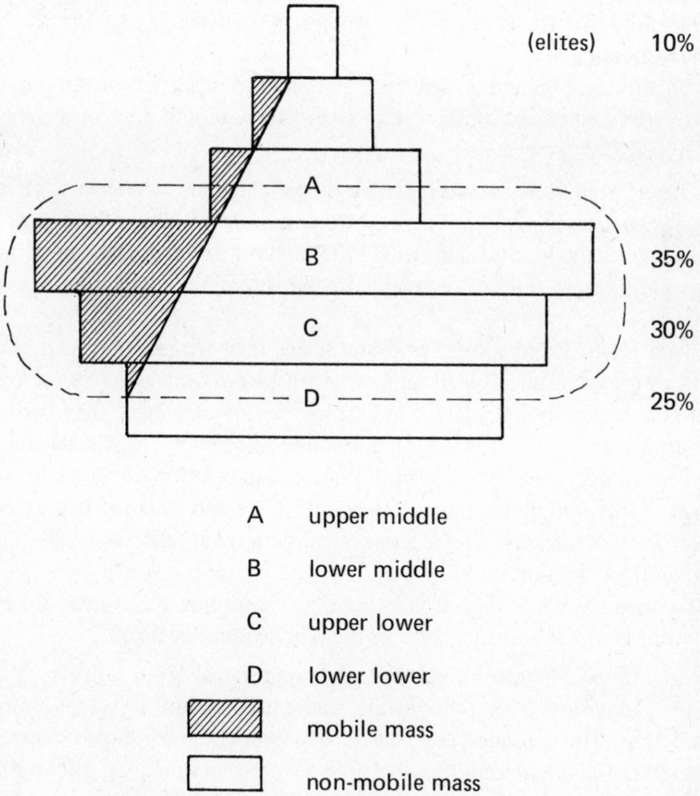

hard and long to control and service the masses, who in turn are going to 'take it easy' on a progressively shorter work week, in jobs which de-emphasize brawn and native shrewdness and play up discipline, reliability, and trained intelligence. This possibility holds great import for both the class structure of our society and its level of social integration.

At the top, the styles of life of business, professional, political, military and cultural elites will involve much mixing of business and pleasure. These elites will continue to have strong work commitments. They will develop an evermore cosmopolitan pattern of participation and consumption. Strong role integration among them will, as before, sustain their conformity, give their collaboration some coherence, and encourage their expression of core values.

Below the elites, the major distinctions will be between those who aspire to enter the elites or are sensitive to their values, on the one hand, and those who are non-mobile and non-aspiring, on the other hand.

Rather than clearly delimited social strata with contrasting subcultures, the society would develop a more homogeneous mass whose work-week and income permit choice of a wide range of behaviour. The society would provide expanded opportunity for social mobility through the cultivation of prestige-giving patterns of leisure.

In this situation, the most and least mobile segments of the population and those most and least committed to their work, should develop sharply different life-styles:

1. The most mobile, whatever their social class and whatever their work commitments, will develop a 'pseudo-community' life-style characterized by many lightly held attachments–the shallow roots I mentioned before. The stronger their career commitments the more they will integrate leisure and work.
2. What about those mobile and ambitious men whose status claims and aspirations are blocked at work and who withdraw from work as an arena for the status scramble? If they retain their status strivings, they will develop a pattern of status-compensating leisure. They will use the leisure ladder for their climb–seek offices in voluntary association, union, political party, spend their money in the Veblenian style, and become dedicated fans and active spectators. Others, however, will give up the race and join the vast majority–the non-mobile mass.
3. The person in the non-mobile mass will continue the retreat from work and withdraw further into family or neighbourhood localism.

Already there are indications that the withdrawal from work as a central life interest, long noted for the working class, is spreading to a vast majority of the population. The evidence is by no means overwhelming, but it seems impressive to me. The facts on trends in the time devoted to work, together with historical and survey data on the meaning of work, despite the eager 'moonlighter' and recurrent reminders that work still functions to keep men among the living, give cogency to the main argument: with continued economic development, and among men far enough above the poverty line, choices between leisure and income are increasingly resolved in favour of leisure.

Many scholars have observed that this leisure for the working class is to a large extent local–centered in family and neighbourhood–and this, too, is spreading upward. Why?

We return to changes on the work front. To the extent that men are exposed to disciplined work routines yielding little gratification and have careers which do not necessitate wide community participation, their retreat from work will be accompanied by a withdrawal from the larger communal life.

Does the task offer little variety? Is there little discretion in methods, pace, or schedule? Then, like dentists and assembly-line workers, our non-mobile man-in-the-middle will do his job in a reliable way, go home, segregate his work from life, and retire into the heartwarming circle of kin and friend.

Does the job yield no readily-visible status claim? Then it is as neighbour and family man that he will find his chief identity. Ask a 'hindleg toenail remover' what he does and he will tell you that he works at Swifts, but the white-collar 'console operator,' too, will name the company, not the job, because nobody has heard of this latest example of automation. The work role, if it is status-invisible, will be checked at the work-place door.

Is the work history punctuated by unexpected periods of unemployment, disorderly shifts among jobs, occupations and industries? Then the kind of life plan afforded by the established professions and crafts, the civil service and military establishment is impossible, and stability will be sought in primary relations off work.

Finally, is it a career which does not necessitate sustained cultivation of customer or client? Then one of the principal motives for getting into civic affairs is removed and participation in fund-raising drives and good works will be left to the ad man, the lawyer practicing on his own, the executive on the make.

In sum: for men in these work situations, middle-class or working-class, there is little motive and opportunity to use occupational identity as a status-winning device, little motive and opportunity to elaborate the work role beyond the work-place.

Where ties to occupation and work-place become weak, the quest for alternative ties is intensified. Therein lie both the danger and the promise of the newer patterns of labour and leisure.

De Tocqueville foretold the danger. On the one side stands the individual in his narrow circle of kin and close friends, immersed in his parochial concerns, with an almost bucolic contentment, retreating from a world of multiplying crises, grown too complex. On the other side stand a powerful state and the great mass organizations of the city–corporation, political party, trade union–centrally controlled by officials and an active minority, as distant from the rank-and-file as the media of mass communication. And nothing stands between.

In the absence of effective mediating ties, of meaningful participation in voluntary associations, the population becomes vulnerable to mass behaviour—more susceptible to personality appeals in politics, more ready for the demagogues who exploit fanatical faiths of nation and race.[15]

The danger is there; the promise less certain. Withdrawal from work and an intensified search for substitute sources of identity and solidarity may result in new leisure commitments more personally satisfying and socially integrating than the ones usually reported in the sociological news. Or the critics of industrialism may be right: progress may produce a nation of apathetic if reliable workmen and ardent consumers—all family locals, seeking life's meaning in the eye-level oven and the split-level home, men who in politics are available for anything—anything, that is, but the entanglements of citizenship.

For those who enjoy polemics such as these, the hazards of research are many. Perhaps students of leisure, more than most, are subject to the general temptation to range too widely, assemble trivia, and rest content with anecdotes. Yet, they have an unusual opportunity to tell us something about social structure and change. They can avoid sin and maximize virtue if they blend traditions of theory and research from the sociology of work, industrial relations, stratification and family research, focus their attention on routines of labour that emerge in leisure style, and gather data pin-pointing the ties that bind men to the Great Society.

8 *Holger R. Stub*

THE CONCEPT OF STATUS COMMUNITY

In recent years the literature of stratification has manifested increasing discontent with the use of the concept of "social class" in analyzing stratification phenomena of modern industrial societies. This paper will attempt to show how the concept of *status community* can serve as a conceptual tool in dealing with

[15] These hypotheses, relating mobility and work commitment variables to patterns of social participation, consumption, and media behavior form the focus of our 1959-60 survey of the middle mass in Detroit. They are elaborated in a companion paper, "Social mobility, life-style and mass behavior," which examines the debate between mass society theorists (who are concerned with the debilitation of culture-bearing elites and the proliferation of anti-democratic mass movements) and their empirically minded critics (who have rediscovered the limits of naked power and the viability of primary groups, and have explored the barriers to media manipulation).

some of the descriptive and theoretical problems arising from the use of the traditional social class approach to stratification.

Most literature on social stratification has employed the concept of social class as the focal point for description and theorizing. As the major concept in one of the most comprehensive stratification theories, Marx's definition has gained a preeminence in the conceptual armory of the theorist. The legacy of Marx and his followers has been so potent that it seems to have impelled us to use a concept that has, in fact, lost a great deal of its former utility.

In addition to retaining the concept of social class, the sociological literature dealing with inequality exhibits substantial confusion regarding the meaning of the concept of stratification. As mentioned in the "Introduction," various measures of inequality have failed to distinguish between social class analysis and social ranking. The former refers to a hierarchy of groups established over time and possessing a "class consciousness," or mutuality of interest, and is often restricted to those possessing appropriate and valued characteristics. Social ranking, however, involves, essentially, the designation of aggregates having similar income, education, occupational prestige, or combinations thereof. M. G. Smith states:

> Stratification is often conceived as the evaluative ranking of social units. Some theorists regard it as an abstract necessity of all social systems. Concretely, it refers to empirical distributions of advantages and benefits in specific societies. Analytically, it connotes the abstract possibilities of evaluative rankings on any number of special scales. As observers, we can construct as many stratification scales as we wish by employing any criteria we choose separately or together; but we should not confuse these abstract possibilities or analytic artifacts with empirical systems of social stratification.[1]

A large proportion of the research on social classes consists primarily of data that merely ranks various types of population aggregates. Such ranks, or aggregates, often give some evidence of possessing common life styles, consciousness of belonging together, traditional norms, values, status symbols, or other identifying behaviors; all of which have been characteristics serving to define social classes. Nevertheless, the traditional rhetoric of stratification resulting from the sophistication of Marx's overall theories has given the concept of social class a deep-seated place in sociology.

Although the Marxian concept of class, and the analysis of certain aspects of class phenomena, is of great importance, Marx's theory of stratification is inadequate. The feature of Marxian theory that seems most vulnerable in light of the changes that have taken place in modern societies is the insistence on the existence of two basic classes–a top class (capitalist) and a bottom class (prole-

[1] M. G. Smith, "Pre-Industrial Stratification Systems," in Neil J. Smelser and Seymour M. Lipset, *Social Structure and Mobility in Economic Development* (Chicago: Aldine, 1966), p. 142.

tariat). Although Marx wrote about other classes, his theory of class development ultimately allowed for only two, both of which, in pure form, develop class consciousness, identity, and cohesion. That is, each in turn becomes a class in itself (*fur sich*). This situation then leads to polarization between the two classes and results in the class struggle. Such a two-class view of stratification has caused difficulty in dealing with the apparent rise of new strata, categories, communities, and groups that are seen to comprise the middle levels of modern society.

Marx's primary distinction between the classes was based upon the control of the means of production. The capitalists owned the means of production and tended to exploit the proletariat, or workers, who had no such control. However, a considerable proportion of the rapidly expanding middle levels of modern society cannot be accurately categorized as being either capitalist or proletariat. The large number in the middle who have developed professional roles and expertise in such critical areas as science and engineering, business management, education, health, social and governmental services, and the arts are, in terms of the means of production, neither dependent upon nor independent of the "controllers" or "the controlled." Rather, they are more often the "kingpins" in maintaining the *interdependence* of all the diverse elements of the social system in the modern industrial state.

There are sound theoretical reasons why Marx did not give the middle portion of the social structure a permanent place in his class system. This segment possesses status characteristics that are either part capitalist, part proletariat, or, as implied above, a mixture that conforms to neither. This heterogeneity of status characteristics among the middle level creates a high degree of status inconsistency; and heterogeneity in terms of status inconsistency, social mobility, religious and ethnic variability, occupational mobility, political orientation, and variation in life styles seem to make the middle levels incompatible with the Marxian theory. In order to maintain the notion that class conflict was inevitable and an important aspect of the dynamism of society, Marx had to maintain the dichotomous view of stratification despite the emerging empirical evidence that this view was incongruous with reality.

This attack on the Marxian concept of social class is in no way intended to eliminate it from stratification theory. One of the bases upon which this discussion rests is that there may, in fact, be identifiable *classes* at the top and bottom of the stratification structure of modern industrial society but that the middle portion of the structure is such that the concept of class is inapplicable. It is in this context that Weber's conceptualizations provide the bases for a useful reformulation.

A considerable part of Weber's work was done in response to Marxian theory. Weber's brilliance has given him a place of importance in the search for better conceptual tools in the field of stratification. His concept of class as one of three major dimensions of stratification (along with status and party) offered an alternative to Marx's all-inclusive concept of class. This stimulated, particularly among American sociologists, a predominant interest in status and all of its ramifications.

Stanislaw Ossowski's work is probably the most important effort at clarifying some of the persistently murky areas of stratification conceptualization and theory. He has posed some significant questions for this discussion:

> Do we follow Marx in placing the main emphasis on the system of privileges and discriminations, on exploitations and in general on asymetrical relations of dependence? Or do we follow [James] Madison or Max Weber (when he is speaking of class structure) in stressing the distinctness of interests? Or again are we at one with modern American sociologists in acknowledging class consciousness as the most socially-important fact in the domain of inter-group relations, and do we, in describing a "class" society—despite the suggestive terminology—give primacy to the characteristics which Weber links with his concept of an estate, not with the concept of class.[2]

There appears to be an increasing movement away from a social class analysis toward the "Madison-Weber" conception, which stresses distinctness of interests. Weber's concept of status groups, which is similar to the concept of status community as delineated in this article, is relevant. Weber states:

> In contrast to classes, *status groups* are normally communities. They are, however, often of an amorphous kind. In contrast to the purely economically determined "class situation" we wish to designate as "status situation" every typical component of the life fate of man that is determined by a specific, positive or negative, social estimation of honor . . . In content, status honor is normally expressed by the fact that above all else a specific style of life can be expected from all those who wish to belong to the circle. Linked with the expectation are restrictions on "social" intercourse (that is, intercourse which is not subservient to economic or any other of business' "functional" purposes).[3]

A pertinent discussion of Weber's theory of community warns that a status community exists only if there is more than a manifestation of common responses or feelings about a given situation and the consequences that flow from it. "It is only when this feeling leads to a mutual orientation of their behavior to each other that their relationships may be termed 'communal'."[4] It is the apparent existence of a "mutual orientation" among members of many middle level occupational groups and professions that supports the possible utility of

[2] Stanislaw Ossowski, *Class Structure in the Social Consciousness* (New York: The Free Press, 1963), p. 139.

[3] Hans Gerth and C. Wright Mills (eds.), *From Max Weber: Essays in Sociology* (New York: Oxford, 1946), pp. 186-187.

[4] J. Winkelmann (ed.), *Wirtschaft und Gesellschaft*, 4th ed. (Teubingen: Mohr, 1956), pp. 30-31, as quoted by Gertrud Neuwirth, "A Weberian Outline of a Theory of Community: Its Application to the 'Dark Ghetto,' " *British Journal of Sociology*, 20 (June, 1969), p. 154.

the concept of status community in dealing with the inadequacies posed by the concept of social class.

Though Weber figures most prominently in the origin of the idea of status community, a considerable number of other social scientists have contributed to the awareness that traditional class analysis is open to serious debate. De Tocqueville's discerning eye, during his travels in the United States, took note of the importance of status in modern society.[5] Durkheim recognized that industrial society was leading to a multiplicity of occupational groups, which developed their own norms and ethics.[6] Veblen, one of the earliest students of America's stratification system, exposed the phenomena of status striving, the *nouveau riche*, and those dynamic aspects of society that tied life style and status to pecuniary considerations.[7] More recently Drucker made much of the fact that the separation of the worker from the means of production, plus the increasing importance of industrial organizations in the productive process, has disrupted the status system of society.[8] The old divisions of owner and laborer no longer seem applicable. These early observations on the changing social and economic order have generated specific criticisms of stratification theory.

For several years a small number of dissident voices have been raised objecting to the use of the social class concept in the United States.[9] One of these belongs to Robert A. Nisbet, who made a very pointed criticism when he wrote that the concept of social class had approximately "the same relation to the data of stratification that the Ptolemic view once had to celestial phenomena."[10] Roger Brown has more recently raised questions about the use of social class as a concept for studying stratification in American society.[11] He concludes that:

> the various kinds of inquiry that ask people to talk about social life without directly suggesting social class do not reliably elicit talk about class . . . Most respondents do explicitly mention things related to social evaluation–in-

[5] Robert A. Nisbet, *The Sociological Tradition* (New York: Basic Books, 1966), pp. 183-193.

[6] Emile Durkheim, *Division of Labor in Society*, George Simpson (trans.) (New York: Macmillan, 1933).

[7] Thorstein Veblen, *The Theory of the Leisure Class* (New York: Random House, 1934).

[8] Peter F. Drucker, *The New Society: The Anatomy of Industrial Order* (New York: Harper & Row, 1962).

[9] Robert A. Nisbet, "The Decline and Fall of Social Class," *Pacific Sociological Review*, 2 (Spring, 1959), pp. 11-17; Arnold M. Rose, "The Concept of Class in American Sociology," *Social Research*, 25 (1958), pp. 53-69; Kurt B. Mayer, "The Changing Shape of the American Class Structure," *Social Research*, 30 (1963), pp. 458-468; Dennis H. Wrong, "Social Inequality without Social Stratification," *The Canadian Review of Sociology and Anthropology*, 1 (1964), pp. 5-16; Don Martindale, *American Social Structure* (New York: Appleton-Century-Crofts, 1960), pp. 452-456; and Joseph Bensman, "Status Communities in an Urban Society: The Musical Community," a paper read at the annual meeting of the American Sociological Association in Miami, 1966.

[10] Nisbet, "Decline and Fall," p. 12.

[11] Roger Brown, *Social Psychology* (New York: The Free Press, 1965).

> come, occupation, race, etc. It looks as if differential social value, rankings, of some kind, are a profound social and psychological reality, but it does not look as if this reality were consciously structured as a small number of classes.[12]

The stimulus for the present discussion grew out of Kurt B. Mayer's attempt to show that the shape of the American class structure has changed, and, as a result, the concept of social class appears inapplicable to the middle part of the stratification hierarchy.[13] He claims that the middle socioeconomic levels of American society do not form a class or classes because middle level jobs provide avenues for demonstrating achievement and ability, and, thus, inheritance as a factor is of diminished importance. It follows that traditional life styles, status symbols, associations, easily recognizable social distance, and other transmitted criteria of class membership are ignored or modified to the extent that traditional status identities become blurred. Rapid social change involving a greatly increased amount of division of labor, social differentiation, a breakdown in ideologies supporting traditional status ranks, and a general democratization of behavior patterns has destroyed the clear-cut status distinctions of an earlier time. These changes are, to a degree, reflected in the increasing range of occupations now available—the *Dictionary of Occupational Titles* lists over 40,000 different occupations in the United States.

Industrialization and urbanization have resulted in a substantial increase in social mobility. The breakdown of status lines is hastened by increasing intermarriage between status levels, increasing geographic mobility, and the decline in the influence of traditional patterns of socialization and child-rearing. As Mayer points out, the result has been the disappearance of what might once have been called the "middle classes." leaving any semblance of social classes only at the top and bottom of the stratification structure. A society oriented toward consumption rather than saving means that the inheritance of class positions is less likely to occur, at least among the middle levels. As large segments of a society develop life styles that emphasize the consumption of goods, a family's remaining in a given stratum can not be based, to any marked degree, on the inheritance of the parental class position by the following generation. High consumption rather than the predisposition to save is backed by the cultural norms. In fact, high consumption becomes institutionalized through the increased material needs and the availability of family credit; these needs eat up potential capital that could otherwise serve as a legacy.[14]

In his work on social distance, prestige, and intimate association among occupational groupings, Edward Lauman reports that occupational prestige and friendship are two very important determinants of social interaction in urban

[12] Brown, *Social Psychology*, p. 17.

[13] Mayer, "Changing Shape of American Class Structure."

[14] Joseph Schumpeter, *Imperialism and Social Classes* (New York: Meridian Books, 1955), p. 119.

America. Also, intimate interaction tends to cluster in identifiable occupational groupings. His findings seem to support Mayer's contention that the middle levels of the American stratification structure show the least evidence of classes, in contrast to the upper and lower extremes. Lauman states:

> Only at the extremes of the occupational hierarchy do we find evidence of more crystallized groupings . . . The middle occupational categories, on the other hand, show considerable differentiation in subjective social distance preferences along prestige lines and relatively weaker tendencies to confine social relationships with status equals. In other words, the middle level occupations reveal less self-selection within their own occupational categories . . . Class-like features best characterize the situation at the extremes of the occupational hierarchy, while a more fluid, differentiated situation obtains for the middle levels of the hierarchy. Yet it is noteworthy that the middle levels are not completely unstructured and merely strung out along the status continuum.[15]

Dennis H. Wrong shows that the traditional social class analysis approach to inequality and stratification is inadequate. Drawing on Ossowski, Lipset, Marshall, and Dahrendorf, Wrong shows that rather than defining American society as stratified by classes, it is actually a "nonegalitarian classless society."[16] Although a full scale nonegalitarian classlessness has not yet occurred in the United States, and less so in Europe, the trend seems apparent. Wrong states that classes are being transformed into "ghost" communities, which represent attempts to preserve traditional status distinctions and class behaviors.[17]

> The emerging social structure of post-bourgeois industrial society can best be understood if, except for secondary purposes and for historical analysis, we abandon the concept of social class and redefine much of the work done under this label as a contribution to the sociology of equality and inequality.[18]

Wrong, Mayer, and Ossowski have presented provocative arguments against the traditional rhetoric of class and analysis of inequality in modern society. Their work seems to dovetail with others pointing directly or indirectly to the possibility of using the concept of *status community*, particularly in dealing with the middle strata, which, as Mayer implies, is that portion of the social structure least amenable to class analysis. The trend Wrong points to is that any real semblance of class boundaries and fully inherited social position is on the wane both at the top and bottom of the social structure. Thus, it will be necessary to

[15] Edward Lauman, *Prestige and Association in an Urban Community* (New York: Bobbs Merrill, 1966), pp. 141-143.

[16] Stanislaw Ossowski, *Class Structure in the Social Consciousness* (New York: The Free Press, 1963), pp. 100-118.

[17] Wrong, "Social Inequality," p. 9.

[18] Wrong, ibid., p. 11.

use a concept such as status community in dealing with the kind of collectivities that manifest similar life styles, adhere to somewhat specific status distinctions and symbols, and whose members feel they belong together.

The concept of status community is a part of Weber's legacy. It has been used most recently by Don Martindale in analyzing American society, and by Joseph Bensman in discussing the place of the musical community in urban society.[19] In commenting upon the utility of the concept of "social class" and its relation to Weber's concepts of class, status, group, and party, Martindale makes the following observations:

> While there is considerable loss of explanatory power whenever one substitutes the concept of social class for the concept of class, status group, and party, there are values to be lost in the abandonment of the concept "social class" or ideas similar to it in that they refer to a fusion of positions across the hierarchies of esteem, wealth, and power. A social class combines positions of esteem and wealth. Even more valuable is the concept of "status community," representing a fusion of positions on all three hierarchies. Thus it is possible to drop the idea of social class, retaining the ideas of class, status group, and party for social units of the separate hierarchies and the idea of status community for fusion of all three.[20]

Martindale defines status community as "a number of persons consolidating the same levels of access to esteem, wealth, and power, and turning these into a monopoly of the in-group, giving them the form of a specialized 'community' within the community."[21]

The most important work using the concept of status community is that of Bensman. He illustrates how the musical community of a large city comprise a status community. In contrast to the classical concept of community, he defines a status community as "a *consensual* community, in which the individual chooses to live out his major life interests within a framework of institutions, culture, practices, and social relationships that are consistent with his adherence to a set of values."[22] As the reader will note in studying Bensman's article, reprinted on page 113 in this text, he also introduces the concept of prestige, or status audience, using it to further clarify and delineate the concept of status community and to add sophistication to his analysis.

G. P. Stone and W. Form, who do not explicitly use the concept of status community, do present arguments that support the adoption of a conceptualization that avoids the rather rationalistic hierarchical description implied by the

[19] Martindale, *American Social Structure*, pp. 452-456; Bensman, "The Musical Community," chapter 24 in this volume.

[20] Martindale, *American Social Structure*, p. 455.

[21] Martindale, ibid., p. 456.

[22] Bensman, "The Musical Community, p. 113.

use of a social class analysis.[23] They add their voices to those of Mayer and Wrong who, observing the broad middle portion of the American social structure, find a multiplicity of wealth, prestige, and power situations; so much so, that not only do they seldom use the term "middle class," but they consider it inappropriate as a theoretically meaningful label. These authors use Weber's concept of status group and devise one of their own by defining what they call status aggregates. Stone and Form further challenge the social class approach by not only failing to delineate classes, but also by showing empirically that the status arrangements are unstable at the middle level of the urban community in which they conducted their study.

As stated previously, the great weakness in a class analysis occurs in attempting to make sense of the phenomena of inequality, power, and privilege in the middle levels of modern society. The analogy of the mosaic has, at times, been used to describe certain aspects of American society. It seems that the so-called middle mass may be characterized as a kind of mosaic of collectivities, for which status factors might be used as criteria of delineation. There seems to be a contradiction in first referring to the middle *mass* and then proceeding to define specific units within this mass. However, in reality, the broad middle levels of American society are not simply a mass of unattached and undefinable particles flowing hither and yon in social space as the forces of fashion and fad dictate. Rather it may *appear* like a mass because neither our conceptual tools nor our observational efforts have been capable of dealing with the variety of collectivities that intuition and close examination seem to reveal. Our perceptions as social scientists have been stimulated by unexplainable inconsistencies. For instance, if the vast majority of Americans did, in fact, belong to an undifferentiated mass, the discernible variety in values and life styles exhibited by such occupations as musician, small businessman, construction worker, librarian, and school teacher, all of whom share similar income levels, would not make sense.

Modern society is characterized by a considerable amount of social differentiation, coupled with a high degree of division of labor. This has resulted in an increase in the surpluses available for use in society. Lenski has based his heroic attempt to synthesize prevailing stratification theory by using history and anthropology to illustrate the relationship between inequality and surplus goods and services in societies ranging from hunting and gathering types to the modern industrial state.[24]

The great increase in surplus goods, the tremendous proliferation of occupations, and the attendant specialization have helped to create a situation wherein a great variety of values and life styles can emerge. The middle level of modern

23 Gregory P. Stone and William Form, "Instabilities in Status: The Problem of Hierarchy in the Community Study of Status Arrangements," *American Sociological Review*, 198 (1953), pp. 149-162.

24 Gerhard Lenski, *Power and Privilege* (New York: McGraw-Hill, 1966).

society seems to be the level at which new functions and occupations emerge most readily. The nature and newness can lead to specialized ideologies and life styles. And these emerge in conjunction with new and generally unknown occupations.

In making their debut, the members of a new occupation will generally experience a substantial amount of status inconsistency in terms of class, status, and political power. Very seldom does a new function command the same salary, prestige, or power during its early, developmental state as it will when it has become a common occupation, with its own ideology and status audience: that is, when it becomes fully institutionalized.

The social value placed on an occupation or function may vary from one part of society to another. And this makes it likely that there will always be some discrepancy between class, status, and political power in all sectors of the occupational status structure. This implies that the distinction between the new and the not-so-new occupational categories, and the ideologies and life styles that may come to be associated with them, can only be seen by closely scrutinizing them in terms of the interaction among all three of Weber's dimensions.

With the emergence of many new occupations annually, a society such as that of the United States can be characterized as consisting of a vast array of coexisting, cooperating, competing, and conflicting occupational or status communities. The effects will be a constant alignment and realignment of these communities in terms of class, status, and political influence. Not only will many of the members of occupational-status communities experience discrepancies in class, status and political power, but the importance of any one of the three variables, for a particular occupation, may change from one period to the next. Dramatic changes can be seen in the history of many occupations, for example, the medical doctor. Compare the rather primitive, often death-dealing, "saw bones" of the American frontier, who had relatively low class and status, with the high status and wealth of doctors of the 1950's and 1960's.[25]

With ever increasing bureaucratization, and the fact that most middle level occupations are carried on within bureaucracies, the Weberian dimension of class may decline from its preeminent position as the most important of the three variables. Bureaucratization tends to narrow the range of salary differentials between occupational types. Similar middle level, white collar jobs demanding similar educational credentials (i.e., similar in time–years of college, etc.) are moving closer together when it comes to income. The superrational norms of bureaucratic structures dictate that men with obvious similarities of work demands, education, and experience earn a similar salary. The large size, power, and rationalized structure of the giant corporations and government agencies results in the dominance of bureaucratic salary scales. Ultimately, the salaries of

[25] Impressionistic evidence seems to indicate a current decline in the status and prestige of medical doctors without, however, any corresponding lowering of their class level.

nonbureaucratized occupational types are brought into line with the dominant levels.[26]

As economic class levels become similar, the status and political power variables of the Weberian triad become more important. The apparent utility of the concept of status community implies that the dimension of status becomes most important for differentiating between units within the broad middle "mass." The willingness to assign primary importance to the status dimension, rather than choosing political power or avoiding a choice between the two, rests on perceiving the function of status and political influence in the everyday lives of the members of society. The *status* situation in which men find themselves is determined by the social honor, or deference, they experience. This, in turn, is granted or denied as a result of the person's life style. The fact that life styles, and the social honor connected with each, develop and are perpetuated in the context of social groups and communities is crucial; it makes the group assume critical importance to the individual and his family.

Political influence (party), is generally expressed in a manner demanding involvement in specific political decisions that are backed by the coercive power of the state. Political influence, emanating from collectivities such as parties or voluntary associations, demands a *self-conscious* involvement in acts of persuasion, compromise, image building, consensus building, as well as other acts of social and political manipulation. In contrast, the status dimension concerns the sharing of a given life style and is to a considerable extent internalized and not self-conscious behavior. That is, a large portion of the behavior related specifically to status honor and life style is the behavior of *everyday life*. Hence, as class differences diminish, the status dimension increases in perceived importance, at least for the middle levels. In this respect Lipset states that:

> Weber regarded economic class as important primarily because it is perceived as a cause of status. Since it is usually easier to make or lose money than it is to gain or lose status, *those in privileged status positions seek to dissociate status from class, that is, to urge that status reflects factors such as family origin, manners, education, and the like–attributes that are more difficult to attain or lose than economic wealth.*[27]

The middle level not only has the greatest variety of available occupations, but it is also the level at which the majority of new occupations emerge in highly developed industrial societies. In addition, middle level occupations, whether old or new, generally demand certain kinds of individual performance or achievement prior to entry. The necessity for education or training and related credentials make specific demands on the individual. The ability to meet these demands

[26] For example, the income of the medical doctor is currently under scrutiny. Witness the concern voiced by the federal government over the large sums medical doctors have been collecting from Medicare and similar health plans.

[27] Seymour M. Lipset, "Social Stratification," in *Encyclopedia of the Social Sciences* (New York: Macmillan, 1968), p. 302. [Italics mine.]

is closely related to the social context in which the person has lived during his formative years. The child-rearing practices and socialization that take place within the family, kinship group, peer groups, neighborhood groups, and school groups contribute to the perpetuation and gradual change of the status community to which the family belongs.

The middle segment of the social structure probably constitutes the most dynamic portion of the overall structure of modern societies. The proliferation of status communities acting and reacting upon one another, plus the wide variety of life styles open to the young stimulates a portion of the dynamism. The perpetuation of a given status community and its life style cannot be based on lineage and kinship group solidarity. Its survival can only be assured if it can appeal to the oncoming generation as an acceptable life style. Such acceptability will be based on its *functional relevance* for the rest of the social structure, and its *societal value*, or perceived importance, as expressed in general prestige or notoriety and income level. At present, the proportion of sons who are willing or able to follow their fathers into the currently most institutionalized status communities (those that exist among the traditional professional occupations such as medicine, law, and the clergy), constitute considerably less than the majority of each new generation of professionals.[28] Thus, many in each new generation of the established professional occupations are recruited from other status communities. The individual desires, achievements, and history of each new occupational cohort insure a high degree of potential dynamism at the middle levels.

In his discussion of status community, Martindale states that:

> the community-forming principles of completeness and closure operating with respect to esteem, wealth, and power tend to consolidate the three types of values in the same hands and freeze access to them in the in-group.[29]

This may be true in general, but there are many exceptions; the vast proliferation of occupations, the changes within older occupations, and the emergence of new ones create the aforementioned dynamism that places limits on the degree of closure possible for status communities that develop within the middle level. On the other hand, there is no doubt that wherever it is possible for a status community to monopolize sources of either increased class, status, or political influence, closure will be attempted and, to some extent, may prove successful. However, it seems less and less likely that such closure will involve strict endogamy, lineage, or other characteristics of traditional status restrictions. With continued bureaucratization of society at the middle level, income variations diminish and curtail the effect of differences in the purchasing power of families. That we are going to have societies wherein status, class, and political differences

[28] This is partly due to the tremendous increase in the number of professionals in all industrial societies during the recent past.

[29] Martindale, *American Social Structure*, p. 455. In this statement Martindale has substituted his preferred terminology of wealth, esteem, and power for Weber's class, status, and party.

will disappear is doubtful. However, a rather definite change from the past seems to be in the offing. We cannot, of course, readily divest ourselves of many of the effects of our collective past. A history does not "go away" like a bad cold.

As Ossowski clearly recognizes, the conceptions of social structure over the centuries show that the ideological notions relative to class structure can endure independently of their specific social manifestations.[30] As such, it is not my intention to imply that the fragmentation into status communities at the middle levels of modern society will signal the end of the "ideological superstructure" present in men's beliefs. There are people who seem to be very distant socially and who seem to occupy extremely high or low positions in comparison to the majority of men. Whether modern man will continue to employ the rhetoric of class by placing such people into an *upper class* or a *lower class* will depend on the *range* of class and political power differences between the top and the bottom. If these class and power differences are significantly diminished, and there is greater equality among people, then the rhetoric of class may disappear. At such a point, however, one might hypothesize that the variation in life style, characterized by variation in consumption patterns, social values, and political ideologies, will increasingly promote the retention and formation of a wide variety of status communities, and their corresponding status audiences.

Despite the possible validity of David Riesman's reference to the "standard package" in discussing the consumption behavior of Americans, Weber's earlier statement on the character of American democracy coincides with the kind of societal setting that probably had to precede the development of status communities.[31] "In the past and up to the present, it has been a characteristic precisely of the specifically American democracy that it did *not* constitute a formless sand heap of individuals, but rather a buzzing complex of strictly exclusive, yet voluntary associations."[32] Weber noted the exclusiveness of American associations. The trend in the 1960's, however, seems to be away from exclusiveness at least in terms of criteria such as race, religion, or national origin. Nevertheless, the voluntary associations remain an integral aspect of status community formation.[33] As such, Weber's characterization was not only accurate, but referred to a phenomenon that would lead to further change from the class structures of Europe to a "mosaic" of status communities.

Weber's three dimensions of stratification are very useful in demonstrating the existence of status inconsistency. An example of this inconsistency is a situation in which an individual or family may be high in economic class position, but low in status position and political influence. This might be the case for

[30] Ossowski, *Class Structure*, p. 180.

[31] David Riesman, *Abundance for What? And Other Essays* (New York: Doubleday, 1964), pp. 111-146.

[32] Gerth and Mills, *From Max Weber*, p. 310. [Italics mine.]

[33] Gertrud Neuwirth, "A Weberian Outline of a Theory of Community," p. 150.

an immigrant who has been very successful economically. Modern industrial society creates conditions that result in substantial status inconsistency, and persons who experience such inconsistencies are usually in the middle levels of the status structure. Status inconsistency is, in principle, not possible at either the *extreme* top or the *extreme* bottom of the structure, since at those levels, class, status, and political influence are highly intercorrelated.

The presence of large numbers of people who experience status inconsistency creates an added degree of heterogeneity at that social level. The social situation of those can vary widely in terms of Weber's three dimensions. Table 1 presents the variety of social types that one might expect to find.

Table 1
Possible Types of Status Inconsistency

	Status	Class	Political Influence
Upper Class	High	High	High
	High	High	Low
	High	Low	High
Middle Level	High	Low	Low
	Low	High	Low
	Low	Low	High
Lower Class	Low	Low	Low

Noting the number of pure types in the table, it is obvious that there are three times as many possible combinations at the middle level as at the top and bottom of the structure. Since reality provides great variation *within* the three dimensions, the number of *actual* combinations that may be found in a complex industrial society would be even greater. Moreover, since Weber's three dimensions often do not fully account for variations in ethnic, racial, and religious factors associated with stratification, the middle level is further elaborated. It seems obvious that heterogeneity in stratification characteristics is a key factor in describing the middle level, despite the superficial implications of the concept "middle mass." Heterogeneity of this type implies a fragmentation of this level into some kinds of collectivities, such as status communities.

If, as it appears, income variation at the middle level is diminishing, then the symbolic manifestations of the life style of a particular status community will involve status symbols that are not tied to their monetary value and are more and more limited to providing prestige. Many current status symbols are unknown outside of a particular status community and its status audience. The members of each status community, even though their overall income may be roughly similar, may have quite different modes of spending their discretionary income.[34] The choices made by a given family about whether they invest a high proportion of their "extra" income on education, travel, sports, fashionable clothing, home decoration, entertaining at home or elsewhere, gambling, and so on, would be in accordance with the norms of their status community.

Modern conditions of life give the status community a dynamism not previously encountered by human collectivities. Every status community, whether institutionalized or merely in a developmental stage, is in a state of constant change. Time and the age of the participants are important elements in the changing pattern of status arrangements *within* a given community as well as *between* status communities. It is evident that the great increase in the life expectancy of man has enhanced the complexity of these changes. Age has become increasingly important in determining status and in the formation of the life style that comes to characterize given status communities. The concerns of a person change decidedly as he grows older. And these concerns have consequences for consumption patterns, and the acquisition and retention of status symbols, many of which are closely related to the variable of age. For example, the world's best dressed women are generally quite beautiful or at least attractive and generally not old. Dior or Heim gowns are not of the same importance to a 75-year-old dowager as to a 40-year-old socialite. Yet, there may be numerically many more prominent 75-year-old than 40-year-old socialites, because of the great increase in longevity. Similarly, a newly married couple may find a small apartment very satisfactory, whereas a 45-year-old couple will probably be much more concerned with the importance of their home as a symbol of membership in a status community and as offering evidence of their class or political influence or both.

At a particular point in a person's life, a sorting process takes place in which he is sorted into a status community. This is somewhat synonymous with that point in life that is often labeled as "maturity." In social and economic terms it generally occurs at the point in young adulthood when a person has completed his education or training, found a mate, and gotten employment in the occupation most suited to his social and economic background. Of course, for some, changes may occur after this point, connoting social mobility.

Occupation is probably the most important determinant of the status community in which a family or individual ultimately falls. As Williams has stated: "It is through the *similarity of circumstances* and through the *interaction* this occasions that both occupation and income level tend to evoke and index similar cultural characteristics among persons of similar objective conditions."[35]

A word of caution must be noted in regard to the importance of occupation. Status community refers to considerably more than simply an aggregate of

[34] A family has discretionary income when a portion of its total income can be used as the members wish (that is, extra income not necessary for basic needs).

[35] Robin Williams, *American Society* (rev. edition) (New York: Alfred Knopf, 1963), pp. 106 n.

persons in the same occupational category. The comprehensive and rather illusive concept of *life style* is the key to the delineation of a status community. Wilensky found that

> traditional indicators of social class–present income and occupational category of self or father–no longer discriminate among styles of leisure and degrees of social integration for a growing middle mass. As determinants of social relations, media exposure, and consumption, these "class" variables are becoming less important than career patterns, mobility orientation, and work milieu–and the associated educational experience.[36]

That is, "career pattern, mobility orientation, and work milieu" may be more closely related to life style than are "present income and occupational category." Although some occupational categories are clearly indicative of life style, others are not. For example, the professions clearly connote specific life styles, whereas many bureaucratic or entrepreneurial occupations do not. Among some middle level occupations, not only are inequalities less publicly visible, due to the esoteric nature of the occupations, but there is a lack of readily ascertainable occupational prestige. In some instances a given status community may be made up of several different occupational categories–although in income, education, conditions of employment and mobility status there would be many similarities.

The major aim of this discussion has been to generate interest in the potentiality of the concept *status community* in studying the middle levels of modern societies. However, there are a great many difficulties in dealing with such a concept. Whether the difficulties will preclude its active use as a stratification concept remains to be seen.

[36] Harold L. Wilensky, "Orderly Careers and Social Participation: The Impact of Work History on Social Integration in the Middle Mass," *American Journal of Sociology*, 26 (August, 1961), p. 539.

CHAPTER 3

MIDDLE LEVEL STATUS COMMUNITIES

The title of this section does not contain the word *class*. This is, of course, an intentional omission in light of the material presented in the previous section. It seems appropriate at this juncture to discuss the wide range of meanings attached to the terms connoting "middle" or "middle class" in the structure of stratification. Frequently, the terms pointing to groups or collectivities occupying some part of the middle level of society are used as terms of derogation or as actual epithets. Words or phrases such as "middle class morality," "middle class housewife," "straights," "squares," "men in grey flannel suits," along with the earlier ones provided by social critics such as Sinclair Lewis, who referred to the middle class "booster," are generally emotionally charged. Much of what these terms connote is often implied by other derogatory terms related to suburban living. In fact, "middleness" in social position is often used synonymously with "suburbia," which in turn is meant to connote a sterile, conforming, and "saran wrapped" way of life.

At the opposite extreme we find those terms that are used to designate scientific concepts, complete with operational specifications. For example, the *Warner Index of Status Characteristics*, as described in the "Introduction," provides numerical scores that can be used to define class levels. It is essentially a composite of measures of source of income, occupation, dwelling area, and type of dwelling. Hollingshead's modification of Warner's scale provided two middle level categories. They were labeled as class II and class III in a scheme with a total of five classes.[1]

Between the epithets on the one hand and the operational definitions on the other are a range of terms less emotionally loaded and less specifically defined. Using a historical perspective, C. Wright Mills pointed to the differences between an "old" and a "new" middle class, the former referring to small entrepreneurs and the latter, to white collar employees and bureaucrats.[2] Although Mills was more scientifically discriminating than many in his analysis of the middle level of American society, he did contribute substantially to the rhetoric of derogation often used in reference to middle and white collar strata of the population. His view of the contemporary middle class as a shallow remnant of a more substantial past and as a new proletariat has made him a leading critic of the "American middle class."

The middle levels of American social structure are most often seen as manifesting social types and life styles that are viewed as typically American, frequently expressed by the term "American way of life." Exactly which strata or levels within the stratification structure espouse and manifest the so-called American way of life is open to question, if indeed such a "way of life" actually exists. One might conjecture that those in the lower portion of the middle level are most vociferous in providing support for such a conception, whereas the middle and upper levels attempt to live it, while engaging less in verbal support.

The middle levels of urban industrial society exhibit a considerable number of those social characteristics and relations that give modern social structure its dynamism. Reference to the middle as dynamic is not meant to enhance or praise those who occupy the middle, but simply to emphasize a number of features that make possible and foster a degree of dynamism. The middle level encompasses most of the social mobility existent in modern society, and, as such, it is of consequence in any consideration of dynamism in society. The middle level is the goal or destination of the "mobiles" from the lower levels and the point of origin of many of those who climb to the top rung of the social ladder. It is also that part of the social structure that includes a great deal of mobility within itself, from the "lower middle class" to the "upper middle class."

An aspect of mobility that exists within the middle level of society has helped to stimulate the development of status communities: the movement from one status community to another, where the movement may entail little, if any, change in income level, but does greatly affect the overall life style. Hence, values and attitudes involving child rearing, education, leisure time activities, associations, religion, ethnic identity, consumption norms, and life goals may

[1] August Hollingshead and Frederick C. Radlich, "Social Stratification and Psychiatric Disorders," *American Sociological Review*, 18 (April, 1953), pp. 163-170.

[2] C. Wright Mills, *White Collar: the American Middle Class* (New York: Oxford, 1951).

change and constitute a very different life style—but one that continues to fall within the middle level.

The middle level has become that level within which education, both lower and higher, is viewed as a paramount concern. It is a concern precisely because it is perceived as the crucial device for maintaining the next generation's class and status level, as well as being the key activity in preparing for *upward* mobility. This is true whether the path to upward mobility is perceived to be best achieved through hard work and professional training or by attending an elite school and marrying upward (which is most applicable to women).

Social dynamism expressed by mobility as well as the remnants of what was once called the "ideal of progress" are probably some of the most characteristic features of the middle level. Although the conservative or reactionary "forgotten American," who began making himself felt at the end of the 1960's, belongs to the middle level, his reaction is not one that simply connotes traditionalism or long term conservatism. His *reaction* is seemingly one that reveals a grave concern over losing the fruits of recent mobility. The perceived slandering by "beats," "hippies" or "yippies," of a life style that he has fought for and become accustomed to has put him on the defensive. It can be argued that such a reaction may promote social change, though the ultimate outcome may be simply an increased conservatism.

The general expansion of occupational opportunity in the professional, managerial, and sales categories has meant the continuation of a relatively high level of social mobility in the United States. This expansion has led to the formation of a series of wholly new occupations, which in turn has meant the development of new life styles or, in other words, new status communities. All of the new service industries, the space, armaments, and electronic industries, the expansion of jobs in the social service sector (education, health, conservation, etc.), have created new paths for mobility, new occupational norms, and ultimately, new life styles. These developments in the occupational structure have contributed to an increasing heterogeneity of social types and life styles rather than the often presumed homogenization that has been subject to so much attack from critics of the middle class and suburbia. That one can and probably should be critical of the content and quality of modern urban life is in the nature of a truism. But why, how, and in what terms criticisms are made has consequences for both the conceptualization and explanation of social phenomena. Explanation of social phenomena can only come with some degree of clarity and precision in the formulation of important questions for research and the definition and categorization of empirically ascertainable instances of social behavior.

The middle level of modern society is that sector of the social structure that contains the bulk of the highly educated population, as well as the intellectuals. Various groups and status communities within the middle level serve as the developers and transmitters of most of the nonfolk values that are an important aspect of new and unique elements in the life styles of these collectivities. The artistic, intellectual, scientific, moral, recreational, and humanitarian values and ideas of modern industrial society are learned, taught, changed, and fought over by individuals and groups holding a place in the middle level. Whatever rise or decline takes place in these areas of life is in large measure the result of the varied activities of the members of the middle level of the social structure.

Although the middle level manifests a considerable amount of variety, Herberg argues that a "common religion" has emerged. His characterization of it is almost identical with many popular descriptions of the so-called American middle class.

> The American Way of Life is individualistic, dynamic, pragmatic. It affirms the supreme value and dignity of the individual; it stresses incessant activity on his part, for his is never to rest but is always to be striving to get ahead; it defines an ethic of self-reliance, merit, and character, and judges by achievement; "deeds not creeds" are what count . . . The American believes in progress, in self-improvement, and quite fanatically in education.[3]

The readings in this part were chosen to illustrate some of the existing variety in life styles, as well as the lack of any clear-cut or scientifically useful delineation of a single middle class.

[3] Will Herberg, *Protestant, Catholic, Jew: An Essay in American Religious Sociology* (New York: Doubleday Anchor, 1960), p. 79.

9 *Joseph Bensman*

STATUS COMMUNITIES IN AN URBAN SOCIETY: THE MUSICAL COMMUNITY

In a complex urban society, the systems of social stratification have many dimensions.[1] The basis of prestige and social honor varies widely, in some instances being known, visible, and relevant to large numbers in the society, and in others being relevant perhaps to only a few.

The relative prestige of old successful Yankee stock may be high, traditional, and symbolic to a wide "audience" in our society at large. By contrast, the prestige accruing to a professional musician is more recent, affects a relatively smaller "audience" and is, on the average, lower. To put it another way, prestige in a total society is a function of both the number of persons who assign honor to a person or position and the amount of prestige so assigned. Since the dimensions of prestige are not of equal relevance or intensity to all members of a society, the so-called average prestige rating of a position, group, or "social class" is an elusive concept. A group's prestige rating can be based either on the universality of its social honor or on its social ratings among smaller segments in society or on both. The danger is that the rating may conceal a relatively high status group whose status is confined to a relatively narrow social circle, and thus obscure the diverse underpinnings of prestige in a complex society.

To understand the many-faceted aspects of prestige, we must set aside the concept of an average prestige rating, and analyze its components. This is all the more necessary because one can hypothesize that the average prestige rating results both from claims for higher prestige and the dissemination of those claims to a wider and wider audience. The prestige-claiming process may go on simultaneously for a large number of groups, at different stages in their development. Therefore both the diverse nature of prestige and the idea of an average prestige rating conceal a wide variety of institutional processes which must be described in detail.

Paper read at the National meeting of the American Sociological Association, August 1966, by permission of the author.

Joseph Bensman is professor of sociology at City College and the Graduate Faculty of the City University of New York. He has done a number of studies in the sociology of the arts and in social stratification. His latest book (with A. J. Vidich) is *The New American Society* (Quadrangle Books, 1971).

1 See Arthur J. Vidich and Joseph Bensman, *Small Town in a Mass Society* (Garden City, New York: Doubleday Anchor, 1960), pp. 94-95. Paul Hatt, "Occupation and Social Stratification," *American Journal of Sociology*, 55 (May, 1950), p. 539. Much of the mode of analysis employed here parallels that used by Alfred McClung Lee in "Attitudinal Multivalence in Reaction to Culture and Personality," *American Journal of Sociology*, 60 (November, 1954), pp. 294-99.

THE PRESTIGE AUDIENCE

The term "audience" suggests the population to which a prestige claim, acceptance, or rating is relevant, and as we have already noted, only a part of society or of the community is relevant or accessible to a prestige claim or rating.

Prestige claims involve fundamental attachments to values. Persons or groups confer prestige by accepting a prestige claim. They do so because they value highly that quality, function, or attribute which the claimant exemplifies or says he represents. This process, of course, is not always so simple. Elementary and high school teachers who claim prestige because of the value of their function may be denied it by educated parents who place a high value on education but nevertheless may feel superior to teachers in educational attainment.

One can define a prestige audience, then, as all those who accept as highly valuable a given complex of attributes, characteristics, qualities, or functions. Thus, the simplicity or complexity of prestige is a function of the degree of unity and integration of the values in a society, and the consensus of various populations in accepting or adhering to these values. A pluralistic system of social stratification simply reflects a lack of consensus, or disagreement over values.

To the extent that it supports claims for superiority of a given set of values and to the degree it gains in the number of relative supporters, the prestige audience affects the prestige system of the total society.

This conception raises a number of problems. The first concerns the interrelations between various prestige audiences as they affect the society at large; the second relates to the individual as he internalizes values that provide the basis for a variety of prestige audiences; a third relates to the internal dynamics of a single prestige audience.

THE "PROFESSIONAL" AND THE PRESTIGE AUDIENCE

It is to this last problem that we wish to address ourselves first. The prestige audience may consist of both producers and consumers. Some individuals who assert and exemplify the predominance of a value are bound organizationally and occupationally to that value. The professional musician, for example, having made his choice of a career, has committed himself to the relative superiority of the value of music.[2]

This is true as well for the psychiatrist, the clergy, the military man, the

[2] This discussion is based, for illustrative purposes, on an extended series of interviews, discussions, and observations of members of half a dozen musical circles, which include professional musicians employed in symphonic orchestras, soloists (primarily piano), freelance instrumentalists who play both as soloists and in ensembles, arts' managers, music teachers, and devoted amateurs who are attached to musical circles that are primarily composed of professionals.

artist, the businessman, etc. Each professional becomes the bearer of the status claims of a set of institutions and of the values that underlie those institutions.

Surrounding the professionals are the amateurs. They do not "live-off" the status-conferring institutions but closely identify with its aspirations and achievements. Included with the amateurs are special groups of intellectuals, managers, critics, and academicians. Although they are not practicing members of the profession, they articulate its values and disseminate them to lay publics.

The lay publics serve as the ultimate validators of claims to status. They do so by joining and adhering to institutions that embody the values at the root of status claims; by imitating the behavior of those who exemplify or claim to exemplify these values; by purchasing the products of the producer groups, whether they be tickets, records, instruments; and by responding to an entire gamut of symbols, culture, speech, dress, and consumption styles that become characteristic of the prestige audience. In short, belonging to a status audience means adapting to ways of life claimed to be superior by an elite group of its proponents.

THE STATUS COMMUNITY

The formation of status communities is closely related to the process of creating a status audience. A status community, however, is smaller and more inclusive. It includes individuals who make adherence to a complex of value, the organizing principle for their entire life style.

MacIver's definition of the community (one that reflects the entire classical sociological tradition) focused on the smallest *territorial* unit within which all the life functions of the individual can be sustained. By contrast, status community is a *consensual* community, in which the individual chooses to organize his major life interests within a framework of institutions, culture, practices, and social relationships that are consistent with his adherence to a set of values. Obviously it differs from a territorial community if that territory is not relevant.[3] The professional musician may be more at home in the concert halls of Aspen, Moscow, Salzburg, and New York than he is in the apartment of his next door neighbor. In addition, adherence to a status community is voluntary.

One usually gains acceptance into a status community by demonstrating those technical, social, and symbolic skills and loyalties upon which the status community bases itself.

The status community is important in the process of social stratification because (1) it develops and articulates the culture, symbols, and life styles for the status audience, perhaps even more than does the critic, publicist, and impresario, and (2) it becomes a major focal point (along with formal organizations and associations) by which the claims for prestige are advanced.

[3] Robert M. MacIver, *Society: Its Structure and Changes* (Ray Long and Richard R. Smith, Inc.: New York, 1932), p. 10.

It has been amply demonstrated that the territorial community is practically a nonexistent institution in the western world. The growth of mass institutions and society have destroyed those spatial limits that constitute local or "natural" boundaries for a life style or life organization. In their place, individuals have been forced to create "communities" that provide psychological boundaries in which they can live their lives. A status community is such a community.

We contend that within urban societies a vast number of status audiences and communities exist, at every level, each based upon a relatively narrow set of values, but collectively embodying a vast array of values, which in their totality may be unrelated, and often in conflict.[4]

We believe, further, that these status communities represent the major vehicle for organizing the lives of individuals in an urban society. It is precisely because of these often unrelated ad hoc status communities that the breakdown of a simple overall societal structure does not result in anomie. Individuals organize their lives around status communities which prevent them from having to deal with the totality of an apparent infinity of social relations. Among other things, the complexity of society manifests itself in the multiplicity of its status communities, and not necessarily in the complexity of life for a particular individual. Pure anomie may exist only in the absence of affiliation to a status community, either because of social isolation or the inability of the individual to anchor himself in any one status community.

Members of a status community limit their discretionary social contacts, in varying degrees, to those individuals who adhere to and exemplify the same preselected values. Professional musicians, for example, will draw their friends mainly from among other professional musicians and devoted amateurs, will frequently marry musicians or music students, and will raise children who become seriously interested in music. Their contacts outside the status community are primarily with family members who are not musicians, or old friends from their premusical years. They also maintain necessary but minimal contacts with neighbors, officials, and the "civilian" population.

THE STATUS COMMUNITY AS A TOTAL INSTITUTION

In these extreme respects, the status community may resemble a total institution. The "civilian population" may be a group of outsiders, with whom it is difficult to be at ease, and to whom one can most easily relate by demonstrating the esoteric and exotic knowledge of one's craft and institutional surrounding.

[4] Peter Berger describes the existence of "counter-societies," "sub-worlds," and "sub-cultures" as characteristic of the urban society. Both his language and his examples imply that these sub-communities are deviant. While we agree with his general point that the city can contain a myriad of sub-worlds, we would emphasize that the urban "sub-worlds" need not be "deviant" in the pejorative sense of the word. Indeed one might argue that there are only sub-communities in the urban world and no one community serves as a "norm" from which others can deviate.

Thus, when he deals with the layman, the professional musician alternates between embarrassment at being regarded as a freak, and exhibitionism—for the same reason. In this respect he is like the psychiatrist, the college professor, the atomic scientist, the medical doctor, or any professional whose craft is inaccessible to others in a world of specialists. Whether he likes it or not, the role he plays with laymen is almost always a caricature of his professional role.

But the status community is unlike a total institution, in that the values that unite its members pervade every level of the community's life and result in contacts of greater depth and frequency. Since many, though not all, members of such a community choose to confine social contacts to their own status group, it tends to make their commitment all the more total.

The process of creating a status community, then, is a two-fold one: members limit their discretionary social contacts but compensate for this through the density of their contacts with other members. Musicians will have friends who are either musicians or who love music. They will entertain each other, they will play together for "kicks" when they are not performing, rehearsing, or practicing professionally. When they have the leisure, they will attend concerts by other musicians, or listen to records, or the FM radio. In addition, the professional musician is likely to appear in the role of teacher of music students. He may, however, have a nonmusical hobby such as gardening, painting, or craftsmanship in household repairs, in which he takes particular delight as proof of his nonprofessional humanity.

Although he may read magazines, journals, and books related to music, the performing musician frequently will object to musicology and criticism as an attempt to substitute literary values for musical ones. The performer may argue that music is to be played and heard. He frequently resents those within the musical community who make capital out of music but who do not perform or compose it.

THE CULTURE OF THE STATUS COMMUNITY

As a result of this combination of isolation from the nonmusical world and a relative density of social relations within it, professional and amateur musicians create a culture that gives character, quality, texture, and context to the musical community. Some elements of this culture will be described below:

1. Mastery of the technology, skills, rhetoric, and technical symbolic systems upon which music is based is a necessary prerequisite for full-fledged entry into the community, a set of prerequisites which it takes years to accumulate and to reduce to a "second nature."

2. A system of gossip and knowledge of persons and events which can come only from long habituation. Almost every professional musician has played with, or at times known, hundreds of others who have moved through many musical organizations and local musical communities that differ from his own. This experience represents a source of anecdotes, gossip, and speculation which

allows a vast number of musicians to find a common basis for social intercourse. They can exchange anecdotes, and in referring to different experiences in different musical settings, develop a knowledge of the musical environment, personalities, and events in distant organizations and communities. Through such networks of personal interchange, for example, a member of the New York Philharmonic may have a working knowledge of the Cleveland Orchestra, the London Philharmonic, the Philadelphia Orchestra, or the Vienna or Berlin Philharmonic, as well as of the soloists who perform with these orchestras. It is in this sense that the musical community in London may be closer and more familiar to the New York musician than the events in his immediate neighborhood.

3. Through his union, or guild, the musician has a vast fund of technical information related to his salary and modes of payments. He is alert to special legal arrangements in this area, and will have special interests in the organization that pays his salary, the hours, wages, vacations, rehearsal time and pay, and to the financial arrangements which make these possible. If he plays the tympany in a symphony orchestra he knows not only the approximate fee he will receive in a similar group but what he can expect for performing in the pit during a Broadway musical.

He has a vested interest in salary scales within his own orchestra if and when these exceed the minimum. A string player may object to the salaries paid the woodwinds, the brasses, or the tympany, since the salaries of these are substantially higher per note than his own. Musicians who do not play string instruments feel that they deserve the higher pay, since they tend to play more solos than other musicians and also participate a great deal in smaller intra-orchestral ensembles. Their mistakes are thus more noticeable. They therefore conclude they should be paid for quality, not quantity.

Some instrumentalists appear to be able to bargain more effectively than others as individuals. They are paid far above the union minimum scale. When their salaries are known, the relative justice or injustice of the financial power they command constitutes an additional source of the musical culture within an orchestra.

4. The musicians have institutional enemies as well as friends. The major enemies appear to be conductors and critics. The performances of individual conductors always stimulate dissection, comment, and anecdotes. The conductor who cannot maintain a beat, who loses his place, who "hams it up," or who abuses his orchestra or a particular instrumentalist, or who loses control of his orchestra or of his temper will be the source of a countless number of anecdotes that circulate through the international music community.

The musician often perceives the conductor as an arbitrary, capricious martinet, whose knowledge of music is eclipsed by his egotism, megalomania, and flair for histrionics—qualities he can indulge to the fullest when he ascends the podium.

The nature of the conductor's position invites these responses, for the conductor is required to control, direct, and discipline simultaneously, in a public setting, as many as a hundred or more specialists, each of whom in his own specialty feels he is more competent than the conductor. Each, then, will resent the discipline to which he is subjected, especially if it is administered unskillfully.

The instrumentalists tend to feel that the conductor gets the credit for a good performance; the performers, the blame for a bad one. The conductor of course is better paid and is a celebrity. In the latter role he is often perceived by the musician as a social climber and a traitor to "music."

The conductor is likely to feel that his instrumentalists are lazy, incompetent, obstructive, and obstreperous. He may regard them as children who resist the discipline necessary to create an ensemble. If a firm hand is not used, he may reason, they can wreck the orchestra and himself. Both conductor and instrumentalists can cite illustrations.

Another institutional enemy of the musician is the critic. He is more the enemy of the soloist than of the orchestra member, though he is an enemy of both. The critic is a member of the musical community by virtue of his concern with musical values, and is important to others in that community. His valuation, however, is ambiguous. He is endowed with vast powers over the lay audience and is seen as having the power to wreck the career of a soloist, a conductor, or the success of an entire orchestra. At times, musicians regard the critic as arbitrary and capricious; to the extent they are sometimes convinced he is bent on destroying a performer, conductor, or ensemble. Musicians tend to see each review of a performance as part of a campaign, whose cumulative effects are greater than a single review. To the soloist a bad and possibly unjust review or one based on an "off night" is too final or has too much weight.

Musicians often view critics as untalented performers whose failure as musicians has led them merely to talk and write about music and to compensate for their failures by attacking those musicians who have not given up. The musician, therefore, sees the work of the critic as an act of resentment against creation and creators.

At the same time, the imputed or actual power of the critic does produce mixed feelings. The critic can also elicit satisfaction and glee when he castigates the performance of a rival or an institutional enemy. In addition, the potential power of the critic forces the performer to treat the critic with respect, deference, and sometimes obsequiousness.

The critic is usually thought of as being a finer type, more relevant than the music historian or musicologist, unless the musicologist happens to be working on specific problems of performance or the unearthing of valuable lost manuscripts.

5. Other institutional enmity takes the form of rivalries. Every major performing group and, we suspect, individual performer selects one or more partners for special rivalry almost in the same way as do college football teams. For the rivalry to be meaningful or to permit the possibility of self-definition by

comparison, the ideal rival has to be almost equal in reputation. At times, each performer or performing group will develop special characteristics or reputations which serve as a basis of pride or defensiveness. These special characteristics will form the basis for rivalries in both a positive and negative sense. Thus, regardless of the music played, the Philadelphia Orchestra will be viewed as either having the richest singing tones in its string section or as being overblown, overcolored, and excessively romantic. The New York Philharmonic will be regarded as a source of great individual performers or as a collection of disruptive individualists who are often underrehearsed, overperformed, and directed by too many different and not always competent conductors, all of whom they seem bent on destroying.

The Cleveland Orchestra will be viewed by other musicians as being one of the most disciplined groups in the world, whose tempo and drive often exceed the score or the intentions of the composer.

The Boston Symphony is sometimes viewed as the most balanced orchestra and occasionally as a most dull and academic one.

Among soloists, similar distinctions are made: some are known for tone (and oversentimentalizing the music); others for virtuosity (and playing too fast, loud, and inaccurately); some are authentic (and too cold and academic); while others are poetic (and too mannered or personal in their styles).

Each performer thus has an armory of terms that provide sources of self- and institutional differentiation and identification. And each can devalue rivals by use of these self- and counter-stereotypes.

PRESTIGE SYSTEMS WITHIN THE STATUS COMMUNITY

The discussion of these stereotypes suggests that there is a great deal of categorical thinking within the musical community. The music community is so large and its culture so varied, that it is necessary for the members of that community to develop categories for the identification and placement of others. These may be conscious or unconscious, but they suggest the way that members of that community divide their world. Some of these categories will be briefly suggested:

1. *Instrumental type*: i.e., strings versus all other; brass versus all other; tympany; woodwinds, and so forth.
2. *Instrument*: violin, horn, oboe, voice (tenor, bass, etc.)
3. *Function in music*: performer, conductor, critic, manager, teacher.
4. *Performance type*: soloist, orchestra, chamber group, accompanist, opera "star," etc.
5. *Attachment to group*: an annual or longer contract; shape-up via union hall, via agent.
6. *By position in orchestra*: first, second, third desk or chair.
7. *By kind of musical group*: symphonic orchestra; pit player attached to "musicals," the ballet, opera, etc.

8. *By size of fees.*

9. *By recording contracts.*

10. *By affiliation with music schools, conservatories, universities.*

11. *By imputed skill.*

12. *By membership in a particular group*: the New York Philharmonic, the New York Pro Musica, the Julliard String Quartet, etc.

13. *By teacher*: Lhevinne, Rubenstein, Casals.

14. *By adherence to a particular style of music or composer*: especially a neglected master or a new style which has not yet been fully recognized.

Each of the 14 musical categories, in addition to being sources of both self-identification, and self-differentiation within the musical community, also serve as bases of prestige within the musical community. Traditional stratification theory makes this distinction between prestige and esteem: esteem is granted by peers on the basis of the performance of function; prestige is granted by outsiders on the basis of evaluation of function.

The distinction does not appear to hold within the extended status community. Individuals, it is true, gain esteem for their immediately observable performance. The musical community, however, is so large that insufficient opportunities exist for making personal evaluations and thus assigning esteem. The categories described above serve as a basis for prestige evaluations *within* a status community. Thus, regardless of the social status of the musician in the society at large, another system of social status exists within the smaller community which is more relevant to the members of the status community than their status within the larger society.

Conductors, soloists, and opera stars are at the pinnacle of the prestige structure. This is true for conductors despite the institutional hostility that performers have for them. Prestige then does not necessarily mean affection. Part of the prestige of conductors, soloists, and "stars" appears to derive from the necessary qualities they project to the lay public. In part, the critic derives prestige for the same reason. Stars and soloists derive their prestige partly from the unique skills and personal qualities that convert a highly talented professional into a "star." There appears to be relatively little envy of great performers by able performers who are not stars.

Among soloists, size of fee is likely to help determine prestige. Victory in such competitions as the Leventritt, Chopin, or Tchaikowsky music festivals bestows prestige, as well as the possibility of a performing career at fees that can sustain a successful career. Ownership of a valued instrument, a Stradivarius, Guarnieri, or Amati, confers prestige on the string player.

Conductors, soloists, ensembles, composers, and even critics and musicologists, may receive prestige by the type of music they are identified with. One conductor's reputation may rest on his advocacy and interpretation of new or experimental music. Another may be known as the foremost conductor of Beethoven, Mahler, or French Impressionist music. The same applies to soloists and smaller ensembles. A soloist or ensemble may revive a previously forgotten master, such as Alcan or Telemann, or rank as the foremost interpreter of a composer, style, or composition. Ensembles may specialize in baroque or renaissance music or in minor works by great masters. Some critics are more able than others to write intelligently or knowingly about a particular composer. A musicologist or a critic may be responsible for a revival or a cycle, and a composer may similarly adapt a neglected or forgotten style.

If the musician, as lobbyist, succeeds in establishing a reputation for such specialization, or leadership in stylistic movements, he acquires the prestige of the musical style, composer, or type of music, and sometimes independently of his technical or performing skill. This does not necessarily mean, however, that the acquisition of such prestige was the intention of the musician or the source of his interest in the composer or in neglected music. Whatever the motive, however, such interests are important in shaping the culture of the musical community and giving it new content and form.

A secondary level of prestige is based on the type of performing group. In general, small permanent ensembles, such as trios and string quartets, bestow more prestige on their members than larger ensembles. We might regard this as an extension of the prestige continuum of the soloist, the conductor, and the star. Anonymity, in the sense of being "lost" in the welter of sound created by a large performing group, diminishes prestige. The rating of "share-of-total" performance intersects with the social rating of the performing group.

The great American symphony orchestras have high prestige, as do about a dozen chamber groups. As we indicated previously, rivalries about the exact prestige ratings of these ensembles operate at all levels.

Types of instruments are also a basis of prestige. The strings and piano are high prestige instruments followed generally by the woodwinds (especially the oboe), with lower prestige assigned to the brasses and tympany. Within these instrumental groups, desk or chair is important, and the position of concertmaster bestows high prestige position.

Age is important both with respect to position in the orchestra and the prominence of the soloist. The musician who achieves a high position at an uncommonly early age is the beneficiary of special prestige. The child prodigy, for example, has unusual opportunities in music, which he must live down as he grows older. Since musical performance also involves physical skills and equipment that deteriorate as the performer ages, unusual prestige accrues to individuals who retain their performing skills long after the age of expected deterioration.

Recording opportunities are also a source of prestige for both the soloist and the ensemble. Within the symphony orchestra, recordings are frequently played by less than the full orchestra. An invitation to perform as a member of the reduced orchestra (the "Mozart orchestra," for example), or as a soloist within the ensemble, is a prestigeful event.

Accompanists have lower prestige than featured performers. This includes orchestral accompaniment of the ballet, opera, or musical, as well as the soloist.

But the prestige of the accompanist is directly related to that of the soloist. An accompanist to an outstanding soloist may have even higher prestige than a soloist of middle rank.

With some exceptions, music teachers are also of relatively low rank. The teacher who is also a performer receives the prestige of his performing role and not of his teaching role (which helps him as a teacher). The teacher of soloists and outstanding performers receives part of the prestige of his students. The teacher affiliated with a conservatory or music school receives the prestige of the school (if he has no higher source of prestige). The student or aspiring soloist will receive prestige from affiliation with a teacher of high rank and distinction.

The teacher who does nothing but teach and who has not previously made a reputation as a performer is low man on the prestige scale. This is a source of anxiety and chagrin to music teachers' guilds, as well as a reason for their existence.

The piano tuner and instrument repairman may have borrowed prestige from his clientele and esteem for his skill within his craft, but generally occupies the same position as the pharmacist does with respect to medical doctors. There is, however, an autonomous prestige system among piano tuners and instrument repairmen of which musicians are only dimly aware.

The complexity of the prestige system within the musical community suggests that while it is possible to rate the social position of some individuals (whose position or personal reputation are known throughout the community), other positions and personalities and performing ensembles are less salient, less known, and more subject to ambiguity. We suspect this is true for the composer, whose prestige depends more on who performs his work and how he makes a living, than on his function as a writer of music. His social rating (we except "star" composers) will thus be a function of differential knowledge, and access to him by particular musicians.

The many-sided quality of prestige within a status community reflects the musical community's division into smaller subcommunities, each of which is highly specialized and has its own subculture and its own internal system of prestige.

Thus every performing group and every supporting and educational group allied with it has its own culture. Moreover, every type of musical expression has its own culture. This is true because the individual musician moves from organization to organization within the same type, and music "fans" also frequently attach themselves to a particular genre such as the opera or even to a specific organization.

Some musical communities are entirely separated from the groups described above. Folk, popular, jazz, and ethnic music are each the basis of separate status communities which have their distinctive cultures and systems of social honor. An individual in the classical music community may be related to these other communities in ways that are not unlike those of any other layman.

THE LAY AUDIENCE AND THE STATUS COMMUNITY

In describing the musical community as a status community we have concentrated on the professional, who tends to live in a psychologically total institution. The lay audience for music is also part of the musical community. It shares in its culture, its technology, and its symbolic systems, and makes prestige evaluations which are important to that community.

But the lay audience is rarely devoted to one musical form. Witness, for example, the attachment to opera among lower class Italians and, for other reasons, upper class Protestants. Others may be almost exclusively devoted to one performing group or organization. Other members of lay audiences may have a wider range of musical tastes. But it is precisely these general audiences, who are also interested in a multitude of cultural forms, including the theatre, ballet, fiction, painting and sculpture, and essays, criticism, and the subject matter of social and physical science, that are significant to the social rating of the entire musical community and the individual unit within it. To the general, lay audiences, interest in music in general, or in particular music in general, or in particular musical organizations is only one element in a wide range of interests.

These lay audiences are members of a wide variety of status communities whose consumption of artistic production helps to shape their cultural life as well as their own prestige aspirations. They receive prestige from like-minded groups for the quality of their knowledge and their taste in the arts. But prestige for artistic consumption is usually but one basis for membership in their lay status communities. Such communities may be organized around an occupation, a professional organization, a neighborhood group, past attendance in a college, ethnic identification, a voluntary organization, or a purely "social" status group. In these instances the individual makes his primary attachment to a status group on grounds other than his interest in artistic consumption, but imports his artistic interests into that group, if those interests are congenial.

Lay audiences for music, therefore, are not merely a segment of general artistic audiences but part of a vast variety of other communities. The musical community is linked at many levels through different channels with a host of other status and psychological communities by common patterns of membership.

The individual member of the lay musical community occupies separate status positions in the wide spectrum of organizations and communities of which he is a member.[5] He may have high status at his place of work, low status in a musical subcommunity composed of a "high level" artistic clique of his wife's

[5] See: Everett C. Hughes, "Dilemmas and Contradictions of Status," *American Journal of Sociology*, 50 (March, 1954), pp. 353-359, and Thomas E. Lasswell, *Class and Stratum* (Boston: Houghton Mifflin, 1965), pp. 93-95. Lasswell's summary of literature in this area indicates a concern with the congruency, consistency, and crystallization of status positions of the individual. The same phenomena when seen sociologically would indicate membership in related or unrelated status communities.

friends, and high status for the very same qualities among his lower brow friends. His richer brother-in-law may think of him as a semipauper and his artistic or intellectual brother-in-law may think of him as a vulgarian. His neighbors may think of him as a well-rounded fellow. Precisely because of the fluid nature of belonging to many status communities, the individual's social status may alter radically in a complex urban society. In a simple or more static society one role (the social role of the family) may be the master social role of the individual. In a complex urban society, no one role necessarily becomes the master role, unless one is a "star" known to the society at large, or unless the individual forcefully and successfully defines himself in a certain way. In some social circles, a psychiatrist may choose to define himself as a music lover and denigrate his professional role. In some New York hospitals, a desirable qualification for employment and advancement is ability to occupy a chair in a hospital orchestra.

To state this, in Goffman's terms, an individual, by choosing his stage-setting and the role he wishes to play, can become a different person simply by entering a new arena. He may attempt to live off his alleged status in another play, even if it is necessary to enlarge the appearance of his role in it. He can manipulate his audiences by acting the expert in an area with which no member of his present audience is familiar. He not only risks exposure from the unknown expert in his audience but the inability to identify with any role he plays. He risks being humiliated when individuals do not recognize or evaluate positively the roles that he projects. In a complex society in which pluralistic status communities predominate, management of one's identity becomes an important problem for the individual. He has many opportunities stemming from his discretionary action to remake himself. But he also suffers great anxieties and risks when he is not able to do so.

SOCIETAL STATUS AND THE STATUS COMMUNITY

We now return to an analysis of the relationship between the status community and social status in the society at large. We have indicated that one can receive prestige both within a status community and within the society at large. The prestige one receives in the society at large is based upon the prestige of one's status community or that status community with which one is primarily identified and the imputed position of the individual in the status community. In both status community and society at large, prestige is pluralistic.

The extent and character of the overall system of social stratification in the society at large depends upon the extent to which a given status community is prominent or relevant to the society at large, and the degree to which it commands a positive or negative valuation.

In a society with a multiplicity of groups and competing claims for prestige, both the salience of the community and its valence are based on the dissemination and acceptance of its underlying values.

Professionals in the status community initiate the prestige-claiming process by asserting those values. Intellectuals, educators, managers, and professional associations disseminate them in explicit, organized terms. Business organizations (both profit and nonprofit), through advertising and selling, disseminate the values implicit in the product or its producers.

Such value orientation and dissemination represent at most only the raw materials of a status system. The end product—prestige—is the result of different processes.

The processes determining the actual distribution of prestige in society are rooted in the acceptance of these prestige claims by potential lay audiences who together constitute the population of the society at large.[6]

These processes derive only incidentally from prestige or honor per se; they spring from the penetration of values and value complexes among a population. Thus, any process or set of circumstances that results in changes in ascendancy or value complexes in a society, leads further to a change in the societal relevance and appeal of the associated prestige system, i.e., the bearers of these values. Changes in the predominance of sacred religious values, for example, altered the prestige of the clergy, and the penetration of science into society has raised the prestige of scientists.

All groups tend to claim some degree of superiority in value and prestige in relation to others. The validation of that claim, however, is based less on the claim itself than on the ability and willingness of others to experience and evaluate favorably the activities, characteristics, and institutions buttressing the claim. In this sense, prestige is a by-product of the total operation of society.

A major vehicle by which prestige claims become transmitted into "realities" is institutional growth. We have indicated elsewhere that prestige claims are embodied in great institutions that organize the activities surrounding a value complex. The prestige claim surrounding these value complexes are validated in society with the expansion and growth of its central institutions. The prestige of business rose with the growth and ascendance of business and the corporation; the professional soldiers with the permanent large-scale army; the academicians with mass college and postgraduate education. Institutional growth and ascendancy validate claims for the functional indispensibility of institutions and leadership classes, because the latter demonstrate their claims by their success. Such growth also attracts new audiences to those institutional values.

The decline of institutions or the slowing down of institutional growth, however, does not necessarily result in the loss of prestige. When this occurs, the declining class bases its claims to prestige on other values such as lineage, character, moral worth, leadership, taste, and identification with the historical roots of the society. The older classes may be successful if they succeed in disseminating these non economic functions and values, and if they co-opt sufficient numbers

[6] For an extended treatment of this approach see Joseph Bensman and Bernard Rosenberg, *Mass, Class, and Bureaucracy* (New York: Prentice Hall, 1963), pp. 191-244.

of the newly ascendant classes to allow the latter to feel their efforts are recognized.

The prestige systems of society also change because of transformations in the character and composition of the population. For example, the white collar revolution, which has increased the number of college graduates, produces new consumers of art, music, books, etc. As a result, the producers of these valued products gain wider prestige for activities they performed in substantially the same manner in the past.

MASS COMMUNICATIONS AND THE ELITE STATUS COMMUNITY

Finally, changes in the system of communication within society vastly alter the prestige systems of society. In a society devoid of mass communications, the dominant prestige systems are local in character, generally slow in changing, and are based on family reputation. Nationwide elites exist but are less visible and are smaller in number. The mass media makes "stars" in all institutional areas—persons who become visible as celebrities. A great turnover among celebrities as stars becomes the result of differential attention to celebrities by the mass media. At the same time, local elites become devalued, if only because of their relative decline in visibility. Local elites continue to exist, but they suffer from comparison with national "stars" and elites who are professionally talented and trained in projecting finished and polished images as personalities, as leaders, and as "characters." The brilliance of the heads of state intimately recorded by TV in the receptions following the funeral of President Kennedy must inevitably make local leaders seem dull and untalented.

The leaders of such psychological or status communities and its stars thus become focal points for the mass media. The head of a small union who can, through a strike, halt the routine functioning of a vast segment of a whole society becomes a celebrity, a public relations personality. In the same way, an outstanding musical star, an instrumental soloist, or an opera singer becomes the focus of television reportage, guest appearances, articles, news and gossip column items, about both his public and private life. An orchestra conductor or a comedian may become a social lion, the friend of kings, queens, and presidents' wives, and—through the mass media—a household word.

This selecting-out by the mass media of stars and elites of the various status and psychological communities in society constitutes a basis for the integration and coordination of the various elites, and for the integration and coordination of society itself.

THE INTEGRATION AND COORDINATION OF SOCIETY VIA STATUS AND ELITE COMMUNITIES

We have indicated that each of the status and psychological communities within the urban society is so specialized that many of their members can live almost totally insulated from social contacts with members of other status communities. At the lower level of the status communities, some integration occurs because the lay publics and the dedicated amateurs are members of more than one status community.

At the top of each status community there is also integration and coordination of leadership because stardom, leadership, and "elitehood" become a generalized status position. The elites of all fields become aware of the parallel nature of their roles. Despite the vast substantive differences in their vocations, their formal organizational and symbolic status is quite similar and they respond to each other in those terms.

Mobility in almost any technical area requires the top leadership in any field to communicate with the public and with out-groups.[7] As a result, stars, leaders, and elites of dissimilar and unrelated fields begin to socialize with each other. They form status communities whose common entrance requirement is stardom, leadership, or elitehood. The result is that the generalized status community of the highest rank in society is based not on institutional specialization or on the sphere of value itself but, rather, on high position within a status community or an organization. All the traditional ways of ascribing status–wealth, education, talent, source of wealth, ethnic background, family background, past consumption styles–become of secondary importance to stardom, leadership, and elitehood in these communities. The heads of old wealthy families will entertain and be entertained by society prostitutes, ex-junk dealers, band leaders, ethnic politicians, and entertainers. If in their own organization or status communities they are stars, leaders, or members of an elite, the sons of immigrants and the descendants of slaves become social equals with the traditional upper classes.

By such means the respective elites of various status communities sustain each other. A vast exchange of social status takes place. Through membership in the elite community, the *arriviste* star receives social support from the members of the old upper classes who are also members of the elite community. The latter, in turn, derive considerable psychic income from their exposure to the values embodied by the *arriviste* star: the sense of organizational power, smartness, the rewards of publicity and recognition, and a feeling of being "where the action is." Each shares in the excitement of knowing others who make the key decisions in their respective spheres. Each can eschew narrow specialization and its accompanying feelings of isolation and feel that he is participating in the whole of a complex society.

But much more than this is accomplished. A major result of such leadership communities is the organizational integration and coordination of a segmented society.

As part of this exchange the very wealthy serve on the governing boards of various specialized organizations in the society. They contribute financial sup-

[7] Israel Gerver and Joseph Bensman, "Toward a Sociology of Expertness," *Social Forces*, 32, 3 (March, 1954), pp. 231-233.

port to these organizations and they lend the prestige, influence and authority of their respective spheres to the support of other spheres in exchange for the social prominence, recognition, acceptance, and personal meaning that such support affords. The stars, performers, and entertainers assist in fund raising by guest appearances, by allowing their names to be used, and by appearing as officers in voluntary organizations whose major purposes lie outside their special field. In politics, the entertainer, the institutional star, and the community leader become important sources for dramatizing support for a candidate, issue, or policy.

The mutually supporting relationship of stars, elites, and leaders alienates them from the specialized professionals working within the organizational and status communities in their fields. As a result, the narrow professionals often feel that the leaders, stars, and elites are traitors, frauds, and fakes who use their specialized positions to secure personal and social advantages at their own expense. At the same time, they publicize the respective values and institutions of their status community.

The terms "establishment" and "power structure" reflect this feeling. The middle and lower ranking specialists feel that an establishment exists—a combine of all those favored in various status and institutional communities of the society. And the dominant perspective of the establishment reflects the social cohesion of an elite community rather than loyalty to a specific status community.

Members of a powerless or pariah community, however, may not react in this way. The acceptance of their organizational or symbolic leaders by the elite community may be viewed as substitute compensation for their own deprivation. Thus, a labor union or an ethnic leader may become a hero on the basis of such acceptance even if, in the process, he appears to neglect the interests of his followers.

The one apparent misunderstanding of the theory of "power elites," power structure, the "establishment," or status communities appears to be the ascription of total coordination, integration, and the coalescence of the elite communities. Mills and Hunter, who have ventured similar theories, have been severely criticized on this basis, despite the fact that nowhere do they specifically assert the unity of all status or power elites. We must reassert that the vast complexity of urban, mass society prevents such unity. The number of status communities that produce candidates for the elite community is too large and is still uncounted.

As a result, a huge number of subcommunities of social circles exist among the elites. They are not organized in any specific or formal way but depend on the mutual co-optation of stars, leaders, and elite members. Subcommunities may possess overlapping memberships. Some may be based on membership in only a few institutional and status communities; others will be drawn from different value and institutional spheres and embrace different members from the same sphere. An individual may be a member of a number of subcommunities and be excluded for personal or other reasons from some elite subcommunities.

Some will be organized for specific purposes to support a given organization, policy, or person and may dissolve or change membership and character in relatively short periods of time. They may compete for attention, may divide on major issues, or simply be unrelated to each other.

As a result, it would be difficult to support the charge that the elite community is an organized, unified conspiracy. Individual elite subcommunities may, of course, be organized for specific purposes and, therefore, appear to contain elements of a "conspiracy." Their purposes, however, may be purely social, political, or cultural. They appear to be a conspiracy because they are temporary alliances of "men at the top" who, by virtue of their self-selection practices, exclude men at the middle or the bottom from all roles but those of complying or serving. Resentment is "natural" and human.

These patterns of organization of the elite communities explain in part how it is possible to coordinate a society so complex that the vast majority of its members can live in only one or a few of an untold number of status communities. The theory of status communities, however, does not supersede theories which explain societal coordination in terms of formal associations, political parties, interest groups, classes. It merely adds a new dimension to these traditional bases of explanation. The status communities derive from these other sources but once in operation, work through, around, and between the formal associations to achieve separate and distinct results.

Moreover, the theory of elite communities, by itself, does not explain the ultimate source of participation in elite communities. The growth rate of various organizations, spheres of value, and lay audiences, coupled with the effectiveness of the underlying status communities and specialized organizations in presenting prestige and power claims, determine much of the overall shape and character of a society.

10 *Thomas E. Lasswell*

INTELLECTUAL STATUS

[A. W.] Kornhauser considered how clusters of statuses and correlated factors might persist through generations by means of a kind of Darwinian selection process.[1] Drastically oversimplifying his argument to illustrate our point, he said that *other factors being equal*, persons with higher intelligence will be selected more frequently than persons with lower intelligence for the more highly valued positions in society. Hence, at any given instant, we might expect to find that in any hierarchy (or situs) of positions–political, industrial, agricultural, and so on–the median I.Q. of persons in the highest positions is higher than that of persons in the lowest positions. Several theoretical points are present. One is that the system of selection is rational. Another is that it is efficient. Another is that the selectors *believe* that high intelligence is preferable to low intelligence in the connection indicated. Still another is that the selectors are free to (and wish to) carry out their beliefs. There are many others. Kornhauser went on to suggest that the repetition of such a selection over a period of many generations would tend to produce (provided a hereditary tendency to inherit the intellectual capacity of one's ancestors exists) a class or stratum of persons who would possess *both* high intelligence and high positions at one end of the continuum, and another stratum of persons who would possess *both* low intelligence and low positions at the other end.

[J. R.] Platt's observations agreed with Kornhauser's. He added:

> We may be beginning to get larger numbers of people at the top as a result of our strong intellectual selection in marriage.
>
> It is all the result of coeducation. The smartest 10 percent of our young people, the 120's and 130's [I.Q.], are now selected and thrown together in college at the most susceptible age for romance. About half the college men marry college women. Almost all the college women marry college men or, alas, remain unmarried.
>
> The important thing is that these college marriages produce bright children. It is not certain whether the intelligence of a child is more a matter of inheritance or of early stimulation, although some psychologists now suspect the latter. But whatever the explanation is, it looks today as if the children of the college marriages are clustering about the average of their

[1] Arthur W. Kornhauser, "Analysis of 'Class' Structure of Contemporary American Society –Psychological Bases of Class Divisions," in George W. Hartmann and Theodore Newcomb, eds., *Industrial Conflict: A Psychological Interpretation* (New York: The Congdon Co., 1939), pp. 211-214.

> parents' abilities, scattering above and below in much the same way that children of unselected parents scatter above and below the average of the whole population. If this proves to be so, it has the remarkable consequence that these marriages are now producing *five or ten times* the total number of 150's, for example, that we would get from perfectly random marriages in a normal population![2]

As a speculative exercise, we might explore the possibility that the ordered statuses suggested by Kornhauser and Platt give evidence of the emergence of a social class in the United States at the present time. . . . we can gather our impressionistic evidence under the general headings of culture, selective association, power and authority, interpersonal behavior, and demographic indications of a "general status" category.

It is our impression that there is an identifiable microculture becoming established which is widely recognized as distinct from and superior to the great culture. [A very] careful distinction [has been made] between society, population, and culture, so that if we label this particular microculture the "intellectual culture" [it] will not [be] confuse[d] with a society of intelligentsia or a population category of persons with specified amounts of schooling, even though both of these may have a close relationship to it. It is our further impression that this intellectual culture is rapidly replacing the bourgeois culture and its lingering predecessor, the noble-gentle culture, as the ascendant microculture in our general cultural time-space. It is, in other words, becoming the most valued and most envied style of life. Our intellectual culture is distinguishable because it has its own appropriate language, art forms and criteria for appreciating art, rituals, social systems, mythology, artifacts, games, and other culturally distinctive characteristics. As is generally true, the host acculturating agency may be the family of orientation, but its alternate or secondary host agency is commonly thought of as the university. The acculturating function of the university is to the intellectual culture what the acculturating function of the club and "Society" were to the bourgeois culture, and what the court was to the noble-gentle culture.

Although selective association occurs, and just as Platt has pointed out above becomes involved in preferential mating, formal restrictions with regard to association appear to be declining on most fronts. This may lead to a decline in intergenerational social control over association. On the other hand, while the university is more heterogeneous than its predecessors with respect to many population qualities it is becoming more restrictive with respect to one quality: intelligence. Thus the formally controlled associations in our hypothetical ascendant class furnish the setting for informal associations by giving them the advantage of proximity to a restricted population. Informal cliques, within this

[2] John Rader Platt, "The Genius Explosion," *Context: A University of Chicago Magazine*, 2 (Winter, 1964), p. 22.

population or without it or mixed between the two, seem to be a human universal and no diminution of their exclusiveness or their numbers seems conceivable or desired by anyone.

The political strength of our hypothetical class is not clearly established at this point in time. Certainly it does not comprise a monolithic power structure about to assume the privileges and responsibilities of national sovereignty in the United States. The term "egghead" has been used with deprecatory intentions as an opprobrious epithet designed to reduce the chances of election of an identified intellectual to public office. He was not elected, although the precise contribution of the epithet to his defeat is difficult to assess. On the other hand, it is our impression that there is increasing public awareness of the powerlessness of the uneducated. Parents show signs of great anxiety about the eligibility of their children to enroll in institutions of higher learning, with the concern apparently focused on the limitation of the child's opportunities for social ascendancy. It is our further impression that the influence of consultants from the intellectual domain upon both government and business policies is increasing.

It is also difficult to assess changes in interpersonal behavior in response to cues which are symbolic of the intellectual person or of the intellectual culture. Not enough research has been done on the mass stereotypes involved to justify even the most guarded kind of general statement about their import. There does not appear to be any acknowledged or defined ideology manifest at this time which produces a general effect on the interpersonal acts of intellectuals or of nonintellectuals.

Finally, are there demographic indicators of the presence of a stratum such as we have hypothesized? There are, indeed, although not all of the boundaries are as distinct as one might wish. We have seen that the median incomes of college graduates are clearly superior to those who have not continued their educations so far. Our impression is that a disproportionately large amount of the country's private wealth is in the hands of college graduates. The intellectuals have high intelligence, too, and the most schooling. And regardless of weaknesses in evaluating occupations, it is clear that the top categories are disproportionately populated by our hypothesized stratum.

We can conclude from our exercise that intellectuals do indeed comprise a social stratum, and that they have (as well as we can comprehend that muzzy quasi-concept) high general status. They are, however, short of being demonstrated to be a social class, as we understand the term. They are short because they have not fully qualified themselves on two of our dimensions; power and ideology. Should these two become manifest, intellectuals will constitute the upper class in the United States (in [Gideon] Sjoberg's frame of reference of upper class, lower class, and outcaste). There is no indication that such is likely to occur in the immediate future.

11 *Seymour Freedgood*

LIFE IN BLOOMFIELD HILLS

Perched on a wooded eminence not far from Detroit is a community that has perhaps the densest concentration of working rich in the world. This is Bloomfield Hills, a five-square-mile suburban municipality that over the past decade has supplanted Grosse Pointe, Detroit's older and much more sedate high-income suburb, as the chief haven of the auto industry's ranking executives and their chief suppliers. The roster of families living in the Bloomfield area reads like an *Almanach de Gotha* of the U.S. auto industry: of the hundred-odd top officers (vice presidents and above) of the four big companies, well over half, including all four of the presidents–General Motors' John F. Gordon, Ford's John Q. Dykstra, Chrysler's L. L. Colbert, and American Motors' George Romney–live either in Bloomfield Hills or within a few minutes' drive of it.

Side by side with these men and scores of their chief aides dwell the top "peddlers," Bloomfield Hills' generic term for those who supply the auto industry with parts and services: manufacturers' representatives; proprietors of tool, die, and metal-fabricating shops; leading members of Detroit's banking, law, engineering, and insurance firms; advertising and media men (of whom more are said to reside in the Bloomfield area than even in Westport, Connecticut). Since at least some of the peddlers, and almost certainly those who own their own companies, are as well-to-do as the auto executives, the median income of the 670 families in Bloomfield Hills proper comes to about $50,000 a year. It is the automotive elite, however, who are the core of Bloomfield Hills' working rich and who provide the town with its special flavor. And by their presence there, they have made it the summit of worldly ambition to many of their subordinates.

THE HUDDLE IN CAMELOT

Quite properly for such an eminence, it has the appearance, viewed from Detroit's flat plain, of being up in the air. Twenty miles north of the city, just off Woodward Avenue, the main highway between Detroit and Pontiac, it is reached by ascending what are in effect a series of suburban steps–Ferndale, Berkley, Royal Oak, Birmingham. These are the "waiting towns," the communities made up in large part of middle-rank and junior executives employed either by the auto industry or by the many manufacturing and service firms that supply it. These corporate nomads have in many cases worked for their firms in five, six, or even ten other localities before being summoned to Detroit headquarters. Most, of course, will never get to Bloomfield Hills.

Just beyond Birmingham, which is the last and grandest of these suburban towns, lies Bloomfield Center, a twentieth-century jumble on the highway, which both services Bloomfield Hills and is its main gateway. It is a municipal rather than a shopping center–Bloomfield Hills does its shopping in Birmingham–but the center's dozen or so buildings do include, in addition to a combined city hall and police and fire station, two flourishing taverns and a small but phenomenally busy liquor shop. There is also a fourteen-lane bowling alley.

Minutes away, hidden in a region of low-lying, thickly wooded hills, is the auto industry's Camelot. In abrupt and dizzying contrast to Bloomfield Center and the "waiting towns," Bloomfield Hills resembles an English village whose cottages some Merlin has blown up to gigantic size and magically transformed into Tudor mansions, French châteaux, and Colonial manor houses. Dominating the settlement is a handsome, "modernized" English Gothic church, Christ Church Cranbrook (Episcopal), and connecting it is a network of narrow, winding lanes–Dunston, Church, Martell–whose contours, like their names, seem more suited to the stagecoach than the automobile age. At the heart of Bloomfield Hills is Cranbrook itself, a 300-acre estate named by the late George G. Booth, publisher of the Detroit *News*, after the little Kentish town his father came from; in the 1920's Booth built a number of cultural and educational institutions there, among them an Academy of Art and two preparatory schools, one for boys and one for girls.

There is also a sense of huddle: although Bloomfield's houses are obviously big and expensive–some have twenty or more rooms and are priced up to \$300,000–they are built on relatively small plots; the average is two acres. While inflated real-estate costs are mainly responsible for this–prime building sites are now selling at \$30,000 an acre–it is plain that Bloomfield's auto executives enjoy living side by side and would not have it otherwise. "The way things are here," one of them explained recently, "I have all the privacy I want and at the same time a hundred yards away there are neighbors I can talk to if I want."

Considering the fact that his neighbors are probably officers of rival, bitterly competing companies from whom he must keep his business affairs secret at all costs, his urge to live in the neighbors' shadow would be inexplicable were it not for two large facts about auto executives. The first is the work strain that is a living presence in their households, clubs, and social lives–a strain so intense that apparently it can be alleviated only in the society of men similarly burdened. A related fact is their lifelong preoccupation with the automobile industry, which leads them to prefer the company of auto executives–even rivals–to that of "outsiders."

Their strained absorption in their jobs can be explained, in part, by their backgrounds. The millionaire managers who run Detroit's auto companies today come almost entirely from poor families. By and large, they have spent their entire working lives in the auto industry, probably with the same company. They are self-made men, but of a very special kind. In contrast to their immediate predecessors, that rough-and-tumble breed of master mechanics and financiers who revolutionized industry by inventing mass production, and who were primarily entrepreneurs, these are "organization men." They are members of the first generation of auto-industry managers to have grown up in, and fought their way to the top of, the assembly-line world. As a result, the former nomads who are now settled in the big, fancy houses around Cranbrook are overwhelmed by the fact that (as one of them observes) "the company made us. Now that we *are* the company it's hard to think about much else."

THE DEDICATED CAVE DWELLERS

Their dedication inspired a young clergyman from a nearby church to comment recently, "These men are monks—monks who've traded in their prayer books for a production line. From the way they work, I sometimes think they want to overwhelm God with their cars. It may sound odd for me to say this, but I don't give as much of myself to my church as many of them do to General Motors and Ford and the rest."

Most of their wives would agree. "My husband and I," one of them noted recently, "haven't been out together after nine for six months. He's away on business a lot and when he's home he leaves the house before seven and he gets back to dinner exhausted. Then he goes to bed. For all he gets out of it," she said, looking about her well-appointed living room, "we could be living in a cave."

The U.S. auto executive may indeed be the hardest-working manager on earth. From the company president down, he is at his desk by eight every morning, and during the annual model changes—the industry's season of crisis—he will be there until late at night. "To tell them to slow down," says a Bloomfield Hills physician, "is just like telling a dog he shouldn't raise his leg at a fire hydrant. When they're racing that model deadline, the new model becomes God. All these people stop being human beings. They exist for that deadline."

Why do they work so hard? In part, it would appear, because of the sheer size of their jobs. In addition to managing some $14 billion worth of assets—a lot of them oppressively on view in the Detroit area—these men are responsible for the current investments of an industry that grosses some $20 billion a year. Moreover, these investments must be made in a business dominated by grinding competition and the vagaries of public taste. As one vice president put it, "None of us is really secure in our jobs, not even when we're on top." The man in charge, the vice president continued, cannot escape the fact that "one bad goof on his part, say a wrong bet like the Edsel, or even a lousy tail fin," may mean not only a huge loss for the company and the loss of his own job but the jobs of thousands of men in his division. In the auto business, as elsewhere, younger men attach themselves to a rising executive. The vice president who makes a big mistake will probably find another job, usually in another industry, but the men who worked for him may "find themselves out on their tails, losing all seniority."

WHERE THE MONEY WENT

A more obvious reason for insecurity is money. Once a man has won top executive rank, a Bloomfield executive explained, "the money sounds so impressive and the stature that goes with it is so pleasant that people work all the harder to hang onto what they've got." Keeping the big salary is an obsession with some even though, in the experience of many who have it, the money isn't all that good. "None of us is solely motivated by money," another vice president declared recently. "If we were, we wouldn't be working for an auto company on a salary. Believe me," he said feelingly, "you can't get to first base on a salary, even if it's $180,000. It's hardly enough to maintain a reasonable standard of living."

He thereupon proceeded to show where his money went. Last year, when he did indeed earn $180,000, including salary and bonus, he asked the company to defer payment of $57,000 until after his retirement, when it would be taxed at a lower rate. After federal income taxes on the remaining $123,000, his take-home pay came to $49,000. Of this he contributed $14,000 to the support of his aged mother and mother-in-law, who maintain separate establishments. He allocated $10,000 for the "capital account"–improvements on his house, a new car, savings. This left him with a total of $25,000 with which to maintain himself, to pay for the maintenance of his house, his housekeeper's salary, his daughter's college tuition, clothes, living expenses, etc.

The case is, of course, an extreme one: the man is a widower who cannot take advantage of the split-income provision in the federal tax code and move into a lower tax bracket. Nevertheless, his complaint is widely shared. Since the typical auto executive has no inherited wealth, his salary provides him with the chief source of income–and many overextend themselves financially in order to maintain the style of life required by their station. One vice president, for example, with two sons at Ivy League colleges and a third at an eastern boarding school, notes that he was recently forced to borrow on some of his stock to pay their tuition. Then he had an exasperating experience when one of his sons won a $2,000 scholarship. "That sure would have helped. Then, when the committee heard what my salary was, they said the boy could keep the scholarship medal but was ineligible for the money."

The executives are haunted by another money worry. As members of the salaried rich, they are painfully aware of the fact that, no matter how hard they work, few of them will be able to pass on substantial fortunes to their children. Unlike some of their predecessors, auto executives no longer retire with a hundred million dollars or more. Under present conditions, and assuming he has good luck with his stock options, the $150,000 executive at the point of retirement probably has accumulated net assets worth between $2 million and $3 million. If he dropped dead the day he retired, one such man points out, his wife and children would get from $1,700,000 to $2,500,000 after taxes. While this is not exactly a pittance, his children would have to supplement the income from it with their own earnings if they were to maintain the standard of living to which he has accustomed them. What troubles him, he says, is that "I've raised them to expect more than they can probably attain. The chances are that none of them will ever make anything like the salary I do, and they won't be able to bring up their children as comfortably as they were brought up. I suppose what I should have done," he added, "was to go into business myself, then sold it and realized a capital gain. That's the only way to make important money nowadays."

The Bloomfield Hills elite stand up under the financial and other strains remarkably well. Happily endowed (as a Detroit industrial psychologist puts it) "with above-average nervous and emotional stability, and less given to mental illness than the general public," they appear to thrive under pressures that would break most men down. "Any other line of work would bore me," the head of one big auto division confessed recently. "Here, each day is crammed with excitement. You're always on deadline. Long before you're producing this year's models you're working out the production problems of next year's. Always there's the hope that next time around you'll hit that jackpot. There are no sabbaticals in this business. You're at it twenty-four hours a day."

Some executives, of course, have an uneasy sense that their total preoccupation with the job has made them rather one-sided. "You don't ever have time to sit back and reflect on what you're doing, much less be serious about other things," an attorney for one of the auto companies complained at a recent Bloomfield Hills gathering. "And even if there were the time, and assuming the company allowed us to speak up as individuals on important issues—for example, the advisability of integrating our southern assembly lines—I hesitate to think what positions some of the men would take." He then spoke of the "rigid, uninformed, locker-room conservatism" of many of his colleagues.

One other man at the gathering muttered that the attorney was a maverick who had joined his company late in his career, and might be happier in the employ of Bloomfield's archenemy, Walter Reuther. The other guests did not seem terribly interested in the discussion, but the attorney kept it going. He said that although most of the executives are college-trained men, their education hasn't helped them to see their jobs in perspective and he included himself in the general indictment. "Wherever we are—at dinner parties, on the golf course, in bed—the talk is automobiles. We talk business all the time. My wife tells me it's gotten so that when she goes to church she expects to see a car up on the altar. And when we do talk about anything else—the important issues of the day, public affairs, how to deal with the Communists in Cuba or the Congo—it's always in terms of the effect on business." He looked around him bleakly. "Sometimes I think we work so hard because we can't enjoy anything else."

The majority, however, at least of the men, seemed to echo the sentiments of another executive, who observed, "We're geared to this pressure and we love it. We wouldn't want to change any of it a bit."

This is not to say that the executives do not take time out to relax, or that they and their wives do not find anything about Bloomfield Hills that is pleasurable and rewarding. For one thing, having spent most of their married lives in the mass-produced "waiting towns" of lower suburbia, there is the sheer pleasure of living in one of the commodious houses on the lanes near Cranbrook. Consider, for example, a more or less typical two-story, eighteen-room establishment owned by one of Bloomfield's top auto executives and his wife. It is, of course, admirably equipped. Opening off the spectacular kitchen, with its two back-to-back refrigerators, is a dining room large enough for formal entertaining and, beyond that, a spacious living room furnished by a Detroit department-store decorator in Chinese Chippendale. There is no library: the typical Bloomfield Hills family reads magazines, not books. But there is an "activity room" in the basement fixed up to resemble a Wild West saloon, a swimming pool out back, and a five-car garage. The last shelters the limousine, which the company provides as an executive benefit and changes every six months; a station wagon for the wife; a convertible for the oldest boy; and a "classic" Locomobile touring car, circa 1920, which the family keeps because it is fashionable and occasionally uses for picnics. The fifth slot in the garage is for whatever new model the head of the house may decide to try out. Sometimes, like many of his fellows, he will drive home in a truck.

In addition to this elegance at home, there is Bloomfield's club and social life. The typical executive is almost certainly a member of the Bloomfield Hills Country Club, the most august of the half-dozen or so golf clubs in the immediate vicinity, and the one to which all recent arrivals automatically apply. (His company ordinarily picks up the tab for at least one of the executive's club memberships; at the Bloomfield Hills Country Club this runs to about $1,500 a year plus the initial fee of $4,800.) In addition, a considerable number of the auto executives become "horsy" after reaching the summit and join the Bloomfield Open Hunt. In contrast to the somewhat somber country club, which concentrates on golf and high-level business discussions and discourages children on the premises, the Hunt is Bloomfield's family club: it gives riding instruction; provides quarters where horses may be stabled and exercised; maintains a hunt master and several packs of hounds; and conducts periodic "open hunts" for fox across the neighboring farm country.

THE GRAPE-JUICE DRINKERS

Even if the newly arrived executive was not a church-goer before, his family will probably join one of Bloomfield Hills' churches: Christ Church Cranbrook, the Presbyterians' Kirk-In-The-Hills, and the Roman Catholics' St. Hugo of the Hills, all of them heavily attended. Although Bloomfield's churches, like its clubs, are the centers–a vestryman at one of them calls them "hurricane centers"–of a great deal of community activity, many auto executives seriously feel the need to go to a quiet place to pray. "Those who attend my church," says one clergyman, "are the most pious group I've run across. They come out of genuine need and with honest devotion."

It is not hard to detect the imprint of business on much of Bloomfield Hills' social life. At the many informal and formal dinners, dances, receptions, and other entertainments at the clubs and churches, one can see the auto men courted and deferred to by those other members of Bloomfield Hills' business elite–the top "peddlers" and their wives. The auto executive is apt to sip his liquor carefully at these social occasions, or even drink grape juice. While Bloomfield Hills probably drinks as heavily as any posh suburb in the country, the ranking auto executives as a whole are an abstemious lot, at least in public: they seem, indeed, to have some sense of being semi-public figures, of always being watched. In the safety of their own houses over the weekend, they are less inhibited, of course. Some try to unwind from the week's pressures by opening their bars early Saturday and keeping them open until late Sunday night.

In addition to golf, which is their "quick" sport, many are ardent hunters and fishermen, some boat or ski, others garden or do woodwork, some collect antique cars, and one executive actually hooks rugs. There are, in addition, many business trips that are not all work. Although most Bloomfield men will insist that there is little truth in the stories of executives' living high off the hog on business trips, their style of life can hardly be regarded as Spartan. It is not their own expense allowances that make the difference. Explains one executive: "We're sought after. When the big boss comes to town, somebody, if it's only the plant manager, is going to roll out the elephants. The guys who need the big allowances are the peddlers. The peddlers," he added, "have really been sweating since Washington began looking hard at the expense account. A lot of them have begun to cut down on the flossier kind of stuff and some are even thinking of pulling out of their duck blinds."

AN EVENING ON THE SUMMIT

In Bloomfield Hills late one workday afternoon recently, a retired executive, who will be known here as Bill Burck, invited a house guest to accompany him on some social rounds. The tour began with a visit to the Kingsley Inn, one of the two taverns in Bloomfield Center.

The dark, cavernous taproom was about half full when they groped their way in. Seated around one large table was a group of well-dressed women, most of them, Burck explained, auto executives' wives who had probably spent the afternoon in the nearby bowling alley and were now having a cocktail while waiting for their husbands to come home. Seated alone at another table was an equally well-dressed woman who seemed to have spent the afternoon less profitably: from the debris in front of her, it was plain she had an addiction for creme de menthe with beer chasers. Crowded alongside one another at one end of the bar were about twenty dapper men, predominantly martini fans, whom Burck quickly identified as "peddlers"–for the most part advertising and media men. After shaking hands with several of them, and permitting one to stand him and his guest a round of drinks, Burck spotted a couple of other men at the far end of the bar. These, too, he was able to identify: they were, he muttered somewhat disapprovingly, a pair of General Motors purchasing officers who he believed lived in Birmingham, and were presumably on their way home. The "important" executives, he explained, rarely stopped by for a drink after work: they would drive straight home for an early dinner and, if possible, a good night's sleep.

The guest was then taken to call on a couple whom Burck referred to as Tom and Daisy. Tom, he explained, was the production boss of a major auto-company division. Strolling up to the entrance of their white-shingled, Cape Cod house, he knocked on the screen door and asked the uniformed maid if the boss was in. He was, and moments later he invited the two men to join him and his wife in their living room. Tom was a squat, square-faced man in his late fifties, dressed somewhat oddly in a sweatshirt, slacks, and blue sneakers; he explained that he had just got home from the office and was about to have his usual workout before dinner. He led his guests downstairs to the "activity room," where three punching bags were lined up against the wall, tapped one after the other, soon had all three going at once. He banged away happily for a couple of minutes, then subsided. "My doctors tell me I'm crazy to do this," he panted. "Maybe so. But in my job you've got to find some way to work off steam." Suddenly looking anxious, he laughed loudly and clapped his friend on the shoulder. "Come on, let's go upstairs and have a snort."

THE BOYS FROM PAW PAW

The auto families that live in the Bloomfield Hills area, and provide its special flavor, can be taken as typical of the Detroit auto-industry elite. Of the 100-odd executives (vice presidents and higher) who are now at the top, sixty live in or at the edge of Bloomfield Hills. A *Fortune* study of these 100 executives discloses, among other things, that their average age is fifty-four, so that most of them were born in the years just before Henry Ford moved his first auto off an assembly line. The typical top executive came from a small farm or factory town–towns with names like Paw Paw, Ishpeming, Crete, recur in the survey–somewhere in Michigan, Illinois, or elsewhere in the Midwest, usually within a 500-mile radius of Detroit. If he was born in a big city like Chicago, or in Detroit itself, it was probably in a working-class section.

His parents were poor. His father was probably a mechanic, a small shopkeeper, or a traveling salesman who (as one of the executives put it) "sold just about everything, although not very much of it"; the family was large and the chances are that it was the mother who kept it together and got the children fed, clothed, and educated. The chances are even better that the executive was raised in the Baptist or some other evangelical church and has since become a Presbyterian or an Episcopalian. In one case out of ten, he is a Roman Catholic of Irish or Italian ancestry. None of the 100 top auto executives is a Jew, and no Jewish families live in Bloomfield Hills proper.

The boy from Paw Paw got off to an early start. He stayed around home just long enough to finish high school, then took his first step upward by enrolling in college, perhaps as a "co-op" student who worked in a plant by day and took classes at night. (This was in the mid-1920's, when only 37 percent of all U.S. high-school graduates went on to college; but almost all the executives in *Fortune*'s survey attended some college or other.) In selecting a college, however, he stayed well inside the American heartland. His choice was most probably the University of Michigan, or some other midwestern state university or college; only about fifteen of the group attended Ivy League colleges. In almost all cases, he helped pay his way by working part time and through the summer. When he graduated, and over 75 percent of those who started college did, it was probably with a degree in business administration.

He was now twenty-one, the year was 1928, and the auto industry was booming. Degree in hand, he soon afterward made the most important commitment of his life: his first job after school was with the auto company at which he is still employed, or with a company that was later absorbed by his present employer. (This was the history in well over half the cases surveyed.) Since his earliest bosses were pioneer auto men, many of whom had quit school at twelve to go to work and who considered "college boys" somewhat effete, his academic training was of little help to him at the start. He probably began work at 20 cents an hour as an assembly-line hand, a specifications clerk, or some kind of bookkeeper. The dozen exceptions to this would include lawyers, like Chrysler's Colbert, and a half-dozen others, like Ford's T. O. Yntema and General Motors' Lawrence R. Hafstad, who come to the industry with advanced degrees in economics or other specialties. These, by and large, did not join their companies until they were in their thirties and forties, after they had earned reputations for administrative ability or technical competence elsewhere. On the whole, the typical top executive started on the factory floor and moved to the top through a series of jobs in production supervision and sales.

He probably got married during the hard times of the early 1930's when everybody's future, including his own, was in doubt. His wife, too, would have been born in a small town of a not particularly well-to-do family, and she most likely did not go to college. In the years of depression and war, as he scrambled up the corporate ladder, she made a home for him and their children in as many as a dozen factory towns across the nation, until his company finally transferred him to Detroit headquarters and he bought a house—perhaps in Birmingham. Then, a couple of years ago, when the company made him a vice president in charge of one of its divisions, he moved his family to Bloomfield Hills. Today, a little more than three decades after he joined the company, he may be making upwards of $150,000 a year. The company is working him harder than ever but he appears to revel in this, and to be pretty well satisfied with everything–except the prospect of retirement.

Since many of the auto executives do not appear to feel entirely alive except when they are working, it is not surprising that many of them dread quitting almost as much as death. "That's the toughest move of all," one recently retired Bloomfield Hills man observes, "when you've got to give up. For years you've been on top. You've had the power and responsibility of investing hundreds of millions. Thousands of livelihoods have depended on whether or not you bet right. All the company's facilities have been at your disposal–fleets of airplanes, guys holding your hat, guys holding your coat, guys meeting you at the airport with the limousine, other guys driving you back. And suddenly, all you've got sitting beside you is your wife, if you've still got one."

THE PLIGHT OF THE WIVES

The pressures on the men of Bloomfield Hills naturally affect their wives. According to a local physician, a lot of the wives have become "totally dependent on alcohol as a tension releaser." The women, he added, "also seem to need a lot more tranquilizers and 'happy pills' than the executives–they feel the pressure more."

There is no doubt that the top-executive way of life in the auto industry makes heavy demands on the wives. "The poor things," says one woman who knows a lot of them well, and may or may not be objective, "have a lot of things to be responsible for. Some just can't take prosperity–they simply haven't been educated for it. Their husbands expect them to run their big houses as if they'd been to the manner born; that isn't easy, even if they're lucky enough to find a good cook and maid. For business reasons, they have to entertain people who are impossible. They have to throw big parties, and they get caught with obligations to take part in charitable enterprises. I've seen them throw parties when they were nervous enough to throw up." Many of her friends, the same lady declares, live in constant dread of a phone call telling them their husbands have had a heart attack.

The wives who are the happiest are those who have a talent for civic and charitable work–the program chairmen, the fund raisers, the party givers. They find plenty to do. In the Bloomfield Hills-Birmingham area there are some 120 women's clubs and organizations of one kind or another. The ladies try to bring the same efficiency to the management of community projects that their husbands do to business, although at least one observer doubts that they quite succeed. "If half of the organizations functioned as well as they should," says Paul Averill of the leading local newspaper, the *Birmingham Eccentric*, "we'd have Utopia here."

Many of these organizations–e.g., the American Cancer Society–have serious social purposes. Others, like the recently formed Bloomfield Art Association, are devoted to culture. Overnight, says a local architect, "all the women have become painters and sculptors. They take art lessons, and they get a kick out of attending the association's bi-weekly parties. It's something to do." Those who still have energy to spare may take it out in bowling; one day each week a large group of exquisitely coiffured, impeccably dressed auto wives–some in their sixties–take over Bloomfield Center's fourteen-lane bowling alley for a morning of vigorous league play.

But there are some wives, according to one local critic (female), who "never get beyond lunch cocktails. They can't cope with their husbands' long hours and absences and the club life bores them. Those are the ones who just sit there and drink."

THE SERIOUS GENERATION

One preoccupation that Bloomfield Hills parents share with most others has to do with their children. The auto executives and their wives appear to be deeply ambitious for their sons and daughters, and determined to provide them with the best schooling. They send them to private schools: well over half of the top executives' children in the Bloomfield Hills area are either graduates of, or are now enrolled in, one or another of the better independent preparatory schools. Cranbrook School for boys and Kingswood, the local school for girls, draw most of these, but an increasing number are now going east–the boys to Exeter, St. Paul's, Hotchkiss, and other such New England institutions.

Surprisingly, in view of the transient and non-intellectual households the youngsters grew up in, they often appear to flourish at these schools as serious students. On the whole, says a Bloomfield Hills clergyman who specializes in adolescent counseling, the auto executives' sons and daughters are "disciplined, serious children, extremely anxious to get ahead." To be sure, Bloomfield Hills, like many another affluent suburb, has its episodes of schoolboy shenanigans. In the parking lot of one of the nearby secondary schools there is a watchtower to which a policeman is permanently assigned; one of his duties is to stop rival gangs of well-to-do boys from slashing the tops of each other's convertibles after football games. The youngsters also appear to do a certain amount of bravado drinking: the most frequent charge made against Bloomfield Hills boys arrested by the police is "possession of alcoholic beverages."

Yet an instructor at one of the Cranbrook schools noted that never before in her many years of teaching had she "met a group of children who consistently drove themselves so hard." Perhaps because they come from such highly competitive, high-pressure families, "they are their own harshest taskmasters. They are very tense. They've got to win. They are very competitive, but the competition is with themselves." In addition to being extremely serious about their studies, she added, they "have become deeply concerned during the past years over the state of the world and the welfare of our country–perhaps more concerned than some of their parents. These are very serious children, members of a very sober generation."

This seriousness is reflected in the colleges they are able to enter. Over a third of the Bloomfield Hills executives' ninety or so sons and daughters who are now eighteen years old or older have been able to meet the tough standards required for admittance to Harvard, Smith, Yale, Mount Holyoke, and other leading eastern men's and women's colleges.

Their determination to succeed is undoubtedly inspired by their fathers' example, yet it often seems to be fueled by a kind of silent protest against their fathers' way of life. This becomes clear when they select their careers. The Bloomfield executives' sons tend to avoid jobs with the auto companies, and indeed with any big corporation. Of some thirty young men now working, about a dozen have either joined the professions, become research scientists, or gone into government work. Several have shown unexpected career preferences: to the considerable astonishment of his parents, one son is doing graduate work in animal husbandry, and plans to get a job as a ranch manager in the Southwest; the son of another couple is engaged in oyster raising. Those who go into the more conventional businesses seem to prefer working on the sidelines of the auto industry: the majority have become auto dealers or distributors or taken jobs as "peddlers." Few, in any case, are trying to become corporation chiefs.

"THEY'VE GOT OTHER IDEAS"

The executives, for the most part, seem pleased with this state of affairs. "When the men start boasting about their kids at the club," says one Bloomfield Hills father, "it's not the guys whose boys have become dealers and distributors that sound off. The proudest is usually the one whose boy is becoming a brain surgeon or something like that." The fathers also appear to sympathize with their sons' disenchantment with the top-executive life. At present, says one executive, "the kids have no desire to earn $150,000. Because they've lived in this atmosphere, they don't want to duplicate it. They've got other ideas about how they want to live." For this man, in any case, the principal reward for his own lifetime of effort lies in the fact that he is now able to support his twenty-six-year-old son, who is married and a father himself, while he gets a post-graduate medical degree in neurology. "The boy won't have any earning capacity for four or five years anyway. The payoff for me is that he has adopted the career he has and that I can help him."

CHAPTER 4

LOWER LEVEL STATUS COMMUNITIES AND SOCIAL CLASS

Current public interest in social stratification and its consequences centers on the lower end of the scale of inequality. The various problems and pathologies identified with the lower stratum or class, notably that of poverty, is high on the priority list of those who deal with social problems.

Adam Smith's economic theory of laissez faire indicated that the arena of work and economics should be left to the rational laws of economics. Since these were *rational* laws, intervention was deemed not only futile but disastrous. One item in this theory decreed that poverty was both necessary and inevitable in the normal functioning of the economic system. We have now reached the point where poverty is something we actively fight rather than simply tolerate.

During the Middle Ages, principalities and communities enacted laws and rules restricting the use of certain behaviors and status symbols by those at the bottom of the stratification structure. For instance, laws regulating the distribution of clothes made from homespun cloth to the peasants and artisans, while reserving colorful silks, satins, and brocades to the upper classes, were in force in Europe until modern times. Behaviors indicative of either "commoners" or "gentlemen" remain an important part of our legacy of manners and etiquette, even though these distinguishing labels have lost much of their original meaning. We no longer write legislation regulating specific status symbols, but we are deeply involved in passing laws that attempt to manipulate social conditions so that certain symbols and behaviors may become accessible to certain strata of the population. Whereas the sumptuary laws of an earlier time were mostly aimed at pleasing the rich and well born, the legal machinery has now been turned to legislating the lower levels out of poverty. This has apparently been almost accomplished in some countries today, such as Sweden.

Although much controversy surrounds discussions of poverty, the issue is not *whether* we should or should not try to get rid of poverty but, rather, *how*. Our theories of human behavior cannot fully explain how or why families cannot avoid poverty or, if they do become impoverished, how they might overcome it. This has led a number of scholars and researchers to question whether or not poverty leads to the development of a culture of poverty. That is, does poverty have such all-pervasive consequences that when a collectivity shares the condition of poverty the result is a way of life that not only tends to be passed on from generation to generation, but also prevents a family from altering its fate.

The search for a culture or subculture of poverty is, in part, prompted by the apparent similarities in the human response to very low income. Economic deprivation is presumed to be of such a fundamental and pervasive nature that it results in social norms, values, and expectations that, over time, result in the development of a subculture. This implies that the stratification variable of class (economic level), as defined by Weber, is the most crucial variable in determining the consequences of stratification at the lower levels; whereas the other two of Weber's interrelated startification variables, namely status and political influence, are of lesser importance. Such an assertion would, however, move too close to an essentially economic "determinist" position–a position that has serious theoretical weaknesses. The high degree of interrelationship existing between class, status, and political influence makes it difficult, if not impossible, to determine which of the three elements of Weber's analytical scheme takes precedence. For example, in analyzing the interrelation of the three variables relative to poverty, it would be difficult to determine conclusively that low class (lack of economic power) is not intimately tied to a lack of political influence and status honor.

That low class is the most obvious or visible aspect of poverty is true; but its theoretical weight is another matter. A social policy that commits a society to raise the economic level of the poor may also recognize that changing the class level is the most effective or, at least, the quickest way of getting some of the desired results associated with the elimination of poverty. As such, of course, the variable of class attains the position of seeming to be the most important variable. However, one of the critical aspects of stratification at the lower level is that connected with the status and prestige of the occupations available to those who occupy the lowest ranks. Simple, unskilled, short-term, menial (even demeaning), and unstable jobs dominate the labor market of the poor. In turn, these kinds of jobs are low in prestige and status and, hence, command the lowest wages. Moreover, low *class* level and low occupational *status* combine very effectively to decrease the possibilities of developing political influence.

One of the most theoretically important characteristics of those who occupy the lowest rung of the social ladder is that they share a low position on *all three* of Weber's stratification hierarchies (class, status, and political influence). This can be viewed in contrast to the situation in the broad middle level of modern industrial society in which we find many instances of status inconsistency among the three.

Empirically there are numerous instances of the type of inconsistency experienced by a clergyman, for example, who has *low class*, relatively *high status*, and middle to low political *influence*; or, as a second example, an American Indian who has very high *class* level (due, for example, to ownership of oil wells in Oklahoma), but low *status* and low *political influence* due to social prejudice and discrimination. The existence of a great deal of inconsistency at the middle level supports the kind of heterogeneity that is implied by the use of *status community* in describing the mosaic of life styles occurring in the middle of the stratification structure.

In a country such as the United States, the concept of lower class has almost been synonymous with certain ethnic and social identities, particularly in urban areas. In many instances, time and social mobility have changed the constituency of the urban poor; but the various negative statuses (minus prestige) held by members of these types of minorities has been a persistent and important element in the structure and functioning of the American stratification system.

Migration, both transoceanic and as rural-urban, has been an important component in determining the composition of the lower levels. In general, most of the immigrants from Europe were from the bottom of the stratification structure in their homelands. There was, however, considerable variability in the class characteristics of the immigrants. The range of differences extend from the starving, oppressed, and pauperized Irishmen, who responded to the famine of 1846-47 by emigrating to America, and the migrants who not only paid their own passage but had enough left over to buy homesteads in the West.

There has also been a long and continuous rural-to-urban migration. Technical and economic changes in agriculture, a civil war, and two world wars all contributed to the migration. Not only did the "Okies," who said they had been "tractored off" the land, make their way to the city, but also the numerous extra sons and daughters of successful farmers. Since this nation's beginning, rural birthrates have been higher than urban; and since, the turn of the century, there has been a continuous decline in the number of farms. The economics of rural life sent thousands into the cities, many of whom joined the ranks of the poor.

Another element in the poverty phenomena of the United States is that of age. The age distribution has changed substantially during the history of the country. The median age of Americans jumped from 16 years in 1800 to 30 years in 1960.[1] America has been progressively becoming an older man's country. However, in the process of "aging," the norms and values have been slow to respond to the new and varied needs of an older population. As such, poverty has characterized the declining years of a great many Americans. The aged, along with one-parent families and the physically and mentally disabled, account for a substantial proportion of those living in poverty. Much of this is due to changes in age at time of death, as well as faulty or insufficient social services. These kinds of social phenomena are partially a product of social change, rather than basic features of the structure of stratification.

It was stated in the "Introduction," and theoretically developed by Mayer in his paper on "The Changing Shape of the American Class Structure," that if social classes existed in the United States it was only at the top and bottom of the stratification structure that they were discernible. Although the article by S. M. Miller, presents a typology of families to be found at the lower levels, it does not preclude the definition of a social class at the bottom of the structure. Nevertheless, a serious theoretical and methodological question remains unanswered: in light of Miller's types of lower class families, at what point would we draw the line between the lower social class and the middle level, which is, in our estimation, best characterized as constituting a considerable number of status communities. One possible point at which such a delineation might be drawn is the level of the "working poor." Such a category might include all of those who work at jobs that pay wages at, or slightly above, the federal minimum.[2] This is not meant to imply that the economic criterion is the key variable in describing the lower class; but, rather, that it can serve as a useful measure for a point of departure in the job of delineating between a lower class and the middle level status communities. A serious lack of the material means of life is certainly an important characteristic of the lower class. As Miller states:

> Lower class life is crisis-life, constantly trying to "make do" with strings where rope is needed.

[1] Murray Gendell and Hans L. Zetterberg, *A Sociological Almanac for the United States* (New York: Scribners, 1961), p. 42.

[2] The minimum wage of $1.60 per hour would provide an annual income of about $3200. This is at or near the official poverty level.

12 *S. M. Miller*

THE AMERICAN LOWER CLASS: A TYPOLOGICAL APPROACH

IDENTIFYING THE "LOWER CLASS"

... Two approaches, not always clearly noted, are employed in defining the "lower class." One approach emphasizes the definition of groups in terms of "class" characteristics, especially economic role or income. The other employs "cultural" or "status" criteria such as style of life. The Hollingshead index, based on occupation, education and place of residence, is in the tradition of the first approach.[1] Walter Miller's discussion[2] of the "lower-class subculture" is along the lines of the second. Social workers' discussion of the "lower-class client" and the "multi-problem family" almost always employ style of life indicators.

The two approaches intertwine but seem to make independent contributions to elucidating the characteristics of the "lower class" or the poor. Consequently, I have brought them together in an effort to move away from a broad and vaguely defined "lower class" into a specification of types of lower-class individuals. The effort is to utilize class and status variables in categorizing a population. The combination of the two produces problems, but these may be outweighed by the difficulties and obscurities produced by the current shifting between the two sets of dimensions in discussing groupings and issues: Walter Miller's "lower class"[3] is not Lee Rainwater's.[4]

Obviously the other dimensions like education or region should also be employed. Class and status dimensions should be more carefully marked off than in the following discussion. Unfortunately the material to do an adequate job is

Reprinted from *Social Research* 31 (Spring, 1964), pp. 3-5, 6-14, 19-22, with permission of the author and the publisher.

Author's Note: I am indebted to the Louis M. Rabinowitz Foundation for financial assistance in the preparation of this paper. I have benefited from the suggestions and comments of Frank Reissman, Bernard Kramer, Bernard Goldstein, Helen Icken Safa, and Jerome Cohen. A version of this paper was presented at the annual meeting of the American Sociological Association, Los Angeles, August, 1963.

[1] August B. Hollingshead and Frederick G. Redlich, *Social Class and Mental Illiness: A Community Study* (New York: John Wiley & Sons, 1958), pp. 387-397.

[2] Walter B. Miller, "Lower Class Culture as a Generating Milieu of Gang Delinquency," *Journal of Social Issues*, 14: 3 (1958), p. 6, footnote 3.

[3] Ibid.

[4] Lee Rainwater assisted by Karol Kane Weinstein, *And the Poor Get Children* (Chicago: Quadrangle Books, 1960). See also the distinction made within the lower-lower class by Martin Loeb, "Social Class and the American Social System," *Social Work*, 6 (April, 1961), p. 16.

lacking. The purpose here is to show one way of approaching the problem of differentiation among the poor in order to direct more attention to the recognition of variations among the poor.

The Class Criterion

The advantage of using an economic indicator in defining the lower class in that it specifies a political-economic category to which legislation and other remedial programs could be devoted. Emphasis on style of life indicators can be confusing because the meaning of attitudes or behavior or what they lead to can be quite different for the rich, for the middling well-off, for those "getting by," and for the poor. The same behavior may have different roots and consequences in varying milieus.

On the other hand, the class or occupational criterion is not as clear-cut as it appears. Some unskilled workers have stable, fairly well-paid jobs and are thus not a pressing social or economic problem. (This is particularly true where the unskilled worker is employed in a unionized, mass-production factory). Many semi-skilled and fewer skilled workers suffer some degres of irregularity of employment, especially due to seasonal factors. Another problem is that a considerable number of poor families (35 to 50 percent) have no member in the labor force.

Consequently, I would suggest that an income criterion is more useful today than an occupational criterion in the definition of the lower class. The recent analyses of poverty in the United States can be employed for this purpose. They show remarkable agreement, despite their different procedures, in estimating that one-quarter to one-fifth of the United States population lives below the poverty line. The level of income defining poverty varies depending on family size, composition, age, region, and type of community. For our purposes we can ignore these complexities and put the poverty line at a $4,000 family income, following Keyserling. It is the population falling below this line which, if we want to use the term, could be called "lower class," or "low income," or "the poor." . . .

The income criterion has several components: the level of income, the stability or regularity of income, and the source of income (employment or welfare). A number of observers believe that it makes a difference, holding income constant, whether a family is supported by welfare or not. The knowledge for making a refined classification of these components is lacking. I have resorted therefore to combining them into one indicator of economic security (roughly combining income and stability), and then dichotomizing this indicator into the two simple dimensions of high (security) and low (insecurity). Lumping together these components and dichotomizing them is inadequate.[5] But we cannot at

[5] Not all families receiving welfare assistance should automatically be classified in the economically insecure category. For the aged, perhaps, welfare assistance does not constitute a lack of security. In general, however, the fact of welfare assistance would put a family in the economically insecure category.

present describe each of the cells of what should be an 8-cell or 16-cell table. I think, however, that the cells of a 4-cell table can be usefully discussed. This capsulated table should rapidly be expanded as we acquire more knowledge and understanding.

The Style of Life Criterions

The style of life variable also offers difficulties. It refers at least to attitudes and behavior in the areas of family relationships and consumption patterns. A major difficulty is that the content of the "lower class style of life" is debatable. Further, evaluative judgments (as implied in the concepts of "family disorganization," "social disorganization," or "family instability") are invariably involved. As yet, it is not possible to formulate a clean-cut classification which avoids cultural biases and still is of use in formulating a judgment about the impact of life-style on individuals. For example, does the absence of a permanent male figure mean that the family is inevitably "unstable," and that children are necessarily psychologically deformed by living in such a family? Assessments such as these are difficult to make because much of our knowledge and theorizing about fatherless families is based on middle-class situations.

I employ the notion of "familial stability/instability," a dichotomization of style of life, to summarize a variety of elements. Familial stability patterns are characterized by families coping with their problems—the children are being fed, though not necessarily on a schedule; the family meets its obligations so that it is not forced to keep on the move; children are not getting into much more trouble than other children of the neighborhood. These are not satisfactory indicators; they are, at best, suggestive of the kind of behavior which is characteristic of stability among the low income population. The aim is to be able to describe the degrees of effectiveness of different styles of life in handling the same environment, granted that our vocabulary is inadequate for this task.

Class and Status

The two approaches can be welded together by cross-classifying the two dimensions of the two variables of economic security and familial stability in a 2 X 2 table:

Table 1
Types of Economic Security and Familial Stability

		Familial Stability	Familial Instability
		+	—
Economic Security	+	+ +(1)	+ —(2)
Economic Insecurity	—	— +(3)	— —(4)

Cell 1 is referred to as the stable poor; cell 2, the strained; cell 3, the copers, and cell 4, the unstable.

To some extent, life-cycle stages may be involved here, as some young people escape from cell 4 via cell 2 or cell 3 to cell 1, representing a more stable pattern, and beyond. Or families may drop with age from cell 1 to cell 3, where they have lowered economic security but maintain family stability.

Each of the cells contains many variants. While I believe the four types are an improvement over analysis in terms of *the* lower class, it is important to recognize that each type has many variations. One kind of variation is determined by whether the family is stationary in its particular pattern or moving to greater or less security-stability. *My general orientation is to emphasize flux, rather than assuming a permanent position in a pattern.*

Cell 1 (the stable poor) is characterized by stability, economically and familially. This cell points to the regularly employed, low-skill, stable poor families.

The rural population, both farm and non-farm, undoubtedly make up the bulk of the stable poor, since this is the majority of the American poor: a recalculation of Morgan's data suggests that only 30 percent of the poor live in metropolitan areas. The majority of all the poor and of the stable poor are white rural Southern populations. In addition, the non-urban poor are probably represented in this cell to a greater extent than they are among all the poor. Aged persons are also over-represented and constitute a large part of the poor who suffer from downward mobility, since most of them were better off at earlier points in their lives. Leftover third-generation immigrant populations in large cities are probably under-represented.

A number of [black] families are of the stable poor. They have higher social status in the [black] community than their economic counterparts have in the white community because of the general scaling down of incomes and occupational levels of [blacks] in the United States. For reasons discussed below, [blacks] and other groups affected by discrimination are probably becoming more important politically as well as in relative size among the urban stable poor.

The children of cell 1 families are of all the children of the poor those most likely to be educationally and occupationally mobile. Cell 1 might be considered the "take-off" cell, representing the phase necessary before many can really make a big advance. But this is a dangerous metaphor, for obviously many youth from families in more difficult circumstances are able to make considerable gains.

The stable poor, then, are a varied group; one component, the aged, has a poor economic future, except to the extent that social security and old-age payments improve, and a declining future as an intact family unit.

Cell 2 (the strained) portrays a secure economic pattern, but an unstable family pattern. This might involve a life-cycle problem i.e., at certain points the families of low-wage, unskilled workers are likely to exhibit unstable patterns. Examples might be "wild" younger workers or alcoholic older workers who disturb family functioning. Or, the pattern could manifest the begining of a move into cell 4, as a low-income family finds increasing difficulty in maintaining its economic security because of family and personal problems or the economic situation. Obviously, the two possibilities may be closely connected.

Movement may be viewed intergenerationally as well as in terms of life-cycle patterns. Many of the off-spring of strained families "may fail to match the economic security of their parents" and experience inter-generational skidding.[6]

Strained familial relations may not, however, result in skidding. In earlier periods, immigrant groups faced considerable internal strain arising from the conflict between the younger and older generations in the course of acculturation. Nonetheless, the second generation generally improved its economic circumstances. The instability of today's strained families is regarded as more "pathological" than that of the immigrant populations, although some social work accounts of families at the turn of the century differ little from current reports of "poor family functioning." The current stress is on parents' fighting and drinking, illicit sexual relations of parents, and neglect or brutality towards the children. Whether the economically secure and familially unstable are characterized by these patterns is not clear. If they are not, the offspring of the strained family may not be a prey to skidding. Further, not all children of deeply conflicting or hostile families are inevitably unable to maintain or improve their economic position.

I have looked at cell 2 as a transitional condition. This view may be misleading: many families persist with a low but steady income and a great deal of internal strain.

The copers of cell 3 manifest economic insecurity and familial stability—families and individuals having a rough time economically but managing to keep themselves relatively intact. This group probably increases considerably during periods of extensive unemployment. Probably a considerable number of [blacks] are in this group and their children are more likely to be mobile than those living in cell 2-type situations.

This cell probably contains a disproportionate number of families affected by downward mobility. Both Morgan[7] and I[8] have shown the sizable number of sons of non-manual workers who end up in manual (and sometimes low-income) positions. In Great Britain 40 percent of those born in non-manual families move into manual occupations. Many of these downwardly mobile persons are probably more likely to retain a stable family style than others in the same economic predicament. As in other situations, however, a minority of the downwardly

[6] Dennis Wrong, in a personal communication, has influenced this and the following paragraph. "Skidding" is discussed in Harold Wilensky and Hugh Edwards, "The Skidder: Ideological Adjustments of Downward Mobile Workers," *American Sociological Review*, 24 (April, 1959), pp. 215-231.

[7] James N. Morgan et. al., *Income and Welfare in the United States* (New York: McGraw-Hill, 1962).

[8] S. M. Miller, "Comparative Social Mobility," *Current Sociology*, 9:1 (1960), pp. 1-89.

mobile may manifest extreme familial instability, which would place them in cell 4. Limited data suggest that children of downwardly mobile families have a better chance of rising occupationally than children of families which have been at this low level for some generations.[9]

In cell 4, the unstable have neither economic nor personal stability. It is this group which is probably most generally called "lower class," and Jerome Cohen has suggested to me that the term "lower class," might be usefully restricted to this group. Since this recommendation is unlikely to be consistently utilized by social workers, economists, sociologists, political scientists and others interested in low-income populations, I have not adopted it, preferring to focus attention on the varied segments of the low-income population. Within the unstable group there are degrees of stability and strain–*not every family is a "hard-core case" or has a "multi-agency problem."* Nor do we have sufficient data over time to assert that once in cell 4, always in cell 4. It may be that families and individuals occasionally manifest both economic and personal instability, then overcome these problems for a while. Later they may again suffer from illness, unemployment, emotional upset or familial instability.

As important in some ways as distinguishing cell 4 from the other three cells which make up the lower class, is it to note that cell 4 contains an extremely varied grouping. In it are partially urbanized [blacks] new to the North and to cities, remaining slum residents of ethnic groups which have largely moved out of the slums, and long-term (inter-generational) poor white families, the declassés of Marx. Also included are the physically handicapped and the aged who have dropped through the class structure. *The low-income class generally and the unstable in particular comprise a category of unskilled, irregular workers, broken and large families, and a residual bin of the aged, physically handicapped and mentally disturbed.*

In some cases, social characteristics handicap the low-income groups: for example, recent rurality (resulting in unfamiliarity with urban problems and lack of appropriate skills) and discrimination. These groups–[blacks], former mountaineer whites–have the worst problems. They also have perhaps the greatest potential because removing their social limitations would lead to major change. Their handicaps are less self-inflicted and self-sustaining. This may not be as true for mountaineer whites as for [blacks]. Aside from people dropping into the poverty class along the life-and physical cycle, the whites in the lower class who have no good *i.e.*, social, reason for being there, are most likely to be intractable to change.

Hylan Lewis[10] has suggested the categories of clinical, pre-clinical and sub-

[9] Ibid., pp. 32-33.

[10] Hylan Lewis, "Child Rearing among Low Income Families," Washington Center for Metropolitan Studies, June 8, 1961. This paper and others by Lewis are among the most stimulating on the problems of low-income patterns. Also see Hyman Rodman, "The Lower-Class Value Stretch," *Social Forces* 42 (December, 1963).

clinical to delineate patterns among the poor. I would substitute the word "chronic" for "clinical." The chronic poor refers to the long-term dependents, part of whom are the "hard-core"; the pre-chronic poor are a high-risk group who are moving toward a chronic situation but have not yet become chronically dependent. The sub-chronic poor are those who have many characteristics of dependence but have a greater ability to cope with their problems.

A number of forces can lead individuals into chronic dependence. *Lower-class life is crisis-life constantly trying to "make do" with string when rope is needed.* Anything can break the string. Illness is most important—"Got a job but I got sick and lost it": "We managed until the baby got sick." The great incidence of physical afflictions among the poor—frequently unknown to the victim—are obvious to any casual observer. Particularly striking are the poor teeth of many. The tendency of lower class people to somaticize [sic] their emotional difficulties may be influenced by the omnipresence of illness.

Familial and personal instability may be the sources as well as the consequences of difficulties. While some frequent concomitants of low income life such as matrifocality do not inevitably produce grave difficulties in family life, they frequently do. Alcoholism, an inability to handle aggression, hostility or dependence—one's own or other's toward one—can deeply disturb family functioning. A variety of direct personal aid may be necessary.

Sophistication along these lines of analysis has frequently tended to denigrate the importance of structural factors in producing "personal inadequacies," "social disabilities," and "familial instability." The work of Raymond Smith[11] and Edith Clarke[12] strongly suggests that illegitimacy is related to economic conditions—the better the economic conditions among the "lower-class" [blacks] of the Caribbean, the lower the rate of illegitimacy. Kunstadter[13] similarly argues that matrifocality as a "lower-class" trait is related to a particular set of economic characteristics.

Prolonged unemployment, irregular employment, and low income are important forces leading to a chronic pattern. Low-paid and irregularly employed individuals do not develop an image of the world as predicable and as something with which they are able to cope. The control or direction of events appears to be (and frequently is) an unattainable achievement. When these individuals suffer long-term unemployment, they are less likely than other unemployed, who have had the experience of fairly regular employment, to maintain personal stability. (Maslow[14] has argued that those who have had a stable past are more able to manage in disastrous circumstances than those who have had

[11] Raymond T. Smith, *The Negro Family in British Guiana* (London: Routledge & Kegan Paul, Ltd., 1956).

[12] Edith Clark, *My Mother Who Fathered Me* (New York: Humanities Press, 1957).

[13] Peter Kunstadter, "A Survey of the Consanguine and Matrifocal Family," *American Anthropologist*, 65 (February, 1963), pp. 56-66.

[14] A. H. Maslow, *Motivation and Personality* (New York: Harper & Row, 1953), pp. 80-106.

considerable prior deprivation.) A high-employment economy has relatively fewer hard-core cases than a low-employment economy. The American community studies suggest that the low class is smaller in number in times of prosperity than in periods of depression. Peter Townsend in an informal lecture recently declared that during the 1930's in England it was believed that 500,000 to 1,000,000 of those not working were unemployable. In 1940, with the pressures of the war, it was discovered that only 100,000 were really unemployable.

CONCLUSION

A good deal of the tone of discussions of the lower class, even by sociologists, has a negative quality. On the other hand, a few seem to have a romantic feeling about the lower class, particularly its juvenile delinquents, whom they see as rebels against the horrors of middle-class, conformist America. The former view suffers from the assumption that the lower class has little potential for change; the latter, that there is nothing better in present-day America to which it can change.

Among other things, the glorification theme ignores, as Frank Riessman has pointed out, the impact on the lower class of its limited education.[15] The negative view frequently confuses, as Keyserling has noted, cause and consequence. The personal instability of many lower-class persons may be a consequence of economic instability as well as a cause of it. The chain of cause-and-effect over time frequently becomes blurred. An effective way of cutting into the chain so that change will occur becomes the key issue. My feeling is that structural forces have been under-played recently as a mode of change, while the "culture of poverty" has been over-stressed.[16]

The negative view has the danger of not seeing positive elements in lower class life. By ignoring these elements, social policies can frequently worsen them. For example, in an exciting study of a Puerto Rican slum, Helen Icken Safa has analyzed the community and familial solidarity of the residents of a slum barrio. When families were moved into public housing, community ties were weakened. Perhaps this was because the project social workers centered their efforts on the wife, while the husband's role and responsibility in the family and community diminished.[17]

[15] Frank Riessman, *The Culturally Deprived Child* (New York: Harper & Row, 1962).

[16] Harrington seems frequently to write and speak as though all low-income persons are bound in an immutable chain of apathy and ineffectiveness, characteristics of "the culture of poverty." He has obviously extended this term beyond the intent of Oscar Lewis who introduced it in his *Five Families* (New York: Basic Books, 1959), and in *The Children of Sanchez* (New York: Random House, 1961). Warren Hagstrom has countered this view in his "The Power of the Poor" (Syracuse University Youth Development Center, 1963).

[17] Helen Icken Safa, "From Shanty Town to Public Housing" (Syracuse University Youth Development Center, 1962). The peculiar stresses of public housing life may be functional equivalents of the economic conditions of matrifocality discussed by Kunstadter.

It is perhaps a "heuristic" fallacy, as Riessman has said, to believe that lower-class people are willing and capable of positive change. This is not always true, but if professionals and social reformers lack confidence in the poor, little can be accomplished either in the social services or in political action. An optimistic outlook may not insure success, but without optimism, it is doubtful if anything can be moved. Frequently, disenchantment and cynicism capture accurately a slice of life, but they are also immobilizing, for they ignore the constructive and energizing role of hope.[18]

A clearly defined "lower class" does not exist. As Peter Townsend has noted, the population embraced by this term is a varied, changing group:

> "A misconception is that in a relatively prosperous society most individuals have the capacity to meet any contingency in life. Only a poor and handicapped minority need special protection or help. This ignores the infinite diversities and changing conditions to be found in any population. Men gain or fall in status and living standards; at one stage of their life their dependencies are minimal, at others unduly numerous; sometimes they need exceptional help to achieve qualifications and skills held to be desirable by society; and at all times they are susceptible to the vicissitudes of prolonged ill health, disability, redundancy of unemployment, and bereavement, which they are usually powerless to control or even reasonably anticipate. Unanticipated adversity is not the peculiar experience of one fixed section of the working class.[19]

In England, Dahrendorf contends,[20] the unskilled category represents a temporary condition; individuals at various stages of the life cycle may drop into it, but for only a comparatively few is it a permanent position. In the United States this is not as true, and if caste pressures grow, it will be even less true.

The changing economy of America is producing new property relations; at the same time it is producing new working classes and lower income classes.[21] The analysis of data and the development of our concepts have not kept up with the increasing differentiation within these populations. Many pressures and counter-pressures exist in any stratum. Despite a modal pattern, considerable variety in values and behavior occurs. Since cross-pressures affect the lower class to a considerable extent,[22] we should look for *types* of behavior patterns even

[18] Cf. S. M. Miller and Frank Riessman, "Working Class Authoritarianism: A Critique of Lipset," *British Journal of Sociology,* September, 1961.

[19] Peter Townsend, "Freedom and Equality," *New Statesman,* 61:1950 (April 14, 1961), p. 574.

[20] Ralf Dahrendorf, *Unskilled Labour in British Industry,* unpublished Ph.D. thesis, London School of Economics, 1956, pp. 492-530.

[21] S. M. Miller, Poverty, Race and Politics," in Irving Louis Horowitz, (ed.,) *The New Sociology: Essays on Social Values and Social Theory in Honor of C. Wright Mills* (New York: Oxford University Press, 1964).

[22] See Miller and Riessman, "Working Class Authoritarianism," and Hylan Lewis, "Child Rearing."

among people apparently very similar in objective characteristics. Those at the social bottom see only a vague and ill-defined "them" above them, and those above believe that those below are all rather similar. But those at the top know how much differentiation actually takes place; those at the bottom are aware of much more differentiation than are the outsiders looking in. In particular, what has been taken as typical of the most unstable bottom group has been generalized to apply to all who are poor or who are manual workers.

The label "the lower class" increasingly distorts complicated reality. We must begin to demarcate types of poor people more sharply if we are to be able to understand and interpret behavior and circumstance and to develop appropriate social policies. Evaluation of commentators are frequently masked as description. The interpretation of behavior frequently assumes that all outcomes are necessarily desired and normatively prescribed. Anti-social behavior is viewed as heavily sanctioned rather than as the interaction of weak sanctions and difficult reality conditions.

The resurgence of interest in the poor augurs well for a rethinking of the new kind of poverty in the "welfare state," which is unlike the mass unemployment of the 1930's or the grinding poverty of the employed workers of the nineteenth century. Our "received wisdom" should be superseded by new categories and concepts. New wine is being poured into old conceptual bottles and the special quality of the new is being lost.

13 *Albert K. Cohen and Harold M. Hodges, Jr.*

CHARACTERISTICS OF THE LOWER-BLUE-COLLAR CLASS

This paper deals with the characteristics of the "lower-blue-collar" or "lower-lower" class. (For brevity, we shall use the conventional abbreviations, "LL," "UL," etc., in referring to the various classes.) Our data are drawn from the findings of a comprehensive study of social class on the San Francisco Peninsula, under the direction of Harold M. Hodges. One purpose of the present paper is to contribute to our descriptive knowledge of the LL class. Its main purpose, however, is to suggest theory to account for some of the characteristics of that class.[1]

A complete and detailed report of all the findings obtained in the Peninsula research will be presented in a later publication by Hodges. In the present paper we shall be concerned only with those findings with respect to which the lower-blue-collar stratum differs, to a statistically significant degree, from all other strata. Even on this level we shall not attempt to be complete; otherwise the paper would be prohibitively long. We have not, however, knowingly omitted any findings that would tend to contradict our descriptive generalizations or to impair the plausibility of our interpretations. This, however, is a matter of judgment. When the full data are published, others will no doubt see some implications in them for the present subject that we do not. The reader will note, however, that the findings are in general consistent with previous research. Those that are peculiar to this study usually concern attributes or response patterns whose linkage to the lower-blue-collar class has not been the subject of previous research.

In the section immediately following we briefly describe the sampling and instruments. Then we set out what seem to us four crucial aspects of the work-

From *Social Problems*, Vol. 10, No. 4 (Spring (1963), pp. 303-34. Reprinted by permission of the Society for the Study of Social Problems.

[1] This study resembles, in one way or another, those of (1) Knupfer [Genevieve Knupfer, "Portrait of the Underdog," *The Public Opinion Quarterly*, 11 (Spring, 1947), pp. 103-114], (2) Inkeles, (3) Walter Miller, and (4) S. M. Miller and Frank Riessman [S. M. Miller and Frank Riessman, "The Working Class Subculture: A New View, *Social Problems* 9 (Summer, 1961), pp. 93-94.], all of whom are cited below. However, (1), (2), and (4) are based on data which have in turn been derived from numerous studies by different investigators on different populations. Furthermore, (1) is primarily concerned with description or portraiture; (2) is concerned with testing a set of inferences from theory; (3) is a brilliant attempt to characterize lower class culture in terms of six "focal concerns" but does not deal systematically with their dependence upon current life conditions of the class; (4) is primarily concerned with the characteristics of the "stable working class." The present study is based on a single population; it is primarily concerned with the lower lower class and with explanation; and our interpretations are frankly post facto attempts to make sense of our data. Reference must also be made to the comprehensive and well-known writings on the characteristics of the social classes by W. Lloyd Warner and A. B. Hollingshead. No attempt will be made to cite all these authors at every point where they might be relevant; their relevance is too pervasive.

aday roles and experiences of the LL. Following that, we set forth what we believe to be the most important characteristics of the "typically LL" adaptation to these roles and experiences—important in the sense of setting the framework for the next and longest section of this paper, the presentation and interpretation of the research findings. . . .

SAMPLING AND INSTRUMENTS[2]

Primary sources of the data were six sets of self-administered questionnaires, three open-ended questionnaires, and one Rorschach schedule. Left with respondents by student interviews, the questionnaires were designed to elicit information relating to approximately thirty basic variables.[3] These pertained to such diverse matters as infant training and child rearing, religious values, self concepts, status concern, career orientations, familistic loyalties, sex norms, leisure time activities, and various "attitudes" for which there were available standardized scales.

The project involved six waves of interviewing, and each respondent filled out one of the nine schedules utilized. Aside from the Rorschach and open-ended procedures, the questionnaire items were largely limited to the forced-choice type.

Approximately 2600 male heads of families residing in three tiers of counties (San Francisco, San Mateo, and Santa Clara) comprised the sample. The sample in turn consisted of a series of sub-samples resident in contiguous sub-areas, each sub-sample received one or more questionnaires. Within each sub-area every hundredth residence within every fifth census tract was contacted.[4] Responses to control items repeated in questionnaires administered to different sub-samples did not differ significantly in their distribution by social class. Nor did the responses of [black] and Mexican-American respondents to selected items differ significantly from the responses of non-ethnic respondents. On the basis of these preliminary tests, we did not deem it necessary to control for ethnicity on the remaining items. The rate of non-response (refusals consistently ranged between 18 and 22 percent in each tract.[5] Not-at-home respondents were eliminated from the population after two unsuccessful calls and interviews were then obtained from the nearest adjacent households. . . .

[2] This description of the data-gathering phase of the research has been kept as brief as possible. A fuller description of the instruments and procedures can be obtained by writing to Harold M. Hodges, Department of Sociology, San Jose State College, San Jose, California.

[3] These were derived from the most frequently posited class-linked traits in the literature (experimental and theoretical).

[4] In order to ensure sufficient representation from each class level, a stratified random sampling procedure was employed for the final two interview waves.

[5] Slightly more than 50 percent of the initial nonrespondents filled out questionnaires in subsequent follow-up analyses; comparison of their questionnaire responses with those of the original respondents yielded no statistically significant differences.

THE LL'S LIFE SITUATION

1. Simplification of the experience world

The LL has experienced a relatively narrow range of objects and situations and of perspectives from which to define, classify and evaluate them. In comparison with other strata, the various stages of the LL's career have not subjected him to expectations nor provided him with opportunities to move in a variety of social and cultural worlds, with correspondingly various roles, styles of living, aspirations and perspectives. His workaday roles entail less complex and heterogeneous role sets, less various and novel interests to be encountered and balanced, less diverse criteria and expectations to which he must be responsive. This is not true only of his experience world insofar as it is directly shaped by his work roles. He is also relatively exempt from the expectation that he assume and he has fewer opportunities to assume "public service" roles and the perspectives that go with them. Not only his direct but also his vicarious experience is limited. His meager education, the relative inutility to his workaday roles of information about diverse, remote events, and the limitation of his circle of intimates, on and off the job, to people very like himself neither facilitate nor encourage vicarious encounters with other, contrasting worlds.

2. Powerlessness

More precisely, we have in mind here "powerlessness in the universalistic-achievement sector," i.e., in those interaction settings in which goods, services and status are dependent upon the assumption and performance of impersonal, functionally specific roles, insulated from claims based upon particularistic ties or membership in ascribed categories. Societies differ in the extent to which facilities and rewards are distributed in accordance with such impersonal mechanisms; our society approaches one pole. If we mean by power, in this context, the ability to manipulate such mechanisms to realize one's goals, the LL is relatively powerless. He is powerless because his bargaining power is weak: he is the most easily replaceable, the marginal utility of his contribution to the productive process is least, his skills are the least esteemed, and he has the least access to and control over strategically important information. He is powerless also because, as one moves down the status hierarchy in the work situation, the institutionalized definitions of work role progressively narrow the range of autonomous decision and of aspects of the work situation that are subject to negotiation until, at the pole approached by the LL's position, the alternatives are limited to simple compliance, withdrawal, or rebellion.

3. Deprivation

By this we mean poverty of resources relative to felt needs and levels of aspiration. It cannot, of course, be taken for granted that deprivation in this sense is more sharply felt at the lower levels of the status hierarchy. Since the upper limits of the level of aspiration are, in principle, indefinitely expansible, it is possible to feel deprived at any level. Furthermore, there operates a counter-tendency to curtail the level of aspiration in accordance with the levels of realistic expectation. However, there is evidence, both from our own study[6] and from others,[7] that the LL is chronically more deprived, in our sense, than persons on other status levels. This felt or experienced deprivation is consistent with what we might expect, especially in a society such as ours. (a) Our culture stresses, to an unusual degree, both the right and the moral obligation of members of all classes to "better themselves," and the propriety of maximizing one's "universe of comparison," that is, the range of persons with whom one might legitimately compare himself. (b) Ours is an economy that is dependent, to an exceptional degree, upon mass markets; to a corresponding degree, vast energies and resources are directed to the stimulation and elevation of levels of aspiration. (c) Not only does our culture emphasize the meritoriousness of upward mobility, we do, as a matter of fact, have a relatively high rate of upward mobility from all class levels. This means that the LL, although his actuarial probabilities of upward mobility, measured either in income or status, may be small, has some knowledge of persons *starting from the same initial level* who have "gotten ahead." The significance of this lies here: Persons who are relatively removed from our workaday world and the groups with whom we identify with will be relatively weak as reference objects. We ordinarily compare ourselves with people who we perceive to be "like ourselves." But if those whom we perceive to be like ourselves come to acquire larger shares of income, deference, and power, while we stay behind, it is difficult to preserve, without ambivalence, a stable low level of aspiration.

4. Insecurity

By this we mean the irregular and unpredictable occurrence of deprivation. (By contrast, the inmate of a correctional institution may experience deprivation without corresponding insecurity.) No society and no social level is immune to the "aleatory element"–to sickness, death, disability, injury to person or

[6] For example, more of the LL than of any other stratum answered "very much" or "somewhat" (rather than "not at all") to *all* the parts of the following question: "Do you feel that you have fallen short–or might fall short–of your hopes, dreams, and ideals in any of the following: (a) in obtaining the amount or kind of education (schooling) you desire, (b) in doing the sort of work (job) you enjoy most, (c) in living in the sort of home and neighborhood you had hoped for, (d) in enjoying as happy a marriage and home life as you had dreamed of, (e) in earning the amount of income (money) you had hoped to, (f) in saving or setting aside enough money for the future, (g) in making headway (or success) in your work (job or occupation), (h) in enjoying life as much as you had hoped you would."

[7] See Alex Inkeles, "Industrial Man: The Relation of Status to Experience, Perception, and Value," *American Journal of Sociology*, 66 (July, 1960), pp. 1-31 for a review of the relevant survey literature. For a review of studies focusing on work satisfaction, see Robert Blauner, "Work Satisfaction and Industrial Trends in Modern Society," Reprint No. 151, Institute of Industrial Relations, University of California, Berkeley, 1960, reprinted from Walter Galenson and Seymour M. Lipset (eds.), *Labor and Trade Unionism* (New York: John Wiley & Sons, 1960).

property through "acts of God," entanglements with the law and all manner of unanticipated "trouble"–all making extraordinary demands upon one's resources. But insecurity, as distinct from chronic deprivation, besets the life of the LL to a greater degree than it does the members of other strata. (a) The probability of occurrences, such as those enumerated, making extraordinary demands upon his resources is greater. (b) His resources are more meager, they are more rapidly expended to meet current needs, and hence there is less left over to deal with "emergencies." (c) His resources, such as they are, are more subject to unpredictable loss or diminution, because of the instability of his job and because of the paucity of alternative or supplementary sources of income. (d) Our society has, to be sure, established roles and structures to cope with the aleatory element: medicine, public and private charities, unemployment agencies and unemployment compensation, social work, etc. However, these services too are administered through functionally specific roles constrained by legislative and institutional requirements. Either the services must be paid for, or the availability of "free" services to which one has legitimate title depend upon his ability to move knowledgeably and skillfully through impersonal and bureaucratic channels. The LL, because of the simplification of his experience world, lacks the requisite knowledge and skills and consequently assurance and optimism, and the very instrumentalities of his society that are consciously designed to alleviate his insecurities are often awkward and cumbersome for him to manipulate.

THE LOWER-BLUE-COLLAR ADAPTATION

The task of the LL is to evolve a way of life that will reduce his insecurity and enhance his power in ways that do not depend on achievement in the universalistic sector and on command of a rich and sophisticated variety of perspectives. He can do this by forging a network of relationships, with people similarly circumstanced, that is in some ways like a mutual insurance scheme. People linked by such a network provide one another with a sense of status and worth, and also with aid and support in time of need, without regard to fluency, leverage or merit in the formally organized world of work and among the anonymous incumbents of public bureaucracies. Such a network differs from a conventional insurance scheme in that the kinds of benefits to which one is entitled are not specified in advance by any kind of contract or enumeration but consist broadly of "help in time of trouble"; it differs also in that one's contributions to the scheme are not specified with respect to kind, quantity or periodicity but consist of "doing whatever he can," whenever another is in need.[8] If one has a sufficiently extensive network of such relationships, and he has honored his

[8] See Donald E. Muir and Eugene A. Weinstein, "The Social Debt: An Investigation of Lower-Class and Middle-Class Norms of Social Obligation," *American Sociological Review*, 27 (August, 1962), p. 538.

obligations in the past, there is probably someone to whom he can turn if he should ever need help in paying for an operation, meeting burial expenses, finding a place to live, evading a process server, or putting up the children until he is "back on his feet." Title to these benefits is not tied to incumbency of specific roles, approaches through prescribed channels, or conformity to legalistic requirements. On the contrary, the relationships are valued precisely because they are not hedged about by such conditions. In sum, the distinguishing characteristics of such relationships are that they are diffuse, reciprocal, durable, and particularistic. They will define for us a "solidary" relationship.

The LL will tend to move, so far as possible, within such a world of solidary familiars. Within this world he can move with some confidence, some security, some sense of trust, and with dignity. Outside this world he feels weak, uncertain, disparaged and distrustful. The tendency to classify people as either inside or outside this network of particularistic solidarities will, therefore, have a peculiar saliency for the LL.

How do people build up such relationships? Any relationship with people similarly circumstanced can be converted into such a relationship. Kinship, neighboring and adolescent peer-group relationships lend themselves especially to such conversion[9] because they are relationships that are to some degree already insulated from the universalistic-achievement sector, they provide occasions for the exchange of goods and services, and they permit intimate, extensive, and prolonged mutual exploration and testing. Furthermore,[10] LL's are less sophisticated and less differentiated by virtue of specialized educational, occupational, and other experiences than are the members of the other social classes. Hence they have fewer desiderata that must be satisfied and those desiderata are more likely to be found among persons near at hand.

We would expect, of course, to find solidary relationships of this sort on all social levels, because on all social levels people have needs that cannot be satisfied in the universalistic-achievement sector and some that are even generated by it.[11] We may expect, however, to find two important kinds of differences between the LL and other strata.

First, we should expect to find a more nearly *exclusive* dependence, on the

[9] It is true that by cultural prescription kinship relationships are already solidary in the sense defined above. However, within the larger circle of all culturally recongized kin, and even within any given category of kin, the development of effective solidarity is never simply a matter of cultural prescription. There is always some selective strengthening of some and selective attenuation of other relationships, so that different individuals, functioning within the same cultural setting, will develop networks of kinship that differ significantly with respect to the distribution of intensity of solidarity within the network. Looking at *concrete* networks, then, rather than at cultural prescribed ideals, we can meaningful speak of the "conversion," intensification, or extinction of effective kinship solidarity.

[10] Suggested to us in conversations with Seymour M. Lipset.

[11] The theoretical argument for expecting the persistence of extended family ties in the middle class is most forcefully stated by Eugene Litwak, "The Use of Extended Family Groups in the Achievement of Social Goals: Some Policy Implication," *Social Problems*, 7 (Winter, 1959), pp. 177-187.

part of the LL, on such solidary relationships; that is to say, interaction and exchange within such networks should constitute larger fractions of the total interactional and exchange systems of the LL than of the corresponding systems of other strata.

A second difference has to do with the nature of the *units* of such networks. The units can be individuals or they can be collectivities. In the latter case, individuals act not in their own behalf but as agents and representatives of these collectivities. For example, in the middle class newly married persons tend to reinterpret and reorganize their kinship ties in such a way that husband's and wife's *effective* networks–i.e., those kin with whom they sustain active relationships of visiting and exchange–are identical. Those relatives of one spouse with whom the other spouse is uncomfortable or cannot get along tend to drop out of the network of active involvement of *both* spouses. Both spouses gain kin, but there is also a pruning away of kinship solidarities that both spouses cannot sustain as a unit. In the LL stratum, by contrast, each spouse tends to cling to kinship solidarities once formed. Having build up a set of more or less binding relationships, the lower-class person is less prone to suffer their attenuation for the sake of the solidarity of the conjugal tie. For men, prospects in the world of work are not sufficiently optimistic to permit turning one's back on any relationships that might provide some cushion against insecurity. For women, there is not the same assurance as in the middle class, derived from marriage to a stably employed male, of an economically stable future, and they are reluctant to weaken their ties to any trusted and dependable kinsmen. In short, the essential contrast is perhaps not so much one of a lower class extended kinship system *versus* a middle class structurally isolated nuclear family, as it is one of tenacity, in the lower class, of *individual* kinship networks, overlapping but not identical, and relatively resistant to change *versus*, in the middle class, reorganization of the networks of both spouses in the interest of the solidarity and primacy of the conjugal unit. If the reasoning behind this expectation is sound, we should expect to find the same contrast in relationships to neighbors and non-kin peers. We should expect also to find more conflict and instability in the LL family than in the others. On the LL level, parents, grandparents, siblings, other assorted relatives and "friends" are more likely to press their claims, even after marriage, than in the other strata; time and money are more likely to be invested in honoring such claims and in maintaining in good repair the wider network of solidary relationships. Furthermore, the involvement of husband and wife in overlapping but different networks greatly increases the probability of conflict between the demands of their respective networks, of strain and acrimony in the husband-wife relationship, and of the instability of the husband-wife bond. . . .

FINDINGS AND INTERPRETATIONS

Family and Kinship

We shall present our data on family visiting in tabular form, rather than merely summarizing them in the text as will be our practice elsewhere in this paper, for reasons that will be apparent when we turn to the result of other studies.

As can be seen from Tables 1, 2, and 3, our LL subjects say they interact more with relatives both absolutely and also relative to their interaction with other categories. Furthermore, we found that our LL's relatives typically live nearby; almost one-half–in comparison to one-in-ten middle class subjects–claim close relatives living within a four-block radius of their own dwellings. This propinquity of kin obtains whether the LL is a long-time resident of his neighborhood or a recent migrant. At the same time, our data suggest that family life is more unstable and strife-ridden. The LL's are more likely to circle "2" or more in answer to our question: "Of your five closest friends, how many have had one or more marriages broken (by divorce, annulment, separation, or desertion)?" To the question, "What is (or was) the usual relationship between *wife* and mother-in-law?", the LL's more often choose one of the two responses (out of five) at the "negative" pole, i.e., "extreme disharmony and friction" or "so much disharmony they don't even speak."

These data, so far as they go, are consistent with what we would expect in the light of the reasoning in the preceding section, although this reasoning would not require that the LL's have an *absolutely* higher rate of interaction with kin than the other strata. However, the implications of the findings of other studies are not so clean-cut.

There is a considerable literature[12] attesting the frequency, in the lower class,[13] of what has been called the "female-based household" or the "matricentric family." In brief, this is an enduring and highly solidary group of related women who lean very heavily upon one another for aid, comfort and support. In this literature, the kinship involvements of men are not so clearly portrayed, but it is clear that husbands and wives tend to be responsive to quite different networks of solidarity,[14] and that conjugal unions are, and are perceived to be

[12] See, for example, Walter B. Miller, "Lower Class Culture as a Generating Milieu of Gang Delinquency," *The Journal of Social Issues,* 14:3 (1958) pp; 5-19; Walter B. Miller, "Implications of Lower-Class Culture for Social Work," *The Social Service Review*, 33 (September, 1959), pp. 219-236; E. Franklin Frazier, *The Negro Family in the United States*, rev. ed. (New York: Dryden, 1948); Michael Young and Peter Willmott, *Family and Kinship in East London*, (New York: The Free Press, 1957); John Barron Mays, *On the Threshold of Delinquency* (Liverpool: Liverpool University Press, 1959), pp. 165-166; Elizabeth Bott, *Family and Social Network* (London: Tavistock Publications, 1957); John H. Rohrer and Munro S. Edmonston (eds.), *The Eight Generation: Culture and Personalities of New Orleans Negroes* (New York: Harper & Row, 1960).

[13] When we use the expression "lower class" in our references to the literature, it usually refers to the lowest stratum distinguished in the study. However, the studies do not always explicitly distinguish strata within a broader "lower" or "working" class, and the criteria of class vary from one study to another.

[14] The properties of these networks and the different ways husband's and wife's networks may be related have been most intensively analyzed by Elizabeth Bott, *Family and Social Network.*

Table 1

Item: "Roughly how many times *a month* do you (husband and wife) visit: neighbors _______; relatives _______; other friends _______?"

Stratum	N	Mean Visits (Relatives) Per Month
Upper Middle	100	2.07
Lower Middle	223	3.36
Upper Lower	231	3.30
Lower Lower	97	4.06

P: LL *vs.* UL ⩽ .001; LL *vs.* all ⩽ .001

Table 2

Item: "Who are the people you have over to your home (for parties or nighttime visits) *most* frequently or often (check one): (a) neighbors; (b) relatives; (c) friends from work; (d) friends you've met elsewhere?"

N's responding:

Stratum	(a) "Neighbors"	(b) "Relatives"	(c) "Friends (work)"	(d) "Friends (Elsewhere)"	Totals	Percent (b)
UM	12	18	24	59	113	16
LM	5	15	21	31	72	21
UL	16	49	12	42	119	41
LL	6	24	2	9	41	59

P for Response "b" (Relatives) only: LL *vs.* UL ⩽ .01; LL *vs.* all ⩽ .001

Table 3

Item: "Of your *four* closest friends who live in this area–those you most often have over to your home or whom you visit–how many are *relatives* (of either husband or wife): none _______; one _______; two _______; three _______; all four _______?"

Stratum	N	Mean	Percent Answering "3" or "all"
Upper Middle	144	0.65	22
Lower Middle	285	0.81	28
Upper Lower	135	1.28	42
Lower Lower	101	1.70	56

P: LL *vs.* UL = .05; LL *vs.* all = .001

fragile and unstable.[15] The literature also documents the importance in the lower class and especially among males, of relatively enduring and highly solidary cliques of peers.[16] Finally, much of this literature emphasizes the way such networks of particularistic ties among kin and peers provide both routine services and help in crises that are not so readily available to people in this class from the formally organized and more impersonal institutions of society. . . .[17]

Neighboring

Our expectation is that neighbors, like kin, will figure more importantly in the total relationship systems of lower class people, and especially of LL's, than of the other classes.[18] The interpretation of our data is complicated by the fact that neighborhood, kinship and solidary peer-group relationships may become so intertwined that it is difficult to distinguish meaningfully between them. Perhaps, as a matter of fact, it is precisely one of the important implications of our general position that it should be more difficult to make such distinctions in the case of the lower than in that of the higher classes. We assume that the higher classes, because of their wider range of social movement and their more diversified participation and stakes in the larger social system, are more likely to construct relationships that can be differentiated according to the bases on which they rest and the functions which they perform in their total relational

[15] August B. Hollingshead, "Class Differences in Family Stability," in Reinhard Bendix and Seymour M. Lipset (eds.), *Class Status and Power* (New York: The Free Press, 1953), pp. 284-292, reprinted from *The American Sociological Review* (February, 1946), pp. 31-41.

[16] William F. Whyte, *Street Corner Society* (Chicago: University of Chicago Press, 1937); Walter B. Miller, "Lower Class Culture." Herbert J. Gans, "The Peer Group Society," hectographed, prepared for a staff seminar of the Center for Community Studies, Harvard Medical School and Massachusetts General Hospital; John H. Rohrer and Munro S. Edmondson, *The Eighth Generation.*

[17] The most vivid and forceful portrayal of the security functions of networks of reciprocity among both extended kin *and* peers is Allison Davis, "The Motivation of the Underprivileged Worker," in William F. Whyte (ed.), *Industry and Society (New York: McGraw-*Hill Book Company, 1946), ch. 5.

[18] "Intensity of social interaction between neighbors tends to decrease as one moves from working class areas to upper income bracket residential suburbs. In the tenements of working-class people borrowing, exchange of services, and assistance in sickness are a necessity, and gossiping and visiting, at least among housewives, are typically frequent." Rudolf Heberle, "The Normative Element in Neighborhood Relations," *Pacific Sociological Review*, 3 (Spring, 1960), p. 7 and passim. It is taken for granted, of course, that women and small children are far more heavily implicated in neighboring relationships than men. It would be interesting, however, to investigate whether there are class differences in the extent to which neighbors tend to be integrated *as individuals* into the network of *one* spouse, or as *household collectivities* into the network of the *conjugal family* analogously to the models suggested here for kin and peer networks. In other words, do the attitudes described in the following report of a group discussion with London working-class families vary with social class? "Both Mr. and Mrs. Newbolt used the term 'friend' as if it applied only to men. The term 'neighbour', on the other hand, seemed to refer only to women. Mr. Newbolt looked rather shocked when I asked him if he saw much of the neighbours." Elizabeth Bott, *Family and Social Network*, pp. 68-69.

systems; and that the lower classes, by contrast, tend more toward a fusion or "de-differentiation" of solidary kin, close neighboring relationships, and old friends. We have seen some indication in the preceding section of the tendency of LL kin to seek propinquity and it is a reasonable surmise, based on impressions from the literature although not a firmly established finding, that lower-class peer-groups are more likely to contain kin-related persons and to be based on and oriented to the neighborhood or local community.

We have seen (Table 2) that LL's have *relatives* over to their homes more often, as compared to neighbors, friends from work, or friends they have met elsewhere, than do any of the other strata. LL's and UL's also respond more often with "neighbors" to this question than do the other strata, although the two lower strata do not differ from one another in this respect. If we combine the numbers responding either "relatives" or "neighbors," in contrast to either "friends (work)" or "friends (elsewhere)," the differences between the two lower classes and the two upper classes are striking, and the difference between the LL and the UL class, although not so great, is also significant. Equally striking, and of profound relevance to our picture of the relationship of the lower classes, and especially the LL's to the sphere of work is the column representing numbers answering "friends from work." Only two out of 41 LL's give this response, suggesting the degree to which the LL's "private" or "social" life is divorced from his work and the extent of his dependency upon relationships independent of what we have referred to as the "universalistic-achievement" sector.

We find also that on the item referred to in Table 1 . . . , LL's pay significantly more visits per month to neighbors than any of the other strata. On the question, "Of family's (husband and wife's) *four* closest friends, how many live within three or four blocks from your home? 0, 1, 2, 3, 4," the LL's mean and the percentage of LL's answering "1" or more are larger than those of any other stratum. To a question asking how many hours the wife, if she doesn't work outside the home, spends visiting neighbors on an average weekday, LL's encircled a larger figure than any other stratum. One two-part question asks: "Do you and any of your neighbors (a) go to movies, sports events, picnics and things like that together . . . (b) exchange or borrow from one another such things as books, dishes, food, tools, recipes, preserves, etc . . . ?", with provision for the responses "Often," "Sometimes," "Rarely," "Never." LL's do not differ significantly from any of the other levels on part (a), but they differ from all the others on part (b).

On the other hand, on the question, "Do you and your neighbors entertain (or visit in the evenings): often–occassionally–rarely–never–?", the LL's neighbored *least*. They also neighbor least as measured by the item, "How many of your nieghbors' homes have you ever been in?", with provision for responses ranging from "six or more" to "none." These items may be construed as contradictory to our theoretical expectations, and we so interpreted them at first. Indeed, they may be construed as contradicting the results of other questionnaire items, such as, "Roughly how many times *a month* do you (husband and wife) visit . . . neighbors?" On second consideration, however, the contradictions are not so clear. The *emphasis* in the first question is on a specific type of interaction, "entertaining," with parenthetical reference to "visit" and "evenings." The responses to this question, taken in conjunction with the responses to the other questions discussed in this section and that on kinship, suggest a class of people who engage relatively little in the "purely social" kind of activity connoted by "entertaining," but who, insofar as they do engage in such activity, do so primarily with relatives and neighbors. The responses to the second question, taken in conjunction with the responses to the others, suggest a class of people who, even with neighbors, are slow to establish even superficial relationships, as measured by getting through their doors, but who, insofar as they sustain a social life with anybody other than kin, are heavily dependent upon neighbors. In sum, the data strongly suggest people whose level of "social" activity is in general low and whose relational networks are shrunken, relative to the other strata, but who build such relationships as they do sustain mostly out of the materials of kinship and propinquity.

Participation in voluntary associations

Consistent with the findings of other studies,[19] the LL participated least in voluntary associations. He *belonged* to fewer organizations including the fraternal, church-related and trade-union associations in which his UL counterpart participated relatively heavily, and he was the most likely to *attend* no organization meetings at all. (In general, differences in participation between LL and UL were greater than those between UL and LM.)

We may suppose that people invest their energies in such participation for two sorts of reasons: first, because they feel that they have a stake in the goals of the organization and that their own participation is instrumental to the attainment of those goals and, second, because they derive satisfaction from the social relationships that they enjoy by virtue of participation. On both these counts, the LL's motivation to participate should be expected to be low.

Voluntary organizations characteristically, although in varying degrees, are concerned with the affairs of a larger community. To be able to appreciate these concerns assumes an ability to envisage events relatively remote from the immediate concrete situation and a relationship between such events and one's own destiny. The severe limitation of the experience world makes it difficult for the LL to think in these terms. In comparison to other strata, his image of the world outside his immediate concrete situation is fragmentary, uncertain, and obscure. Except in the case of organizations like labor unions, where the payoffs are relatively immediate, direct and tangible, it is difficult for him to visualize

[19] The literature is reviewed in Charles R. Wright and Herbert Hyman, "Voluntary Association Memberships of American Adults: Evidence from National Sample Surveys," *American Sociological Review*, 23 (June, 1958), pp. 284-294.

the relationship between the goal-directed activities of the organization and his own interests. And finally, . . . even though he values the goals of the organization and believes in giving it generalized "support," he does not feel that his influence within the organization is great enough that his active participation would make any important difference in how things turn out.

The satisfactions that derive from participation itself consist largely of respect and deference, which in turn are linked to the exercise of power, the occupation of honorific positions, and the quality of performance of one's organizational roles. These latter, in turn, rest upon the possession of relevant skills and personal qualities: knowledge about the goals of the organization and the aspects of the larger social scene that are relevant to attainment of those goals; fluency in discussion and argumentation; special combinations of discipline, restraint, initiative and sensitivity that are necessary to perform successfully in committee operations; certain technical skills: parliamentary, clerical, bookkeeping, fiscal. These are the same kinds of skills and personal qualities that the LL, in comparison to other strata, has the least opportunity to acquire, cultivate and practice in the world of work and the universalistic-achievement sector. . . .

Preference for the familiar

One of the clearest outcomes of this study is an image of the LL as one who is reluctant to meet new people and new situations, to form new social relationships, and above all to initiate interaction with strangers. On the contrary, he values and seeks out, more than anybody else, the routine, the familiar, the predictable. Our findings on this matter are worth reporting rather fully because of the light they add to current controversy about the meaning of "other-directedness" about where, if anywhere, among the various social strata this property principally resides.

> LL's more often agreed with the following statements: "I am not the sort of person who enjoys starting a conversation with strangers on a bus or train"; "It is easiest not to speak to strangers until they speak to you"; "I don't enjoy going to large parties where there are many people I don't know"; "[I much prefer] sticking with my old friends" [to making new friends]; [main reason doesn't want to change job:] "having to get acquainted with new people;" "I find it hard to 'warm up' to most of the people I meet—to feel close to them and enjoy their company." Our instruments also include Rorschach items and some open-ended questions. Unfortunately, the Ns on these instruments were too small to permit separate analysis of the LL and UL responses. These were, accordingly, combined, but some of the results do seem pertinent and worth reporting. Rorschach responses of combined-lower-class subjects were most often interpreted, on blind reading: "finds it especially trying to adjust to new people and new situations." To the open-ended question, "What things bother you most in everyday life?", these subjects most often answered to the effect that things and people are too

unpredictable, they prefer the routinized and familiar. To the question: "who do you prefer as friends," they most often answered "relatives" and "neighbors."

It seems clear that this neophobia does not express an *indifference* to "popularity" and "acceptance." In this respect, the LL is at least as "other-directed" as any of the other strata:

> LL's most strongly agreed with the statements: "One of the most important things that can be taught a child is how to get along with others–how to mix well, make friends easily, and be popular"; "It is more worthwhile to be popular, well-liked, and friendly than it is to get ahead in the world at the risk of making enemies and being disliked"; "It is difficult, when in a crowd of strangers, not to be concerned about how I look to them–about the sort of impression I am making." When asked to note the "things in life which worry you most," LL's and UL's combined most often mentioned things akin to "being well-liked by fellows at work," or "by others."

The LL is not the citadel of old-fashioned "inner-directedness":

> LL's agree most often: "If a person has strong but unpopular likes or dislikes, he should keep them to himself instead of letting others know how he feels"; "It is hard for me to speak out and say what I think if I have to run the risk of being taken for an 'oddball' or character."

The hypotheses most consistent with *all* of the foregoing findings are these: the LL cares greatly what others think of him; he lacks confidence in his ability to say and do "the right things" in encounters with strangers, he is therefore anxious and uncomfortable in such encounters; and he seeks comfort and security in a circle of "old-shoe" relationships. His description of the qualities he values in friends *and in himself* is consistent with the foregoing.

> He agrees most often that "the personality he admires most in others is 'strong, quiet, calm.' " (More often than members of any other stratum, he tells us that the movie actor he most admires is John Wayne.) To open-ended questions, LL's and UL's combined most often list as qualities they would most like to have in their closest friends: "quiet," "calm," "easy-going," "not loud"; and as qualities they would most like to have in themselves: "quiet," "calm," "steady," "reliable."

In short, the LL likes people (and presumably his friends like people) who don't "rock the boat," who don't make excessive demands upon a limited capacity to shift perspectives and adopt new roles.

This relative inflexibility of role-taking, which is implied in the simplification of the LL's experience world, would seem to be central to the entire pattern of response. Indeed, the LL agrees most often with the statement: "I find it difficult to 'change my personality' easily when talking with various sorts of people." This discussion is, in a way, an extension and documentation of the theme of the preceding sections, the dependence of the LL upon kin and old friends. . . .

Anti-intellectuality

The LL expressed least admiration of intellectuals, professors, writers and artists. Typically, indeed, he treated them with disdain or suspicion. From lists of occupations he was least likely to choose occupations in these categories as representing what he would want to be if he had to start life over again, or to list them among the four occupations he would rate highest in prestige. Those who expressed a hope that their sons or daughters might go to college were more interested than were the other levels in the practical, financially remunerative aspects of education as compared to its esthetic or intellectual aspects. LL's most disliked symphonic, ballet and operatic music. They most strongly agreed that the country would be better off if people tried to "be more 'down to earth' and less intellectual and 'high-brow.' " They were most likely to indicate that they "would probably be deeply hurt" if they "were to learn that friends or acquaintances secretly thought they were 'too intellectual' (high-brow or 'egg-head')." They most strongly agreed that "Our government would be sounder and better run if there were fewer intellectuals involved in it and more hard-headed, down-to-earth businessmen." They reacted most negatively to what, from their standpoint, are "high-brow" television programs (quiz shows, plays, panels).

It would seem natural that people should be distrustful of what they do not understand, disdainful of skills they do not possess, and threatened by modes of reasoning and interaction in which they cannot participate creditably. The more general formulation that underlies these assumptions is that people tend to disvalue standards of evaulation whose application would result in the disparagement of the self. This interpretation of the LL's anti-intellectuality would seem to fit well with the general argument of this paper. It is also likely that art and intellectuality are most disdained in the lower classes because these classes are most preoccupied with masculinity–indeed, according to Walter Miller "masculinity" is one of the "focal concerns" of "lower-class culture"–and art and intellectuality are tainted with connotations of femininity. . . .

Authoritarianism

Our LL subjects agreed most strongly with Adorno F-Scale items. This scale is often interpreted as a scale of authoritarianism. Needless to say, this interpretation is open to some question. However, Christie, in his critical re-examination of the literature bearing on the behavioral correlates of F-Scale scores, concludes that "the reports available on social behavior of individuals accepting these items indicates that they behave in a manner which is characteristically authoritarian." He also concludes that "the relevant research indicates a sizeable negative correlation between scores on the F-Scale and various measures related to socio-economic status."[20] In any case, we wish to emphasize that the face implications of the F-Scale for authoritarianism are less ambiguous for some items than

[20] Richard Christie and Marie Jahoda (eds.), *Studies in the Scope and Method of "The Authoritarian Personality"* (New York: The Free Press, 1954), pp. 149-194.

for others, and that our imputation of authoritarian trends is based primarily upon items that emphasize rather explicitly the necessity for leaders to be strict, the division of people into two classes: the weak and the strong, the importance of obedience and respect for authority in children, and a belief in harsh and punitive repression of deviants. The last point is additionally supported by several other items in our questionnaire not derived from the F-Scale. Finally, mention should be made of Lipset's comprehensive review of the evidence, from a variety of sources, of "working-class authoritarianism."[21]

We offer three distinct, but complementary, kinds of interpretations.

1. The first is essentially that offered by Lipset,[22] who argues, in effect, that "working-class authoritarianism" is not so much a primary commitment to authoritarianism per se, as it is a special manifestation of a more general characteristic. To wit, "other things being equal, [the working class] will prefer the least complex alternative." This preference would seem to follow from the simplification of the experience world. People who, by comparison with members of other social levels, have had little occasion and less necessity to assume, on any given issue, a variety of perspectives, to envisage a variety of possibilities, to take into account and attempt to balance a variety of interests might be expected to develop a characteristic style of decision-making–namely, to proceed directly to simple, unqualified, easily comprehended solutions. And the least complex alternative is usually the authoritarian one. It means you have to answer only one question: Whose word goes? There is no simpler way of resolving an issue.

2. However, the experience world of the LL is not only simpler than that of the other strata; it is also qualitatively different in respects that, it seems to us, must make a difference in the ways power and authority are perceived and evaluated. In the world of work above all, but not only there, the LL is most likely to confront others in the role of a subordinate subject to express demands. These demands are likely to have the following characteristics. (a) They are formulated in relatively concrete terms: *"Do this"*–rather than in terms of broad goals, to be implemented in ways that commend themselves to his discretion. He is not expected, to the same degree as members of other strata, to "exercise judgment," which means to weigh and balance alternatives, consider the circumstances, and reconcile conflicting principles. (b) The demands are less likely to be justified or rationalized to him in terms of more ultimate goals or principles. The authority of those who issue the demands is supposed to be enough to legitimize them. (c) The alternatives, when confronted with these demands, are few: compliance or defiance or, in some cases, withdrawal.[23]

[21] Seymour M. Lipset, *Political Man* (Garden City: Doubleday and Company, 1960), pp. 97-130.

[22] Ibid.

[23] See the excellent review by Blauner, "Work Satisfaction," pp. 342-349, of the literature on the patterning of control, responsibility, autonomy, etc., in working-class occupations. See also Katherine Archibald, "Status Orientations among Shipyard Workers," in Bendix and Lipset, *Class, Status and Power* pp. 395-403, for a vivid description of attitudes toward authority among shipyard workers.

> A job inevitably involved a hierarchy of authority. There was always a boss, and it was accepted shipyard dogma that it was the worker's place to do what the boss commanded and to do it without hesitation or question. "What a fellow learns on his first job, if he learns nothing else," I was told by an old-timer "is to take the boss's orders and to keep his own mouth shut. I used to try and tell a boss if I knew he was wrong about a job, but after being tossed out on my ear a time or two, I soon learned better. Now I do the thing just like the foreman tells me to, even if I'm sure it will get torn down and have to be put in different when the real big shots come snooping around. The way I figure it, that's the boss's worry and none of mine."[23a]
>
> . . . although servility toward the boss was accompanied by much antagonism and criticism, nobody ever questioned the legitimacy or inevitability of the *system*, of the idea of an hierarchical structure of power and privilege.[23b]

In short, role relationships are more likely for the LL to be defined in terms of somebody responsible for making decisions and giving orders, and somebody responsible for carrying them out. Putting it more bluntly still, the decisive question in "real life" situations is, for the LL, more than for anybody else, "Who's boss?" We are assuming that the pervasiveness of this kind of experience in the social world of the LL produces a generalized set or disposition to conceptualize issues and to resolve them in terms of power and authority.

3. One other consideration seems to us relevant: the degree of symbolic fusion of *status* and *authority*. By "status" we understand here the show of respect by one party to another. People who exercise authority or power over others are likely to command respect from the others as well, but the extent to which these are correlated as incidents of the same role relationships can vary considerably. The ability psychologically to differentiate between status and authority or power should vary, presumably, with the extent to which they are, in one's experience, de facto fused or differentiated.

In comparison to the world of the blue-collar class, and especially the lower-blue-collar class, the world of the middle-class person is more likely to be one in which differentials of status are not associated with corresponding differences in authority. The whole sphere of the learned professions, for example, and the sphere of "technical staff" in industry, government and commerce is a sphere of relatively high status accorded to people with prized abilities or people who occupy valued roles, but who do not necessarily exercise conspicuous authority over others. To put it differently, their ability to command respect does not depend upon or correlate strongly with their ability to issue commands, to inflict sanctions or grant indulgences. This dissociation in actual experience facilitates the conceptual distinguishing between authority and status.

23a Archibald, "Status Orientations," p. 397.

23b Ibid., 401-402.

This is less true in the lower-class world—or the same world from the perspective of the lower-class person. The status-graded relationships most familiar to the LL—e.g., relationships with employers, landlords, work supervisors, law enforcement officials—are more likely to be correlated with gradations of power. Although the powerful are not always respected, they can usually exact at least the outward show of respect; and the respected are usually powerful. Under these conditions we should expect a less complete differentiation of power and status, on a symbolic or perceptual level, than in the middle class. This means that status without power will be felt as dubious and uncertain status. To deny the right of a person to exercise power will be felt as a denial of status. Contrariwise, the effective exercise of power, the show of compliance by others, will be the most effective validation of status.

If this is so, we should expect that the LL, to a greater extent than other classes, will tend to measure status by power, and to validate his own claim to status, where he feels entitled to it, by asserting a claim to power. An illustration will be provided in our discussion in the section on "patriarchy."

Insofar as this mechanism operates, it should produce "authoritarianism" in the specific sense of *a tendency to take a person's power as a measure of his status;* and, as a psychological corollary of this, a tendency to claim power in proportion to one's claim to status.

Intolerance

Although the study's LM stratum proved least forgiving of violations of what we may call "conventional morality"—*i.e.*, hetero-sexual misconduct, drunkenness and swearing—the LL was most harsh in condemnation of other sorts of deviants: the atheist, the homosexual, the "un-American," the radical, the artist-intellectual. But it was above all toward the ethnic minority group that he directed his animosity. Whether assessed in terms of a modified Bogardus ethnic distance, the Adorno "E-Scale," or standardized measures of ethnic and racial intolerance, this lower-blue-collar antipathy was consistently apparent. We suggest two mechanisms to link this with the life conditions of the LL stratum.

1. The LL's tendency, of which we have already spoken, to the simplification of alternatives would include, with reference to the world of social objects, simplified categorization in terms of in-group and out-group, "we" and "they," such that people fall unambiguously in the one or the other. In addition to a general tendency to categorize dichotomously and unequivocally, a further implication of the preference for the simple is a reduction of incongruity, in the sense of the assignment of people to a "favorable" category on one modality and to an "unfavorable" category on another. Such assignment implies seeing the same people from different perspectives, which, we have argued, does not come so easily to the LL as to middle-class persons.

2. In our remarks on "anti-intellectuality" we offered the proposition that "people tend to disvalue standards of evaluation whose application would result in the disparagement of the self." Therefore, where a culture provides a set of

possible criteria for evaluating persons, sub-groups will tend to develop subcultural emphases on those criteria on which they fare relatively well and to de-emphasize those criteria on which they do poorly. They will grasp, so to speak, at status straws, and make much of them. We have also said that the LL's claim to status on the basis of universalistic, achievement-related criteria are weak, relative to the claims of the other strata. It follows that the LL will tend to de-emphasize these criteria and to place relatively more emphasis on the "ascriptive" components of social identity, like race, nationality, and ethnicity. If this line of reasoning is correct, the "prejudice" of the LL is not *in spite* of the "American creed" but partly *in consequence* of it. The "American creed" implies one kind of criterion for measuring the worth of a person. The more consistently it is applied, the worse does the LL fare, and the greater his tendency to seek *other* bases for differential evaluation in our cultural tradition, bases that will yield different results and go part way toward redressing the balance. This would then be a special case of a component of a cultural value system generating behavior and attitudes incongruent with those same values.

Pessimism-Insecurity

"A body just can't take nothing for granted; you just have to live from day to day and hope the sun will shine tomorrow." No theme more consistently runs through the pattern of the LL's responses and distinguishes him from the others. In his view, nothing is certain; in all probability, however, things will turn out badly as they generally have in the past. The theme stands out most clearly in his agreement with Srole "Anomie" items–e.g., "Nowadays a person has to live pretty much for today and let tomorrow take care of itself"; "In spite of what some people say, the lot of the average man is getting worse, not better"; "It's hardly fair to bring children into the world with the way things look for the future"; and so on.[24]

From one point of view, there is nothing less problematical than this pattern of response. After all, we have described the LL as powerless, deprived, and insecure. Are not these responses of his simply a realistic recognition of his life situations and his life chances?

However, one could also argue as follows: The LL's world view is disproportionately black. After all, lots of LL's can and do, by steady work habits, self-discipline and frugality, achieve a higher and more dependable income, reduce their vulnerability to the aleatory element, move into the upper-blue-collar class, and, in general, render their own lives and prospects less bleak. The actual situation of the LL is, to be sure, an unhappy one, but this is determined only in part by his objective insecurity and powerlessness; it is also determined by his *adaptation to* that insecurity and powerlessness, by a style of life marked by improvidence, unsteady work habits, and other characteristics calculated to

[24] For comparative data see Inkeles, "Industrial Man," pp. 18-31.

insure his continued occupancy of what Knupfer calls his "underdog" status. In short, his world view is not a realistic perception. It is, rather, a rationalization of failure and frustration that are attributable as much to his personal limitations as to his objective circumstances; it is also a self-fulfilling prophecy, for the belief motivates a style of life that insures the experience of failure and frustration.

It would be hard to prove that either the "pessimistic" or "optimistic" view of things is more realistic. It is true that some LL's do "make it," and often as a result of rational, disciplined effort. The LL has seen others "of his own kind" achieve what, from his perspective, is a tolerable situation of security and comfort. So there is an objective basis for "optimism." On the other hand, we have already remarked that the actuarial probability for any given LL to "better himself" is probably small; at any rate the probability that the pay-off will be commensurate with the effort and discipline is problematic. There is, then, an objective basis for "pessimism" as well.[25] Furthermore, if a LL makes the more optimistic assumption and the corresponding commitments of his slender resources to "bettering himself," and is *then* thwarted, the sense of disappointment, frustration, and pessimism can be even more poignant. It could be argued, then, that the "pessimistic" world view is also *adaptive* for most LL's, in that it tends to inhibit the development of levels of expectation that are likely to be disappointed, and therefore to protect them against the consequent frustration.

The LL's world view is also a defense against moral criticism. The assumption that it is possible to "better oneself" and that one's misfortune is self-inflicted and a sign of one's lack of moral fibre runs deep in the American cultural tradition. From the standpoint of many of his fellow citizens, including many of his "respectable" upper blue-collar neighbors, the LL is a failure; his failure creates the presumption that he is morally inadequate; and his style of life provides his critics with "objective evidence" of his moral inadequacy. A view of the world in which the role of chance is selectively noted and exaggerated both justifies his style of life and explains the distribution of the world's goods in ways that do not reflect on his moral adequacy.

If we are correct, then, we have all the essential terms of a vicious circle: (1) A set of life conditions characterized by powerlessness, deprivation and insecurity. (2) The adoption of a view of the world as bleak and uncertain, partly a matter of realistic perception and partly an adaptive protection against disappointment. (3) On the basis of this world-view, the adoption of a style of life characterized by "improvidence," etc. (4) In consequence of the style of life, the more certain recurrence of the experience of powerlessness, deprivation and insecurity. (5) A further intensification of the pessimistic world view, partly on the basis of the fact that things *did* turn out badly after all, and partly to protect the self against the criticism of having brought about one's plight through one's own moral defect.

[25] S. M. Lipset and R. Bendix, *Social Mobility in Industrial Society* (Berkeley: University of California Press, 1962), chs. 6 and 7.

Misanthropy

LL's, more than the members of any other stratum, are cynical and distrustful. For example, disproportionate numbers of LL's "strongly agreed" with these Rosenberg Misanthropy items (which we cite, not because they come from a scale labeled "Misanthropy" but because of their prima facie connotations): "many people are out to cheat or outwit others, and if you don't watch yourself, people are liable to take advantage of you"; "nine people out of ten are basically selfish and more inclined to look out for themselves than they are to help others"; "you have to be careful with strangers; very few can be trusted and many are inclined to take advantage of your weakness and generosity." This "people are no good" theme was substantiated by responses to several other items. Economic and occupational success, they most often agreed, is accomplished by "friends or connections," "luck or chance," "pull or manipulating," or "cheating or underhanded dealing" (in contrast to "daring and taking risks," "education" or "hard, day-by-day work"); they most often agree that television repairmen, politicians, doctors, auto mechanics, butchers, union officials and businessmen are not trustworthy. The LL's image of the world resembles a jungle. We suggest two sources of this image.

1. The more obvious of these sources is simply realistic perception of the fact that he *is* an object of exploitation. The LL is, by virtue of his relative powerlessness, the least able of all our subjects to protect himself against exploitation. Among persons, each of whom has something valuable to withhold from the other, or is in a position to inflict some damage upon the other, or is in a position to invoke the agencies of the law for the protection of his rights and the redress of grievances, a certain mutual consideration tends to prevail and the more obvious types of fraud and coercion to be tempered. In brief, when the powerful deal with the powerful, it pays, within limits, to observe the rules of the game to which they claim to subscribe, and the assumption that people can be trusted and that they mean what they say is a more realistic assumption than when the powerful deal with the weak. Furthermore among those who are least powerful—whose own resources are least and who enjoy only fitful and imperfect protection under the ragged edges of the umbrella of justice—the vulnerability to force, fraud and exploitation of all kinds from members of their own stratum is great. [Black] neighborhoods in American communities in which people are left to settle their own disputes, as long as they do not infringe upon the interests of white people, provide a particularly clear-cut example. Although the LL's image of the world no doubt often exaggerates the component of malice and treachery, his cynicism and distrust cannot be dismissed as "projective," in contrast to a more "realistic" view of people as good and benevolent.

2. The foregoing interpretation is couched in the crudest terms of power and the presence or absence of countervailing power. We suggest also that this "misanthropy" reflects a certain moral attitude toward the world. . . .

What we are suggesting is that "misanthropy" is not merely a picture, in the mind of the LL, of the universe as a kind of amoral, Hobbesian jungle, but a way of classifying people that is implied in a particularistic morality. For the LL, a decisive feature of his world is that it consists of friends and strangers. Your friends will stand by you, as you are obligated to stand by them. Strangers are not to be trusted (although it is assumed that they too are bound by obligations to *their* friends), nor do you expect them to trust you. But most people are strangers. In sum, we are suggesting that what our research instruments may have tapped is not a unitary, pervasive, characterologically rooted distrust of all humanity, but *one* facet of the LL's particularistic morality.

It is interesting that, notwithstanding his misanthropy, however we choose to interpret that expression, the LL is also *credulous* in the sense that he most readily accepts the written or printed word at its face value. Of all our subjects he least often indicates that he finds it hard "to believe in the truth of most television commercials I see" or the truth of magazine or newspaper advertisements or television commercials stating that "most doctors agree that Brand X is best." It is one thing to feel a generalized distrust in human beings, their motives and their claims; it is another to form an attitude on a specific claim or message where one has few independent criteria for evaluating the content of the message, little awareness of specific alternatives, and little disposition to weigh evidence. It is one of the best established findings of social psychology that "suggestibility" and "gullibility" are maximized when the cognitive field is "unstructured," *i.e.*, when the actor has no independent frame of reference for forming a judgment. Needless to say, the availability of such independent frames of reference depends heavily on the richness of one's direct and vicarious experience.

Extrapunitiveness

This caption suggests another perspective from which to view the findings we have discussed under "pessimism" and "misanthropy." In the psychological literature, the term suggests a fund of aggression that accumulates in response to frustration, and which has to "go somewhere," either inward or outward. People "high on extrapunitiveness" characteristically "handle their aggression" by "directing it outwards"; intropunitive people direct it inwards. We make no assumption here about the psychohydraulics of aggression. We are concerned, however, with the visible datum that, when things go wrong, some people more characteristically "pin responsibility" on themselves, others on circumstances outside themselves. This becomes fairly explicit in the disproportionately frequent agreement of LL subjects with the statement: "When things go wrong at home or work I find it easy to blame others instead of myself." We have few items that go to the issue as straightforwardly as this, but certainly our data as a whole strongly suggest that LL's find it easier to impute the fault for faulty outcomes to something outside the self.

We have already referred to the function that such a view of things may perform by helping to protect the self against criticism. However, it is important to point out that this "extrapunitiveness" of the LL may also "reflect social reality" in a fairly direct way–the social reality in this case being the actual distribution of authority and responsibility when people come together in inter-class relationships.

We take our lead from Henry and Short, *Suicide and Homicide*. Where blame will be perceived to lie, they suggest, depends on the objects to which it may legitimately be imputed. This, in turn, depends on "the strength of external restraint over behavior."

> As the role of others in the determination of behavior increases, the right to blame others for unfortunate consequences also increases. When the role of the self in determining behavior is great relative to the role of others, the self must bear responsibility for the consequences of behavior."[26]

In contrast to lower-class persons, middle-class persons are more likely to be required by their roles to relate to others either as superordinates, as colleagues, or as independent operators. The important thing about these roles is that the expectations that attach to them are not merely expectations of conscientious performance of detailed assignments received from others, but that they are expectations that one will, without minute directives, close supervision, or threats of punishment, exercise good judgment, make appropriate decisions, and carry them out. In short, one is expected to provide his own discipline and assume responsibility for his decisions and their consequences. The legitimacy of one's claims to middle-class roles rests, as a matter of fact, largely upon the claim–albeit an implicit one–that one is capable of such initiative, decision, self-direction and self-discipline. To assert such a claim, however, is to deny to oneself the right to blame others for things that go wrong. . . .

Patriarchy

Lower-blue-collar men agreed most often with the statement, "Men should make the really important decisions in the family." Let us take agreement with this statement as our operational definition of "patriarchy." We must then distinguish this from the actual, operative structure of decision and control in the home, for LL subjects also report that LL women actually take the major share of responsibility for budgeting, bill-paying and child-care–to a greater degree, in fact, than is true in the other class levels.[27]

Elizabeth Bott suggests that the inconsistency is only apparent and that the "patriarchal" sentiments of lower-class male "heads" are really expressive of a family with a rather rigid division of labor in which each parent has authority and responsibility in his own sphere. Her argument is especially interesting be-

[26] Andrew F. Henry and James F. Short, Jr., *Suicide and Homicide* (New York: The Free Press, 1954), p. 103.

[27] There is another sense, which we shall not discuss here, in which the LL's are most "partriarchal": they agree most strongly with statements affirming that women are out of their place in the world of business and politics and that the proper place of women is in the home.

cause it relates this division of labor to the kinds of social networks we discussed in the section on kinship.

> ... If both husband and wife come to marriage with such close-knit networks, and if conditions are such that the previous pattern of relationships is continued, the marriage will be super-imposed on these pre-existing relationships, and both spouses will continue to be drawn into activities with people outside their own elementary family (family of procreation)... Rigid segregation of conjugal roles will be possible because each spouse can get help from people outside ... If husband and wife come to marriage with ... loose-knit networks or if conditions are such that their networks become loose-knit after marriage, they must seek in each other some of the emotional satisfactions and help with familial tasks that couples in close-knit networks can get from outsiders. Joint organization becomes more necessary for the success of the family as an enterprise.[28]

Therefore, Bott argues, the common tendency to describe the working-class family as both "male-authoritarian" (or "patriarchal") and as "mother-centered" is not paradoxical. They are, indeed, both, depending upon the functional area which one is attending to.

James H. Robb comments on the disagreement as to who is the "real head" of the working-class family.

> ... The disagreement seems to be based on a sharp division of labour between men and women and a difference of opinion as to which role is to be regarded as the more important. One consequence of the man's economic importance is that so long as he remains in work he can claim, if he wishes, almost complete exemption from all other tasks connected with the family. Again, it is essential for the well-being of the family that he should be kept as fit for work as possible. Therefore, he tends to get first consideration ... in the comforts and amenities of the home ... On the other hand, his abdication from responsibility for activities within the home leaves his wife in a central position as far as closer relationships within the household are concerned.[29]

In any case, it is clear from these and other descriptions of lower-class family life that the lower class male is *not* a patriarch within the ordinary connotations of the term. At the same time we are left with a strong feeling that the repetition of the themes of "woman's place" and "the man is (or should be) boss" expresses more than a simple recognition of a division of labor. It might be that if we had items that discriminated sentiments about the relative authority of husband and wife in different spheres, we would have obtained differences that are not revealed by responses in the form of agreement and disagreement with the "blan-

[28] Bott, *Family and Social Network*, p. 60.

[29] James H. Robb, *Working-Class Anti-Semite, A Psychological Study in a London Borough* (London: Tavistock Publications, 1954), p. 60.

ket" statement put to our subjects. Pending such more discriminating research, however, it seems to us reasonable to assume, on the basis of responses to our own questionnaire item and impressionistic reports of lower-class family life, that the LL male really feels that he *should be* the boss, the ultimate authority, in his household in a general and not a functionally circumscribed sense. . . .

Toughness

LL subjects were more "tough-minded" on selected items from Eysenck's T-Scale.[30] We are not here concerned, however, with interpreting scores on Eysenck's "T-factor," which are compounded from responses to 32 scale items. We limit ourselves to a consideration of three connotations of the term "toughness" which are sufficiently distinct to merit separate consideration and which are based on responses to both Eysenck and other items in our questionnaires.

1. There is "tough-mindedness." in the sense of subscribing to a "dog-eat-dog" ideology, expressed in agreement with this questionnaire item: "If a person hopes to get ahead in this world he can't help stepping on others' toes, and he can't let this bother him." This item is representative of several other items to the same effect, to all of which the LL agrees more frequently than do subjects of any other level. This is, of course, an aphorism, a formula, part of the LL's "vocabulary of motives," not necessarily a description of what he does, and it must be interpreted guardedly. There is good reason to believe that it is often qualified, implicitly because it is taken for granted, by a phrase to this effect: "excepting, of course, certain kinsmen and good friends." Interpreted in this way, it becomes another expression of the LL's particularistic orientation to the social universe, and there is little more that need be said that we have not said under our discussion of "misanthropy."

2. A second connotation is not so much a callous indifference to the woes of others as an ability to "take it," whether "it" is physical pain, suffering, or a sea of troubles. We have two items, with which the LL's most frequently agree, that seem to tap this sentiment: "A really strong man doesn't let his feelings or emotions show," and "One of the most important things that a teen-age boy should learn is how to 'take it' without crying." If men ever make virtues of necessity, we should certainly expect toughness in this sense to be accounted a virtue among the LL's. We expect this, however, not only because the occupational tasks of the LL require stamina, fortitude, and endurance, and because he is subject to deprivation and insecurity, but also because his value to those who depend on him—his fellow workers, his family, and friends—depends on his ability to "take it."

3. Finally, there is a third connotation of "toughness": a general posture of truculent self-assertiveness, defiance, "don't-push-me-around" touchiness. The

[30] H. J. Eysenck, *The Psychology of Politics* (London: Routledge & Kegan Paul, 1954), chs. 4 and 5 and pp. 276-280; *The Structure of The Human Personality* (London: Methuen, 1953), ch. 7.

LL's agree most frequently that "No really strong or manly man will let other people push him around." This kind of toughness is exaggerated and romanticized in many lower-class folk heroes and movie and TV criminals, who are eventually destroyed, to be sure, and whose toughness itself may be the instrument of their destruction; however, there is something about their refusal to grovel to any man and their contempt for the trouble they invite that apparently elicits a kind of fascination and even admiration in their audiences. "Toughness," in this sense, is apparently equivalent to Miller's "autonomy," one of his six "focal concerns" of "lower-class culture."[31] However, we have also described the LL as "authoritarian," as tending to conceive of social relationships as naturally hierarchical, in which there is always somebody who dominates and somebody who is dominated. It may even be true, as Miller himself suggests, that the LL's overt insistence upon autonomy "runs counter to an implicit seeking out of highly restrictive social environments where rules, regulations, and edicts exert close control over all his behavior. . . ."[32]

We have already suggested two polar types of response to the authoritarian relationship. One is compliance, obedience, surrender of autonomy; in short, one can build a self around the role of the "good soldier." This is one of the ways the possibilities of the relationship can be exploited for the enhancement of the self, at the same time that it has the tangible gain of minimizing "trouble." The polar alternative to this is "toughness" in the sense in which we are now using it. This is the refusal to surrender autonomy, ranging from outright defiance to surly or sullen compliance, by which one serves public notice that one's will has not been broken. Whatever the gains of this role, it obviously has its costs; it invites "trouble." We therefore find also various compromises and combinations constructed out of the materials of compliance and resistance: putting up a show of resistance and allowing oneself to be overcome by superior force, or complying for the most part but occasionally "blowing up" in the face of some "provocation." Another possibility is "playing it cool" *i.e.*, compliance with authority but making it clear to one's self and one's peers that this compliance is purely expedient and does not rest on respect for authority or on ego-involvement in conformity. A closely related alternative, which fuses subtly into "playing it cool," is "conning" the powers that be—that is, disarming their suspicion by the show of compliance or deference, and exploiting the consequent trust. Of all these, the openly belligerent posture is perhaps the least common because it is the most dangerous, and perhaps for that very reason the most "heroic."

But the most common compromise of all, probably, is to *perform* in the style of one role but to talk in the style of another, in a muted or not-quite-serious way where it is dangerous, and more boldly when the situation permits. Much of the "toughness" of the LL and his insistence on autonomy is undoubt-

[31] Walter B. Miller, "Lower Class Culture," pp. 12-13.

[32] William C. Kvaraceus, Walter B. Miller, et al., *Delinquent Behavior: Culture and the Individual* (Washington: National Education Association, 1959), p. 67.

edly "tough talk" that is very different from his performance and that makes it possible for him to enjoy some of the gratifications of more than one pattern of adaptation to authority.

Consumption Patterns

The prevailing market value of the LL's car, television, and basic appliances averages almost 20 percent higher than the average value of equivalent upper-blue-collar possessions, despite a median family income that is fully one-third lower. A number of explanations readily suggest themselves. However, the very surfeit of explanations should make one wary. Furthermore, the dangers of a middle-class ethnocentric bias, always great, are nowhere greater than here. The middle-class person's attitude toward the spending patterns of the LL is frequently a combination of patronizing amusement, moral indignation, envy, and resentment. It would be surprising if this attitude did not color the motivations that are imputed to the LL, or even distort the perception of the facts about spending themselves.

Perhaps the most popular explanation of the LL's spending is that it is a compensatory response to status insecurity. We are dealing here with that stratum whose claim to status in the larger social system on the basis of generally valued attainments or positions is weakest. A disproportionate investment of his slender resources in "loud," showy, expensive artifacts, especially those touted by the mass media, would be the most efficient "status equalizer." (A higher percentage of LL's own Cadillacs–no doubt mostly second-hand–than of any other level.)

An alternative line of thinking would suggest that the differences among the social classes are not as great as they appear to be. It could be that the important difference between the middle class, for example, and the LL, is that the middle class spends substantial amounts on innumerable details of their backdrops and accoutrements: clothes, cosmetics, car, house, lawn and garden, curtains, rugs, silver, objects d'art, gourmet foods, etc., and that they spend it for much the same reasons as the LL, but attribute this spending to taste and breeding. It could be that the LL, having so much less money to dispose of for "status spending," can get a larger net status dividend by concentrating his spending on a few expensive, highly visible objects, rather than by spending small sums on each of a larger number of "cheap," inconspicuous objects. In brief, it may be that the marginal status utility, so to speak, of the consumer dollar may be maximized in different ways depending on the total amount that is available to be expended.

There is no question but that possessions are enviable, and their display brings status. But the possibility also suggests itself that the "disproportionate" expenditure on "creature comforts" is not altogether an expression of striving for status or need for reassurance thereof. It could be also that it is a simple and logical implication of the LL's pessimistic world view that we have described. If one despairs of materially improving his status, if husbanding one's resources seems futile, if scrimping and economizing determine the future much less than do "the breaks," if nothing seems certain but the present, then the resources one has are "freed" to be spent in ways that promise immediate gratification. What the middle-class person might censor as "improvidence" might appear to the LL as a sensible way to live in an uncertain world.

Whatever explanation we favor, we must come to terms with the additional fact that the LL seems to have defaulted his pride in his home. With more "leisure" time available than any other stratum, he seldom effects the simplest of repairs or improvements, nor does he often boast of a garden or even a lawn. Certainly the "home" is a "status symbol" par excellence. If the LL is so preoccupied with status, why does he invest so little in this highly visible symbol? Why do the other classes, and notably the middle class, presumably less anxious about status, invest so much of both their money and their time in defining, beautifying, cultivating and improving the home? Let us speculate on this, at the cost of adding to our surfeit of hypotheses.

It may be that the contrast between the LL's valuation of cars and appliances *versus* his valuation of housing is a spurious contrast. In the case of cars and appliances we were speaking of an attitude toward the *purchase* of consumption goods; in the latter case, we were speaking primarily of an attitude toward the *care and husbandry* of property once acquired. It may be that the same "improvident" style of life—a low level of rational, deliberate, disciplined planfulness—expresses itself in *both* spending patterns *and* "care" patterns. Our data do not permit us to generalize about patterns of care regarding cars and appliances, but it may be that, were such data available, they would reveal the same casualness about care as obtains with respect to housing. On the other social levels, by contrast, what we may have is a generalized pattern of careful husbandry of property that expresses itself in housing but also in all other classes of possessions.

However, there is one further possibility that we cannot ignore. If the house, and especially its external visage, is a symbol, what precisely does it symbolize. Surely the house, to a greater degree than any other possession, symbolizes the status and the "personality" of the *family* that occupies it. It is a presentation of a *collective* self, of the common identity of the conjugal family. The more highly its members value this common identity to the exclusion of other identities, the more their self-conceptions are at stake in the public image and reputation of the conjugal unit, and the fewer the competing solidarities, the more willing they will be to lavish money and time and work on the preservation and enhancement of the visage they present in common. Where the conjugal family is seen as and is in fact a precarious entity we should expect a greater reluctance to invest so heavily in this presentation of the collective self.

We are not prepared ourselves to do more than offer these speculations. Hopefully they will provide the materials from which it may be possible to construct an adequate theory of the distinctive consumption patterns of the LL.

CAUTIONS AND QUALIFICATIONS

1. This paper does not present a "portrait of the underdog." It is specifically concerned with the respects in which the LL *differs to a statistically significant degree* from the other strata. Our comparisons do not necessarily contrast a majority of the LL's with a majority of each of the other strata. Viewed from another perspective, many of the "characteristically LL" responses of this study would turn out to be differences in emphasis on a set of common cultural themes.

2. Our statistical treatment does not deal with the range of variation within the LL stratum, nor with the extent to which the same subjects are responsible for the differences obtained on different comparisons. Both for the sake of descriptive knowledge and of the advancement of theory, it would be useful also to investigate *patterns of adaptation within the same stratum.*

3. Had we concentrated on certain sub-groups within the LL stratum, or had we studied LL's in some other setting, our findings might have turned out somewhat differently. For example, much of our discussion had concerned the relationship between characteristics of the conjugal family and characteristics of the social networks. When Young and Willmott[33] followed their lower-class families from Bethnal Green to a housing estate in the suburbs, where husband and wife are isolated from their kin and life-long friends and neighbors, they observed significant changes in the relationships between the spouses. . . .

4. For the sake of making a point, many of our comparisons are overdrawn. For example, although we have made much of "deficiency in role-taking ability," it would be flying in the face of common experience to assume that LL's are clods incapable of seeing more than one perspective. The "peasant shrewdness" of the lower classes is not "animal cunning" as contrasted to "role-taking ability." It is a pejorative term for role-taking ability. The skills employed by the servant, whether faithfully to serve or craftily to manipulate the master, are role-taking skills.

5. It is worth repeating that this paper is concerned with the lower blue-collarite, not the blue-collar or "working" class in general. The findings reported here, with exceptions noted, contrast the LL to his upper-blue-collar compatriots as well as to members of the other strata. The stably employed, economically secure, relatively prosperous working-class—such as the Ford workers described by Bennett Berger—live under a very different set of life conditions. . . .

6. Reference should be made to the problem of comparing questionnaire and interview responses by subjects of different social classes. . . .

In brief, it is possible that interview and questionnaire techniques are more

[33] Richard A. Cloward et al., *Theoretical Studies in the Social Organization of the Prison,* Social Science Research Council Pamphlet 15 (New York: Social Science Research Council, 1960), chs. 7-10.

likely, when applied to LL respondents than when applied to respondents of the other strata, to produce caricatures in which the half-tones and shadings, present in the subject, are obliterated in the image.

7. Are there, among the LL themes we have delineated, a dominant few, closely linked to the life conditions, which in turn determine the remainder? Have we, indeed, performed a kind of informal factor analysis? Retrospectively, a few themes do seem to stand out as relatively prepotent: e.g., a poverty of perspectives, a preference for particularistic relationships, a tendency to view the self as a victim of circumstances beyond one's control. . . .

14 *Jack L. Roach*

THE CRAWFORDS: LIFE AT THE BOTTOM [1]

The Crawford family consists of Frank, age 30, his wife Viola, age 27, and their six children ranging from 11 years to 4 months. A premarital pregnancy resulted in a shot-gun marriage when she was 17 and he, 20. In addition to the six children Mrs. Crawford has had at least two miscarriages during the 10 years of their marriage. (She claims she has tried birth control but somehow slip-ups occur, for which she blames her husband.)

The family has a number of health problems. Most of the children badly need dental care. Both parents will probably require full extractions in a few years. The children seem to be constantly bothered by respiratory disorders. This condition is serious enough to warrant visits by the Public Health nurse. Mrs. Crawford is especially beset with health disorders. For several years she has needed corrective surgery for what she calls "female trouble" and for varicose veins. She appears to be chronically exhausted and looks closer to 40 than in her late twenties.

The Crawfords began marriage with no savings and with money owed for a car he purchased shortly before they wed. They set up housekeeping in a two-room, furnished apartment, remaining there until the second child was born, at which time they found a semifurnished flat. Although they have moved five

Jack L. Roach, "The Crawfords: Life at the Bottom" in Jack L. Roach, Llewellyn Gross, and Orville R. Gursslin, *Social Stratification in the United States.* © 1969. Reprinted by permission of Prentice Hall, Inc., Englewood Cliffs, New Jersey.

[1] From case files of Jack L. Roach.

times in the past 10 years (twice their dwelling was condemned by the health department; twice they were evicted for nonpayment of rent), they have remained within the same eight-block slum section. At present the Crawfords live in a five-room flat, haphazardly constructed from a former garage. Although they are cramped for space and the plumbing and heating are defective, better housing would be too costly for them.

Mr. Crawford is employed as a general laborer in an industrial plant. He had a variety of jobs–assembly-line worker, truck driver, construction laborer, cab driver, gas-station attendant–none of which required much in the way of skill or training. He quit school when he was 17. Because of frequent unemployment, short work weeks, and marginal wages, Mr. Crawford's income has frequently been inadequate to cover the family's basic daily needs. Consequently the Crawfords have turned to public assistance several times in the past 10 years. One application was necessary when Mr. Crawford traveled to a neighboring city to find a better job and remained away from his family for several months. He was charged with desertion and placed on probation. The probation department in turn referred the Crawfords to a family agency for counseling.

Below are excerpts from three tape-recorded interviews with the Crawfords. These interviews were part of a larger study of lower-class families. The interviews were semistructured. Most questions were open-ended, allowing the Crawfords to enlarge upon their responses if they desired. The interview data are organized under question headings, phrased in the same way they were presented to the Crawfords.

What kind of work do you usually do? What kind of work would you like best?

Mr. Crawford: For about six months now I've been on the bullgang of the ironworks factory here. You know that's like a catchall job. We fill in, do the odd jobs . . . the heavy work that the lift truck and that can't get at. We're like Chinese labor.

If I had a chance I would take a night watchman or guard job. That's steady work. No piecework where you break your back to make an extra buck. You know what you earn and that's that. It may not be the biggest pay, but it is always coming in and no more of this one week a big check and the next week two days pay. I had a chance at a night watchman job a couple years ago, but I thought I'd be better off sticking it out with construction work. I thought maybe I'd get a chance at one of those big machines like a 'dozer or a power shovel, but I hurt my hand and couldn't do much of anything for a while. Then they laid off and I was out. And like I said before I've been mainly in factory work lately. You know, on the bullgang and things like that. Sometimes on the assembly line.

Since I got out of school when I was 17–I got sick of them teachers always yelling–I've done practically every kind of work. I've driven a truck, pick-up, dump, all kinds. I was a bartender for a while. I've been a kitchen helper. Been in business myself–haulin' things with a big pick-up truck. But that didn't pan out.

No business. I've been in and out most of the factories here. Mostly on the assembly line or as a laborer. They hire and lay off. Once I told the foreman he could shove his job and walked off just when the line started. He begged me to stay, but I had it there. The longest I was at was the Rogers steel plant. I stayed there three years. I was set for a soft spot on the line when things got slack and they cut our hours down. I left for a dockworker job and strained myself there. I was on sick leave for half a year from that. I must have had a dozen different jobs since I began working. Once I think I switched three or four times in one year. I got to watch myself now. I figure this is a good plant I'm in now. If I can stick it out on the bullgang till the end of the year, maybe I can switch over to a sweeper. Who knows, maybe a watchman job will come along. You gotta keep your eyes open and grab when the grabbin's good. I shoulda did that long time ago. Or else you gotta know some Big Wheel to suckhole around.

How are you doing as a family, with each other as well as raising the kids?

Mrs. Crawford: I do what I can with them. If they would just stay out of trouble. We have enough of that without them getting mixed up in something. The oldest boy–he's 11–he's a big mouth and always knows better. The school warned me they can't stand him. Well, I can't stand him either. I've told him I'll put him someplace if he doesn't straighten out. He even started to hit me back last week when I slapped him for lying. The others are bad enough, but they're younger and don't try that stuff. I can lock them in a room or something when they get on my nerves. I try to tell Frank to get after them more but he thinks all he has to do is to whip them once a month and then I'm supposed to take care of everything. If it wasn't for the way those kids are always at me, and Frank and his beer money, things would be a lot better.

How do you mean how are we getting along with each other? I get disgusted with things a lot but I guess we're gettin' by. Anyways we have stood it for ten years now.

Mr. Crawford: It's up to the wife to keep them kids in line. What am I supposed to do, kill them everyday? I will too if any one of them ever raises a hand to me. I've got enough headaches without arguin' about those damn kids all the time. Whatta they care anyways. Even the three-year-old all he knows is gimme, gimme! What do they care about their old man. All I ask is just give me a little peace and quiet when I come home. Why do I gotta listen to all that about the kids this and the kids that!

Except for naggin' about money all the time–what should I do, go rob a bank?–we get by. She's gotta put up with me, who else is she gonna find to put up with her and her temper like I do (said "jokingly" to his wife who gives him a sour look). Anyways, what do them marriage counselors know? We went there twice (his wife interjects: "You mean I did!"), and they couldn't find nothin' wrong. All I know is the wife's still the same. Still crab, crab, crab.

What sort of plans or hopes did you have when you first got married? What about now?

Mr. Crawford: For a long time now I've been wantin' to get into the junk business. I was thinkin' I could rent that empty lot around the corner. I would build a fence or something in the front so the city wouldn't squawk. There's a lot of junk and used stuff layin' around that people throw out or will sell for a buck or two. Like old stoves, washers, and things like that. Mostly metal things is what brings the money. Furniture you have to have a shed for. There's even some junk cars that are left here and there. I could rent a truck to haul things or maybe even buy an old one cheap. Whan I was 18 another guy and I were really going to do this and then . . . well, one thing led to another and we never got around to it. I still have that in mind. All I need to do is get a few bucks ahead—then I think the finance place will let me take a hundred or so to get going. I've always wanted to be in some kind of business where you'd be your own boss. No one to keep telling you this or that and you can earn as much as you want to put time in. I know a guy who after the Korean War bought a couple of dump trucks. Now he's livin' in a big place of his own, got everything he wants, and he doesn't have any college degree either. In fact, I don't think he got finished with high school.

Mrs. Crawford: I've heard that junk business for how many years now? Anyways, we got no money to go buying a truck or renting some lot. I thought when we first got married that maybe somehow we could get our own place in a couple years. There's places around with empty grocery stores in front and a flat in back. You could buy something like that and pay it off with the grocery business. There's a need for a store like that here. The only one here now is that booky-joint place. All they got is rotten vegetables and they're always out of anything you want. Now we gotta go about eight blocks to the supermarket. And they don't give any credit.

I never looked into how much money they wanted for one of those stores. Anyways its too late now. We ain't got a dime, and the way I feel and with this bunch of kids how can I run a grocery business? I never did plan on all these kids I'll tell you! Sure I wanted some kids, anybody does. Why do you get married anyways? But I didn't want all these many. No more I say if I got something to say about it. I'm the one whose insides gotta be operated on. With the man, that's it, its fine and dandy. He don't have all this body trouble—afterwards.

I don't plan on nothing now. If you plan you just borrow trouble.

What would you say are your worst troubles, the things that bother you the most?

Mrs. Crawford: Money troubles! I get a headache thinking about it. I'm sick of bill collectors. Half the stuff I don't think we owe on anyways. Sometimes I feel like packin' up and clearing out. Now we even have the land-lord squawking even though I told him there was a short pay and he'd have to wait. If he tries eviction, we'll tell the health department about his toilets leaking through the floor. And then they say I'm suppose to give the kids . . . how much more milk and things every day? On top of that we got a car that was driven less than a month and it broke down, and yet we have to pay through a garnishee on Frank's pay. But the company won't do right by the guarantee.

I'd say next to money the kids are the next big bother. They're gonna drive me to the bug house.

Mr. Crawford: I was figurin' I could rent a trailer for the car I bought last month and do odd jobs, carting and things. Now all I got is a clunker sittin' on the street which has to be moved or I get a fine. Why don't they bother some of those big deals with their big convertibles over on Rodney Street? Now either I take a bus to the plant and get up an hour early or I pay $4.50 a month for a car pool. It's the same old crap. You try to do something to save a buck and wind up all the worse. All I know is if there's going to be any clearin' outta here, I'm the one who'll do it. (The next remark is prompted by his wife's comment that the best way to save a dollar would be to stay away from the bars.) All I can say is that when it comes to a time when I can't have a few bucks a week for beer money then I've had it. I earn the money, what do I get–nothin'? (He ignores his wife's retort that $10 is a lot of beer money.)

Well, anyways, if I could put together two straight months of the pay I'm gettin now, we might see our way clear and get rid of some of these bills and even get some more furniture and also a decent TV. I'm sick of that thing and its flip-flop picture. And I'm sick of this stinkin' chicken coop. Now the owner is coming around saying he has to raise the rent but he won't fix the damn toilet.

What about relatives, neighbors, and friends? Do you see much of them or visit often?

Mrs. Crawford: My sister lives over on Spring Avenue about three blocks from here. I see her once in a while at the A & P. She used to come around to the house every so often, but then she began to argue about the old man, my Dad, I mean. She was insistin' that I was supposed to give her some money because he was stayin' at her house. That's pretty good. She never gave us a dime when he stayed here a couple of months last winter. Well, let her see how it is with his drinkin'. Anyways, she came around at Easter with her kids. I also got a brother someplace in Florida last I knew. I guess he's just bumming around down there. He's 21. I also have a brother in the Stillwell School (an institution for the mentally retarded). He's 18 and I don't think he'll ever see the outside. I should go see him sometime.

I have a girl friend a couple doors up the street. She comes over a lot. Her husband took off in August. She's got two kids, and they're always sick with this or that. She's on welfare. She's got a raw deal from that rat husband of hers. She's about the only one I have over. The rest around here are a bunch of louses. They're always looking for trouble and looking for ways to get you mixed up in it. Two years ago one of them squealed to the welfare workers that we had money somewhere hidden in some bank or somethin'. They knew it was a lie, but they just did it to be miserable. So I stay away from them and mind my business.

Mr. Crawford: Her father is always comin' around trying to borrow a buck or sponge a meal. Why should I give him anything just for him to go booze it up? My parents live in Pennsylvania, where I come from. They split up a couple of years ago. I heard from my mother a while ago. She's working for some family there. I don't know what's going on with my old man. I also got a couple brothers and sisters in P.A. I don't hear from them. They're all married now so I hear.

I don't monkey much with the neighbors around here. Some of them think they're too good for anybody. It beats me why, they're nothin' and will never be nothin'. I go up to the gin mill every so often and have a couple beers and shoot the breeze with the bartender (as he is saying this his wife is shaking her head and making exasperated noises). I went to school with him. Once in a while I help him out, cleaning up and taking care of the bar sometimes. I don't like the place anymore though. They're gonna close up and get out, the owner says. The place is gettin' full of them Spics–you know, those Puerto Ricans. They stand around and jabber and act like they own the place. Why don't they go back where they came from? Who asked them around here anyways? The place is getting dead anyways. There used to be some guys there I knew that hung around there before I was married. I dunno if they ain't got no money now or the wives make 'em stay home or they're dead or what. I don't see 'em around much anymore.

Can you see yourself in about ten years? What do you think you will be like in ten years?

Mrs. Crawford: I have enough trouble with things now without thinkin' about ten years from now. Besides the Bible says take no thought for tomorrow. You never know if you are gonna be here tomorrow, to take thoughts for tomorrow. I don't even wanna bother about that sort of thing. If you fret about something, sure enough it'll happen. So I keep my mind off the future. I suppose I'll have a bigger pack of kids by then. (Said with a grimace to her husband.) I'll be a wreck when I am 40 if I ain't already that. Things can't be no worse I know that. So maybe I'll just blow my top and they can drag me off someplace, and someone else can try to put two and two together around here.

Mr. Crawford: I don't believe in that day-dreamin' business. Anyways I'll be shot by then. I'm half shot now. At least maybe I won't have teeth trouble then, they'll be all gone by then. We got enough worry about each day or maybe worry about a week ahead. How the bills are gonna get paid and all that. As my wife says, the Bible says let the future take care of itself. Who knows anyways about the future? I don't know, and I don't care. I've had enough bad luck now.

I suppose I will see myself as a bum in ten years. They say I'm a bum now, so what's the difference? Anyways who knows if anybody will be around in ten years. Maybe the Chinese or Russians will blow up the world.

CHAPTER 5

UPPER LEVEL STATUS COMMUNITIES AND SOCIAL CLASS

The upper levels of the stratification structure are rarely viewed as a social problem or blamed for the ills of the society, other than by a relatively small number of radicals or dissidents. This may help to explain why these levels have seldom been systematically studied by social scientists. There is, however, a substantial body of literature, including society gossip, novels, autobiographies and muckraking pieces or exposés, that describe certain features of upper level life styles. But the sources of much of this kind of information are usually biased in one direction or the other. Reliable data and unbiased analysis are rarely found among the writings on the members of the upper end of the structure of inequality. This scarcity is attributable to the difficulty of gaining access to valid information, since the powerful are able to maintain a high level of privacy.

As mentioned previously, the aim of this volume is to show that it is theoretically appropriate to use the concept of social class to characterize the *top* and *bottom* levels of the American social structure, but not the middle levels. In the case of the latter, the concept of status community seems most expedient. Of all the parts of the stratification structure of the United States, it is apparent that the top level can be most readily viewed as a social class.

A number of individuals exist sharing an equally high place on Weber's three hierarchies of class, status and political power, and these individuals and their families can be said to form a social class. Defining them as a class is further substantiated by the fact that they attend the same preparatory schools, intermarry, conform to a similar life style: similar places of residence, types of housing, vacation resorts, and club memberships.

In contrasting the upper *class* with the middle level, one finds the occurrence of inconsistency between class, status, and political power much more frequent in the middle levels. It would seem that it is explicitly the existence of all types of inconsistencies and combinations thereof that has contributed to the necessity of substituting the concept of status community for social class in analyses of stratification at the middle level.

In distinguishing an upper class as distinct from other collectivities, it can be argued that inherited wealth and some reference to lineage are important criteria of upper *class* membership. The basis for such an assertion rests on the fact that *time* is a factor in the development of life styles. Possessing wealth over several generations allows for a more articulated style of living than does acquiring wealth in one's own generation, especially after attaining adulthood. It takes time for a collectivity to decide about which status symbols are important, to build and people exclusive residence areas, private schools, clubs, churches, and summer resorts. Participation in the development and maintenance of any part of these aspects of an accepted and exclusive style of life is probably the sine qua non of a family that moves into the upper class and *remains* at that level for several generations. Very few families last indefinitely as members of the top rank in the stratification structure. Time, on the other hand, along with the effect of social, economic, and political factors, in terms of the membership of a given upper class family usually leads to an ultimate decline from upper class to somewhere in the middle and lower levels of the stratification structure.[1] Although families may rise, decline, and rise again, there is no known *cyclical* pattern for this kind of phenomena.[2]

The question of the existence of an upper class need not necessarily be complicated with the further question that concerns itself with the existence of a "ruling class" or "power elite." Although the article by Domhoff, included in this section, attempts to illustrate some of the connections between upper class position and power, the two are not always closely correlated. Baltzell points out, in reference to Philadelphia's "aristocracy," that involvement in the ultimate power sector of society, politics, was a rather uncommon pursuit of Philadelphia gentlemen. Instead, Baltzell emphasized a life style revolving around lineage, education, religion, club membership, and exclusive residence and primary group life reflecting "intimate access to one another." At the outset of his book, *Philadelphia Gentlemen,* Baltzell states quite flatly that, in the last analysis,

[1] For a discussion of this "percolator" phenomenon in stratification, see Joseph Schumpeter, *Imperialism and Social Class*, (New York: Meridian Books, 1955), pp. 113-124.

[2] The observation that some families go "from shirtsleeves to shirtsleeves in three generations" may well be true in some cases, but it does not establish a cyclical pattern for such phenomena.

power over other people is the indispensible mark of high social status, and the primary function of an upper class is the exercise of power."[3] Nevertheless, the exercise of power is not the only, nor necessarily the most important function of an upper class. In fact, to designate power as one of the "primary" functions of an upper class obscures more than it reveals. If power is the function of the upper class, what is the function of the lower class, middle status communities, jet sets, intellectual elite, financial elite, athletic elite, etc.? The wielding of power, however much an individual group or collectivity commands by way of resources or skills, is one of the aspects of life that is of prime importance in determining position in the structure of inequality. Power wielding is no more the *function* of the upper class than of any other collectivity in the stratification structure. The difficulty of determining the interrelation between an upper class and a ruling or power elite is highlighted in Chapter VIII by Arnold Rose's discussion of "Contrasting Theories of Political Power in the American Society."

A problem in dealing with the upper levels of the status structure is one of adequately defining and categorizing these who are said to be celebrities, and are labeled as the "jet set," or "international nomads." It is readily apparent that aristocratic and celebrity status are not coextensive. A recent study reveals that in a sample of celebrities, defined as such by being written about in a leading society gossip column, only 23 percent were listed in the *Social Register*, whereas 33 percent were listed in *Who's Who in America* and 15 percent in *Who's Who*.[4] Moreover, only 17 percent of the "richest of the rich," as listed by *Fortune* magazine, were included among the celebrities.[5] As such, they are difficult to define in terms of the usual kinds of criteria. As with the "working rich" of the motor industry, and so-called intellectual or artistic elites, many celebrities comprise upper level status communities and are not necessarily members of a national upper class. It is obvious that a given person may hold membership in both the upper class and also be a celebrity. Nevertheless, in such instances it would appear that the individual's celebrity status would ultimately decline, whereas his upper class status would not, since it is not determined or maintained by publicity or notoriety.

3 E. Digby Baltzell, *Philadelphia Gentlemen* (New York: The Free Press, 1958), p. 60.

4 From an unpublished study by the editor of this volume.

5 Arthur Lewis, "America's Cantimillionarie," *Fortune*, 7 (May, 1968), pp. 152-157.

15 *E. Digby Baltzell*

AN AMERICAN ARISTOCRACY

Conceived in a new world which was free of the traditional authority of an established church and a feudal nobility, and born in a revolt from the tyranny of a centralized government symbolized in the British monarchy and mercantilism, American institutions have, virtually from the beginning, been shaped in a laissez-faire capitalist climate. The merchant, mining, manufacturing, railroad, and finance capitalist, each in their day, were the most powerful members of the elite in nineteenth-and early twentieth-century America. As "old family" is usually found to be synonymous with "old money," the leading capitalists in the pre-Civil War period were the "old-family" founders in America. In the 1870's, the families of these men and their descendants formed local business aristocracies in the older cities such as Boston, New York, and Philadelphia. Living near one another, on the gentle slope of Murray Hill in New York, on Beacon Street in Boston, or around Rittenhouse Square in Philadelphia, the members of these families knew "who" belonged with this formal and well-structured world of polite society.

In the last two decades of the nineteenth century, these provincial aristocracies of birth and breeding (old money) merged with a new and more conspicuously colorful world known as "Society." It was in the 1880's that New York Society with a capital "S," then moving uptown to the newly fashionable Fifth Avenue district, came under the tutelage of Mrs. Astor and her right-hand man, Ward McAlister. It was Mr. McAlister who coined the snobbish term "Four Hundred" and finally gave his official list to the New York *Times* on the occasion of Mrs. Astor's famous ball on February 1, 1892. During this same period, as millionaires multiplied and had to be accepted, as one lost track of "who" people were and had to recognize "what" they were worth, the *Social Register* became an index of a new upper class in America.

But this new upper class was soon to be organized on a national rather than a local scale. In an age which marked the centralization of economic power under the control of the finance capitalists, the gentlemen bankers and lawyers on Wall Street, Walnut Street, State Street, and La Salle Street began to send their sons to Groton, St. Mark's, or St. Paul's and afterwards to Harvard, Yale, or Princeton where they joined such exclusive clubs as Porcellian, Fence, or Ivy. These polished young men from many cities were educated together, and introduced to one another's sisters at debutante parties and fashionable weddings in Old Westbury, Mount Kisco, or Far Hills, on the Main Line or in Chestnut Hill, in Dedham, Brookline, or Milton, or in Lake Forest. After marriage at some fashionable Episcopal church, almost invariably within this select, endogamous circle, they lived in these same socially circumspect suburbs and commuted to the city where they lunched with their fathers and grandfathers at the Union, Philadelphia, Somerset, or Chicago clubs. Several generations repeat this cycle, and a centralized business aristocracy thus becomes a reality in America. The *Social Register*, first published in 1888, lists the families of this business aristocracy and their relatives and friends, in New York, Chicago, Boston, Philadelphia, Baltimore, San Francisco, St. Louis, Buffalo, Pittsburgh, Cleveland, Cincinnati-Dayton, and Washington, D.C. In 1940, approximately one-fourth of the residents of these twelve metropolitan areas who were listed in *Who's Who* in that year were also listed in the *Social Register*. Thus the members of this contemporary American upper class, descendants of leaders in American life from colonial times to the present, had considerable influence on the elite in 1940.

It is important to stress once again the fact that, while there are many middle and lower classes in America, and in Philadelphia, there exists one metropolitan upper class with a common cultural tradition, consciousness of kind, and "we" feeling of solidarity which tends to be national in scope. The origin and development of this inter-city moneyed aristocracy in America quite naturally paralleled the rise of rapid communications and the national corporate enterprise. Moreover, just as economic control of the various local firms in the "Yankee Cities" and "Middletowns" of America have gradually gravitated to such metropolitan centers as Boston, New York, or Chicago, so upper-class prestige has, over the years, become increasingly centralized in the fashionable metropolitan suburbs.

The growth and structure of this national upper class has, in turn, been supported by various institutions. First and most important, of course, are the New England boarding schools and the fashionable Eastern universities. Whereas the older generation of Proper Philadelphians were educated at home or in local schools and colleges, at the turn of the century, and especially after the First World War, these national upper-class family-surrogates began to educate the children of the rich and well-born from all cities in ever-increasing numbers. At the same time, the Episcopal Church also developed into a national upper-class institution. By the end of the nineteenth century, the process of upper-class conversion, which had actually begun in the previous century, was virtually complete. In the twentieth century, the fashionable descendants of staunch New England Calvinists or pious Philadelphia Quakers almost invariably worshipped in the Episcopal churches in the metropolitan suburbs of America. And the Episcopal Church is also an important part of the summer social life at such fashionable resorts as Mount Desert which do so much to foster inter-city family alliances.

Several things follow from the development of this national upper class and its supporting institutions. On the whole, of course, the family is weakened and increasingly replaced by an associational aristocracy. The family firm gives way to the large and anonymously owned corporation with the attending consequences of declining family pride and responsibility. The entrepreneur who founded the family firm and fortune is replaced by the hired executive, and the corporation soon becomes an impersonal source of dividends which conveniently supports a suitable style of life. At the same time, the fashionable school, college, and club replace the family as the chief status-ascribing institutions: often isolated geographically as well as socially from the rest of the community, these fashionable associations tend to make for less social contact between classes than was the case in an earlier day when the members of polite society, although undoubtedly protected by a formal social distance recognized by all classes, may well have interacted more frequently in the local community with the members of the middle and lower classes. George Wharton Pepper, for instance, met and befriended a Negro boy while he was growing up in the neighborhood of stiff and fashionable Rittenhouse Square; his grandsons, reared in the social homogeneity of the Main Line and a New England boarding school, were more geographically isolated even though born in a more egalitarian age. Finally, the Episcopalianization of the whole American upper class also tends to foster uniformity and class isolation. This is, of course, part of a general trend throughout Protestantism. The Catholic Church has traditionally been an altar before which men of all walks of life bow down together, but the various Protestant denominations have, almost from the beginning, been organized along class lines. Certainly most Protestant churches today are social centers where families of similar backgrounds assemble together for worship. One often wonders if fashionable Episcopalians, in their aversion to the middle-class drabness of the "Protestant ethic," have not thereby substituted a convenient conventionality for their ancestors' more rigid convictions. At any rate, these developments in upper-class institutions tend to make for an increasing conformity and uniformity, a decline in local color and originality, and perhaps, at the same time, a new snobbishness which inevitably follows the increasing importance now attached to proper association affiliation.

16 *G. William Domhoff*

THE AMERICAN UPPER CLASS

Underlying the American upper class are a set of social institutions which are its backbone—private schools, elite universities, the "right" fraternities and sorori-

G. William Domhoff, *Who Rules America?* ©1967. Reprinted by permission of Prentice-Hall, Inc., Englewood Cliffs, New Jersey.

ties, gentlemen's clubs, debutante balls, summer resorts, charitable and cultural organizations, and such recreational activities as foxhunts, polo matches, and yachting.[1] The private school is an excellent starting point, for its rise to importance was coincident with the late-nineteenth-century development of the national upper class. Baltzell emphasizes that at that time the proper school replaced the family as the chief socializing agent of the upper class: "The New England boarding school and the fashionable Eastern university became upper-class surrogate families on almost a national scale."[2] Educating the big-city rich from all over the country is only one of the functions of the private schools. They serve several other purposes as well. First, they are a proving ground where new-rich old-rich antagonisms are smoothed over and the children of the new rich are gracefully assimilated. Then too, they are the main avenue by which upper-class children from smaller towns become acquainted with their counterparts from all over the country. Perhaps equally important is the fact that the schools assimilate the brightest members of other classes, for such assimilation is important to social stability. Sweezy calls the private schools "recruiters for the ruling class, sucking upwards the ablest elements of the lower classes and performing the double function of infusing new brains into the ruling class and weakening the political leadership of the working class."[3] Indeed, many private schools employ persons to search out talented members of the lower classes.

The most prestigious of the private schools for boys are probably Groton, St. Paul's, and St. Mark's, but Choate, Hotchkiss, and St. Andrew's are not far behind. Descendants of 65 of the 87 great American fortunes studied by [Gustavus] Myers [*History of the Great American Fortunes*, New York: Modern Library, 1937] attended either Groton, St. Paul's, or St. Mark's between 1890 and 1940. The best known of the schools, however, are Phillips Exeter and Phillips Andover, which have a greater number of scholarship students and a sizable minority of rich Jewish students. Other leading schools for boys included St. George's, Kent, Taft, Middlesex, and Deerfield in New England; Lawrenceville in New Jersey; Hill in Pennsylvania; Shattuck in Minnesota; and Episcopal High and Woodberry Forest in Virginia.

There are necessarily more than just a handful of these schools, some more

[1] However, these are by no means the only institutions which are the basis of the American upper class. Such financial and economic institutions as corporate stock and corporation boards, which are its economic basis, will be discussed in the next chapter. Intermarriage, the all-important institution that is the result of interaction in the above-noted institutions, will be discussed shortly as part of the evidence that the upper class is nationwide in its scope.

[2] E. Digby Baltzell, *The Philadelphia Gentlemen* (New York: The Free Press, 1958), p. 37. See also Jacob Brackman, "The Gospel According to St. Paul's," *Esquire* (June 1966), pp. 92-94, 135-136.

[3] After quoting Sweezy at length on this matter, Baltzell comments: "What a Marxian finds so dangerous, Tocqueville found desirable." Baltzell believes that the Marxist "rightly see the opportunitarian ideal as the worst enemy of their ideals of equality of conditions." The quote from Sweezy and the quote from Baltzell are both to be found in E. Digby Baltzell, *The Protestant Establishment* (New York: Random House, 1964), p. 344. The comment by Sweezy is in his review of Mill's *The Power Elite*, "Power Elite or Ruling Class?" *Monthly Review* (September, 1956), p. 148.

intellectually challenging, some more liberal, than others. A study by [Lucy] Kavaler, [*The Private World of High Society*, (New York: David McKay, Inc., 1960)] based upon interviews with upper-class women from all over the country led to a list of 130 private schools for young men and young ladies of the upper class. While this list is not perfect, leaving off such important schools as Berkshire, Salisbury, and Scarborough, it is valuable in conjunction with other considerations, such as family background and club memberships.

It is perhaps needless to add that most of these students go on to college. Kavaler estimates that 90 percent of private school graduates attend college, while a spokesman for an association of private schools claims that 99 percent of the female graduates of such schools now continue their education.[4] It is also needless to add that these well-prepared students attend the finest colleges and universities in the country. For example, the 1965 graduates of Lawrenceville went on to the following schools in large numbers: Harvard, 14; Princeton, 10; Yale, 8; Georgetown, 7; University of North Carolina, 7; Brown, 5; Cornell, 5; University of California, Berkeley, 5; Columbia, 4; Bucknell, 4; Penn, 4; Stanford, 4; Vanderbilt, 4; and Wesleyan, 4.[5]

Twenty-five years ago the importance of an Ivy League education could not be overestimated in studying the American upper class, and the chances were excellent that an Ivy League graduate could be so indexed. From 1900 to 1940, Harvard, Yale, Princeton, and several other select Eastern colleges brought together the rich from all over the country, superseding in importance the local universities, such as the University of Virginia, which had trained members of the upper class of their regions for so many generations. The pattern varied only slightly from city to city. Bostonians preferred Harvard, New Yorkers preferred Yale, and St. Louis and Baltimore were Princeton towns. Only two *Social Register* cities continued to favor local schools by a small margin–Philadelphia remained loyal to Penn, San Francisco to Stanford and the University of California at Berkeley. However, with the Second World War, the pattern of concentration at a few Eastern schools began to alter. Population pressures, the GI bill, stiffer entrance requirements, more scholarships for the bright but needy, and the rise in respectability of other universities were all factors in this change, but so were the experiences of the war, which did so much to shake the attitudes and prejudices of many insulated sons of the upper class. Data documenting the importance of the Ivy League schools in the development of a national upper class can be found in the historical studies by Baltzell; data revealing the change in the role of these universities have been compiled more recently by Gene Hawes[6] His study of the New York *Social Register* showed that 67 percent of

4 *Newsweek*, February 9, 1959, pp. 53-56.

5 I tabulated these schools from the Lawrenceville alumni journal, the *Laurentian*, 30:1 (Autumn, 1965), 33-34.

6 Gene Hawes, "The Colleges of America's Upper Class," *Saturday Review of Literature*, November 16, 1963 pp. 68-71.

the adult men who had attended college had received degrees from Harvard, Yale, or Princeton. In contrast, 45 percent of those currently attending a university were at one of the Big Three. On the graduate and professional school level, Harvard and Columbia were the most important, with Yale, a distant third. It will be interesting to note in future studies whether or not Harvard, Columbia, and Yale retain their pre-eminence in graduate training, for these schools have been absolutely essential in the training of the lawyers, physicians, and intellectuals of the upper class. These Ivy League schools, as Baltzell notes, also have been essential in the training of American Presidents:

> In the first half of the twentieth century, five of our eight Presidents were graduates of Harvard, Yale, Princeton, and Amherst. A sixth came from Stanford, "the western Harvard," where the social system most resembled that in the East.[7]

It is not only Presidents who are trained at these elite universities. Mills's study of 513 higher politicians—men who between 1789 and 1953 served as President, Vice-President, Speaker of the House, Cabinet Member, or Supreme Court Justice—revealed that 22 percent of them had attended Harvard, Yale, or Princeton. "If one includes such famous schools as Dartmouth and Amherst, then one-third of all the higher politicians, and 44 percent of those who ever spent any time in college, went to top-notch Eastern schools."[8] The same pattern holds true in the business world. For example, in a study of 476 top executives who went to college, "86 percent had received their undergraduate training at Yale, Harvard, and Princeton alone . . ."[9] A study of all directors in Poor's *Register of Corporations, Directors, and Executives* revealed that 4135 of the directors were from Harvard. Harvard was followed in numerical representation by Yale, Princeton, and the University of Pennsylvania.[10]

There have been changes in the exclusive gentlemen's clubs that are present in every major city, but they remain, as Max Weber said, the essential proof that one is a gentleman.[11] Among these changes is the fact that women have been known to enter the clubroom on occasion, an unheard-of event in the "old days." Then too, being a member of scores of such clubs is no longer the fashion, although some few persons belong to a half-dozen or more. Finally, many clubs have fallen into bad odor because of their anti-Semitism, which has led to public resignations by prominent members of the upper class. Most shocking, many successful executives have become members, leading to the claim by the more hide-bound of the hereditary rich that clubdom is going to the dogs, letting "everybody" into its august portals. For all of these revolutions, the

[7] Baltzel, *Protestant Establishment,* p. 135.

[8] See C. Wright Mills, *The Power Elite* (New York: Oxford University Press, 1956), pp. 400-402. The quote is on page 402.

[9] Baltzell, *Protestant Establishment*, p. 340.

[10] *Congressional Record* (Senate), July 19, 1965, A3870.

[11] Baltzell, *Protestant Establishment*, p. 19.

functions of the clubs remain very similar. They provide an informal atmosphere in which new members of the upper class can be initiated into the mores that govern gentlemanly behavior. They also provide a place in which the ground work for major business deals can be laid, and a place in which economic and political differences can be smoothed over in a friendly manner. Then, too, the clubs are a haven for the traveling businessman where he gets to know his compatriots from other localities, and a tie to the national upper class for the first families of small cities. Baltzell is most convincing when he shows that the "upper uppers" of the small cities studied by sociologists a generation ago are members of one or more of these clubs, if not graduates of the most exclusive private schools.

There are too many of these clubs to be named here. The better known include the California in Los Angeles, the Pacific Union in San Francisco, the Duquesne in Pittsburgh, the Links and the Knickerbocker in New York, the Somerset in Boston, and the Piedmont Driving Club in Atlanta. However, among the most important are the Harvard, Princeton, and Yale Clubs of New York and other major cities. The New York branches of these clubs are especially important, for they provide a place for out-of-town businessmen to see old college friends, and

> . . . in addition, countless small-town boys at Princeton, Harvard, or Yale live at their respective graduate clubs during their first years out of college if they happen to be among that large group of Ivy alumni who seek their fortunes each year among the caverns of Wall Street, or, in more recent years, along Madison Avenue.[12]

These alumni clubs are also important because they are not as anti-Semitic and anti-Catholic as their more stuffy counterparts. Then too, they are more likely to continue the assimilation of bright members of other classes which was begun at the private school and/or the Ivy League college.

Resort living is not what it used to be either, although its functions also remain the same. First, huge, ostentatious "cottages" are no longer the rule. Furthermore, the "in" resorts change slightly over the years, and the style of life at various resorts may vary from "roughing it" to Victorian splendor. Also, foreign resorts have become an integral part of the circuit, and the Georgia and Florida coasts have replaced the Virginia resorts that were the Southern playgrounds of yesteryear. All this said, the resorts continue to be a fertile stamping ground for intercity marriages.

Debutante balls serve the function of corraling the democratic inclinations of libidinal impulses. Or, as Baltzell puts it, ". . .the democratic whims of romantic love often play havoc with class solidarity."[13] These coming-out parties

[12] Baltzell, *Philadelphia Gentlemen*, p. 380.

[13] Baltzell, Ibid., p. 26.

announce that the girl is now available for marriage, preferably to the type of lad tendered an invitation. When the whirl of debutante dances and parties does not achieve its function, which is more than likely in an age when four years of college are ahead for girls as well as boys, the corraling function is taken over by the "right" sororities and fraternities, or such young adult clubs as the Bachelors and Spinsters of San Francisco, Los Angeles, and other major cities. It should be emphasized that discussions of the lavishness and frivolity of such occasions as debutante balls do not do justice to the important function they serve, for a considerable amount of intermarriage is at the crux of a well-knit social class.

To the competitive, hard-working members of the American upper class, the life of the feudal landlord apparently seems almost idyllic. In fact, one of the first acts of many newly arrived members of the upper class is to attempt to achieve the wonderful dreams of landlordism by returning to the land. They buy a farm or ranch, raise cattle or horses, and ride to the hounds. There are scores of hunts in the United States, some more exclusive than others, and so strong is the urge that the foxless Coloradans of Arapahoe gracefully substitute the coyote. The horse also figures in another major diversion for some members of the upper class. It is no mere coincidence that horse racing is called "the sport of kings," and it can be revealed that jockey clubs are not for jockeys–they house members of the upper class. This proclivity on the part of some members of the upper class for raising, riding, and racing horses helps cement the tie between the East, where riding has been a sport for some time; the border states of Maryland and Kentucky, where horses are bred and raised; and the West and Southwest, where riding is a symbol of the rugged frontier existence so recently and totally erased. Horses are also necessary for the game of polo, one sport not likely to join golf, tennis, and bridge in a complete skid to middle-class levels. For example, a handful of rich men from all over the country occasionally fly their horses to the Kleberg family's King Ranch in Kingsville, Texas, to enjoy a weekend of polo, and then return to more worldly pursuits thousands of miles away come Monday morning.[14] Sporting members of the upper class do not spend all of their spare time on horseback, however. There is also the water, where sailing and yachting are still the pastimes of gentlemen. Indeed, sailing gave rise to one of the most famous aphorisms of the upper class, which is repeated in just about every chronicle of high society: "You can do business with anyone," said J. P. Morgan, "but only sail with a gentleman." This is apparently the way aristocrat Franklin D. Roosevelt felt about it, for "he preferred to relax with what Jim Farley, with a touch of resentment, once called

[14] In 1937 Dixon Wecter characterized now-statesman Averell Harriman as an "industrialist and polo player" [The Saga of American Society (New York: Charles and Sons, 1937), p. 137]. We mention Harriman because he is one of the "red threads" that runs throughout our narrative. Industrialist, financier, ambassador, Secretary of Commerce, State Department official, and special emissary for Presidents, he is an ideal prototype of the member of the power elite who moves from command post to command post in different institutional hierarchies.

the 'Hasty Pudding Cabinet' as he watched them sail away for a brief vacation with the President on Vincent Astor's yacht."[15]

Members of the American upper class participate in a great many charitable and cultural organizations. In fact, they control most of these organizations, and the evidence for this is so ubiquitous in the daily press and the works of Baltzell and Kavaler that no attempt will be made to provide systematic documentation. A few examples will suffice:

> Architect Nathaniel A. Owings [SR, SF][16] has accepted the post as Chairman of the President's Council on Pennsylvania Avenue, aimed at sprucing up the nation's Capitol.[17]
>
> Somehow they ["the New Elegants"] find time for charity work, church functions, community projects, and college alumni drives.[18]
>
> Pittsburgh financier Andrew Mellon, a *Social Register* listee, built Washington's $15,000,000 National Gallery of Art in 1937 to house his $50,000,000 art collection. Now his son, Paul Mellon, is planning another public gallery in Washington for his 500-plus works of art.[19]
>
> The late C. D. Jackson [SR, NY] was a leading official of Time, Inc., an adviser to President Eisenhower, and a member of the board of directors of the Boston Symphony.
>
> E. Roland Harriman, Averell [Harriman's] brother, heads the American Red Cross.

THE GATEWAYS TO THE UPPER CLASS

Acceptance into the American upper class of today is not an impossible task, although a passport to its innermost citadels may be issued primarily to succeeding generations. For the newly arrived rich, the first step as a family is participation in charitable and cultural projects. Working on the organization of such ventures, and giving a considerable sum of money to them, will often lead to private dinner invitations in addition to invitations to other upper-class activities. Another important avenue for the aspiring family is to hire a social secretary, who, interestingly enough, we have usually found to be a member of the upper class herself. The social secretary will have many suggestions to make; she will arrange guest lists, caterers, and music for parties to which she will invite her

[15] Baltzell, *Protestant Establishment*, p. 300. The remark by Morgan is on page 36.

[16] *Social Register*, San Francisco. We have adopted this shorthand method of identifying listees in the *Social Register* because of the lack of elegance in such phrases as "socially registered" and "social registerite."

[17] *Look*, April 6, 1965, p. 41.

[18] *Time*, December 4, 1964, pp. 54-67. For the tremendous importance of big businessmen in charity fund raising, see the article on that topic in the January, 1966, *Fortune*, "The Fund Raising Businessmen–Eight Billion Dollars," by Robert Sheehan.

[19] *Time*, December 4, 1964, p. 56.

upper-class friends and clients. The social secretary is especially important for planning debutante parties, for she has guest lists from other clients and from private social enrollment rosters. To be accepted as a client by one of these important persons is almost a guarantee that one is on the status elevator to the social upper class. The importance of this seemingly trivial person cannot be overemphasized, for she functions to screen and mold applicants for membership in the social upper class.

For the man of the family, the most important gateway into the upper class is election into one of the exclusive gentlemen's clubs. Baltzell notes that there is a status order among these clubs, and quotes Allen's *Lords of Creation* to show how each generation is brought a step closer to the inner sanctum:

> The following progress is characteristic: John D. Rockefeller, Union League Club; John D. Rockefeller, Jr., University Club; John D. Rockefeller III, Knickerbocker Club.[20]

Election into a club, as Osborne Elliott (SR, NY) of *Newsweek* points out in his *Men at the Top*, is often one of the first signs that the bright young executive is in line for a significant promotion. For the woman of the family, the most typical gateway to the upper class is the Junior League. Founded in 1901 by Mary Harriman Rumsey (Averell's sister) and other New York socialites, the League, as of the early 1960's, had about 78,000 members in chapters in over 180 American cities. It is not as exclusive as many upper-class organizations, and has been one of the most important in co-opting the wives of the small-city aristocrats and of the successful corporation executives. One of the League's best features is the national structure, for its transferable membership is an important social entree into the new community for the wife of the oft-transferred organization man. In many cities hospital boards serve a similar function.[21]

The attainment of upper-class status is perhaps slightly less painful and self-conscious for the children of the newly arrived rich. Most important, the child is sent to a private school. To be able to afford this is "proof," so to speak, to the hereditary members of the upper class that the upstart has arrived financially, for private schooling is a very expensive proposition. Tuition is often only the beginning; travel expense, room and board, and, occasionally, sheltering a horse can raise the cost as high as $3000 to $5000 per year. Then too, being admitted to a private school often "proves" that one is "well connected," for it sometimes takes recommendations from alumni and friends of the school to be admitted. Attendance at one of the exclusive private schools automatically guarantees that the child will mingle with upper-class children. For one thing, his name is on the school's enrollment list, which will be circumspectly revealed to the nearby private schools for the opposite sex, as well as to social secretaries and dancing classes. This results in invitations to the schools' social functions, to

20 Baltzell, *Philadelphia Gentlemen*, p. 379.

21 J. W. Moore, "Exclusiveness and Ethnocentrism in a Metropolitan Upper Class Agency." *Pacific Sociological Review*, 5 (1962), pp. 16-20.

dancing classes, and to debutante parties. At the school itself the child learns upper-class values, upper-class manners, and most of all upper-class speech, one of the most telltale signs of class and regional origin. From private school attendance it is but a short hop to the debutante parties and social gatherings of school acquaintances; the result is usually intermarriage into the hereditary upper class.[22]

Sweezy, in discussing social classes, states that they have an identifiable core but very vague boundaries. At the fringes, says Sweezy, social classes seem to flow into each other.[23] While this is true at the lower levels of society, leading some social scientist to abandon the rigid-sounding concept of "class" for more permeable-sounding terms such as "social groups," "status groups," or "social strata," it can be seen that social secretaries, clubs, leagues, private schools, and similar institutions give a surprising definiteness to the upper class.[24] It takes a considerable amount of money even to knock on the door of the co-opting institutions, the right contacts to gain entrance, and certain amount of training to gain certification. Once inside the castle there are many rooms, but that should not over-shadow the formidable nature of its moated entrance.

17 *Lucy Kavaler*

THE INTERNATIONAL SET AND CAFÉ SOCIETY

Ask the man in the street to name members of high society. Chances are that he will come right back with the names of those prominent in the international set and cafe society. To the unsophisticated that is what society is.

The reason is not hard to understand. These are the people whose names appear regularly in society columns all over the country.

[22] On tuition, expenses, and sheltering a horse, see Lucy Kavaler, *The Private World of High Society* (New York: David McKay, 1960); on the right connections, see *Time*, July 30, 1965, p. 41; and on the style inculcated at these schools, see Kavaler, 1960, and Brackman, "The gospel according to St. Paul's."

[23] Sweezy, 1953, p. 124.

[24] See Roger Brown's *Social Psychology* (New York: The Free Press, 1966), for an excellent chapter on social class which abandons the concept.

The columnists are not altogether happy about this state of affairs. There is nothing they would rather do than write about old-line society exclusively. Unfortunately, the inner circle does not do enough that is news producing. Members entertain at home, and sometimes even divorce is secret. And so the columnists have been forced to turn to the more flamboyant doings of the international set and café society.

Although the two groups overlap to a certain extent, they are not on a par in terms of prestige. The international set ranks much higher.

Its highly publicized parties, sun-drenched resorting, and lavish expenditure of money are so ostentatious as to appear low class. But the set does include so many bona-fide socialites that it cannot be written off as *nouveau riche* and nothing more. Many heirs to great fortunes do not need to earn a living and can spend their lives in seeking pleasure. They lend the influence of their great names to this group and so attract some hard-working self-made men and women and a number of celebrities.

Who is in the international set? I find it dominated by the figures of the Duke and Duchess of Windsor, Colonel Serge Obolensky, Princess Grace of Monaco, Elsa Maxwell, and the Greek shipowners, Aristotle Onassis, Basil Goulandris, and Stavros Niarchos. Royalty, even minor royalty, is in no danger of being dethroned. There is also a mixture of old and new society, including Margaret (Peggy) Bancroft, the Winston Guests, the Henry Ford II's, the William Paleys, the Henry Luces, Mrs. George F. Baker, the Cornelius V. Whitneys, the Herbert Scheftels, John Mortimer Schiff, and Angier Biddle Duke.

The group is relatively easy to break into. Socialites are welcomed with open arms. Others only need to have money—lots and lots of it. One magazine recently estimated an annual income of at least $100,000 after taxes as the bare minimum. To many in this set that would be living in a very sparse way indeed.

Lady Norah Docker, for example, shows up on the Riviera in a gold Daimler upholstered in leopard skin. I have never been on Mr. Onassis' fabled yacht, the *Christina*, but those who have report that an El Greco hangs in the master bedroom. There are eight guestrooms, each with its own marble bathroom with gold fittings. A mosaic dance floor can be lowered to become a swimming pool. Then there is the White Russian who recently built a villa on the Riviera and felt that the floor simply had to be of pure white marble. His bill for the villa? Estimates hover near the $500,000 mark.

At the Corviglia Ski Club at St. Moritz, the crowd that gathers on the terrace after lunch still likes to remember the exploit of a young heir to a mining and oil fortune. He won a $1,000 bet at a party by climbing up and down a pyramid made of six tables and a chair without spilling a drop from the brimming champagne glass held in one hand.

The international set meets at resorts on a rigid time schedule. In winter it alternates between St. Moritz and Nassau. February is the height of the St. Moritz season—and the Corviglia Ski Club is the place to meet. Some of the group's best-known party-givers—among them Messrs. Onassis and Niarchos—usually stay at the Palace Hotel.

This has given rise to the international set wisecrack: "It's the Greek Grossinger's."

The real Grossinger's in case anyone has missed the publicity, is a lively, celebrity-packed resort right outside New York City.

A somewhat quieter group goes to Gstaad to the Winter Palace Hotel. Others travel to Schloss Mittersill in the Austrian Alps near Kitzbuhel. And La Colmiane in the French Alps north of Monaco also attracts a fashionable crowd.

Nassau is the other favored winter spot.

"British nobility is a tremendous draw for the international set," a keen-eyed vacationer observes.

Many members of this group own cottages at the exclusive club resorts. Others stay nearby at hotels or clubs. A favorite is the Coral Harbour Club at the tip of New Providence. Only a hundred guests may stay there, and admission is by invitation.

The United States itself is permissible resort country. Many spend at least a little time each year in Palm Beach, Colorado Springs, and White Sulphur Springs. As is the way with this group, a number of Palm Beach aficionados were shaken when the Duke and Duchess of Windsor passed it up one season and went to Tucson instead.

Some follow the racing calendar, traveling around the United States, to London, to Paris, and to Ireland, wherever the horses are running.

"It is the thing to alternate between London and Paris in June," a member of the set told me. "The most *wonderful* parties are given in Paris!"

In July the move is on to the Riviera. Many time their arrivals so as not to miss the opening gala of the International Summer Sporting Club at Monte Carlo. Mr. Onassis is in his element as a party-giver on the Riviera.

Key members of the set have villas and/or yachts of their own. Those who have not yet achieved villa rank go to the Carlton in Cannes, the Hôtel du Cap in Cap d'Antibes, or the Hôtel de Paris in Monte Carlo. Much of their time, to be sure is spent on board the yachts of their friends.

In August they pack up again and move on to Rome and Venice. Italy is the scene of some of the most lavish—and at times scandal producing—parties.

When the set returns to America, members meet again at balls to aid exiled White Russians and Hungarian victims of oppression and at benefits for charities in France, Italy, and Greece.

The parties and resorting are carried out on such a lavish scale that they overshadow many other activities of the international set. Some of the major art collectors of today belong to this group. Mr. Goulandris, for example, spent $297,000 for Gaugin's *Still Life with Oranges*. Mr. Niarchos recently lent his art collection to the Knoedler Art Galleries in New York for a showing. Included were the works of Van Gogh, Degas, Toulouse-Lautrec, and many other noted artists.

Somehow the art collecting, business activities, and old-line family connections do not counterbalance the general impression. The public views these people as playboys on a world scale. They are frequently confused with café society.

I find that nothing angers members of the international set more.

"Why, *anyone* can belong to café society," they say scornfully.

And they are quite right. It does not even take a lot of money. Members are not required to maintain luxurious homes in New York, Venice, and the Riviera. They do not need to travel to St. Moritz, Palm Beach, and Monte Carlo in season. The women are not expected to wear "name" jewels and designer clothes–although it helps if they do. And café socialites do not pay off social obligations by giving frequent parties for several hundred people with dash. All that is needed is enough money to go night clubbing several times a week.

Today even that requirement can be circumvented. Businessmen and their wives often go the café circuit on one another's expense accounts.

As for a girl, she does not need to have any money of her own. She simply has to be attractive enough to get a date with a man who can afford to take her night clubbing. No one but the most innocent is surprised to find former models, manicurists, hat-check girls, receptionists, chorus girls, and waitresses bearing some of society's biggest names. How did they meet the scions of the old families? It often happened in the cafés.

Café Society is no longer society at all. But members are apt to be a little wistful about this, remembering the days when it consisted of the younger high society set. Old-timers tell me that it was started before World War I by an inner-circle group influenced by dancers Irene and Vernon Castle. Bored by the staid social lives of their parents, they slipped off to the clubs to dance the turkey trot, bunny hug, and Castle Walk. The term "café society" was coined in those halcyon days by Maury Paul, the original Cholly Knickerbocker.

Society stayed in the cafés right through the 1930's. But since then it has become déclassé. I found a study done in 1937 by *Fortune* magazine. It pointed out that about one-third of café society members were not in the *Social Register*. By today it would be the height of exaggeration to say that one third of its members are *in* the *Register*.

Those who still go to the clubs are attracted by the presence there of celebrities of the movies, television, the stage, and sports. Many of these well-known personalities have infiltrated the cafés in order to gain publicity and to hobnob with socialites.

"Society rings the cowbell that attracts celebrities to a restaurant or club," Marianne Strong, the press agent for the Stork Club, tells me.

Conversely, the presence of theatrical personalities brings in socialites. It also is a magnet for out-of-towners, couples on dates, and businessmen on expense accounts.

The press agents of the top clubs are so well aware of the attracting powers of socialites and celebrities that they make every effort to ensnare key members, Yetta Golove, public-relations woman for the Harwyn, told me. They go through the *Social Register* sending out post cards to families who might go to late night spots. The debutante lists published in the newpapers are also carefully studied and selected names are used in mailings. Cards are sent to stage and screen celebrities, urging their patronage.

This practice is a continuous one. As new names appear on any of the lists, they are considered. And the others get reminders. Post cards go out regularly, bearing a message that there is dancing at the club, or that it is open until the wee hours.

"It doesn't matter what the cards say," declares Miss Golove. "Their purpose is to remind people of your existence."

Everyone wants to be near celebrities. When Princess Grace and Prince Rainier were in New York, they visited the Harwyn. For months afterward, Miss Golove reports, the table post cards filled out by guests and mailed by the club contain such statements as: "I am sitting right next to Princess Grace." They ignore the sad fact that by then Princess Grace is thousands of miles away in Monaco. The folks back home will not know that anyway.

The old axiom that position is everything in life applies to café society. The position, of course, is that of the table assigned by the all-powerful headwaiter.

"I always know where to look for the celebrities and big society people," one night-club habitiué said to me. "They are always placed at certain tables."

I am often told an anecdote about a well-known socialite, who once refused to let a friend bring along an extra luncheon guest. The presence of an additional person would have meant that she could not be given her regular table and she would have lost face. (The name of the lady involved changes from time to time, by the way; the story, however, does not.)

Location is taken with such seriousness that I observe that society's magazine *The Diplomat* had to run a report on just where the best tables are. This is what they found: At the Twenty-One Club, the best upstairs tables are those in the foyer at the top of the stairs. The banquettes along the walls of the first room are ranked in descending order from Table One on the right as one enters. Anyone put in the little rooms to the left or in the third room simply does not rate at all. Downstairs, the favored spots are in the front room: the two tables against the left wall and the first one on the right. The nearest right-hand table is known as "Benchley's corner," in honor of the late Robert Benchley, one of its most famous and regular habitués.

At Le Pavillon the best tables are in the busy foyer leading into the main room. Those placed in the barroom or the back of the room have no social distinction at all. The personal attention of owner Henri Soule is considered the final seal of approval.

At El Morocco the key location is the first table on the right by the headwaiter's desk. The banquettes along the right-hand wall are also good. Personal friends of owner John Perona are seated at his big round table. Those on the far side of the dance floor might as well not be there at all, in terms of prestige.

At the Colony restaurant any of the tables at the front of the room are good, with the banquettes on the right especially favored. At the Stork Club any table at all in the Club Room will do. Those in the know look at Table Fifty in the first corner or at the tables near the door.

The rulers of café society are the society columnists. All they need to do is mention a person often enough—and, lo, he becomes a member of the set.

Igor Cassini is the current Cholly Knickerbocker, the name that has come to symbolize the society columnist. His influence is augmented by the fact that once a year he runs a list of New York debutantes. A succession of talented reporters have helped him to gather the news for his column. Mary Elizabeth (Liz) Smith is his current assistant.

Charles Ventura has a wide readership, although he tends to neglect the cafés a bit in favor of the international and resort set. In recent months "Society Today," the New York *World Telegram and Sun's* column by Knickerbocker-graduate Joseph X. Dever and Charles Van Rennselaer, has been winning advocates. Socialites say that it is "surprisingly" accurate. (The choice of the quoted word is theirs.) Another well-known column is Nancy Randolph's "Chic Chat" in the New York *Daily News*. "Suzy," the New York *Mirror's* society column, is now done by Aileen Mehle.

It is the thing for old-line society to look down on the columnists and assert that they are "wrong . . . wrong . . . wrong." But I was quite unable to find one who did not read them avidly. Knickerbocker has the widest readership among this group.

"The problem of writing a daily column has created vast numbers of members for café society," a former columnist reveals.

Nobody knows the trouble the columnist has in filling the space allotted to him—nobody knows, but the press agent, that is. To get some idea of how easy it is for a publicist to have a client mentioned, here is an item recently placed in one of the leading columns: A popular debutante had been wearing her hair shoulder length. She cut it off short. Her mother disapproved. But her boy friend, a well-known (to column readers) playboy, liked it.

And a popular story when press agents get together is about the days when the activities of oil man Roy Crocker and railroad tycoon Tony Lamb were followed by all the columnists. The wild oats being sown by Lamb's daughter, Angela, were described in columns for months. Need I add that Crocker and Lamb were simply creations of a press agent's vivid imagination? Their function was to provide column mentions for the restaurants and night clubs he was handling.

The columnists themselves regularly visit El Morocco, the Stork Club, and others, trying to pick up news. The captains and maîtres d'hôtel are primary sources of information. They hear all, and usually tell all. If a socialite or celebrity is in one of these clubs incognito—possibly wearing a black wig, which is a popular maneuver nowadays—a captain's keen eye will almost surely spot her. News about engagements or their opposites, divorces, are often leaked from the moment of decision.

Almost anyone who really does spend time in the clubs will eventually be rewarded with a mention, then a line, and then an anecdote in the columns. At that point he has his membership badge in the club.

Café society is basically a New York product, but I find that it does exist to a certain extent in any city big enough to have a supper club or even a hotel with room for dining and dancing. Wherever there are celebrities, this type of social life will appear. Personalities have to go somewhere to be seen and photographed. California, with its movie colony, therefore, has, if anything, a more active night life than New York.

But even in cities where supper clubs are unimportant or nonexistent, there is a group that occupies the same social position as the café set in New York. In some parts of the West it has come to be called "barbecue society," and is made up of people rich enough to give lavish parties. This group has money but has won no entree into society.

Joining in café society is sometimes mistakenly believed to be a way to break into real society. This can happen only to girls–and not very often. A young woman can use the opportunity to meet and ultimately marry a scion of an old family. She can even be made into a glamour debutante (not to be confused with the debutante daughters of the inner circle). But the road to the Junior Assemblies and the *Social Register* in most cases detours around the Stork or El Morocco.

Café society is a way of life. Those in it enjoy it for the pleasure of the moment and the publicity of tomorrow–not for the hope of social advancement.

CHAPTER 6

STATUS SYMBOLS, PRESTIGE, AND LIFE-STYLE

The most readily discernible aspect of social stratification is related to symbols of status and prestige. To imagine the existence of a status difference without reference to some kind of symbolic representation of it is difficult. The prestige, honor, and deference that characterize many social relationships are manifested in symbolic form. Initial claims for status are made by the presentation or display of status symbols. These symbols are found in an infinite variety of forms. Status is not only expressed and claimed through nonobjective symbols, such as credentials, occupational labels, titles, and family names, but many consumer goods can symbolize status, as well.

Barber has pointed out that material objects can be viewed as having one or more of the following functions: (1) a utilitarian function, (2) an aesthetic function, and (3) a symbolic function.[1] For example, to some people a Cadillac may fulfill all three functions; a diamond ring or an original painting may have only the latter two; a diploma may possess only the third. Relatively few consumer goods, except very basic foods and certain personal objects (tooth brushes and the like), are exempt from having some kind of symbolic function.

[1] Bernard Barber, *Social Stratification* (New York: Harcourt Brace Jovanovich, 1957), p. 136.

The general affluence, plethora of consumer goods, and diversity of occupational and status communities have resulted in the creation of a vast array of status indicators. These range from nonmaterial behavior patterns and verbal symbols to a great variety of material goods. Speech patterns, manners, and etiquette, as well as titles, family trees, exclusive group memberships, publically bestowed honors, and other verbal distinctions are part of the nonmaterial status structure of modern society. Material symbols are varied; some are found only in homes and in private or semi-private life, such as traditional family objects of veneration, heirlooms of precious metals or stones, furniture, medals, weapons, dogs, objects of art, exclusive summer homes, town houses, or Greek islands. Other status symbols serve primarily in one's occupational setting or other more public areas of life, such as the set of telephones and desk pens that connote status in the Federal bureaucracy, the black Cadillacs of the diplomats, and the executive washrooms, carpeted offices, and jet aircraft of the business executives. In the intellectual, artistic, and entertainment world the public symbols of the published book or article, the motion picture, the painting or sculpture, and the phonograph record are objects that can provide status to their producers. In addition, the sandals and long hair of the hippie as well as the "go to meeting" clothes of the poor hillbilly are symbols of status.

In an urban industrial society with a great variety of occupations resulting from division of labor and specialization of function, and the resulting different styles of life, there is great ambiguity in the assignment and claiming of status. Ambiguity in status arrangements promotes an increased use of status symbols. Status instability in a society will create status insecurities, which, in turn, foster an increased use of status symbols. [2]

That the acquisition and deliberate use of status symbols is closely associated with status striving has often been assumed. If one considers the conceptual relation between status symbols, life style, and status community, the use of status symbols and status striving as two separate, though closely related, phenomena of complex stratification systems seems apparent. Status striving varies by life style. Different status communities create differential levels of status anxiety, which, in turn, create differential degrees of striving. Persons who are overly sensitive to status and allocate a large proportion of their resources to the acquisition and display of status symbols are most likely to be either members of status communities in which status anxiety occurs, or cross-pressured individuals who experience inconsistency between class and status.[3] For example, persons with a low status ethnic identity may have relatively high incomes. A case in point would be an immigrant from southern Europe who is also a millionaire businessman. Such an inconsistency between income and ethnic status may lead to status insecurity and hence susceptibility to increased symbol

[2] Hans H. Gerth and C. Wright Mills, *Character and Social Structure: The Psychology of Social Institutions* (New York: Harcourt Brace Jovanovich, 1953), pp. 315-321.

[3] A given status community may consist of a predominance of cross-pressured individuals.

acquisition and display. Therefore any situation leading to an ambiguous status tends to promote a concern for certain symbols of status.

This concern and insecurity along with the specialization of function has led to the development of an interesting phenomena in connection with status symbol manipulation. E. Goffman points to the emergence of "curator groups" that facilitate symbol manipulation.[4] He states that occupational groups such as fashion experts, models, interior decorators, architects and hairdressers function to develop and service the "machinery of status." Their job is to produce and manipulate status symbols with the intent of maximizing the status of their customers. Goffman refers to this as "an institutionalized source of misrepresentation, false expectations, and dissensus."[5]

Although the manipulation of status symbols is an integral part of most status systems, some symbolic aspects of status are difficult to manipulate. Distinctions in the sphere of language, elaborate manners, and etiquette usually necessitate long training and tend to be quite durable after they are acquired. Shaw's *Pygmalion*, or its latter day musical version, *My Fair Lady*, illustrates the difficulty and the possibility of altering behavior and speech patterns in the hope of achieving a gain in status. Though in most parts of the world one's manner of speaking is clearly indicative of social status, few *readily apparent* dialect distinctions in the United States can be used to identify status levels. There is, however, evidence that differential linguistic behavior in the use of abstractions, multiple frames of reference, and organized description vary by status and class.

Although the rhetoric categorizing Americans as "status seekers" is popular and seems to express an obvious truism for the critically inclined, it is probably an oversimplification. Status striving is a response to status anxiety, which varies from one status community to the next. The most prevalent use of status symbols is as a means of demonstrating identity with one's peers or social equals. That is, symbols may serve a predominant function in "keeping *even* with the Jones'," rather than in getting ahead of the Jones'. Riesman refers to the "standard package" of consumer goods that determines the criteria of need (for consumer goods) among average Americans.[6] The acquisition of the standard package is a major objective and once it is met, striving, as revealed by new and ever more expensive consumer goods may, in fact, decline. At present, the empirical evidence needed to affirm either description of *homo americanus* is not available.

[4] Erving Goffman, "Symbolic of Class Status," *British Journal of Sociology* 2 (1951), p. 303.

[5] Ibid.

[6] David Riesman, *Abundance for What? And Other Essays* (Garden City) N.Y.: Doubleday, 1964, pp. 111-148.

18 *Hans H. Gerth and C. Wright Mills*

THE STATUS SPHERE

Prestige involves at least two persons: one to claim it and another to *honor* the claim. The bases on which various people raise prestige claims, and the reasons others honor these claims, include property and descent, occupation and education, income and power—in fact, almost anything that may invidiously distinguish one person from another. In the status system of a society these claims are organized as rules and expectations governing those who successfully claim prestige, from whom, in what ways, and on what basis. The level of self-esteem enjoyed by given individuals is more or less set by this status system.

There are, thus, six items to which we must pay attention: From the claimant's side: (1) the status claim, (2) the way in which this claim is raised or expressed, (3) the basis on which the claim is raised. And correspondingly from the bestower's side: (4) the status bestowal or deference given, (5) the way in which these deferences are given, (6) the basis of the bestowal, which may or may not be the same as the basis on which the claim is raised. An extraordinary range of social phenomena are pointed to by these terms.

Claims for prestige are expressed in all those mannerisms, conventions, and ways of consumption that make up the styles of life characterizing people on various status levels. The "things that are done" and the "things that just aren't done" are the status conventions of different strata. Members of higher status groups may dress in distinct ways, follow "fashions" in varying tempi and regularities, eat and drink at special times and exclusive places in select society. In varying degrees, they value the elegant appearance and specific modes of address, have dinner together, and are glad to see their sons and daughters intermarry. From the point of view of status, the funeral, as a ritual procession, is an indication of prestige, as is the tombstone, the greeting card, the seating plan at dinner or the opera. "Society" in American cities, debutante systems, the management of philanthropic activities, the social register and the *Almanach de Gotha*—noble titles and heraldic emblems—reflect and often control the status activities of upper circles, where exclusiveness, distance, coldness, condescending benevolence towards outsiders often prevail.

Head roles in any institution may be the basis of status claims, and any order may become the social area in which these claims are realized. We can conceive of a society in which status rests upon economic class position and in which the economic order is dominant in such a way that status claims based on economic class are successfully raised in every order. But we can also imagine a society in which status is anchored in the military order, so that the person's role in that order determines his chance successfully to realize status claims in all, or at least in most, of the other orders. Thus the military role may be a prerequisite to honorific status in other publicly significant roles.

Of course, men usually enact roles in several orders and hence their general position rests on the combinations of roles they enact.

Claims for prestige and the bestowal of prestige are often based on birth into given types of kinship institutions. The Negro child, irrespective of individual "achievement," will not receive the deference which the white child may successfully claim. The immigrant, especially a member of a recent mass immigration, will not be as likely to receive the deference given the "Old American," immigrant groups and families being generally stratified according to how long they and their forebears have been in America. Among the native-born white of native parentage, certain "Old Families" receive more deference than do other families. In each case–race, nationality, and family–prestige is based on, or at least limited by, descent, which is perhaps most obviously a basis of prestige at the top and the bottom of the social ladder. European royalty and rigidly excluded racial minorities represent the zenith and nadir of status by birth.

Upper-class position typically carries great prestige, all the more so if the source of money is property. Yet, even if the possession of wealth in modern industrial societies leads to increased prestige, rich men who are fresh from lower-class levels may experience difficulty in "buying their way" into upper-status circles. In the southern states, in fact, impoverished descendants of once high-level old families receive more deference from more people than do wealthy men who lack appropriate grandparents. The kinship may thus overshadow the economic order. The facts of the *nouveau riche* (high class without high prestige) and of the broken-down aristocrat (high prestige without high class) refute the complete identification of upper-prestige and upper-class position, even though, in the course of time, the broken-down aristocrat becomes simply broken-down, and the son of the *nouveau riche* becomes a man of "clean, old wealth."

The possession of wealth also allows the purchase of an environment which in due course will lead to the development of these "intrinsic" qualities in individuals and in families that are required for higher prestige. When we say that American prestige has been fluid, one thing we mean is that high economic-class position has led rather quickly to high prestige, and that kinship descent has not been of equal importance to economic position. A feudal aristocracy, based on old property and long descent, has not existed here. Veblen's theory[1] was focused primarily upon the post-Civil War period in the United States and the expressions of prestige claims raised in lavish consumption by the *nouveau riche* of railroads, steel, and pork. In a democratic society equipped with mass media we are not surprised to find that many images of upper-status types are diffused. It is also well known that in contrast with feudal elites the American upper

[1] See Thorstein Veblen, *The Theory of the Leisure Class* (New York: Viking, 1924).

classes have not shied from publicity. Society columns and obituary pages chronicle the activities and connections of conspicuous members of the high-status groups.

The prestige of the middle strata in America is based on many other principles than descent and property. The shift to a society of employees has made *occupation* and the *educational* sphere crucially important. Insofar as occupation determines the level of income, and different styles of life require different income levels, occupation limits the style of life. In a more direct way, different occupations require different levels and types of education, and education also limits the style of life and thus the status successfully claimed.

Some occupations are reserved for members of upper-status levels, others are "beneath their honor." In some societies, in fact, having no work to do brings the highest prestige; prestige being an aspect of property class, the female dependents of high class husbands becoming specialists in the display of expensive idleness. But only when those who do not need to work have more income than those who must, is idleness likely to yield prestige. When work is necessary but not available, "leisure" means unemployment, which may bring disgrace. And income from property does not always entail more prestige than income from work; the amount and the ways the income is used may be more important than its source. Thus the small *rentier* does not enjoy an esteem equal to that of a high-paid doctor. Status attaches to the *terms* for income, to its source and timing of payment. Socially the same number of dollars may mean different things when they are received as "rent" or "interest," as "royalties" or "fees," as "stipends" or "salaries," as "wages" or as "insurance benefits." Men striving for status may prefer smaller salaries to higher wages, meager royalties to substantial profits, an honorific stipend to a large bonus.

Among the employed those occupations which pay more, and which presumably involve more mental activities and entail power to supervise others, seem to place people on higher prestige levels. But sheer power does not always lend prestige: the political boss renounces public prestige—except among his machine members—for power; constitutional monarchs, on the other hand, retain and possibly gain public prestige but lose political power. In offices and factories, skilled foremen and office supervisors expect and typically receive an esteem which lifts them above unskilled workers and typists. But the policeman's power to direct street masses does not bring prestige, except among badly frightened drivers and little boys.

The type of education, as well as the amount, is an important basis of prestige; "finishing" schools and "prep" schools turn out ladies and gentlmen fit to represent their class by styles of life which, in some circles, guarantee deference. In other circles the amount of intellectual skill acquired through education is a key point for estimation. Yet skill alone is not as uniform a basis for prestige as is skill connected with highly esteemed occupations.

All the variables which underpin status—descent, skill (on the basis of education and/or experience), biological age, seniority (of residence, of membership in associations), sex, beauty, wealth, and authority—may be quite variously combined and usually in typical ways. These combinations may be and often are quite intricate. For example, the cross-tabulation of descent, wealth, and skill alone logically yields the following types: where wealth and high birth is combined with skill we may find, for example, the experienced statesmanship of a Churchill; but where there is wealth and high birth but no skill, perhaps a publicized heiress, or an hereditary successor to the throne. The self-made man of the nineteenth century in the United States had wealth and skill but low birth; the ignorant black woman who suddenly wins the sweepstakes, has wealth, but low birth and no skill.

Sir Walter Scott, a heavily indebted nobleman who did well as a writer, had no wealth but both high birth and high skill. And famous artists, such as Beethoven, or famous scholars such as Albert Einstein, do not have wealth or high birth, but excel in skill. The Russian refugee nobleman who becomes a waiter in a Paris hotel lacks both wealth and skill although he has high birth. Finally, the Jewish Luftmensch,[2] the hobo, the tramp, or the black farmhand have no wealth, no birth status, and no skill.

Such a panorama may serve to indicate the manner in which one raises questions and classifies observations about the status sphere of given social structures.

We cannot take for granted that to claim prestige is automatically to receive it. Status conduct is not so harmonious. The status claimant may in the eyes of others "overstate" his "true" worth, may be considered "conceited." If he understates it, he may be considered "diffident" or "humble." The conceited status claimant may of course receive the deference he claims, but it is likely to be "spurious deference" for "spurious claims." His conceit in fact, is often strengthened by flattery, sometimes to the point of megalomania, as with despots in a context of priestly or courtier byzantinism or organized mass adulation.

In cases of mistaken judgment people may give genuine deference on the basis of spurious or pretended claims; there are the false Messiahs, the false prophets, the false princes, and the professional charlatans.[3]

Spurious deference for misconstrued claims may be illustrated by referring to the mock coronation of Christ as "the King of the Jews" with the crown of thorns. Genuine respect for genuine claims needs no particular elaboration.

False humility is often transparent as a technique for eliciting deference. We call it "fishing." The bid for good will, with which speakers often open their talks, is often no more than thinly veiled flattery of the audience. Once upon a time kings were flattered; today more often "the people" are. To be sure, such flattery of the people goes hand in hand with open disdain for the European

[2] A man without an occupation, formerly found among Eastern European Jews.

[3] On professional charlatans, see Grete de Francesco, *The Power of the Charlatan* (New Haven: Yale Univ. Press, 1939).

"masses" or the American "suckers." Hitler proved highly successful in allocating to German Gentiles the rhetorical certificate of presumably high birth and ancestral background by calling them each and every one "Nordics."

Thus the extent to which claims for prestige are honored, and by whom they are honored, varies widely. Some of those from whom an individual claims prestige may honor his claims, others may not; some deferences that are given may express genuine feelings of esteem; others may be expedient strategies for ulterior ends. A society may, in fact, contain many hierarchies of prestige, each with its own typical bases and areas of bestowal; or one hierarchy in which everyone uniformly "knows his place" and is always in it. It is in the latter that prestige groups are most likely to be uniform and continuous.

Imagine a society in which everyone's prestige is clearly set and stable; every man's claims for prestige are balanced by the deference he receives, and both his expression of claims and the ways these claims are honored by others are set forth in understood stereotypes. Moreover, the bases of the claims coincide with the reasons they are honored; those who claim prestige on the specific basis of property or birth are honored because of their property or birth. So the exact volume and types of deference expected between any two individuals are always known, expected, and given; and each individual's level and type of self-esteem are steady features of his inner life.

Now imagine the opposite society, in which prestige is highly unstable and ambivalent: the individual's claims are not usually honored by others. The ways in which claims are expressed are not understood or acknowledged by those from whom deference is expected, and when others do bestow prestige, they do so unclearly. One man claims prestige on the basis of his income, but even if he is given prestige it is not because of his income but rather, for example, because of his education and appearance. All the controlling devices by which the volume and type of deference might be directed are out of joint or simply do not exist. So the prestige system is no system but a maze of misunderstanding, of sudden frustration and sudden indulgence, and the individual, as his self-esteem fluctuates, is under strain and full of anxiety.

American society in the middle of the twentieth century does not fit either of these projections absolutely, but it seems fairly clear that it is closer to the unstable and ambivalent model. This is not to say that there is no prestige system in the United States; given occupational groupings, even though caught in status ambivalence, do enjoy typical levels of prestige. It is to say, however, that the enjoyment of prestige is often disturbed and uneasy, that the bases of prestige, the expressions of prestige claims, and the ways these claims are honored are now subject to great strain, a strain which often throws ambitious men and women into a virtual status panic.

19 *David Riesman*

CAREERS AND COMSUMER BEHAVIOR

(with Howard Roseborough)

In the summer of 1954, the Kroger Food Foundation made an experiment. They turned several dozen preteen boys and girls loose in a supermarket, telling them they could have twenty items free, without any limits on what they chose. (According to the sponsors, the idea was based on the rather fantastic suggestion of a "world's fair for children" in *The Lonely Crowd* [David Riesman, *The Lonely Crowd: A Study of the Changing American Character*, with Nathan Glazer and Reuel Denney. (New Haven: Yale University Press, 1950)] a proposal as to how consumer free choice might be developed.) Recorders, human and mechanical, observed the proceedings and a group of social scientists are now examining the results. What was immediately evident, however, was that the children, in addition to picking up watermelon and pop for immediate consumption, filled their carts with the very sorts of things their mothers might have taken, such as sacks of flour and meats and vegetables. They did not select—perhaps in that setting they did not feel quite entitled to—the cameras and other toys which the supermarket, as a one-floor department store, carries in addition to groceries, nor did they pick as much candy and ice cream as had been predicted.[1] It would seem as if anticipatory socialization[2] had occurred, in which these children had been trained, at home and by the media (perhaps at school, too, in the "junior home economics" of a book like *Let's Go Shopping*), to view themselves as prospective householders and to take an adult role. (We don't mean to imply that this socialization was the result of deliberate parental or societal decision—many of the parents would no doubt have been surprised to see how "well" the children behaved when on their away-from-home good behavior.)

At the same time, it may be likely that the parents of these children were involved in what we might term "retroactive socialization," in that meals reflected children's tastes as influenced by the media and each other, with break-

[1] Boys bought slightly fewer, but more expensive, items than girls—a sign perhaps of the future "male" shopper, extravagant but narrow, as if over-detailed or sparing purchasing of household items were "women's work." Boys, of course, would be less likely than girls to identify with their mothers in the role of shopper.

[2] This concept owes much to Robert K. Merton's formulations; cf. his article with Alice S. Kitt, "Contributions to the Theory of Reference-Group Behavior," in R. K. Merton and Paul F. Lazarsfeld (eds.), *Continuities in Social Research: Studies in the Scope and Method of "The American Soldier"* (New York: The Free Press, 1950), pp. 87-89. We may think of anticipatory socialization as a kind of psychological hope-and-fear chest the individual accumulates as he imaginatively transcends his membership group.

fast cereals or Coca-Cola serving both age groups (much as many comic books do). For today, it is our belief, a general lowering of barriers is going on: between the age grades, between the sexes, between regions of the country, and between social classes, with the prospect in view of a fairly uniform middle-majority life-style becoming a major American theme with variations.

The *theme*, a set of goods and services including such household items as furniture, radios, television, refrigerator, and standard brands in food and clothing, shows a considerable uniformity throughout American society: it encompasses the (steadily rising) national standard of living. Some seek to level up to it, and some level down, with the result that quality differences are minor, and expense-concealing rather than class-revealing. The *variations* include both embroideries and elaborations on this standard package and, more importantly, the setting given this package by the home and neighborhood; the neighborhood in turn involves such class-bound services as schools, churches, clubs, and civic amenities. While possession of the standard package, the theme items, carries membership in the broad band of the American middle class, the variations identify one as the possessor of a specific life style, localized by region, subclass, ethnic group, and occupation. Social mobility in America is made easier by the ability of the family, through minor variations (in terms of expense and complexity), to adapt the standard package to a new peer group—much as one can buy parts that will make one's Ford look much like a Mercury.

In childhood and adolescence, one builds the standard package into one's anticipations, and the young married couple will expedite its acquisition—at first, or ordinarily, in an apartment. But by young adulthood anticipation begins to assume, at least in the white-collar strata, a more specific form, for the husband's occupational peers and superiors, and to a lesser extent the wife's neighbors and friends, provide models for what the family's style will be at the peak of the husband's career; it is here, of course, that variations enter. Meanwhile, as the husband advances in his career and as children arrive, the package will be moved, probably geographically, possibly socially, nearer to the community that symbolizes his final occupational status. As we shall see, this destiny is compressed for the skilled worker; it may be protracted until late middle age for the corporate vice-president. Even so, parts of the "dwelling complex"—the schools, clubs, cars, plus inconspicuous elaborations of the standard package—will be acquired in anticipation of the career peak.

This is not the only cycle for consumer behavior: we propose the hypothesis that it is increasingly typical. There are, of course, many Americans even today who have made money faster than they could possibly anticipate; their resocialization does not begin until after they are rich, and often it is painful.[3] Others have their anticipations so structured by their subculture as virtually to eliminate

[3] Some political consequences of this painfulness are suggested in D. Riesman and N. Glazer, "The Intellectuals and the Discontended Class," *Partisan Review*, 22 (January-February, 1955), pp. 47-72; also in *The Radical Right* (New York; Doubleday, 1963).

discontinuities and discretionary areas; for an example, we can refer to a study, which is in some ways the antithesis to the Kroger experiment, by the social psychologist Manford Kuhn.

Kuhn asked a group of Amish and of matched non-Amish children in Iowa what gifts they would most want to have. The "American" children wanted toys: dolls, electric trains, and so on (these being things, of course, their parents expect them to want). The Amish children, rigorously brought up on first-class farms and, save for baseball, not allowed to share in the general youth culture, wanted such things as a team and wagon, an oven, a tractor. Though eleven or twelve years old, they already saw themselves as grownups; indeed, only by anticipatory socialization that deprived them of what many Americans would consider a normal childhood, could the Amish youngsters be kept "to home," safe from the seductions of the urban and secular world. Moreover, for them as for their parents, useful producers' goods such as handsome tractors and barns moderated the consumption asceticism of the sect, and permitted reward of the faithful in fine equipment useful if not essential in agricultural success. Indeed, only in a rural area can children enjoy and use adult equipment in quite this way, in which increasing access to the world of work becomes, like Tom Sawyer's fence, a kind of eventful fair whose pleasures only pall with time; but by then the Amish are mostly hooked, unprepared in tertiary skill or in energizing consumer passions to enter the middle-majority market. They are ready in turn to become unyielding Amish parents, relatively unaffected by retroactive socialization and hence compelling their children to imitate them unequivocally; the age-grade barriers remain firm, and the children, short of occasional instances of revolt, must accept the adult world on adult terms.

The Amish are, we suggest, an exception to many of the generalizations one might develop about the careers of Americans as consumers. But before we leave them aside, we should underline the point about their expensive farm equipment, in order to foreshadow our discussion of "conspicuous production," a kind of corporate consumption in which the energies displaced from individual consumption by sumptuary rules are channeled into impressive or luxurious or stagey ways of doing business. Early observers noticed that American farmers tended to over mechanize, as contemporary observers might notice that American manufacturers may tend to oversplurge on new plants and machine tools, and perhaps the Amish have been ever so slightly of this world in this so-easily rationalized area of producers' vanity.[4] . . .

A number of studies, including those of Kuznets on the shares of the upper-income groups and those published in *Fortune's* series on the Great American

[4] Manford H. Kuhn, "Factors in Personality: Socio-cultural Determinants as Seen through the Amish," in Francis L. K. Hsu (ed.), *Aspects of Culture and Personality* (New York: Abelard-Schumann, 1954). We need not stop to encompass the irony of the Amana Society, whose handsome freezers and refrigerators, products of cooperative asceticism, may often be the prime adornments of an urban housewife's menage.

Market,[5] indicate the increasing pace of homogenization of possessions between the top ranks of factory workers (notably where there is more than one employed person per spending unit) and the lower ranks of the professional, managerial, and entrepreneurial people. A study done by S. Stansfeld Sargent in Ventura, California, indicates that the "dwelling complex" of a skilled worker will not differ in any obvious way from that of an air-plant physicist–even life-style differences seemed minimal.[6] To be sure, those parts of California where everyone is new may be a special case, but we do believe that the differences between the social and occupational strata are coming more and more to lie primarily in consumer attitudes, not in consumer behavior or the objects bought at any given moment; more precisely, the attitudes influence behavior only when the whole life cycle is taken into account. To a degree, for the office and factory workers, the "poverty cycle" that B. Seebohm Rowntree found in York, England, a half century ago[7] still holds, though at a far higher level: an early peak is reached, followed by a plateau and a slow decline–modified, to be sure, by the secular rise in real income, especially among factory workers.[8] However, Warner Bloomberg, Jr., a thoughtful participant-observer of factory life, has commented on differential meanings of the cycle for men and for their wives. He points out that the young man, before marriage, has been well supplied with funds, often living at home: "he may well indulge in tailor-made suits, expensive whiskies, and high-priced restaurants if they also are not high falutin' . . . always more object-than experience-oriented, with fun correlated with expenditure of money, even in sex–the more high-priced the woman, the better she must be."

"This period," he continues, "is usually brief, ending as soon as he marries, though the emphasis on recreation as a highly valued activity remains: that is, he will continue to want to have his sports, his nights with the boys for cards and drinks, his dancing, etc. However, he must now acquire the capital goods of a home or apartment to be furnished (he already has a car). Over a period of time he becomes more and more engrossed and expert in the 'consumption' of these hard commodities and recreation-orientation slowly subsides under the pressure of family obligations and the nagging of his wife. But once the most difficult period, financially, of the marriage is over, the emphasis on recreation returns,

[5] S. Kuznets, *Shares of Upper Income Groups in Income and Saving* (New York: National Bureau of Economic Research, 1953); the Editors of *Fortune, The Changing American Market* (New York: Hanover House, 1955).

[6] S. S. Sargent, "Class and Class Consciousness in a California Town," *Social Problems*, 1 (June, 1953), pp. 22-27.

[7] B. S. Rowntree, *Poverty: A Study of Town Life*, 2nd ed. (New York: Longmans, 1922).

[8] In their valuable paper, "Savings and the Income Distributions," Dorothy S. Brady and Rose D. Freidman emphasize, as Katona's work also does, the importance of the reference group for a relativistic income analysis: if real income rises for "everyone," everyone will think himself no better off and will not save new increments. *Studies in Income and Wealth*, (National Bureau of Economic Research, 1947), pp. 247-64.

especially travel, sports, and the like, although those who acquire home (and the number has been increasing at a fantastic rate) are forever involved in the purchase, repair, and replacement of the hard goods of the domicile and of the car–involved as buyers and users (and stealers, we might add) of tools, since 'do it yourself' has been part of their occupational culture for a long time."[9]

While, for the men, graduation from (or early leaving of) high school brings liberation, even if followed by the gradual constrictions of domesticity, for the girls the end of high school is viewed with real distress, for it means the end of the pleasant round of dates and opening of the unromantic prospect of early marriage (in this stratum, the seamy side of marriage cannot be hidden from the young). While in an earlier day all they expected of marriage was a pay check, a home in repair, and a spouse who behaved himself, they now have learned–anticipatory socialization again–to look forward to wider alternatives; for one thing, they can protect themselves by their own jobs from having to marry the first man who asks them (nor are they, with contraception, so likely to have to marry because pregnant). "More often than not," Bloomberg observes, "the girls who cry at night as graduation approaches have been introduced to a vague but compelling notion of a richer life, mainly through the mass media and the high schools. More than any others in the working class, they are experience-oriented rather than object-oriented. The men, still in the main occupied vocationally by thing-centered jobs and avocationally by the traditional skills of the hunter or the ball player or the homebuilder, are a big drag on the largely unformulated desire of these girls to build into their lives some *expertise* in consumership which, by an emphasis on experience, could provide the variety and alternation in routines which they believe to be enriching.[10] Travel comes the closest to doing things for both of them, and the working people are getting to be great travelers as time and money permit."[11] No wonder that travel agents have begun to be aware of the guidance function they control; a group of them, recently organized for adult education at the downtown branch of the University of Chicago, met with Reuel Denney to discuss the emotional aura in which people increasingly were buying their way, often on the installment plan, "from here to eternity." Travel becomes a recurrent second honeymoon, a compensation for the disillusion built into the first by the contrasting expectations of the worker

[9] Statement in a letter to the authors.

[10] Owing to these attitudes, working-class girls often have an easier time attaining white-collar jobs and lower middle class status than their male compeers do, and their ability to pass their aspirations on to their sons has been a continuing dynamic in the American drive for upward mobility. Mark Benney also reminds us of the "concealed" mobility the lower class girls may have in affairs with men of higher social position–after which the girls are never quite lower class again. Moreover, he has noticed how continuously working girls give each other gifts–at showers and like occasions–and comments that gift buying, in all classes, tends to be the most socially sensitive form of consumption, analogous to the money girls persuade their boy friends to spend on them.

[11] Brady and Freidman, "Savings and Income Distribution."

and his bride; and no doubt the home itself, as the man works his evenings and weekends around it, also reflects these tensions and some "built-in" compensations for them.

To return to the life cycle of the educated strata: here it is not contrasting expectations drawn from the youth culture, but the role of the corporation or other large employer in dictating a specific style of life, that creates adult tensions between the spouses. At one level, brilliantly portrayed by William H. Whyte, Jr.,[12] are the wives of management who cannot drive Cadillacs because the fuddy-duddy president drives a Buick; a little lower down are the wives who must hear their husbands groan on returning from a business trip because the latter must conceal the fact that they live much better "abroad," on the expense account, than their wives can afford to at home, on a mere salary. Still more unhappy are the wives of the [black] school principals described by a student in a recent seminar: These principals are required by their position to live in a large house and to drive a good car (though not too large and too good) but their salaries have not kept pace and they have had to take outside jobs; since these (dairy farmer, trucker, redcap, bellhop, bartender, gas station attendant, and so on) are too lowly for school principals to hold, they must do so under an assumed name and in a neighboring community. The strain on both spouses, caught in a status conflict and in a series of concealments, can well be imagined.

In general, we believe that, despite the foreshortening of time perspectives in all social class, the middle-managerial groups still take a good deal longer than the working classes to acquire the full domestic package; and they also, again unlike the working classes, cut down on the size and housekeeping demands of this package as they age. Thus, a study done under Everett Hughes in Chicago indicated that the middle-class person usually begins his adult life in an apartment, where he may live for the first several years of marriage; then in his late twenties or early thirties he buys a house (and the neighborhood to go with it) in which to raise his children; after the children have grown and flown, the house becomes a heavy burden, and the bereft couple move back to an apartment, though of a different cast, so that the cycle does not quite end where it began. (In Chicago, he is perhaps also more likely than the working-class person to move because [blacks] have "invaded" his neighborhood, for he clings less tenaciously to real estate, including "his" church, and more tenaciously to the values of nonviolence.) Though people when they buy their homes are not fully conscious of the likelihood they will stay in them at most for two decades, the general pattern in their milieu certainly casts its shadow before.

While a house cycle of some sort may be characteristic of the middle class as a whole, at least in large cities, ambivalence about putting down "roots" is especially characteristic of the younger executive groups that Whyte has studied for *Fortune*. He notices that they would engender criticism by premature pur-

[12] See William H. Whyte, Jr., *Is Anybody Listening?* (New York: Simon and Schuster, 1952).

chase of an overimpressive menage (even if a private income, rather than a bet on future advance, could sustain the cost), and that their careers would also be jeopardized by overcommitment to a particular peer group and neighborhood, which might tie them too closely to people whose careers may not prove commensurate with their own. On the other hand, Charlie Grey is invited by his boss to migrate to a fashionable suburb and to join an expensive country club before he feels quite ready to swing it (though the boss has decided, in a self-fulfilling prophecy, that he *is* ready for the move); accepting, he passes the point of no return.

In terms of family life, this means that, while the husband is to some extent stabilized by his career line within or among firms in a given field or set of fields, his wife and children must be prepared for moves and for the domesticity of transiency, though with only limited knowledge of, let alone satisfactions from, the occupational culture that imposes these requirements. As W. H. Whyte has observed, a man's move up is almost always also a geographic move, and if the wife is not to redo her hair and replan her life while she packs, she must subtly anticipate the promotions her husband may or may not get, while not antagonizing the current peers or baiting the current superiors who see in the consumption field no less than in the office the margins that distance them from their prospective successors. In the new locale, the children (whose own life cycle may not jibe comfortably with this) will attend a slightly different school, the parents join a slightly different club, meanwhile rearranging the standard package in the home so that old objects carried by the moving van will combine into a new *Gestalt*.

Those among us who pull up stakes with difficulty should not, of course, read our own malaise into the transients for whom schools and the army have already provided anticipatory experience. Moreover, in the middle strata of which we are talking, the growing interregional uniformity of the country, doubtless in part the product of mobility and migration, and of the effective system for distributing goods and services, makes moving easier financially and psychologically.

To be sure, there remain millions of people, not only Amish, who do not buy the standard package, much less transport it, either because they fall far below the \$4000–\$7500 per year range that *Fortune* speaks of as the Great American Market, or because they have not been trained to want it. Thus, there certainly remain in less free-floating parts of the country many working-class folk who will use increments of income to buy real estate, not for living only, but for social security, and who will reject many of the amenities in and around the standard package as irrelevant. That is, people in the working class do not see the home as an expendable consumer good but as an investment for old age—something like the West Room into which the Irish peasant retires when his heir takes over the farm. Likewise, workers may buy happenstance items that, in a different combination, form part of the middle-class standard package, but these items will reflect special earning-power bonanzas and may even be compensations, as the [black's] Buick or Cadillac sometimes is, for inability to buy the standard package as an entity and an identity.

At the other end of the social scale, the upper end, the standard middle-majority package operates as a different sort of pressure: not as an aspiration, not as something one prepares for in imagination or in childhood paradigms, but as a limitation, as a kind of sumptuary guide. Contrary to the situation described by Veblen, it does not seem to us to be the members of the upper class who dictate life-styles, which then, filter down; these residuary legatees of the past are influenced as much as they influence, and the location of style leadership, like other leadership, is ramified and, to our mind, obscure. The upper Bohemians have a hand in it, as avocational counselors, just as the upper middlebrows have a hand in diffusing high style to the general population through the mass media. The upper-class youngster in school wears blue jeans and drives an old car; on graduation he wears Uncle Sam's jeans; save in a few enclaves, he avoids high fashion. If he enters the hierarchy, it is, already pointed out, his official rather than his genealogical rank that will determine the make of car he drives. (As for the academic hierarchy, we recall the profuse apologies of an instructor at a Kansas college for driving a Lincoln–he explained he had got it cheap; and in Cambridge were heard many wry comments on a colleague who drove a red Jaguar.) On the whole, in a tug-of-war between the occupational culture and the social-class-and-kinfolk culture, the former is likely to win out. The father of one of the authors, a consulting internist, felt compelled to appear for consultations in patient's homes in a car at least the equal of the doctor's who called him in, much as he disliked display; he ironically referred to the car as his "delivery wagon." (In his own office, where other colleagues would be less embarrassed, he could afford shabbiness.) In one of our Kansas City interviews, a housewife bitterly and repeatedly complained about her husband's air-conditioned Cadillac, which he insisted was necessary for selling trips. One investigator recounted the violent objection of a group of clerks in a large city bank when management insisted on their wearing white collars; though many of them had originally come into the bank because of its genteel white-collar aspects, they felt envious both of the salaries and the shirt worn by the working class and if they could not have the one, at least wanted the comfort and economy of the other!

As we have just said, the upper-class person entering on an occupation will have to be careful not to carry with him his class consumption patterns. This is not easy for him since some of these patterns are bred in the bone, so to speak in his accent and the way he looks and carries his body. But he must make the effort because of the still far-from-evaporated cultural defensiveness of the middle-class businessman, for whom a Harvard accent is not only a doubtful idiosyncrasy but an aggressive one. Provided he conforms in the office, the upper-class businessman may find a hobby on which his excess income may be spent without rivalry-creating inflation of his life style; that is, he will early buy the standard package in one of its more elaborate and expense-concealing variations and then look around for something to collect–a cause or charity, possibly–or have more children and educate them better than the average for the class, or even save something. But in general, the standard package operates here as a restriction on gaudiness, in part because the older sorts of conspicuously flamboyant objects (footmen, for instance) are no longer made, and in part because equalitarian ideologies influence people to level down as well as to level up. The main, and not insignificant, difference is that the upper-class person will carry the standard package lightly, expand it more quickly, and renew or discard it more ruthlessly, whereas the person of lesser income and less assured position will strain under the load and be toppled by unemployment, serious illness, or miscalculation.

20 *Erving Goffman*

SYMBOLS OF CLASS STATUS

I

. . . the rights and obligations of a status are fixed through time by means of external sanctions enforced by law, public opinion, and threat of socio-economic loss, and by internalized sanctions of the kind that are built into a conception of self and give rise to guilt, remorse, and shame.

A status may be *ranked* on a scale of *prestige*, according to the amount of social value that is placed upon it relative to other statuses in the same sector of social life. An individual may be *rated* on a scale of *esteem*, depending on how closely his performance approaches the ideal established for that particular status.[2]

Cooperative activity based on a differentiation and integration of statuses is a universal characteristic of social life. This kind of harmony requires that the occupant of each status act toward others in a manner which conveys the impression that his conception of himself and of them is the same as their conception of themselves and him. A working consensus of this sort therefore requires adequate communication about conceptions of status.

The rights and obligations of a status are frequently ill-adapted to the

From the *British Journal of Sociology*, 2 (1951), pp. 294-299, 300, 301, 302-304. Reprinted by permission of the author and publisher.

[1] A modified version of this paper was presented at the annual meeting of the University of Chicago Society for Social Research in 1949. The writer is grateful to W. Lloyd Warner for direction and to Robert Armstrong, Tom Burns, and Angelica Choate for criticism.

[2] The distinction between prestige and esteem is taken from Kingsley Davis, "A Conceptual Analysis of Stratification," *American Sociological Review*, 7 (June, 1942), pp. 309-321.

requirements of ordinary communication. Specialized means of displaying one's position frequently develop. Such sign vehicles have been called *status symbols.*[3] They are the cues which select for a person the status that is to be imputed to him and the way in which others are to treat him.

Status symbols visibly divide the social world into categories of persons, thereby helping to maintain solidarity within a category and hostility between different categories.[4] Status symbols must be distinguished from *collective symbols* which serve to deny the difference between categories in order that members of all categories may be drawn together in affirmation of a single moral community.[5]

Status symbols designate the position which an occupant has, not the way in which he fulfills it. They must therefore be distinguished from *esteem symbols* which designate the degree to which a person performs the duties of his position in accordance with ideal standards, regardless of the particular rank of his position. For example, the Victoria Cross is awarded in the British Army for heroic performance of a task, regardless of what particular task it is and regardless of the rank of the person who performs it. This is an esteem symbol. It rates above a similar one called the George Cross. On the other hand, there is an insignia which designates Lieutenant-Colonel. It is a status symbol. It tells us about the rank of the person who wears it but tells us nothing about the standard he has achieved in performing the duties of his rank. It *ranks* him above a man who wears the insignia of a Captain, although, in fact, the Captain may be *rated* higher than the Lieutenant-Colonel in terms of the esteem that is accorded to good soldiers.

Persons in the same social position tend to possess a similar pattern of behaviour. Any item of a person's behaviour is, therefore, a sign of his social position. A sign of position can be a status symbol only if it is used with some regularity as a means of "placing" socially the person who makes it. Any sign which provides reliable evidence of its maker's position—whether or not laymen or sociologists use it for evidence about position—may be called a *test of status.* This paper is concerned with the pressures that play upon behaviour as a result of the fact that a symbol of status is not always a very good test of status.

By definition, then, a status symbol carries *categorical* significance, that is, it serves to identify the social status of the person who makes it. But it may also carry *expressive* significance, that is, it may express the point of view, the style of life, and the cultural values of the person who makes it, or may satisfy needs

[3] The most general approach to the study of status symbols known to the writer is to be found in H. Spencer, *The Principles of Sociology*, vol. 2, part 4, "Ceremonial Institutions."

[4] See G. Simmel, "Fashion," *International Quarterly*, vol. 10, pp. 130-155.

[5] See E. Durkheim, *The Elementary Forms of the Religious Life*, trans. S. W. Swain (New York, 1926), especially pp. 230-234.

created by the imbalance of activity in his particular social position. For example, in Europe the practice of fighting a duel of honour was for three centuries a symbol of gentlemanly status. The categorical significance of the practice was so well known that the right of taking or giving the kind of offence which led to a duel was rarely extended to the lower classes. The duel also carried an important expressive significance, however; it vividly portrayed the conception that a true man was an object of danger, a being with limited patience who did not allow a love of life to check his devotion to his principles and to his self-respect. On the whole, we must assume that any item of behaviour is significant to some degree in both a categorical and an expressive capacity.

Status symbols are used because they are better suited to the requirements of communication than are the rights and duties which they signify. This very fact, however, makes it necessary for status symbols to be distinct and separate from that which they signify. It is always possible, therefore, that symbols may come to be employed in a "fraudulent" way, i.e. to signify a status which the claimant does not in fact possess. We may say, then, that continuing use of status symbols in social situations requires mechanisms for restricting the opportunities that arise for misrepresentation. We may approach the study of status symbols by classifying the restrictive mechanisms embodied in them.

With this approach in mind, we may distinguish between two important kinds of status symbols: *occupation symbols* and *class symbols*. This paper is chiefly concerned with class symbols.

There appear to be two main types of occupation symbols. One type takes the form of credentials which testify with presumed authority to a person's training and work history. During the initiation of a work relationship reliance must frequently be placed upon symbols of this kind. They are protected from forgery by legal sanctions and, more importantly, by the understanding that corroborative information will almost certainly become available. The other type of occupation symbol comes into play after the work relation has been established and serves to mark off levels of prestige and power within a formal organization.[6]

On the whole, occupation symbols are firmly tied to an approved referent by specific and acknowledged sanctions, much in the manner in which symbols of social caste are rigidly bound. In the case of social class, however, symbols play a role that is less clearly controlled by authority and in some ways more significant.

No matter how we define social class we must refer to discrete or discontinuous levels of prestige and privilege, where admission to any one of these levels is, typically, determined by a complex of social qualifications, no one or two of

[6] Examples would be private offices, segregated eating-rooms, etc. For a treatment of status symbols in formal organizations, see C. Barnard, "Functions and Pathology of Status Systems in Formal Organizations," chap. 4, pp. 46-83, in *Industry and Society*, ed. W. F. Whyte (New York, 1946).

which are necessarily essential. Symbols of class status do not typically refer to a specific source of status but rather to something based upon a configuration of sources. So it is that when we meet an individual who manipulates symbols in what appears to be a fraudulent way—displaying the signs yet possessing only a doubtful claim to what they signify—we often cannot justify our attitude by reference to his specific shortcomings. Furthermore, in any estimate we make of a person's class status, the multiple determinants of class position make it necessary for us to balance and weigh the person's favourable social qualifications against his less favourable ones. As we may expect, in situations where complex social judgments are required, the exact position of a person is obscured and, in a sense, replaced by a margin of dissensus and doubt. Self-representations which fall within this margin may not meet with our approval, but we cannot prove they are misrepresentations.

No matter how we define social class we must refer to rights which are exercised and conceded but are not specifically laid down in law or contract and are not invariably recognized in practice. Legal sanctions cannot be applied against those who represent themselves as possessing a class status which an informed majority would not accord them. Offenders of this kind commit a presumption, not a crime. Furthermore, class gains typically refer to attitudes of superiority which are not officially or too openly discussed, and to preferential treatment as regards jobs, services, and economic exchanges which is not openly or officially approved. We may agree that an individual has misrepresented himself but, in our own class interests, we cannot make too clear to ourselves, to him, or to others just how he has done so. Also, we tend to justify our class gains in terms of "Cultural" values which everyone in a given society presumably respects—in our society, for example, education, skill, and talent. As a result, those who offer public proof that they possess the pet values of their society cannot be openly refused the status which their symbols permit them to demand.

On the whole, then, class symbols serve not so much to represent or misrepresent one's position, but rather to influence in a desired direction other persons' judgment of it. We shall continue to use the terms "misrepresentation" and "fraudulence", but as regards matters of social class these terms must be understood in the weakened sense in which the above discussion leaves them.

II

Every class symbol embodies one or more devices for restricting misrepresentative use of it. The following restrictive devices are among the most typical.

1. Moral restrictions

Just as a system of economic contract is made effective by people's willingness to acknowledge the legitimacy of the rights which underlie the system, so the use of certain symbols is made effective by inner moral constraints which inhibit people from misrepresenting themselves. This compunction is typically phrased in different but functionally equivalent ways. For example, in Western society, some of the persons who can for the first time afford to emulate the conspicuous consumption of the upper classes refrain from doing so on the grounds of religious scruple, cultural disdain, ethnic and racial loyalty, economic and civic propriety, or even undisguised "sense of one's place."[7] Of course, these self-applied constraints, however phrased, are reinforced by the pressure of the opinion both of one's original group and of the class whose symbols one may misemploy. But the efficacy of these external sanctions is due in part to the readiness with which they are reinforced by internalized moral constraints.

2. Intrinsic Restrictions

One solution to the problem of misrepresentation is based on the kind of symbol which perceptibly involves an appreciable use of the very rights or characteristics which it symbolizes. We symbolize our wealth by displaying it, our power by using it, and our skill by exercising it. In the case of wealth, for example, racing stables, large homes, and jewellery obviously imply that the owner has at least as much money as the symbols can bring on the open market.

The use of certain objects as intrinsic symbols of wealth presents a special problem, for we must consider why it is that a very high market value can be placed upon them. Economists sometimes say that we have here a case of "effective scarcity," that is, a small supply in conjunction with a large demand. Scarcity alone, however, does not qualify an object for use as a status symbol, since there is an unlimited number of different kinds of scarce objects. The paintings of an unskilled amateur may be extremely rare, yet at the same time almost worthless. Why, then, do we place great value on examples of one kind of scarce object and not upon examples of another kind of similar and equally scarce object?

Sometimes an attempt is made to account for great differences in the market value of objects that are of similar kind and are equally scarce by pointing to the "expressive" difference between them. (The same rationalization is sometimes employed to explain the difference in market value between "originals" and "reproductions.") In many cases an identifiable difference of this kind not only exists but can also be used to rank the objects on a scale in accordance with some recognized aesthetic or sensuous standard of judgment. This difference in experiential value between relatively similar objects does not, however, seem to be important enough in itself to justify the widely different market value placed upon them. We must account for the high price placed upon certain scarce objects by referring to the social gains that their owners obtain by showing

[7] Moral restrictions apply to many types of status symbols other than class. For example, in Western society, women feel that it is seemly to refrain from using symbols of sexual attractiveness before reaching a given age and to abstain progressively from using them after attaining a given age.

these possessions to other persons. The expressive superiority of an object merely accounts for the fact that it, rather than some other equally scarce object, was selected for use as a status symbol.

3. Natural restrictions

The limited supply of some kinds of objects can be increased with relative ease but is not increased because persons do not have a motive for doing so or because there is a strong social sanction against doing so. On the other hand, the limited supply of certain kinds of objects cannot be increased by any means remotely available at the time, even though there may be a motive for doing so. These objects have been called "natural scarcities."

The natural scarcity of certain objects provides one kind of guarantee that the number of persons who acquire these objects will not be so large as to render the objects useless as symbols for the expression of invidious distinction. Natural scarcity, therefore, is one factor which may operate in certain symbols of status. Again we may note that not all scarce kinds of objects are valued highly. We must also note that not all highly valued scarce objects are status symbols, as may be seen, for example, in the case of certain radioactive minerals. Bases of scarcity in the case of certain status symbols nevertheless present a distinct analytical problem. If we think of it in this way we can appreciate the fact that while scarcity plays its most obvious role as an element in intrinsic symbols of wealth, there are symbols of status which are protected by the factor of natural scarcity and which cannot be directly bought and sold.

On the whole, the bases of natural scarcity may be sought in certain features of the physical production or physical structure of the symbol. More than one basis, of course, may be found combined in the same symbol.

The most obvious basis of scarcity, perhaps, can be found in objects which are made from material that is very infrequently found in the natural world and which cannot be manufactured synthetically from materials that are less scarce. This is the basis of scarcity, for example, in the case of very large flawless diamonds.

A basis of scarcity is found in what might be called "historical closure." A high value may be placed on products which derive in a verifiable way from agencies that are no longer productive, on the assumption that it is no longer physically possible to increase the supply. In New England, for example, family connection with the shipping trade is a safe thing to use as a symbol of status because this trade, in its relevant sense, no longer exists. Similarly, furniture made "solidly" from certain hardwoods, regardless of style or workmanship, is used as a symbol of status. The trees which supply the material take so long a time to grow that, in terms of the current market, existing forests can be considered as a closed and decreasing supply. . . .

Finally, a play produced by a given cast must "play to" an audience of limited size. This is related to the limitations of human vision and hearing. The cast may repeat their performance for a different audience, but the performance cannot be reproduced in the sense that is possible with a cinematic performance. It is only in the cinema that the same performance may be "given" at different places simultaneously. Play-going can thus be used as a symbol of status whereas a visit to the cinema, on the whole, cannot.

4. Socialization restrictions

An important symbol of membership in a given class is displayed during informal interaction. It consists of the kind of acts which impress others with the suitability and likeableness of one's general manner. In the minds of those present, such a person is thought to be "one of our kind." Impressions of this sort seem to be built upon a response to many particles of behaviour. These behaviours involve matters of etiquette, dress, deportment, gesture, intonation, dialect, vocabulary, small bodily movements and automatically expressed evaluations concerning both the substance and the details of life. In a manner of speaking, these behaviours constitute a social style.

Status symbols based on social style embody restrictive mechanisms which often operate in conjunction with each other. We tend to be impressed by the over-all character of a person's manner so that, in fact, we can rarely specify and itemize the particular acts which have impressed us. We find, therefore, that we are not able to analyse a desired style of behaviour into parts which are small and definite enough to make systematic learning possible. . . .

5. Cultivation restrictions

In many societies, avocational pursuits involving the cultivation of arts, "tastes," sports, and handicrafts have been used as symbols of class status. Prestige is accorded the experts, and expertness is based upon, and requires, concentrated attention over a long period of time. A command of foreign languages, for example, has provided an effective source of this sort of symbol.

It is a truism to say that anything which proves that a long span of past time has been spent in non-remunerative pursuits is likely to be used as a class symbol. Time-cost is not, however, the only mechanism of restriction which stands in the way of cultivation. Cultivation also requires discipline and perseverance, that is, it requires of a person that he exclude from the line of his attention all the distractions, deflections, and competing interests which come to plague an intention carried over an extended period of time. This restriction on the improper acquisition of symbols is especially effective where the period from preparation to exhibition is a long one.

An interesting example of cultivation is found in the quality of "restraint" upon which classes in many different societies have placed high value. Here social use is made of the discipline required to set aside and hold in check the insistent stimuli of daily life so that attention may be free to tarry upon distinctions and discriminations which would otherwise be overlooked. In a sense, restraint is a form of negative cultivation, for it involves a studied withdrawal of attention from many areas of experience. An example is seen in Japanese tea ceremonies during the Zen period of Buddhism. In Western society the negative and positive aspects of cultivation are typically combined in what is called sophistication concerning food, drink, clothes, and furnishings.

6. Organic restrictions

Restrictions related to manner and cultivation provide evidence by means of relevant symbols as to how and where an individual has spent a great deal of his past time. Evidence concerning previous activity is crucial because class status is based not only on social qualifications but also on the length of time a person has possessed them. Owing to the nature of biological growth and development, acquired patterns of behaviour typically provide a much less reliable view of a person's past than is provided by acquired changes in his physical structure.[8] In Britain, for example, condition of hands and height in men, and secondary sexual characteristics in women, are symbols of status based ultimately on the long-range physical effects of diet, work, and environment.

III

. . . Six general devices for restricting misuse of class symbols have been outlined. It must be said, however, that there is no single mode of restriction which can withstand too many contingencies, nor is there any restriction which is not regularly and systematically circumvented in some fashion. An example of this is the Public School System in Britain, which may be seen as a machine for systematically re-creating middle-class people in the image of the aristocracy. . . .

The presence of routine methods of circumvention may partly explain why stable classes tend to designate their position by means of symbols which rely on many different types of restrictive devices. It would appear that the efficacy of one type of restriction acts as a check upon the failure of another. In this way the group avoids the danger, as it were, of putting all their symbols in one basket. Conversely, social situations for which analysis of status symbols is important can be classified according to the type of mechanism upon which members of a class may be over-dependent or which they may neglect.

From the point of view taken in this paper, problems in the study of class symbols have two aspects, one for the class from which the symbol originates and the other for the class which appropriates it. As a conclusion to this paper, reference will be made to three of these two-sided problem areas.

1. Class movement

Social classes as well as individual members are constantly rising and falling in terms of relative wealth, power, and prestige. This movement lays a heavy burden upon class symbols, increasing the tendency for signs that symbolize position to

[8] The use of inherited characteristics as symbols of status is typically found, of course, in a society of castes not classes.

take on the role of conferring it.[9] This tendency, in connection with the restrictions that are placed upon the acquisition of status symbols, retards the rise to social eminence of those who have lately acquired importance in power and wealth and retards the fall of those who have lately lost it. In this way the continuity of a tradition can be assured even though there is a change in the kind of persons who maintain the tradition.

. . . We find that sources of high status which were once unchallenged become exhausted or find themselves in competition with new and different sources of status. It is therefore common for a whole class of persons to find themselves with symbols and expectations which their economic and political position can no longer support. A symbol of status cannot retain forever its acquired role of conferring status. A time is reached when social decline accelerates with a spiral effect: members of a declining class are forced to rely more and more upon symbols which do not involve a current outlay, while at the same time their association with these symbols lowers the value of these signs in the eyes of others.

The other aspect of this problem turns upon the fact that new sources of high status typically permit the acquisition of costly symbols before symbols based on cultivation and socialization can be acquired. This tends to induce in the rising group expectations which for a time are not warranted and tends to undermine the regard in which costly symbols are held by members of other classes.[10]

2. Curator groups

Wherever the symbolizing equipment of a class becomes elaborate a curator personnel may develop whose task it is to build and service this machinery of status. Personnel of this kind in our society include members of such occupational categories as domestic servants, fashion experts and models, interior decorators, architects, teachers in the field of higher learning, actors, and artists of all kinds. Those who fill these jobs are typically recruited from classes which have much less prestige than the class to which such services are sold. Thus there are people whose daily work requires them to become proficient in manipulating symbols which signify a position higher than the one they themselves possess. Here, then, we have an institutionalized source of misrepresentation, false expectation, and dissensus.

An interesting complication arises when the specialist provides symbol service for a large number of persons and when the symbol to which he owes his

[9] The extreme case is found in so-called ritual transmissions of charisma. See Max Weber, *Theory of Social and Economic Organization*, trans. T. Parsons (London, 1947), p. 366.

[10] This has been referred to as the problem of the *nouveau riche*, of which the community of Hollywood provides and example. See Leo Rosten, *Hollywood* (New York, 1941), especially pp. 163-180. See also Talcott Parsons, "The Motivation of Economic Activity", *Essays in Sociological Theory* (New York, 1948), p. 215. An extreme case in the U.S.A. is the decrease in social value of the type of expensive car favoured by the rich criminal classes.

employment at the same time carries a strongly marked expressive component. This is the case, for example, with the fashion model and interior decorator. Under these circumstances the curator comes to play much the same sacred role as those entrusted with the collective symbols of a society. It then becomes possible for the improper expectations of the curator to be realized and for the status and security of the patron class itself to be correspondingly diminished.

3. Circulation of Symbols

The systematic circumvention of modes of restriction leads to downward and upward circulation of symbols.[11] In these cases, apparently, the objective structure of the sign-vehicle always becomes altered. A classification of these alterations or modes of vulgarization would be interesting to pursue but is beyond the scope of this paper.

From the point of view of this paper, circulation of symbols has two major consequences. First, those with whom a symbol originates must turn from that which is familiar to them and seek out, again and again, something which is not yet contaminated. This is especially true of groups which are smaller and more specialized than social classes—groups whose members feel inclined to separate themselves from their original social class, not by moving up or down but by moving out. This may be seen, for example, in the attempt of jazz musicians to create a monthly quota of new fashion to replace items of their action and speech which laymen have appropriated.[12]

The second consequence is perhaps the more significant of the two. Status symbols provide the cue that is used in order to discover the status of others and, from this, the way in which others are to be treated. The thoughts and attention of persons engaged in social activity therefore tend to be occupied with these signs of position. It is also a fact that status symbols frequently express the whole mode of life of those from whom the symbolic act originates. In this way the individual finds that the structure of his experience in one sphere of life is repeated throughout his experiences in other spheres of life. Affirmation of this kind induces solidarity in the group and richness and depth in the psychic life of its members.

As a result of the circulation of symbols, however, a sign which is expressive for the class in which it originates comes to be employed by a different class—a class for which the symbol can signify status but ill express it. In this way conscious life may become thin and meagre, focused as it is upon symbols which are not particularly congenial to it.

[11] It is not rare for practices which originate in one class to be adopted by the members of a higher one. Cases in point would be the argot of criminal, ethnic, and theatrical groups and such fugitive social crazes as the Lambeth Walk. In most cases these adopted practices serve only as an expressive function and are not used as status symbols. Sometimes practices of low repute are adopted as status symbols in order to comment on those who cannot afford to be associated with them.

[12] From conversations with Howard Becker.

21 *Dean S. Ellis*

SPEECH AND SOCIAL STATUS IN AMERICA

Language has long been recognized as a symbolic indicator of social class. Barber[1] points out in his text, *Social Stratification*, that in India the ability to use written language, i.e., to read and write, had long been a symbol of Brahman caste membership. In nineteenth-century Russia, the upper classes spoke French, the language of the court, in preference to their native language which they shared with the lower classes. In modern European countries the speech patterns of the different classes are often so gross as to be considered different dialects. The middle- and upper-class Germans are expected to speak "Hoch Deutsch" or high German. But it is acceptable for the working and lower classes to speak a regional variation of "Platt Deutsch" or low German. George Bernard Shaw's play, *Pygmalion*, points out how vital he thought language was as an indicator of social status in England.

The prominence of speech as an indicator of social status in foreign lands seems to be fairly well accepted. However, its prominence in America seems to be more questionable, as is indicated by the statement of Barber:

> In American language and speech, as in so many other kinds of American symbolic phenomena, the symbolization of differences in social class position has been subtle rather than gross. Regional differences in accent and diction are probably greater than differences of social class position. All social classes speak roughly the same except that the better educated upper and middle classes have better diction and grammar. This is a product of their superior education.[2]

The present paper will present research findings which are contrary to Barber's statement. These will be followed by a discussion of additional research findings which show that Americans' speech does, rather nonsubtly, reveal social status and some possible implications of the way persons are affected by the social-status revealing aspect of their speech.

Barber states that regional differences in accent and diction are probably greater than differences of social class position. His statement seems to overlook the fact that listeners may be able to recognize the social-status cues in a person's speech in spite of the speaker's regional dialect.

From Dean S. Ellis, "Speech and Social Status in America," *Social Forces*, 45 (1967), pp. 431-437; published by the University of North Carolina Press, and reprinted by permission.

Note: This research was done while Professor Ellis was a research assistant in the Communications Research Center at Purdue University. It was conducted under the guidance of Dr. W. Charles Redding and with the financial support of a National Science Foundation grant to the Communications Research Center.

[1] Bernard Barber, *Social Stratification* (New York: Harcourt Brace Jovanovich, 1957), p. 151.

[2] Ibid.

Baltzell goes slightly beyond Barber's statement when he suggest in *The Philadelphia Gentleman* that there are some similarities in the speech patterns of upper-class persons which cut across regional dialects, but he limits such cross-regional speech patterns to the upper class.[3] Research findings suggest that there are actually similarities which cut across dialects for the middle and lower classes also. Putnam and O'Hern[4] recorded one-minute samples of speech from 12 [blacks] of different educational and social backgrounds. The speech samples consisted of each speaker telling in his own words the fable, "The Lion and the Mouse." The speaker's social status was determined by the Warner index. After hearing these short recordings, 55 white university student judges produced mean ratings of the speakers' social status which correlated .80 with the Warner index scores. This study shows that "whites" can identify the social status of [blacks]. Putnam and O'Hern in discussing the findings pointed out that the various [black] speakers had a variety of regional dialects such as Southern, Eastern and "General American." Yet, these differences in the dialects of the speakers did not inhibit the judges' ability to identify the speakers' social status.

This same set of tape recordings used by Putnam and O'Hern was used by L. S. Harms in a study in the Midwest (Putnam and O'Hern's study was conducted in Washington, D.C.).[5] Harms found that the Midwestern listeners were as accurate as the Eastern listeners in identifying the social status of the [black] speakers.

A study by the present author also supports the contention that regional dialects of speakers do not inhibit the ability of listeners to identify the speakers' social status.[6] The speakers in this study were 12 college freshmen. Though the majority of the speakers spoke "General American," several speakers had an "Indiana Twang," one speaker had a New York accent and one had a rural Southern accent. The social status of the speakers was determined by use of the Hollingshead *Two Factor Index of Status Position*.[7] Each speaker made a 40-second recording of the fable, "The Tortoise and the Hare." These short recordings of the speakers' voices were played to groups of from 15 to 20 upper

[3] "Accent clearly distinguishes the Southerner from his countrymen in the Middle West or New England. At the same time, there is a subtle upper class accent in America which cuts across regional differences." Taken from *The Philadelphia Gentleman* by E. D. Baltzell (New York: The Free Press, 1958), p. 50.

[4] G. N. Putnam and E. M. O'Hern, "The Status Significance of an Isolated Urban Dialect," *Language* 31 (October-December, 1955), pp. 1-32.

[5] L. S. Harms, Unpublished research, Reported on by Phillip K. Tompkins, "Speaking Ability and Social Class," a paper presented at the 1963 convention of the National Society for the Study of Communication, Denver, Colorado.

[6] D. S. Ellis, "The Identification of Social Status from Limited Vocal Cues," unpublished paper, Purdue University, Communications Research Center, Department of Speech, 1963.

[7] A. B. Hollingshead, *Two Factor Index of Status Position* (New Haven: Yale University Press, 1957), pp. 1-11. The two factors are the education and occupation of the head of the household.

division students who served as judges. The judges produced mean ratings of the speakers' social status which correlated .80+ with the Hollingshead measure. The evidence from the three studies cited here all indicates that persons can identify social status regardless of the regional dialect of the speaker.

A second assumption made by Barber was that, "All social classes speak roughly the same, except that the better educated upper and middle classes have better diction and grammar." Putnam and O'Hern conducted a linguistic analysis of the 12 speakers used in their study. They brought out that the upper-class speakers had a marked sophistication in vocabulary and sentence structure and spoke with a clear, logical simplicity. The lower-class subjects used several sound substitutions such as the use of */ai/* and */aeu/* as allophones of */ai/* and */au/*, respectively, and spoke with great weakening of the consonants, especially the stops. Their grammatical structure was extremely simple.[8] From the Putnam and O'Hern analysis, it appears that though grammar and diction are important status cues, the differences between the speech of upper- and lower-class persons in America is more complex than Barber's statement implies.

. . . Bernstein of the University of London, Department of Sociology . . . , suggests that persons of different classes and different backgrounds do not really share a common language, or as Bernstein states it, a common "code." This same concept is supported by general semanticists such as Wendal Johnson and S. I. Hayakawa.[9] The general semanticists point out that words do not have meanings; only people have meanings, and they assign those meanings to certain symbols, the most common of which we call words. The meaning a person assigns to a symbol depends upon the person's background. It seems obvious that the backgrounds of rich and poor are going to vary greatly. It should, therefore, be just as obvious that the meanings the rich and poor assign to symbols will vary greatly, and, thus, the symbols used by the two groups to express the same concepts should be expected to vary greatly.[10]

Osgood has conducted research, using his semantic differential scales, which has shown that the meanings of words vary from group to group. The semantic differential studies, most highly related to this paper, are those that compare the meanings assigned to words by workers as compared to managers. These studies clearly are comparing the language codes of two different social classes. The findings consistently show that there are gross differences in the codes being used by the two groups.[11]

[8] Putnam and O'Hern, "Status Significances," pp. 27-30.

[9] An excellent review of general semantics can be found in Wendall Johnson's *People in Quandaries* (New York: Harper & Row, 1946).

[10] An example of the difference in the use of words to express an idea would be the two statements "I got'a buck," and "I have a dollar"; or, "He's a cool swinger," and "He's a nice guy."

[11] C. E. Osgood, G. T. Suci, and P. H. Tannenbaum, *The Measurement of Meaning* (Urbana, Illinois: University of Illinois Press, 1957).

The evidence cited above indicates that there are major differences in the speech of different classes of Americans and the differences are neither subtle nor restricted to differences in diction and grammar as is suggested by Barber.

The discussion will now focus on studies which have directly investigated the effect of diction, grammar and other speech cues as indicators of social status.

In the Putnam and O'Hern study, it was reported that the major cues the listeners used in identifying the social status of the speakers were: "inclusion of aberrant vowel and diphthong allophones, consonant articulation, and the degree of sophistication of vocabulary and sentence structure. . . ."[12] They made no attempt to isolate the amount of independent effect any of these variables had in revealing the speakers' social status. They concluded, "Further research is needed to discover just what features are most diagnostic of social status."

L. S. Harms conducted a study using nine Midwestern, white speakers.[13] Instead of telling a fable, his speakers responded to printed cards which said such things as "How are you?" "Ask for the time." Harms pointed out that though his listeners could identify the social status of his speakers, the cues they based their judgments on were not obvious.[14] He stated, "They could be based on word choice, pronunciation, grammatical structure, voice quality, articulation and several other observable variables." The listeners could not indicate whether they based their judgments on one variable or several.

The study mentioned earlier by the present author found results similar to those of Putnam and O'Hern and [of] Harms. The follow-up studies were conducted to partially isolate the effect speech cues—such as diction and grammar—had in revealing social status.[15]

In the follow-up study, instead of telling an impromptu version of the fable "The Tortoise and the Hare," as they had done in the first study, the speakers were instructed to role-play that they were honor students selected to conduct the university President and his guests on a tour of a new dormitory. The speakers were told to use their very best grammar and voice quality, and to try to "fake" their voices to make them sound upper class. The listeners were able to identify the social status of the speakers, in spite of the speakers' attempts at role-playing or "faking." However, the accuracy of the listeners' judgments dropped from a validity coefficient of .80+ in the first experiment to .65+ in this one.

It was assumed that since all of the speakers were college students, they could all use correct grammar and sophisticated sentence structures if they con-

[12] Putnam and O'Hern, "Status Significance," p. 28.

[13] L. S. Harms, "Listener Judgments of Status Cues in Speech," *Quarterly Journal of Speech* 47 (1961), pp. 164-168.

[14] Harms determined the social status of his subjects by using the Hollingshead *Two Factor Index of Status Position*.

[15] Ellis, "Identification of Status."

sciously attempted to. A later analysis of the speech samples proved this assumption to be only partially correct. The subjects all used proper grammar, but their choice of vocabulary, sentence length, sentence structure, and their fluency varied greatly.

This experiment indicated that grammar may be a factor, but not the only factor giving cues to the speakers' social status. It also points out that speakers cannot easily hide or fake the social-status-revealing cues in their speech. A second follow-up experiment was designed which could more rigidly control the speech variables heard by the listeners.[16]

In this experiment the speakers each counted from 1 to 20 at a set rate of speed. This eliminated the speech variables of vocabulary choice, sentence length, sentence structure, grammatical usage, and fluency. Counting from 1 to 20 was chosen in preference to some other list of words because: (a) counting from 1 to 20 requires a person to use almost every common sound in the English language, (b) the pronunciation of the numbers is well known to all classes and should not reflect one's educational background, and (c) the numbers are as well known and commonly used by the members of one social class as another.

The listeners were able to identify the social status of the speakers after hearing each speaker count for only 20 seconds. The ratings of the listeners correlated .65+ (significant at the .01 level) with the Hollingshead status position scores of the speakers.

These findings indicate that some of the cues listeners use in identifying speakers' social status are based on stimuli such as grammar or word choice which were eliminated from this third experiment, since the accuracy of the listeners dropped from a validty coefficient of .80+ to .65+. But, a major part of the cues upon which listeners base their ratings of speakers' social status comes from the way the subjects speak individual words. The cues may be in the pronunciation of the words or in some tonal qualities of the speakers' voices.

In relating these findings back to Barber's statement that "diction and grammar" are the two factors which differentiate the speech of upper- and lower-class individuals, it becomes apparent that his statement is not entirely false, but is rather a gross oversimplification. Even under the broadest definitions of the words "grammar" and "diction," it seems difficult to classify the list of speech variables discussed above which could be used as cues for discriminating between upper- and lower-class speakers.

Barber's explanation of why the grammar and diction of the upper-class subjects is superior to that of the lower-class subjects also seems to lack empirical support. Barber states that it is due to the superior education of the upper-class speakers. Yet, in the three experiments by the present author, the speakers were all college freshmen. This indicates that they all had the same number of years of schooling and all had been in the upper one-third of their

[16] Ibid.

high school class scholastically. The S.A.T. [Scholastic Aptitude Test] scores of the speakers were not significantly related to their social status.

This indicates that formal educational differences, if a factor at all, are not the only factor which affect the social status revealing cues in speakers' voices. Nor is the intelligence of the speaker (as measured by S.A.T. scores) the major factor which determines these status revealing cues. It seems logical to assume that the speech qualities which reveal social status are not a product of anything so simple as "amount of education," but are rather a product of the speakers' total environment. It seems naive to assume that a lower-class rural [black] who is fortunate enough to receive a good education, but returns to work in his rural community, would adopt the speech patterns of the upper classes. It seems far more logical and obvious that a person will speak as the persons he intimately associates with and identifies with speak.

Now that the oversimplifications of Barber's statement about language as a symbolic indicator of social status have been discussed, some additional research findings not related to Barber's statement will be presented.[17]

Harms measured the social status of his listeners as well as the social status of his speakers. He found that there was no significant difference between the way high-status [HS], middle-status [MS], and low-status [LS] listeners rated MS speakers or LS speakers. But he did find that the LS listeners rated MS speakers significantly lower (sig. at .05 level) than did MS or HS listeners. This difference was small and was not explained by Harms.

Harms also had his listeners rate the credibility of the speakers. Again, he found that generally the MS, HS and LS listeners rated the credibility of the speakers about the same. He then correlated the ratings of the speakers' social status with the ratings of the speakers' credibility. He found all correlations to be significant at the .05 level, indicating that high status persons are perceived as being more credible than low status persons.

Highly related to these findings are some of the findings in the series of experiments by the present author. In two of these experiments the listeners rated how well they liked each speaker. These ratings of "likableness" of the speakers correlated with the speaker's Hollingshead Status Position score .76 (significant at the .01 level) and with the listeners' ratings of the speakers' social status .60 (significant at the .05 level). These findings tend to support Harms' findings,[18] i.e., they suggest that when listeners hear even very short samples of

[17] These additional findings are drawn from the works of the four authors already cited, since these authors are the only ones which have reported experiments dealing with status cues in speech. One other study related to this area, but not reviewed here, [has been] completed at the University of Chicago. The study used a sample size of four. And those four were reported to be extreme cases.

[18] These correlations are from the first experiment in the series on social status. In this experiment, the listeners heard the speakers tell a fable. In the experiment in which the listeners heard the speakers count, the correlations were smaller, but still signficant at the .05 level.

a person's speech, they are able to make a value judgment about how well they would like the person. These value judgments of the listeners are highly related to the social status of the speakers.

The present author then constructed a rating scale of "job-type best suited for" to see if his listeners could make a meaningful value judgment about the type of work each speaker is best suited for; and to see if these value judgments are related to the social status of the speakers. The job-type scale used had seven different occupational categories described on it, one to correspond to each of the seven levels or types of employment described by Hollingshead in the *Two Factor Index of Status Position*.[19] The listeners heard the recording of the speakers' counting. The correlation between the Hollingshead Status Position score of the speakers and the listeners' ratings of the job-type the speakers were best suited for was .67 (significant at the .01 level).[20] These findings suggest that listeners, when rating the type of job a person is best suited for, are actually identifying the general level of employment which corresponds to the social status of the person. A discussion of the possible implication of these and the other findings will be presented in the next section of this paper. . . .

To explain why speech should receive special attention as a symbolic indicator of social status, one need only ask himself, how many persons hear me speak every day? Speech is the primary medium which all persons use to affect the society in which they live, and the main medium through which they are affected by that society.

Research by Dusenbury and Knower[21] has shown that auditory cues provide more information about personality traits than do visual cues. And a study by the present author[22] has shown that when raters make judgments about speakers based on both auditory and visual cues jointly, the auditory cues strongly dominate over the visual cues. Barber has stated that they symbolic implications of American speech in relation to social class are subtle, but the research reported in this paper suggests that whether subtle or not they are easily recognized by all classes of Americans, and they label the speaker as belonging to a certain social class. The research further indicates that persons speaking one accent of Amercan English can identify the social status of the speech of persons using different accents of American English. In short, the research implies that how one speaks reveals his social class. This conclusion raises two other major

19 Hollingshead, *Two Factor Index*.

20 This correlation is exactly the same as the correlation reported earlier between the speakers Hollingshead Status Position score and the listeners' (a different group of listeners) ratings of the speakers' social status.

21 Delwyn Dusenbury and Frank H. Knower, "Experimental Studies of the Symbolism of Action and Voice," *Quarterly Journal of Speech* 24 (1938).

22 Dean S. Ellis, "The Effects of Limiting the Amount of Exposure between Interviewers and Interviewees," unpublished paper, Communications Research Center, Purdue University, 1964.

questions: (1) is this label a handicap to the lower-status persons, and (2) if it is a handicap, how hard is it to change one's speech?

There is some research which indicates that the label may be a handicap. The research of Harms and the present author, already reported in this paper, has indicated that listeners rated lower-status speakers as less credible than higher-status speakers. If these listeners make the same type of judgments in a nonexperimental situation—for example, in an interview—the lower-status person would have a disadvantage. There are over 170 million employment interviews conducted in the United States each year.[23] Much research has indicated that interviewers frequently base their decision about whether or not to hire a man on some personal whim, or a mannerism of the applicants which is totally unrelated to their qualifications for the position.[24]

In the series of experiments by the present author, the speakers were all college students. These students' social status was determined by the educational and occupational backgrounds of their fathers (the head of their household). So, in fact, the study shows that the children's voices reveal the status of their family backgrounds. The students in these experiments were all engineering students; in a few years they will all be interviewing for jobs which are classified by the Hollingshead index as upper-status jobs. The evidence thus far presented, though not conclusive, suggests that the student who comes from a lower-class family is likely to be discriminated against at hiring time. A controlled study is needed to investigate whether or not such discrimination really takes place, but a study of engineers by Perrucci lends some support to this concept. He found that engineers from low-status backgrounds earn less than engineers from higher-status backgrounds.[25] However, there are many factors other than voice qualities of the speaker which could account for this difference in earning power, such as individual aspiration and family connections.

Though the evidence is not conclusive, it strongly suggests that the social acceptability of one's speech is a source of discrimination.

The discussion thus far has dealt with only one possible area in which a person may be discriminated against—the interview situation. The variety of other interpersonal situations which exist in our society could all be given as other possible examples: buying a house, joining a club, etc. Just how extensive such discrimination might be is a question which can be answered only by further sociological research.

We now turn to the second question. How hard is it to change the status-

[23] Roger Bellows, *The Psychology of Personnel in Business and Industry* (Englewood Cliffs, New Jersey: Prentice-Hall, 1961).

[24] A review of literature on this topic can be found in Roger Bellows and M. F. Estep, *Employment Psychology: The Interview* (New York: Holt, Rinehart and Winston, Inc., 1954), chap. 8.

[25] Robert Perrucci, "Social Class and Intra-Occupational Mobility: A Study of the Purdue Engineering Graduate from 1911 to 1956," thesis, Purdue University, 1959.

revealing qualities of one's voice? This question cannot be fully answered because research has not yet discovered exactly what the status-revealing qualities of speech are. Putnam and O'Hern's concluding statement to their article is not too encouraging.

> The importance of speech as a mark of social status is a matter of great social significance. It is known that speech habits are not easily altered: the phonetic speech features, which proved to be most distinctive of social status, are probably more resistant to change than non-phonetic speech habits. Persons who grow to adulthood as members of an underprivileged social group may carry a mark of their origin through life and suffer from the various forms of discrimination which society imposes on members of the lower socio-economic classes.[26]

This view seems a little pessimistic. The voices of students in the present author's experiments revealed the social status of these students' fathers. In the Harms, and the Putnam, and O'Hern studies the speech samples were of persons who were the heads of their own households. Their voices revealed their own social status; if any of the speakers in those two studies had fathers of a lower social status than their own, it indicates that with time and change of environment, the status-revealing qualities of one's voice may change to reveal the person's new status. Again no definite statement can be made due to a lack of research.

Harms suggests that voices can be changed, but Harms, who is a speech teacher, warns that, "when making a student aware of the different and unacceptable features of his speech, the teacher has a strong responsibility to assist the student systematically. Otherwise, the loss in confidence may far outweigh the possible gains of a partly learned new dialect."[27]

For the final thought on this subject the lesson from *Pygmalion* seems appropriate as a warning. Professor Higgins was able to change the flower girl's speech, but neglected or was incapable of changing her values. As a result, the girl was left with speech symbolic of the upper class, which, Shaw pointed out, would be as great a hindrance to her with her lower-class friends as lower-class speech would be in an upper-class gathering.

Speech is only one indicator of social class, and though it is an important one which should not be ignored, it should always be viewed in perspective. There is some evidence that the status-revealing cues in speech can be changed, but these changes, if not accompanied by complementary changes in the rest of the person's environment, may create as many problems as they alleviate.

26 Putnam and O'Hern, "Status Significance," p. 23.

27 Harms, "Speaking Ability and Social Class," p. 168.

CHAPTER 7

ELITES AND STATUS CIRCLES

The dissolution of the middle class in modern society has had ramifications in assessing the power of the upper strata. Forces emerging from industrialization, urbanization, and population increase have brought forth a high level of specialization, making it impossible to clearly define many of the power-wielding groups as belonging to an aristocracy or ruling class. The development of new social and economic roles, particularly in the professional and technical areas, has made it necessary to devise new ways of conceptualizing the existence of new forces of influence and power-wielding in modern society. The concept of *elite* is a response to the inapplicability of the older concepts in dealing with the new heterogeneity.

The greater the degree of specialization in modern society, the greater the concern over decision-making processes within and between the various elite groups. Numerous elites tend to share the available power. Power-wielding in modern society can no longer be attributed to a ruling class or an aristocracy. Hence the demands and restraints made in relation to the power-wielders must be applied to certain elites, rather than to a single set of leaders of a ruling class.

Elite means "best," and in stratification study the concept is usually thought of in the plural form, a fact that has important implications for stratification theory. That is, there are considerable numbers who are viewed as "best" in their *particular* activity. The increase in specialization in technologically advanced societies has given rise to the need for expertise. The expert gains his place on the basis of merit, and the most meritorious become members of the elite. Since there are numerous types of experts, a plurality of elites therefore develops.

The apparent theoretical necessity for the use of the concept of elite lends support to the use of the concept of status community. It is, in effect, another conceptual tool in the attempt to handle the fragmentation of society at the upper middle levels of highly differentiated modern societies. The concept of elite is a more specific concept than status community. An elite *may* form a status community, but the term is not synonymous with status community. In Weberian terms, an elite is a positively honored or privileged status group; a status community may be *either* positively or negatively privileged. For example, a Skid Row can be conceived of as a negatively honored status community.[1]

Suzanne Keller has divided the various types of social leadership into five parts: (1) ruling caste, (2) aristocracy, (3) the first estate, (4) ruling class, and (5) strategic elites. In elaborating on "strategic elites" she states:

> In this type of social leadership, several social strata supply personnel to leading social positions. Social functions are elaborated and specialized, and those in charge of these functions are recruited in a way adapted to their tasks. Merit regardless of other attributes—sex, race, class, religion, or even age—is the predominant justification for attaining elite positions or elite status. The notion of all around excellence or overall superiority is gone. Strategic elites are specialists in excellence . . . along with this specialization, diversity, and impermanence of elites, new problems arise—those of cohesion and unity, morale, balance, and a new type of interdependence at the top. No single elite can outrank all others because no one elite knows enough about the specialized work of others.[2]

Although specialization is basic for elite formation, the possibility remains of membership in more than one elite, i.e., overlapping membership. Presumably, a single elite will command the greatest loyalty of the individual, but membership in another may still be maintained. In recent times the top levels of government have been populated by some of these particular social types, for example, Arthur Schlesinger, Jr., Kenneth Galbraith, Walter Heller, Daniel Moynihan, and Henry Kissinger. All of these men belonged to a high level governmental elite of presidential advisors. They also maintained their ties with the academic elites from which they came. In fact, by the very nature of presidential advising, their most enduring elite membership is usually in the academic elites, unless their political involvement draws them out of the academic and into a career in governmental administration.

[1] Don Martindale, *American Social Structure* (New York: Appleton-Century-Crofts, 1960), p. 460ff.

[2] Suzanne Keller, *Beyond The Ruling Class: Strategic Elites in Modern Society* (New York: Random House, 1963), p. 32.

Membership in some elites can be temporary. This is a characteristic that distinguishes the concept of elite from that of ruling class. The recent concern over "conflict of interest" is a by-product of multiple elite memberships as well as the temporary tenure held in some elites, notably those involving political power. Conflict of interest implies that a given individual may attempt to serve several masters at the same time. Membership in two or more elites may result in the situation wherein a decision made in serving as the member of one elite may be conditioned or partially determined by membership in another elite. Such would be the case for a Secretary of Defense whose business connections or position in a business elite is closely connected to a major contractor for military hardware and material.

Since expertise is the prime basis for elite status, educational credentials have become the major criteria for entry into the subelites that provide the recruiting ground for the *strategic* elites, to use Keller's term. To an exaggerated degree, this fact is seen in the new elites emerging in tropical Africa.[3] The need for functionaries in the administration of the new independent African states has put a premium on the educated person. Since a pool of people of proven experience and capability is nonexistent, diplomas and school attendance have became the key to elite membership. In contrast, although a college education may be a necessary requirement for elite status in technologically developed countries, it is by no means a sufficient requirement. Many other criteria, most of which signify some type of merit, act in determining who gains elite status in a modern industrial society. In those few African states in which a military elite exists, a distinct type of elite is formed; one that is more expert than the other major elites. "The superior training of army officers and their seclusion from everyday political life does, however, insulate them from the envy and often the stigma or corruption attaching to the political and very newly rich elite. . . ."[4] That is, the military elite seems to possess a more unequivocal and demonstrable criteria of merit.

The developing states of Africa offer an on-going natural experiment of elite formation and change. Many of these elites are so new that the membership is young and homogeneous relative to age, educational credentials, and previous experience—the latter being generally limited or nonexistent.

Furthermore, these new elites are rapidly expanding in size due to the growing demands for expertise of all types. The drive to "catch up" to the twentieth century by these developing countries insures a "booming" growth in elites. All manner of questions pertaining to the sociology of elites may be asked in contemplating this phenomena. For example: (1) What new criteria will be imposed on the second generation of elite members? (2) What type of status criteria and symbols, coupled with a stable life-style will emerge? (3) What

[3] The following material on Africa is taken from P. C. Lloyd, *The New Elites of Tropical Africa* (Oxford: Oxford University Press, 1966), p. 4.

[4] Ibid., p. 9.

effects will the second generation of elites have on the earlier established elite members? (4) To what degree will some of the elites begin to form a ruling class? (5) Will an aristocracy develop, and to what extent will elite membership be an avenue into such an aristocracy? (6) Will political and economic power in these countries come to rest in the hands of a ruling class, a small number of strategic elites, or in the hands of a multiplicity of elites that serve to fragment the wielding of power and function as "veto groups."[5]

Arnold Rose, in Chapter 24, discusses the question of whether or not political power is lodged in one all-pervasive "power elite," as postulated by C. Wright Mills, or in a multiplicity of elites or power wielding groups. In general, Rose argues that power in the United States is dispersed among a multiplicity of decision makers and elites.

The development and growth of elites in both developing and modern societies challenges the use of traditional class analysis. The existence of numerous elites connote heterogeneity, which, in turn, provide a place for either an analysis in terms of status communities or some other conceptual scheme that recognized the fragmentation of middle levels of modern societies.

22 *T. B. Bottomore*

THE ELITE: CONCEPT AND IDEOLOGY

The word "*elite*" was used in the seventeenth century to describe commodities of particular excellence; and the usage was later extended to refer to superior social groups, such as crack military units or the higher ranks of the nobility.[1] In

[5] David Riesman, *The Lonely Crowd*, (New York: Doubleday-Anchor, 1953), p. 257.

[1] See the *Dictionnaire de Trevous* (1771) where the primary meaning of *elite* is given as "Ce qu'il y a de meilleur dans chaque espece de marchandise"; and it is then added that "ce terme a passe de la boutique des marchands a d'autres usages . . . (troupes d'elite, l'elite de la noblesse)." (Quoted in Renzo Sereno, "The Anti-Aristotelianism of Gaetano Mosca and Its Fate," *Ethics*, 47:4, [July, 1938] p. 515.) In the sixteenth century, according to Edmond Huguet, *Dictionnaire de la langue francaise du seizieme siecle*, the word *elite* meant simply *choix* (a choice); *faire elite* meant "to make a choice." See also, on the early uses of the term itself and of the idea of elites, Hans P. Dreitzel, *Elitebegriff und Sozialstruktur*,

the English language the earliest known use of "elite," according to the *Oxford English Dictionary*, is in 1823, at which time it was already applied to social groups. But the term did not become widely used in social and political writing until late in the nineteenth century in Europe, or until the 1930's in Britain and America, when it was diffused through the sociological theories of elites, notably in the writings of Vilfredo Pareto.

Pareto defined "elite" in two different ways. He began with a very general definition: "Let us assume that in every branch of human activity each individual is given an index which stands as a sign of his capacity, very much the way grades are given in the various subjects in examinations in school. The highest type of lawyer, for instance, will be given 10. The man who does not get a client will be given 1–reserving zero for the man who is an out-and-out idiot. To the man who has made his millions–honestly or dishonestly as the case may be–we will give 10. To the man who has earned his thousands we will give 6; to such as just manage to keep out of the poor-house 1, keeping zero for those who get in . . . And so on for all the branches of human activity . . . So let us make a class of the people who have the highest indices in their branch of activity, and to that class give the name of *elite*." [2] Pareto himself does not make any further use of this concept of elite; it serves merely to emphasize the inequality of individual endowment in every sphere of social life, and as the starting point for a definition of the "governing elite," which is his real subject matter. "For the particular investigation with which we are engaged, a study of the social equilibrium it will help if we further divide that class [the elite] into two classes: a *governing elite*, comprising individuals who directly or indirectly play some considerable part in government, and a *non-governing elite*, comprising the rest . . . So we get two strata in a population: (1) A lower stratum, the *non-elite*, with whose possible influence on government we are not just here concerned; then (2) a higher stratum, *the elite*, which is divided into two: (a) a governing *elite*; (b) a non-governing *elite*." [3]

(Stuttgart: Ferdinand Enke, 1962) and H. D. Lasswell et al, *The Comparative Study of Elites* (Hoover Institute Studies; Series B: Elites, No. 1, Stanford, 1962). The idea that the community should be ruled by a group of superior individuals figures prominently in Plato's thought, and even more in the Brahminical caste-doctrines which regulated ancient Indian society. In another form, which yet has an important influence upon social theories, many religious creeds have expressed the notion of an elite in terms of the "elect of God." The modern, social and political, conception of elites may perhaps be traced back to Saint-Simon's advocacy of the rule of scientists and industrialists; but in Saint-Simon's work the idea is qualified in numerous ways, and especially by his recognition of class differences and of the opposition between the rich and the poor, which allowed his immediate followers to develop his thought in the direction of socialism. It was in the positive philosophy of Auguste Comte that the elitist and authoritarian elements in Saint-Simon's thought, allied with the ideas of de Bonald, were restored to prominence, and so influenced directly the creators of the modern theory of elites, Mosca and Pareto.

[2] Vilfredo Pareto, *The Mind and Society*, (London: Jonathan Cape, 1935), vol. III, pp. 1422-1423.

[3] Ibid., pp. 1423-1424.

It is not difficult to discover, from Pareto's earlier writings, how he arrived at this conception. In his *Cours d'economie politique*[4] he had propounded the idea of a normal curve of the distribution of wealth in a society. In *Les systemes socialistes*[5] he went on to argue, first, that if individuals were arranged according to other criteria, such as their level of intelligence, aptitude for mathematics, musical talent, moral character, etc., there would probably result distribution curves similar to that for wealth; and secondly, that if individuals were arranged according to their degree of political and social power of influence, it would be found in most societies that the same individuals occupied the same place in this hierarchy as in the hierarchy of wealth. "The so-called upper classes are also usually the richest. *These classes represent an elite, an 'aristocracy'*. . ."[6]

Nevertheless, there is an important difference in the formulation of the question in *The Mind and Society*, for Pareto here concerns himself not with a curve of distribution of certain attributes (including power and influence), but with a simple opposition between those who have power, the "governing elite," and those who have none, the masses. This change in Pareto's conception may well have owed something to the work of Gaetano Mosca, who was the first to make a systematic distinction between "elite" and masses–though using other terms–and to attempt the construction of a new science of politics on this foundation.[7] Mosca expressed his fundamental idea in these words: "Among the constant facts and tendencies that are to be found in all political organisms, one is so obvious that it is apparent to the most casual eye. In all societies–from societies that are very meagrely developed and have barely attained the dawnings of civilization, down to the most advanced and powerful societies–two classes of people appear–a class that rules and a class that is ruled. The first class, always the less numerous, performs all political functions, monopolizes power and enjoys the advantages that power brings, whereas the second, the more numerous class, is directed and controlled by the first, in a manner that is now more or less legal, now more or less arbitrary and violent . . ."[8] Mosca explains the rule

[4] Lausanne, 1896-1897.

[5] 1st ed. Paris, 1902; 2nd ed. 1926.

[6] Pareto, *Mind and Society*, p. 28.

[7] Gaetano Mosca, *The Ruling Class* (New York: McGraw-Hill, 1939). This English version, edited by Arthur Livingston, is a conflation and rearrangement of chapters from two separate editions of Mosca's *Elementi di scienza politica* (1st ed. 1896, 2nd revised and enlarged ed. 1923). An excellent recent study of Mosca's work–J. H. Meisel, *The Myth of the Ruling Class: Gaetano Mosca and the Elite* (Ann Arbor: University of Michigan Press, 1958)–makes clear that Mosca had formulated the main elements of his doctrine in his first book, *Sulla Teorica dei governi e sul governo parlamentare: Studi storici e sociali* (Turin, 1884), and shows how this doctrine was elaborated and qualified in his later writings. Meisel also discusses with great fairness (*Myth of the Ruling Class*, chap. 8) the relation between the ideas of Mosca and Pareto and shows that the latter can hardly be convicted of simple plagiarism (as Mosca claimed); nevertheless, Pareto's later account of the governing elite does seem to owe something to Mosca's doctrine.

[8] G. Mosca, *The Ruling Class*, p. 50.

of the minority over the majority by the fact that the former is organized "... the dominion of an organized minority, obeying a single impulse, over the unorganized majority is inevitable. The power of any minority is irresistible as against each single individual in the majority, who stands alone before the totality of the organized for the very reason that it is a minority"—and also by the fact that the minority is usually composed of superior individuals—"... members of a ruling minority regularly have some attribute, real or apparent, which is highly esteemed and very influential in the society in which they live."[9]

Both Mosca and Pareto, therefore, were concerned with elites in the sense of groups of people who either exercised directly, or were in a position to influence very strongly the exercise of, political power. At the same time, they recognized that the "governing elite" or "political class" is itself composed of distinct social groups. Pareto observed that the "upper stratum of society, the *elite*, nominally contains certain groups of people, not always very sharply defined, that are called aristocracies," and he went on to refer to "military, religious, and commercial aristocracies and plutocracies."[10] The point was made more sharply in a study of elites in France by a pupil of Pareto, Marie Kolabinska, who discussed explicitly the movement of individuals between the different sub-groups of the governing elite, and set out to examine in some detail the history of four such groups: the rich, the nobles, the armed aristocracy and the clergy.[11] Nevertheless, Pareto is always inclined to emphasize more strongly the division between *the* governing elite and the non-elite, and it is Mosca who examines more thoroughly the composition of the elite itself, especially in the modern democratic societies. Thus he refers to "the various party organizations into which the political class is divided," and which have to compete for the votes of the more numerous classes; and later on he remarks that "it cannot be denied that the representative system [of government] provides a way for many different social forces to participate in the political system and, therefore, to balance and limit the influence of other social forces and the influence of bureaucracy in particular." This last passage also reveals a considerable divergence between Pareto and Mosca in their interpretation of the development of political systems. Pareto always emphasizes the universality of the distinction between governing elite and masses, and he reserves his most scathing comments for the modern notions of "democracy," "humanitarianism" and "progress." Mosca, on the other hand, is prepared to recognize, and in a qualified way to approve, the distinctive features of modern democracy; in his first book, it is true, he observes that in a parliamentary democracy, "the representative is not elected by the voters but, as a rule, has himself elected by them ... or ... his friends have him

[9] Ibid., p. 53

[10] Pareto, *The Mind and Society*, III, pp. 1429-30.

[11] Marie Kolabinska, *La circulation des elites en France: Etude historique depuis la fin du XIe siecle jusquala jusqu'a la Grande Revolution* (Lausanne: Imprimeries Reunies, 1912), p. 7.

elected"; but in his later works he concedes that the majority may, through its representatives, have a certain control over government policy. As Meisel notes, it is only in his criticism of Marx that Mosca makes a sharp disjunction between masses and minorities; for the most part he presents a more subtle and complex theory in which the political class itself is influenced and restrained by a variety of "social forces" (representing numerous different interests in society), and also by the moral unity of the society as a whole which is expressed in the rule of law. In Mosca's theory, an elite does not simply rule by force and fraud, but "represents," in some sense, the interests and purposes of important and influential groups in the society.

There is another element, too, in Mosca's theory which modifies its original stark outlines. In modern times, the elite is not simply raised high above the rest of society; it is intimately connected with society through a sub-elite, a much larger group which comprises, to all intents and purposes, the whole "new middle class" of civil servants, managers and white collar workers, scientists and engineers, scholars and intellectuals. This group does not only supply recruits to the elite (the ruling class in the narrow sense); it is itself a vital element in the government of society, and Mosca observes that "the stability of any political organism depends on the level of morality, intelligence and activity that this second stratum has attained." It is not unreasonable, then, to claim, as did Gramsci, that Mosca's "political class . . . is a puzzle. One does not exactly understand what Mosca means, so fluctuating and elastic is the notion. Sometimes he seems to think of the middle class, sometimes of men of property in general, and then again of those who call themselves 'the educated.' But on other occasions Mosca apparently has in mind the 'political personnel.'"[12] And later, with more certainty: "Mosca's 'political class' is nothing but the intellectual section of the ruling group. Mosca's term approximates Pareto's *elite* concept—another attempt to interpret the historical phenomenon of the intelligentsia and its function in political and social life."[13]

The conceptual scheme which Mosca and Pareto have handed down thus comprises the following common notions: in every society there is, and must be, a minority which rules over the rest of society; this minority—the "political class" or "governing elite," composed of those who occupy the posts of political command and, more vaguely, those who can directly influence political decisions—undergoes changes in its membership over a period of time, ordinarily by the recruitment of new individual members from the lower strata of society, sometimes by the incorporation of new social groups, and occasionally by the complete replacement of the established elite by a "counter-elite," as occurs in revolutions. . . . From this point, the conceptions of Pareto and Mosca diverge.

[12] Antonio Gramsci, *Note sul Machiavelli, sulla politica e sullo stato moderno* (Milan: Einaudi, 1955).

[13] Idem, from his prison diary (1932), published in *Gli Intellettuali e l'organizzazione della cultura* (Milan: Einaudi, 1955).

Pareto insists more strongly upon the separation between rulers and ruled in every society, and dismisses the view that a democratic political system differs from any other in this respect.[14] He explains the circulation of elites in mainly psychological terms, making use of the idea of residues (sentiments) which he has set out at great length in the earlier parts of *The Mind and Society*. Mosca, on the other hand, is much more aware of the heterogeneity of the elite, the higher stratum of the political class, itself; of the interests or social forces which are represented in it; and, in the case of modern societies, of its intimate bonds with the rest of society, principally through the lower stratum of the political class, the "new middle class." Thus Mosca also allows that there is a difference between modern democracies and other types of policy, and to some extent he recognizes that there is interaction between the ruling minority and the majority, instead of a simple dominance by the former over the latter. Finally, Mosca explains the circulation of elites sociologically as well as psychologically, in so far as he accounts for the rise of new elites (or of new elements in the elite) in part by the emergence of social forces which represent new interests (e.g. technological or economic interests) in the society.[15]

Later studies of elites have followed Pareto and Mosca, especially the latter, closely in their concern with problems of political power. Thus H. D. Lasswell, both in his early writings which are commended by Mosca himself, and more recently in the Hoover Institute Studies on elites, has devoted himself particularly to the study of the political elite, which he defines in the following terms: "The political elite comprises the power holders of a body politic. The power holders include the leadership and the social formations from which leaders typically come, and to which accountability is maintained, during a given period."[16] The difference from the conceptions of Pareto and Mosca is that the *political elite* is here distinguished from other elites which are less closely associated with the exercise of power, although they may have a considerable social influence, and that the idea of "social formations" (including social classes) from which elites are typically recruited is reintroduced into a scheme of thought from which, especially in Pareto's theory, it had been expelled. As we shall see in a moment, the idea of elites was originally conceived in opposition to the idea of social classes. A similar development is apparent in the writings of Raymond

[14] Except that under the influence of democratic sentiments the governing elite is likely to be hesitant and incompetent in its rule. As so often, there is a conflict here between Pareto's science and his political doctrine; in a democratic system there is still, inevitably, a governing elite, and yet Pareto inveighs against democracy as though it were actually a real threat to the existence of such an elite.

[15] Cf. Meisel, p. 303 ". . . like the Marxian classes, Mosca's social forces closely reflect all the changes, economic, social, cultural, of an evolving civilization. With every new need, new social forces rise to meet the challenge and to ask their share of power of the old established interests."

[16] Lasswell, in H. D. Lasswell, D. Lerner and C. E. Rothwell, *The Comparative Study of Elites.*

Aron, who has also been chiefly concerned with the elite in the sense of a governing minority, but has attempted to establish a relation between the elite and social classes,[17] has insisted upon the plurality of elites in modern societies, and has examined the social influence of the intellectual elite, which does not ordinarily form part of the system of political power.[18]

The fresh distinctions and refinements which have been made in the concept of the elite call for a more discriminating terminology than has been employed hitherto.[19] The term "elite(s)" is now generally applied, in fact, to functional, mainly occupational, groups which have high status (for whatever reason) in a society; and henceforward I shall use it, without qualification, in this sense. The study of such elites is fruitful in several ways: the size of the elites, the number of different elites, their relations with each other and with the groups that wield political power, are among the most important facts which have to be considered in distinguishing between different types of society and in accounting for changes in social structure; so, too, is the closed or open character of the elites, or in other words, the nature of the recruitment of their members and the degree of social mobility which this implies. If the general term "elite" is to be applied to these functional groups, we shall need another term for the minority which rules a society, which is not a functional group in exactly the same sense, and which is in any case of such great social importance that it deserves to be given a distinctive name. I shall use here Mosca's term, the "political class," to refer to all those groups which exercise political power or influence, and are directly engaged in stuggles for political leadership; and I shall distinguish within the political class a smaller group, the political elite which comprises those individuals who actually exercise political power in a society at any given time. The extent of the political elite is, therefore, relatively easy to determine: it will include members of the government and of the high administration, military leaders, and, in some cases, politically influential families of an aristocracy or royal house and leaders of powerful economic enterprises. It is less easy to set the boundaries of the political class; it will, of course, include the political elite, but it may also include "counter-elites" comprising the leaders of political parties which are out of office, and representatives of new social interests or classes (e.g. trade union leaders), as well as groups of businessmen, and intellectuals who are active in politics. The political class, therefore, is composed of a number of groups which may be engaged in varying degrees of cooperation, competition or conflict with each other.

[17] Raymond Aron, "Social Structure and the Ruling Class, *British Journal of Sociology,* I (1), 1950. "The problem of combining in a synthesis 'class' sociology and 'elite' sociology . . . can be reduced to the following question: What is the relation between social differentiation and political hierarchy in modern societies?"

[18] See Raymond Aron, *The Opium of the Intellectuals* (London: Secker & Warburg; 1957).

[19] This has also been proposed by Raymond Aron in his article, "Classe sociale, classe politique, classe dirigeante," *European Journal of Sociology*, I (2), 1960; and I follow his suggestions to some extent.

The concept of the political elite was presented by Mosca and Pareto as a key term in a new social science,[20] but it had another aspect which is scarcely less apparent in their writings; namely, that it formed part of a political doctrine which was opposed to, or critical of, modern democracy, and still more opposed to modern socialism.[21] C. J. Friedrich has drawn attention to the fact that the nineteenth-century European doctrines of rule by an elite of superior individuals–doctrines which encompassed Carlyle's philosopy of the hero and Nietzsche's vision of the superman as well as the more prosaic studies of Mosca, Pareto and Burckhardt–were "all offspring of a society containing as yet many feudal remnants," and that these doctrines represented so many different attempts to revive ancient ideas of social hierarchy and to erect obstacles to the spread of democratic notions.[22] The social environment of such doctrines is defined still more narrowly by G. Lukacs, who suggests that the problem of political leadership was raised by sociologists precisely in those countries which had not succeeded in establishing a genuine bourgeois democracy (i.e. in which the feudal elements were especially strong); and he points to Max Weber's concept of "charisma" (in Germany) and Pareto's concept of "elites" (in Italy) as similar and typical manifestations of this preoccupation.[23]

The opposition between the idea of elites and the idea of democracy may be expressed in two forms: first, that the insistence in the elite theories upon the inequality of individual endowment runs counter to a fundamental strand in democratic political thought, which is inclined rather to emphasize an underlying equality of individuals; and secondly, that the notion of a governing minority contradicts the democratic theory of majority rule. But this opposition need not be by any means so rigorous and extreme as appears at first sight. If democracy is regarded as being primarily a political system, it may well be argued, as many have done, that "government *by* the people" (i.e. the effective rule of the majority) is impossible in practice, and that the significance of political democracy is primarily that the positions of power in society are open in principle to everyone, that there is competition for power, and that the holders of power at any time are accountable to the electorate. Schumpeter presented such a view of democracy, which has since been widely accepted, when he defined the democratic method as "that institutional arrangement for arriving at political decisions in which individuals acquire the power to decide by means of a competitive struggle for the people's vote."[24] Similarly, Karl

[20] Both writers insisted strongly upon the positive, scientific character of their studies, and their merits in this respect have been very favourably assessed in James Burnham's *The Machiavellians*: Defenders of Freedom (London: Putnam & Co., 1943).

[21] The critique of socialist doctrines and movements is a prominent feature of Robert Michels' *Political Parties*, (New York: The Free Press, 1949).

[22] Carl J. Friedrich, *The New Image of the Common Man* (Boston: Beacon Press, 2nd ed., 1950).

[23] G. Lukacs, *Die Zerstorung der Vernunft*.

[24] J. A. Schumpeter, *Capitalism, Socialism and Democracy*.

Mannheim, who at an earlier stage had seen in the views of the elite theorists an irrational justification of "direct action," and of unconditional subordination to a leader,[25] came later to regard such theories as being compatible with democracy: " . . . the actual shaping of policy is in the hands of elites; but this does not mean to say that the society is not democratic. For it is sufficient for democracy that the individual citizens, though prevented from taking a direct part in government all the time, have at least the *possibility* of making their aspirations felt at certain intervals."[26]

Moreover, it can equally well be argued that, even if democracy is regarded as comprising more than a political system, it is still compatible with elite theories; for the idea of equality which democracy as a form of society may be held to imply can easily be re-interpreted as "equality of opportunity." Democracy will then be treated as a type of society in which the elites—economic and cultural, as well as political—are "open" in principle, and are in fact recruited from different social strata on the basis of individual merit. This conception of the place of elites in a democracy is actually suggested by the theory of the circulation of elites, and it is stated explicitly in Mosca's writings.

It needs to be emphasized at this point that both the conceptions I have discussed—that of political competition; and that of equality of opportunity—can be presented as corollaries of liberal, or laissez-faire, economic theory. Schumpeter was quite aware of this: "This concept (of competition for political leadership) presents similar difficulties as the concept of competition in the economic sphere, with which it may be usefully compared;"[27] and a more recent writer has stated the connection still more forcefully: " . . . the theory of elites is, essentially, only a refinement of social laissez-faire. The doctrine of opportunity in education is a mere silhouette of the doctrine of economic individualism, with its emphasis on competition and 'getting-on.' "[28] In one sense, therefore, the elite theories of Pareto and Mosca were not (and those of their successors are not now) opposed to the general idea of democracy. Their original and main antagonist was, in fact, socialism, and especially Marxist socialism. As Mosca wrote: "In the world in which we are living socialism will be arrested only if a realistic political science succeeds in demolishing the metaphysical and optimistic methods that prevail at present in social studies . . . " This "realistic science," which Pareto, Weber, Michels and others in different ways helped to further, was intended above all to refute Marx's theory of social classes on two essential points: first, to show that the Marxist conception of a "ruling *class*" is erroneous, by demonstrating the continual circulation of elites, which prevents

[25] Karl Mannheim, *Ideology and Utopia* (1929, English trans. 1936 [London: Routledge & Kegan Paul]), p. 119.

[26] Idem, *Essays on the Sociology of Culture* (London: Routledge & Kegan Paul, 1940).

[27] J. A. Schumpeter, *Capitalism, Socialism, and Democracy* (London: Allen & Unwin, 1943), p. 271.

[28] Raymond Williams, *Culture and Society* (Penguin Books, 1961), p. 236.

in most societies, and especially in modern industrial societies, the formation of a stable and closed ruling class; and secondly, to show that a classless society is impossible, since in every society there is, and must be, a minority which actually rules. As Meisel so aptly comments: " 'Elite' was originally a middle class notion . . . (In the Marxist theory) . . . the proletariat is to be the ultimate class which will usher in the classless society. Not so. Rather, the history of all societies, past and future, is the history of its ruling classes . . . there will always be a ruling class, and therefore exploitation. This is the anti-socialist, specifically anti-Marxist, bent of the elitist theory as it unfolds in the last decade of the nineteenth century."[29] The elitist theories also oppose socialist doctrines in a more general way, by substituting for the notion of a class which rules by virtue of economic or military power, the notion of an elite which rules because of the superior qualities of its members. As Kolabinska says, " . . . the principal notion conveyed by the term 'elite' is that of superiority . . . "[30]

These reflections upon the ideological elements in elite theories provoke some further questions. It is possible, as I have suggested, to reconcile the idea of elites with democratic social theories; yet the early exponents of elite theories were undoubtedly hostile to democracy (although Mosca changed his views somewhat after his experience of Fascist rule in Italy, and became a cautious defender of some aspects of democratic government), and the hostility is still more marked in the case of those, such as Carlyle and Nietzsche, who presented social myths rather than scientific theories of politics. How is this to be explained? There is, first, the fact that these nineteenth-century thinkers conceived democracy in a different way, as a stage in the "revolt of the masses" leading with apparent necessity towards socialism. In criticizing democracy, therefore, they were, in an indirect way, combating socialism itself. It should be noticed, further, that the elite theorists themselves have had an important influence in producing the new definitions of democracy, such as that of Schumpeter, which are then held up as being compatible with the notion of elites. . . .

Another characteristic of the elite theories has been reproduced in many recent social theories which are directed against socialism; it is that, while these theories criticize the determinism which they find especially in Marxism, they themselves tend to establish an equally strict kind of determinism. The fundamental argument of the elite theorists is not merely that every known society has been divided into two strata—a ruling minority and a majority which is ruled—but that all societies *must* be so divided. In what respect is this less deterministic than Marxism? For whether men are obliged to attain the classless society or are necessarily prevented from ever attaining it, are they not equally

[29] Meisel, p. 10.

[30] M. Kolabinska, p. 5. S. F. Nadel, in his essay on "The Concept of Social Elites," *International Social Science Bulletin* VIII (3), 1956, also emphasizes "social superiority" as the distinguishing feature of an elite, without noticing the ideological element in this conception.

unfree? It may be objected that the cases are not alike: that the elite theorists are only excluding one form of society as impossible, while leaving open other possibilities (and Mosca claimed that in the social sciences it is easier to foresee *what is never going to happen*, than to foresee exactly what will happen); whereas the Marxists are predicting that a particular form of society will necessarily come into existence. But one might equally well say that the elite theorists—and especially Pareto—are claiming that one type of political society is universal and necessary, and that the Marxists deny the universal validity of this "law of elites and masses" and assert man's liberty to imagine and create new forms of society. In short, there is in both theories an element of social determinism which may be more or less strongly emphasized.

I mention this question now only in order to bring out the connection between the ideological and the theoretical aspects of the concept of elites. The concept refers to an observable social phenomenon and takes its place in theories which seek to explain social happenings, especially political changes. At the same time the concept makes its appearance in social thought at a time and in circumstances which at once give it an ideological significance in the contest between economic liberalism and socialism, and it spreads widely in doctrines which have an avowed ideological purpose. Even later, even in our allegedly post-ideological age, the concept cannot be regarded as a purely scientific construct; for every sociological concept and theory has an ideological force by reason of its influence upon the thoughts and actions of men in their everyday life. It may have this influence either because it is impregnated with a social doctrine, or because, while it excludes any immediate doctrinal influence, it nevertheless draws attention to and emphasizes certain features of social life and neglects others, and thus persuades men to conceive of their condition and their possible future in one set of terms rather than another. To criticize a conceptual scheme or a theory in its ideological aspect is not, therefore, simply to show its connexion with a broader doctrine of man and society and to oppose another social doctrine to it; it is also, or mainly, to show the scientific limitations of the concepts and theories, and to propose new concepts and theories which are truer or more adequate to describe what actually occurs in the sphere of society . . .

23 *Charles Kadushin*

POWER, INFLUENCE AND SOCIAL CIRCLES: A NEW METHODOLOGY FOR STUDYING OPINION MAKERS

SOCIAL CIRCLES AND THE THEORY OF POWER

Most theorists agree that social power can be studied effectively through the backward approach of locating powerful persons. For whatever their theory or method, observers agree that much social power is exercised in the form of legitimate authority, albeit not necessarily in political institutions. Persons who hold such positions can, in principle, easily be identified through the use of informants, documentary materials, or both. Direct and detailed measurement of power as a way of locating such persons is generally rejected, except by the decision-study school of power elites. Even they tend to back up this direct measurement with several other techniques (Dahl, 1958). [Full references to works cited are at the end of this Chapter.]

The difficulty of measuring power directly stems from its nature as a disposition concept. Any disposition concept, such as attitude, requires the collection of a large number of measurements which must then be reduced with the aid of a mathematical model. The model determines whether the concept is, in fact, uni- or multidimensional. The proper measurement of power requires the examination of a large number of situations in which power is said to be exercised. When more than two units are said to have power, then the data which must be examined are still more complex. The multimeasurement, multidimensional approach to the measurement of power which we suggest has, therefore, generally not been taken. In part, this approach has not been used because power has been viewed as a concept which *should* have a single definition and therefore should be measured with a simple measurement in one dimension. For the moment, we bow to the collective intuitive wisdom of students of the field, for the procedures we suggest would be quite arduous if applied to an entire population. Ideally, measurement of power should be confined to those likely to have some in the first place. Even the most confirmed decision-making theorists of national or community power begin their study with persons in the position to make the decision. This leads us right back to the problem of locating power elites.

As with the study of organizations, there are two systems of power in society at large. One is the formal system, and the other, the informal system.

Reprinted from the *American Sociological Review,* Volume 23, No. 5, October, 1968, by permission of the author and the American Sociological Association.

Note: This paper has benefited from the comments of Terry N. Clark, Lewis Edinger, George Fischer and Juan Linz. This is BASR publication.

The informal linking mechanisms within formal organizations have been fairly well studied. The same is not true of the informal system when society is viewed as a whole.

> The mechanisms through which such extensions take place [from small groups to large units] also apply in extending cohesion from one rank to the whole organizational unit, and, for that matter, to a larger social unit as well, even to society as a whole. The study of these mechanisms seems to be one major direction in which sociology must develop if it is to become less a study of small groups and more a study of society (Etzioni, 1961: 193).

The major informal mechanism which links power persons and powerful organizations is the social circle: the exact counterpart on the social system level of the informal shop system at the organizational level.

The structure and function of informal social circles in power situations is the single most controversial issue in the study of power and elites, though the concept has generally remained implicit. The key issues of the field, reconceptualized in social circle terms, are: (1) whether or not persons in formal positions of power are linked together through informal networks of power or influence; (2) whether or not persons who do *not* hold formal political system power positions are nonetheless linked to the formal positions in such a way that they can systematically influence decisions; and (3) whether or not influential persons who do not hold formal political power are themselves also interconnected. Allied to these questions are further specifications: What is the precise nature of links, if any, and what is the total structure of the linkage system. Further, the answers to these questions are likely to be different for the six aspects of power previously identified.

In community studies, for example, if the elite are closely responsive one to another, then the community power structure is said to resemble a pyramid;[1] if the elite form two or more cohesive circles, then power is said to be factional; if there are separate circles of elite which come together for limited and specific purposes, then power is said to be coalitional. Finally, if it is difficult to identify any coherent power circles, then power is said to be amorphous (Walton, 1966a, 1966b). In studies of national power circles in the Western democracies, Mills (1956), Hunter (1959) and Domhoff (1967), who wrote on the United States, and Guttsman (1963), who wrote on Britain, all found strong linkages between members of the elite. On the other hand, Aron (1966) and Keller (1963), in general reviews, and Parsons (1960), Dahl (1961), Kornhauser (1965) and Rose (1967), all writing about the United States, each for somewhat different reasons, found that linkages were non-existent or highly limited in scope and function. Keller (1963: 149) even found the lack of linkages between the various strategic elites to be a social problem. Domhoff (1967: chapter 7) was content to find

[1] This is obviously just one type of responsive network, but the lack of social circle theory has blinded analysts to other possibilities.

that the "governing class," which controls the "power elite," is mainly recruited from a national upper class. At the same time he suggested that these groups might be split into cliques of unspecified power.

The lack of a clear model of connectedness means that the limited amount of data collected is subject to various interpretations. For example, in the community power field, Walton (1966a: 431) classifies Hunter as having found, in his major study, a pyramidal structure. Yet Hunter himself summarizes his work as follows:

> Every community I have visited or studied has had a well-defined, relatively small group of people who constitute the local power structure. They most often represent the largest local industries, banks, law firms, commercial houses and newspapers. Major projects must have at least the informal sanction of the majority of these policy makers. *But they are not a single pyramid of power*. There are revolving committee clusterings of leaders who link with other committee clusterings on matters of major policy concern (Hunter, 1959: 5, italics supplied).

In a national elite study, Guttsman found that a ruling class existed in Britain and that movements between elite groups tended to *increase* (1963: chapter 11). A similar finding in the United States indicated to Mills that he indeed was dealing with a power circle. But Guttsman noted that in contrast to the nineteenth century, the contemporary elite appears at first sight disparate and lacking unity. Sereno explained that it is precisely because the concept of interpersonal influence is so intractable that he believes there is no such thing as a ruling class (1962: 79).

CHARACTERISTICS OF SOCIAL CIRCLES

Whatever one's favorite method for locating elites and, hence, for studying community or national power systems, the matter of social circle connection must be dealt with systematically. First, some working definition of the phenomenon must be established. A social circle has three defining characteristics, two of which are positive and one, negative: (1) A circle may have a chain or network of indirect interaction such that most members of a circle are linked to other members, at least through a third party. It is thus not a pure face-to-face group. (2) The network exists because members of the circle share common interests–political or cultural. (3) The circle is not formal–i.e., there are: (a) no clear leaders, although there may be central figures; (b) no clearly defined goals for the circle, though it almost always has some implicit functions; (c) no definite rules which determine modes of interaction, though there are often customary relationships; and (d) no distinct criteria of membership.

There are four kinds of common interests that circle members may have, and thus there are four kinds of circles: Cultural circles draw members together on the basis of valuational goals such as religion, psychotherapy (Kadushin,

1966) and other "philosophies of life"; expressive goals such as literature, art and recreation (Kazin, 1965; Wilson, 1964; Podhoretz, 1968); and cognitive goals such as science and technology (Price, 1963; Mullins, 1966; Cole and Cole, 1967). Utilitarian circles are characterized by the need to trade goods and services with other producers in "external economy" industries (Vernon, 1960) such as "Wall Street," or "Seventh Avenue" or "Hollywood". Power and influence circles are exemplified by our current discussion. Finally, there are integrative circles which are elaborations of interaction resulting from some common experience such as ethnic membership, wartime experience, or membership in an occupational community (Lipset et al., 1954).[2]

The structure of these circles tends to differ. Cultural circles have a core of producers of symbols and are surrounded by a periphery of symbol consumers and validators. Utilitarian circles are less concentric in form and more overlapping in nature. Power circles are more pyramidal, while integrative circles are often the most loose and egalitarian in structure. Their linkage to formal organizational structures tends to vary by type of circle. Cultural circles are often completely unattached to formal organizations and hence have often relied on a direct salon or a particular meeting place as a unifying device. Utilitarian circles form connections between formal organizations. Power circles do this too, but also exist as units within some larger and more amorphous political unit, and they may or may not have a coherent or cohesive ideology (Agger, 1964). For various reasons, connections in utilitarian and power circles are more covert and less legitimated. Integrative circles frequently are hung upon or grow into or develop from various forms of voluntary organizations. There are also "super circles" which link the inner core of two or more circles or different types. Frequently, it is asserted that there are "super circles" of a combined utilitarian and power axis.

An exposition of the theory of social circles is beyond the scope of this paper. But it is important to observe that many of the issues warmly debated in the field of power and elite studies are systematically identified within this framework. The issue of super circles and the relation between social circles and formal organizations are obvious problems. More generally, the kind of structure which characterizes different social circles is important to the power field: Are circles closely knit? Are they primarily face-to-face units or are they composed of a string of persons who know other persons? Are there sociometric stars? Are there inner and outer circles? What are recruitment and expulsion mechanisms? Are circles born, and if so, how do they die? Do power and influence circles have, as we claim, structures that are different from other types of circles? Finally, it is evident that the structure of circles depends in part on the nature of a particular social system, so there is no a priori reason to assume that power

[2] These types correspond to Parsons' latent pattern maintenance, adaptation, goal achievement and integrative functions (Parsons et al., 1953: 179-190). A full exposition of these types is beyond the scope of this paper.

structures in all communities will have the same form (Agger, 1964; Clark, 1967a and forthcoming).

The Social Circle Method for Studying Power and Influence

The major issues in the study of power and influence have been reconceptualized as problems of social circle structure, function, and development. If systematic ways of studying social circles of powerful or influential people can be found, then many of the problems of studying power and influence can be located if not resolved. In general, *the problem is to construct an open-ended sociometric*, rather than a sociometric of a closed system. Further, the measurement must allow for indirect as well as direct interaction. The *basis* for the interaction must be specified. Though some of the same persons may be involved, and hence the circles may to a major or minor degree overlap, circles formed on the basis of socio-political influence will not be the same as those formed on the basis of, say, literary influence. Finally, all circles are in various ways linked to formal structures, as suggested above. This means that in any institutional area, the location of informal circles may serve to locate formal structures, and vice versa. Nevertheless, because social circles do not have a formal leadership, positional or formal leadership variables are never altogether satisfactory substitutes.

Any sociometric must decide upon the particular link between persons which is to be studied. "Best friend," "person you would most want to sit next to," and so on, have been traditional linkages. Linkages that have been used in past studies of power include participation in the same decision and general influence. Obviously, discussion of political and economic issues should also be included as linkages. All of this points to using the concept *influence* rather than power in studying linkages. Influence implies informality, the sort of thing we wish to measure with social circles. It also is defined in terms of the *probability* that someone will take into account the wishes of others. This is presumably what is meant by the expectation that "true" power is exerted not by the person in the formal authority position, but by some other persons or class of persons. As long as the person in the formal position *thinks* that he takes another into account, then that other person must be said to have influence. This kind of influence is not "mere" perception as Rose (1967: chapter 18) would have it. This also suggests that some of the best informants about influence must be the very occupants of formal decision-making positions (Katz and Lazarsfeld, 1955). It follows that once a person holding a formal power position is found, he must be asked about other persons who influence him, much as has been done in studies of individual decision-making (Kadushin, 1968a). His perception about who is *generally* influential is also important but is a different matter. On the other hand, a person may unwittingly take the desires of others into account or may be placed in a situation in which the social framework serves to limit severely the course of his action (or inaction). Here the direct use of informants may be of only limited value. It is not so much the individual influencer that is so important as the entire social circle of influencers surrounding the decision-maker and of which he himself is a part. This again has a parallel in studies of individual decision-making. In many individual depth decisions, such as going to a psychiatrist, it is not the overt pressure of a single influencer which makes a person act, but rather the pressure as expressed by the norms of an entire social circle (Kadushin, 1966, 1968b). The concept of social circle changes the notion of influence from one of perception to one of social structure.

Our analysis of current methods of studying elites begins with the one closest to the social circle method. In the reputational technique, a preliminary list of the elite is constructed with the aid of informants and documents. In practice, this first list often consists of a positional elite. Under the assumption that the best judges of influence and power are the power elite themselves, this list is then shown to those named on the list and perhaps to other important persons. The judges may now rank the persons on the list (or "vote" for them) and/or they may be asked to name other persons who should qualify for such a list but were not placed upon it. The other influentials who are named (or who are named sufficiently often) are then interviewed and shown the list, and they too are asked to suggest other influentials. The process stops when some criterion is reached, usually when a significant proportion of the same persons is repeatedly named.

The reputational method obviously meets many of the requirements for circle measurement. Its most important virtue is that it can be considered a *snowball* sample (Goodman, 1961). A snowball sample is a device for obtaining an open-ended sociometric. Starting with a given list, usually a sample of some universe, each respondent is asked to name several others who are then interviewed, and so on. The problem with many reputational studies is that they have not been formally conceptualized as snowball samples and hence have not always maintained adequate controls over the snowball process. The feeling that reputational studies err because the elite play favorites in their nominations of other elite (Presthus, 1964:110) or that they offer only perceptions of power (Rose, 1967) is now seen as an advantage. The "error" helps to trace the linkages in the power circle. On the other hand, some of the most serious critics of the reputational technique stems from the lack of clarity with which the snowball method is used. In particular, the *basis* on which the circle is extended is always clear, for the reputational technique attempts to discover four things simultaneously: the *general formal* structure of power, the *general informal* structure, the *perception* of formal and informal power, and the *particular formal and informal interaction partners* of members of the power circle. In principle, there is no reason why a single study cannot accomplish all these aims, but if the goals have not been properly conceptualized in advance, as they generally have not, the result is likely to be confused.

From a formal point of view, the major competitor of the reputational technique, the decisional method, is simply another kind of snowball. The decision method works not with some general or hypothetical influence links, but with influence upon specific historical issues as linkages. The snowball starting points are drawn in two steps: first, a list is made with the aid of documents and informants of important recent community decisions. Then, with the aid of documents and/or informants, a list is drawn of persons who are thought to have participated in the decision. Again, this is often a positional list. These persons are then interviewed or documentary evidence is consulted, in part to ascertain their exact role, if any, in the decision or series of decisions. While reputational studies usually ask respondents to rate the importance of other respondents, most decisional studies do not do the analagous thing—they do not ask respondents to rank the importance of the various decisions (though see Agger, 1964). But they do ask respondents for a list of others who participated in the decision in certain ways. Should new names not previously on the investigator's list be derived from the interviewers, these new persons are also interviewed. Again, the process stops when some criterion of repetitiveness is reached. Once a decision study is seen as an open-ended sociometric a number of new problems emerge. By failing to conceptualize decision studies as snowball samples, investigators have tended not to conceptualize the role of the decision-maker respondent. He may be asked to act as an informant and to name people who generally participated in a decision. But he may also serve as a respondent and may report the person who influenced him, whom he influenced, and with whom he interacted in particular ways at particular times in the decision. Although these distinctions may not matter much in a very small power elite, more complex situations will yield quite different lists of people for different modes of interaction and influence. Decision methods thus tended to give a false sense of precision. They too are subject to sociometric "error," and since the dimension upon which the snowball is expanded is usually not clearly noted, it is difficult to ascertain the grounds upon which persons are drawn into the sample. Curiously, only to the extent that respondents are asked to act *exclusively* as purely "objective" informants are the data both limited and confused. In any case, the network aspects of decision-making is usually unavailable in decision studies. At best, the data are examined only in terms of the overlap between participants in one decision and participants in another. Finaliy, the problem of sampling decisions has been often noted.

Even positional methods of studying elites have used social circle methods. In the most ambitious application, closed system sociometrics are used. The entire list of positional or decisional elite derived from a previous research step is shown to those on the list who are then asked to indicate whom they know and in what capacities (Bonilla and Silva-Michelena, 1968; Hunter, 1956; Agger, 1964). This method indeed gives closure, but aside from its cumbersomeness (examination of the list may use up a major part of the hour or so one can get from most elites), this very closure creates problems. One of the chief characteristics of a social circle—its informal boundaries—is lost. In practice, this means that once assembled, the initial list cannot be self-correcting in the fashion of a snowball sample. There are many *indirect* ways of demonstrating common social circle membership, however, and positional studies have proved most ingenious in tracking these down, though no one study has used all methods. Most of the indirect measurements are based on some functional consequences of circle membership or upon some set of circumstances that might lead to a high probability of membership in a common circle.

One may assume that social circle membership is identical with membership in a given subculture or social class. Studies which attempt to show that members of a power elite come from an upper class are of this type. Merely demonstrating this common origin is usually insufficient since most studies wish to talk about the *interconnection* of the elite. Thus an attempt is made not only to show common values and origins but also participation in common organizations or, even better, common activities or instances of having been in the same place at the same time. Common schools, clubs, resorts, coffee houses and recreational or cultural interests, even appearances in the same journals, have all been used as indirect evidence of the connection between elites. Some positional studies use the organization as a unit of analysis and produce "organizational power sociometrics" by showing that the same person is a member of two or more organizations. (This method was used by Young and Larson, 1965: 926-934, to measure the structure of an entire small community.)

In sum, once the social circle character of elites and power elites has been recognized, and once it is seen that most studies have, in fact, relied on this characteristic to gather their data, it is necessary only to formalize these techniques to gain superior data. Sociometric techniques should be used both to locate the sample and to analyze its interconnections.[3] The more varied the bases for the sociometric questions, the richer the material and the more easily can some of the issues outlined above be resolved. Items pertaining to general influence, discussion partners, and actual decisions should be included. The distinction between members of the same type of circles and members of other types should be maintained so as to allow for the analysis of both functional circles and super circles. There remains, however, the question of selecting the right starting points for the snowball. If the elite is at all cohesive, then it presumably makes no difference where one starts, since all who count will eventually be named. But this assumption is often exactly what one wishes to

[3] The methods of analyzing the sociometrics of a snowball sample are somewhat different from those used with closed system samples. If most of the sample is drawn as a snowball rather than as a positional sample, then by definition the density of interconnections will be higher, since to be a member of the sample in the first place one must have been named by at least one person. The concept of a biased net is appropriate. For a review of appropriate models, see Abelson (1966), Coleman (1964: chaps. 14 and 17), and Rapoport (1963). It must be admitted that at present none of these models is altogether satisfactory for our purposes. The lack of techniques, much less models, for handling sociometric data has probably been responsible for the failure formally to analyze network data collected in such studies as Linz (1967) and Bell (1964), which have used snowball and circle approaches. Agger (1964) represents a sophisticated attempt to combine decisional, nomination and informant data to arrive at a comparative study of power circles, but the snowball method is not formally applied.

test. In such a case, a positional or decisional elite as a starting point may be the only recourse. Unfortunately, there is no substitute for knowledge of the social system for selecting the appropriate institutional "command posts" or the important decisions for the initial sample. This is the kind of information which can best be given by informants (Zelditch, 1962) or which can be obtained from documents, though as Bonilla and Silva-Michelena (1968) point out, a list of positions is, in fact, a "reputational" study of positions.

The advantage of a snowball study of the elite is that it is largely self-correcting. Nonetheless, different elite structures and different sample strategies can yield quite different results, and the procedure can become quite complex. Let us suppose that we are planning a study of economic and governmental elites in a moderate-sized country. We construct an initial "universe list" composed of all first and second officers of all enterprises above a given size, all legislators, and all civil servants above a given level. We take a proportional sample of these lists as our initial starting points and perhaps weight according to size of firm and importance of governmental position.[4] Two dimensions govern possible outcomes of nominations for the second wave of a snowball sample with this design: Whether the nominations are contained within the the initial "universe" list or not, and whether they tend to come from the same institutional area or to cross over into the other one. Nominations largely confined to the same institutional sectors and the initial list confirm the existence of two fairly tight circles. Nominations cross-cutting the institutional sectors show a tight super circle. The disproportionate "vote" received by [a] certain individual can confirm or correct the weighting scheme. If the nominations tend to fall outside the initial universe list, then there are basically three possibilities: the initial starting points were simply wrong; the initial list was incomplete; or a "kitchen cabinet" phenomenon is operating in which powerful persons name their close advisors who themselves have no formal power position. Subsequent waves can check some of these possibilities. If relatively few names are added on subsequent waves, then the new universe list formed by the initial list plus all new names mentioned say, by at least two or three persons, is likely to be the right one. Constant expansion of the lists shows a diffusely structured elite. The discovery of new circles which nominate each other on subsequent waves but which rarely refer to anyone on the initial list would be of special interest and, depending on other information, would suggest that the "true" centers of power are "behind the scenes," that a self-delusional group has been found, or that second levels in a society form their own circles. These are not all the possibilities and only one basis for linkage is assumed, but some notion of the richness of data obtained in this way has been given. It is possible to generate empirically grounded hypotheses about elite structure that might otherwise have never been even considered, much less verified.

[4] As with all sociometric and structural studies, there is the issue of general coverage versus structural density. The resolution of this problem must always be at the level of expediency, given the resources at hand.

Once the sample is obtained, then the elite's degree of power or influence should be checked according to reports of what they say they actually do. That is, what are their inputs and outputs. Properly developed, information in these areas provide the materials to fill in the reduction statements about power and influence. No doubt some persons obtained in the snowball will not be producers of opinions which influence others, nor will they have made decisions or produced position papers which have had an impact on societal processes. These matters can be solved by considering the entire classification of reduction statements about power which we earlier derived from the literature. A full consideration of the methodology for measuring power *after* the elite has been identified is impossible here. In any case, it will be apparent that a multidimensional index of power, influence, and opinion-making ability is likely to emerge from such an effort. Some of those drawn into the elite sample may score so low that they will be eliminated. Thus the index serves as an additional sample control, as well as a variable to explain and analyze . . .

REFERENCES

Abelson, Robert P. "Mathematical models in social psychology." 1966 pp. 1-25 in Leonard Berkowitz (ed.), *Advances in Experimental Social Psychology*, Volume 3. New York: Academic Press.

Agger, Robert, et al. The Rulers and the Ruled. New York: Wiley, 1964.

Aron, Raymond. "Social class, political class, ruling class." 1966. Pp. 201-210 in Reinhard Bendix and S. M. Lipset (eds.), *Class, Status and Power* (2nd ed.). New York: Free Press. First published in *European Journal of Sociology* 1 (1960): 260-281.

Bachrach, Peter and Morton S. Baratz. "Two faces of power." *American Political Science Review* 56 (December, 1962): 947-952.

Bell, Wendell, et al. *Jamaican Leaders: Political Attitudes in a New Nation.* Berkeley: University of California Press, 1964.

———. *Public Leadership.* San Francisco: Chandler, 1965.

Bonilla, Frank and J. A. Silva-Michelena. *Politics of Change in Venezuela. Volume I: Strategy of Research on Social Policy.* Cambridge: Massachusetts Institute of Technology, 1967.

Bottomore, T. B. *Elites and Society.* New York: Basic Books, 1964.

Cartwright, Dorwin. "Influence, leadership, control." pp. 1-47 in James G. March (ed.), *Handbook of Organizations.* Chicago: Rand McNally, 1965.

Clark, Terry N. "Power and community structure: Who governs, where, and when?" *The Sociological Quarterly* 8 (Summer, 1967a): 291-316.

———. "The concept of power: Some overemphasized and underrecognized dimensions." *Southwestern Social Science Quarterly* (December, 1967b): 271-286.

———. "The concept of power." Pp. 45-87 in Clark (ed.), *Community Structure and Decision Making.* San Francisco: Chandler, 1968.

———. "Community structure, decision-making, budget expenditures and urban renewal in 51 American communities," in Charles M. Bonjean, Clark, and Robert L. Lineberry (eds.), *Community Politics:* New York: Free Press. Forthcoming.

Clark, Terry N., et al. "Discipline, method, community structure and decision-making." *American Sociologist*, forthcoming.

Cole, S. and J. R. Cole. "Scientific output and recognition: A study in the reward system in science." *American Sociological Review* 32 (June, 1967): 377-390.

Coleman, James S. *Introduction to Mathematical Sociology*. New York: Free Press, 1964.

Dahl, Robert A. "A critique of the ruling elite model." *American Political Science Review* 52 (1958) 463-69.

———. *Who Governs?* New Haven: Yale, 1961.

Danzger, Herbert. "Community power structure: Problems and continuities." *American Sociological Review* 29 (October, 1964): 707-717.

Domhoff, G. William. *Who Rules America?* Englewood Cliffs: Prentice-Hall, 1967.

Edinger, Lewis J. *Political Leadership in Industrial Societies*. New York: Wiley, 1967.

Etzioni, Amitai. *A Comparative Analysis of Complex Organizations*. New York: Free Press, 1961.

Freeman, L., et al. "Locating leaders in local communities: A comparison of some alternative approaches." *American Sociological Review* 28 (October, 1963): 791-798.

Friedrich, Carl J. *Man and his Government*. New York: McGraw-Hill, 1963.

Goodman, Leo A. "Snowball sampling." *Annals of Mathematical Statistics* 32 (1961) 148-170.

Guttsman, W. L. *The British Political Elite*. New York: Basic Books, 1963.

Hempel, Carl G. "Fundamentals of concept formation in empirical science." P. 24 in *International Encyclopedia of Unified Science* (Volume II, No. 7). Chicago: University of Chicago Press, 1952.

Hunter, Floyd. *Top Leadership, U.S.A.* Chapel Hill: University of North Carolina Press, 1959.

Kadushin, Charles. "The friends and supporters of psychotherapy: On social circles in urban life." *American Sociological Review* 31 (December, 1966): 786-802.

———. "Reason analysis." Pp. 338-343 in the *International Encyclopedia of the Social Sciences* (2nd ed.). New York: The Free Press, 1968a.

———. *Why People Go to Psychiatrists.* New York: Atherton, 1968b.

Katz, Elihu and Paul Lazarsfeld. *Personal Influence*. New York: Free Press, 1955.

Kazin, Alfred. *Starting Out in the Thirties.* Boston: Little, Brown, 1962.

Keller, Suzanne. *Beyond the Ruling Class: Strategic Elites in Modern Society*. New York: Random House, 1963.

Kornhauser, William. " 'Power elite' or 'veto groups,' " pp. 210-18 in Reinhard Bendix and Seymour M. Lipset (eds.), *Class, Status and Power* (2nd ed.). New York: Free Press, 1966.

Lasswell, Harold. *World Politics and Personal Insecurity*. New York: Free Press (originally published, 1934), 1950.

---. "Introduction: The study of political elites." P. 4 in Harold Lasswell and Daniel Lerner (eds.), *World Revolutionary Elites: Studies in Coercive Ideological Movements*. Cambridge: Massachusetts Institute of Technology Press, 1965.

Lasswell, Harold D. and Abraham Kaplan. *Power and Society*. New Haven: Yale University Press, 1963.

Linz, Juan. "Local elites and social change in rural Andalusia." Unpublished report (July, 1967).

Mills, C. Wright. *The Power Elite*. New York: Oxford University Press, 1956.

Mullins, N. C. *Social Networks among Biological Scientists*. Harvard University Ph.D. dissertation, 1966.

Lipset, Seymour M., et al. *Union Democracy*. New York: Free Press, 1954.

Parsons, Talcott. "The distribution of power in American society." Pp. 199-225 in Parsons (ed.), *Structure and Process in Modern Societies*. New York: Free Press [first published in 1957, World Politics 9 (October).], 1960.

---. "On the concept of political power." Pp. 240-65 in Reinhard Bendix and Seymour M. Lipset (eds.), *Class, Status and Power* (2nd ed.). New York: Free Press [first published in Proceedings of the American Philosophical Society 197 (June).], 1963.

Parsons, Talcott, et al. *Working Papers in the Theory of Action*. New York: Free Press, 1953.

---. *Toward a General Theory of Action*. Cambridge : Harvard University Press, 1954.

Podhoretz, Norman. *Making It*. New York: Random House, 1968.

Presthus, Robert. *Men at the Top: A Study in Community Power*. New York: Oxford University Press, 1964.

Price, Derek. *Little Science, Big Science*. New York: Columbia University Press, 1963.

Rapoport, Anatol. "Mathematical models of social interaction." Pp. 495-545 in R. Duncan Luce, et al. (eds.), *Handbook of Mathematical Psychology*. New York: Wiley, 1963.

Ricker, William. "Some ambiguities in the notion of power." *American Political Science Review* 58 (June, 1964): 341-349.

Rose, Arnold M. *The Power Structure*. New York: Oxford University Press, 1967.

Rosenau, James N. *National Leadership and Foreign Policy: A Case Study in the Mobilization of Public Support*. Princeton: Princeton University Press, 1963.

Rustow, Dankwart A. "The study of elites: Who's who, when and how." *World Politics* 18 (August, 1966): 690-717.

Sereno, Renzo. *The Rulers*. New York: Praeger, 1962.

Spinrad, William. "Power in local communities." *Social Problems* 12 (Winter, 1965): 335-356. Also, pp. 218-231 in Reinhard Bendix and S. M. Lipset (eds.), *Class, Status and Power* (2nd ed.). New York: Free Press, 1966.

Vernon, Raymond. *Metropolis, 1985*. Cambridge: Harvard University Press, 1960.

Walton, John. "Discipline, method and community power: A note on the sociology of knowledge." *American Sociological Review* 31 (October, 1966a): 684-689.

———. "Substance and artifact: The current status of research on community power structure." American Journal of Sociology 71 (January, 1966b): 430-438.

Wilson, Robert (ed.). *The Arts and Society*. Englewood Cliffs: Prentice-Hall, 1964.

Young, Ruth C. and Olaf F. Larson. "A new approach to community structure." *American Sociological Review* 30 (December, 1965): 926-934.

Zelditch, Morris, Jr. "Some methodological problems of field studies." *American Journal of Sociology* 67 (March, 1962): 566-576.

24 *Arnold M. Rose*

CONTRASTING THEORIES OF POLITICAL POWER IN AMERICAN SOCIETY

The belief that an "economic elite" controls governmental and community affairs, by means kept hidden from the public, is one that can be traced at least as far back in American history as the political attacks of some Jeffersonians on some Hamiltonians at the end of the eighteenth century. Scarcely any lower-class political movement in the United States has failed to express the theme that the upper classes successfully used nondemocratic means to thwart democratic processes. Perhaps the widest popular use of the theme was achieved by the Populist movement in the decades following 1890. Anarchism and Marxism were imports from Europe that accepted the theme as one of the essential elements of their ideologies.[1] The history of the United States also provides ample factual examples to strengthen credence in the theme. The literature of exposure, especially that of the "muckrakers" in the first decade of the twentieth century, provides details as to how economically privileged individuals and groups illegally bought and bribed legislators, judges, and executive heads of government to serve their own desires for increased wealth and power.

The belief is not entirely wrong. But it presents only a portion of relevant reality and creates a significant misimpression that in itself has political repercussions. A more balanced analysis of the historical facts would probably arrive at something like the following conclusion: Segments of the economic elite have violated democratic political and legal processes, with differing degrees of effort and success in the various periods of American history, but in no recent period could they correctly be said to have controlled the elected and appointed political authorities in large measure. The relationship between the economic elite and the political authorities has been a constantly varying one of strong influence, cooperation, division of labor, and conflict, with each influencing the other in changing proportion to some extent and each operating independently of the other to a large extent. Today there is significant political control and limitation

[1] That the orthodox communist viewpoint regarding power in the United States today is still in terms of dominance by an economic elite was made evident in a series of interviews Walter Lippmann had with Premier Nikita Khrushchev in April 1961. When Lippmann said that decisions regarding foreign policy would be made by President Kennedy, "Khrushchev insisted that the forces behind the president would determine his policy. These forces behind the Kennedy administration he summed up in the one word: Rockefeller." It was also Khrushchev's opinion that Kennedy could not accelerate American economic growth "because of Rockefeller" and then added, "DuPont. They will not let him." (Walter Lippmann, syndicated columns, *Minneapolis Morning Tribune*, April 17, 18, 1961).

of certain activities over the economic elite, and there are also some significant processes by which the economic elite uses its wealth to help elect some political candidates and to influence other political authorities in ways which are not available to the average citizen. Further, neither the economic elite nor the political authorities are monolithic units which act with internal consensus and coordinated action with regard to each other (or probably in any other way). In fact there are several economic elites which only very rarely act as units within themselves and among themselves, and there are at least two political parties which have significantly differing programs with regard to their actions toward any economic elite, and each of them has only a partial degree of internal cohesion.[2] On domestic issues, at least, it is appropriate to observe that there are actually four political parties, two liberal ones and two conservative ones, the largest currently being the national Democratic party, which generally has a domestic policy that frustrates the special interests of the economic elite. This paragraph states our general hypothesis, and we shall seek to substantiate it with facts that leave no significant areas of omission. Merely to provide it with a shorthand label, we shall call it the "multi-influence hypothesis," as distinguished from the "economic-elite-dominance" hypothesis.

These two hypotheses are not to be equated with what in the social science literature is often called the "opposing theories of consensus and conflict." Both hypotheses fall under conflict theory, and the difference is that the multi-influence hypothesis depicts social reality as a far more complex conflict than does the economic-elite-dominance hypothesis. The latter sees conflict merely between a more or less unified elite and largely unorganized "masses," and if by some chain of events the latter could become better organized, conduct the conflict more effectively and *win*, there could ensue a society with a substantial consensus (ranging–in the writings of the varying proponents of the theme–from traditional agrarianism to communism). The multi-influence hypothesis sees conflict as often multilateral, with large proportions of the population often not involved, with the sides changing at least partially from issue to issue, and with consensus being achieved only temporarily and on a limited number of issues (except when naked force imposes an apparent consensus). The multi-influence hypothesis holds this to be true at least for heterogeneous, industrialized societies; it begs the question as to whether its own image or the "consensus theory" is more applicable to small "primitive" societies.[3]

[2] The two political parties sometimes agree on almost identical specific pieces of legislation, but mainly in the areas of foreign policy and national defense, practically never in regard to their programs or actions with respect to an economic elite.

[3] The functionalists in anthropology have used a consensus theory to explain the societies they typically study. When they, or the functionalists in sociology, use a consensus theory to explain heterogeneous, industrialized societies, our multi-influence hypothesis is opposed to theirs as well as to the economic-elite-dominance hypothesis. But we shall not deal here with the consensus or functionalist theory. I have considered sociological functionalism in

The distinction between the two hypotheses we are considering is also not to be equated with another distinction found in the social science literature—that between "social force" explanations and "powerful men" explanations. Sociologists generally are inclined to adopt the former and reject the latter, whereas proponents of the economic-elite-dominance hypothesis openly embrace the latter, at least much of the time. For example, Ferdinand Lundberg, the author of one study using the economic-elite-dominance hypothesis, wholeheartedly accepts the "powerful men" explanation in attributing complete power in the United States to "sixty families."[4] C. Wright Mills, the author of a . . . [later] and more scholarly exposition of the economic-elite-dominance hypothesis,[5] is too much of a sociologist and too much of a Marxist to reject "social force" explanations completely. After making the distinction between the two sorts of explanations, which he calls the "drift" and the "conspiracy" explanations, Mills comes out in favor of a combination of both of them, while concentrating on the latter for the purposes of the study in hand. In now presenting the multi-influence hypothesis and the evidence for it, I accept the general need for balance between "social force" and "powerful men" explanations, and even recognize that for a study of political power it might be desirable to stress the "powerful men" explanation. I believe it is necessary to use terms like "elite" and "leaders," and to recognize that the truly active and innovative people in any group activity are relatively few in number (although probably not so few as Lundberg and Mills suggest). But it is not necessary to consider all "powerful men" explanations as "conspiracy" or "secrecy" theories, as Lundberg and Mills do. While it may be true that not everything about power meets the eye, it does not follow that most things that are open to observation are false. Conspiracy and secrecy theories of power are theories based on inference, with very little fact, and their authors justify the absence of facts by stating that the important facts are kept hidden. This assertion might have a degree of plausibility if empirically supported explanations were offered as to the means of linking the conspiracy to the observable facts of power. But the conspiracy theorists who adopt the economic-elite-dominance hypothesis do not offer such explanations as far as the observable facts of political power are concerned. If facts regarding means and processes are not to be offered, then plausible and rational hypotheses must be presented; lacking even these, the social scientist must be skeptical about conspiracy and secrecy theories of power. In sum, in the hypothesis of this . . . [study] I am willing to admit a large element of a "power-

three other publications: *The Institutions of Advanced Societies* (Minneapolis: University of Minnesota Press, 1958), ch. 1; "On Merton's Neo-Functionalism," *Alpha Kappa Deltan*, 30 (Spring, 1960), 14-17; and "A Current Theoretical Issue in Social Gerontology," *The Gerontologist*, 4 (March, 1964), 46-50.

4 *America's Sixty Families* (New York: Vanguard, 1937).

5 *The Power Elite* (New York: Oxford University Press, 1956); see esp. pp. 24-27.

ful men" explanation of power, but not much of a "conspiracy" or "secrecy" explanation.

The multi-influence hypothesis differs from the economic-elite-dominance hypothesis both in it conception of the elite and in its conception of the masses. The latter hypothesis envisages society as a vast pyramid with the people of wealth in control at the top. They may or may not be seen as interspersed with a military elite. At a somewhat lower level are said to be their "lieutenants"—politicians, hired managers, small businessmen, and perhaps a few lesser categories who accept the orders of the economic elite and operate the control mechanisms and institutions that manipulate the rest of the society. Still lower are the "local opinion-makers," persons who constitute the mechanisms of control, who respond more or less automatically to the will of their superiors and who have a "grass-roots" following. At the bottom is the great bulk of the population, envisaged in the hypothesis as inert masses deprived of their rights and exploited economically and politically to serve the interests of those on top.[6]

There is also a "contrast-conception," an ideal of what an alternative structure of society would be, envisaged by those who hold the economic-elite-dominance hypothesis: this is of a classless, equalitarian society, in which the dominant groups have been eliminated or merged as equals into the masses, and the masses have been organized into functional groups that have a social structure for operating a society without the present controllers.[7] Those who hold this hypothesis usually imagine that their theoretical opponents are setting forth their own contrast-conception as the present reality and that they are declaring that a society without classes presently exists in order to fool the masses and keep them acquiescent.

While there are undoubtedly some among the wealthy who do deny a class system as a means of fooling the "masses" and trying to keep them satisfied with the status quo, this is not the view of most of those who hold the multi-influence hypothesis. The latter hypothesis, which is expounded and empirically supported in the present study, conceives of society as consisting of many elites,

[6] There is some difference of opinion as to the nature of the masses among the various proponents of the economic-elite-dominance hypothesis. C. Wright Mills depicts them as inherently passive and disorganized in the American system, completely unable and unwilling to resist their exploitation. The theorists of a communist bent, however, see them constantly resisting and struggling against their exploiters, but unable to take effective action because they have no access to the instruments of control. This theoretical difference is well expressed in the book by the communist theoretician Herbert Aptheker, *The World of C. Wright Mills* (New York: Marzani and Munsell, 1960).

[7] This contrast-conception ranges from the "communist stage" of Marx through the guild socialism of Mills (best expressed in his 1948 book, *The New Men of Power*) to the "social fascism" of some of the latter-day populists like Representative William Lemke of North Dakota, who, with the Catholic priest Charles Coughlin, sought in the mid-1930's to build a political movement around the goal of "social justice."

each relatively small numerically and operating in different spheres of life, and of the bulk of the population classifiable into organized groups and publics as well as masses. Among the elites are several that have their power through economic controls, several others that have power through political controls, and still others that have power through military, associational, religious, and other controls. While it is true that there are inert masses of undifferentiated individuals without access to each other (except in the most trivial respects) and therefore without influence, the bulk of the population consists not of the mass but of integrated groups and publics, stratified with varying degrees of power. "Integrated groups" are defined as numbers of individuals operating on the basis of common, "traditional" meanings and values, with networks of communication among themselves, with internal divisions of labor in role and function, and resistant to control by any elites who "pressure" them to behave in ways contrary to their common meanings and value. "Publics" are similar, but much less structured internally, more open to ideas from the outside, whether from an elite or from any other idea-generator (including Marxists), and much more specialized in that they have a very small range of common interests about which their members interact. Constituted mainly of integrated groups and shifting publics, as well as of an undifferentiated inert "mass," the bulk of the population is seen as much more differentiated and much less susceptible to control by any elite in the multi-influence hypothesis than in the economic-elite-dominance hypothesis.

Both hypotheses recognize the role of impersonal forces—such as economics and geography—as having significant influence over the course of society, but there is a difference between the hypotheses in how they view the nature and manner of influence of these impersonal forces. The economic-elite-dominance hypothesis holds economic forces as setting the course of history, and at the present time giving predominance to those private owners and managers of the means of production and media of mass communication they call the economic elite. The multi-influence hypothesis recognizes the importance of economic forces but considers that there are also semi-independent forces of social change in technology, cultural contact and conflict, and concrete and diffuse social movements. It further recognizes resistances to social change not only in economic vested interests but also in law and custom and in social structure generally. Both the impersonal forces of social change and of resistance to social change set marked limits to the power of any elite group to control the actions of society. For example . . . [in considering] the effort, in 1956–1965, to institute a federal program for financing medical care through Social Security . . . , [it can be seen] that a most significant new factor that promotes this is improvement in medical technology, which markedly reduces death through acute illness and leaves an increasing number of older people prone to heavy medical expenses through contracting the chronic illnesses. Social movements and elites then come into operation to promote or retard the formation of a federal program, and elements of existing social structure—such as private insurance plans and the committee system of Congress—play their roles in determining the final outcome. Thus, the multi-influence hypothesis holds that each social change or decision occurs in a matrix of social forces and social resistances, of cultural elements and social structures. Only some of which are or can be deliberately controlled or manipulated by elites.

CHAPTER 8

SOCIAL MOBILITY

Social mobility is a critically important characteristic of technologically advanced societies. Relatively high rates of both intergenerational and intragenerational mobility generally characterize such societies, and are key elements in determining the type of stratification structure that develops and the kind of social change that takes place.[1] For example, a society where the lower and middle levels have a readily perceptible possibility for upward mobility will have a less clearly defined status structure than one with very little social mobility. Class consciousness, which was such a crucial element in Marx's theory of stratification, fails to develop under conditions of high social mobility. Thus, social mobility may act to retard the formation of social classes.

Social mobility appears to be a concomitant of rapidly developing societies. Under conditions of urbanization, industrialization, and the attendant differentiation and specialization of occupations, a relatively high rate of mobility generally occurs. In order to have mobility, there must be both some place to move to, but there must also be room at that place. A society with a clearly delineated

[1] Intergenerational mobility refers to mobility between generations–a change from father to son–whereas intragenerational mobility refers to social mobility experienced by a single generation–a person changing his class or status during his own life time. The latter is sometimes referred to as career mobility.

class structure and class consciousness usually exhibits substantial barriers and inhibitions to movement. As a society develops toward increased differentiation, the clarity of status barriers declines with the development of new occupations, new life-styles, and an expanded range of income distribution. As class lines recede mobility increases, primarily because the occupational structure has new and intermediate places available for those ready to take advantage of the opportunity to move.

Certain structural features are important in determining the degree of mobility, or openness, of any society. Six such features are: (1) The *number* of occupations at the middle and upper levels toward which a mobile person may move. (2) The *size* of these openings. Are they spread over numerous occupations or merely over a few? For example, in a given period there may be a great and continuing shortage of social workers but an oversupply of teachers, accountants, office managers, draftsmen, and similar occupational types. This is not as open a situation as when the needs of each of these occupations are similar and the availability of openings are spread among all of them rather than being concentrated in the one (social work). (3) The birth and retirement or *turnover rate* for an occupation. (4) The degree of ethnic identity, kinship group solidarity, and locality ties existing in a society. (These factors generally inhibit intergenerational mobility and career mobility, though not necessarily occupational inheritance or group mobility.) (5) The social, political, and legal conditions affecting the job market as well as the restraints and rules determining the entry into the various occupations. (This is a two-edged sword. Racism and ethnic discrimination are currently some of the most important inhibitors to mobility. Sometimes these constraints are supported by political or legal rules, although in other, less frequent, instances political and legal circumstances may increase potentialities for mobility. The current high demand for black educators and scholars is a case in point. The existence of unions and other types of occupational protective associations is another structural feature influencing movement into certain occupations. (6) And, paradoxically, the development of bureaucracy and advanced technology in modern industrial society encompass opposing characteristics for social mobility. (Although bureaucratization increases career opportunities and orderliness in pursuing careers involving upward mobility, the orientation toward the use of technology and the commitment to change that characterizes certain types of large bureaucracies create many instabilities in career building, at both the upper and lower white collar and executive levels.[2])

In addition to these structural factors that influence mobility, there are the more specific personal variables. The most important of these is probably that of *father's occupation*. In actuality, father's occupation is a central element in determining other variables, such as family status, income, attitude toward edu-

[2] William H. Form, "Occupation and Careers," in *International Encyclopedia of the Social Sciences*, David L. Sills, (ed.), vol. 2, (New York: Macmillan, 1968), p. 253.

cation, consumer behavior, political affiliation and other factors combining to determine the life-style of the family in question. *Educational level* is another crucial factor in determining mobility. This too may be significantly related to father's occupation and its resultant life-style. Other variables include such personal characteristics as physical appearances and psychic energy. The latter may be important as the basis for various kinds of motivation and susceptibility to chronic disease and mental disability. Certain kinds of native ability or intelligence have a bearing on mobility potential. However, as currently measured, intelligence is correlated to some degree with family status and educational level. There are also a number of factors that may inhibit mobility. Although racism was mentioned above in relation to the structural aspects of mobility, one's race (among blacks the darkness or lightness of pigmentation)[3] has been a factor determining the probability of success in achieving upward mobility.

In attempting to measure the social mobility of a population, social scientists have generally compared the occupation of fathers and sons. In the study of mobility an important consideration is the movement from blue-collar to white-collar employment. Although most emphasis is paid to the jump from blue-collar to white-collar work, movement occurs in both directions. A substantial number of the sons of white-collar workers experience downward mobility and become blue-collar workers. In some cases the consequences of this kind of downward mobility may vary. Some white-collar pay scales are quite low, whereas certain blue-collar work pays very well.

The above discrepancy refers to two aspects of mobility, class, or economic mobility and status mobility. A man's occupation often accounts for his economic class as well as the status and life-style that results from the work he does. However, in a rapidly changing modern society, class, or economic, mobility is probably easier to achieve than status mobility. The only systematic approach to a rapid rise (i.e., within one's lifetime) in status is either through advanced higher education or the display of conspicuous talent or skill.[4] Mobility involving a great change in life-style and unlimited financial resources is relatively infrequent; so much so, that such occurrences still make good magazine copy.

Most social mobility, even in a rapidly changing society, is relatively limited. Most mobility occurs *within* either the blue or white collar occupational categories. The relatively short distance moved by most mobile people would seem to preclude the notion that their mobility is from a lower *social class* to a higher one, at least as social class has been defined in the classical Marxian sense. A better description of the most prevalent type of economic and occupational mobility would be one utilizing the concept of status community. That is, most mobility is more fittingly described as movement from one status community to

[3] Donald Cheek, "Black Ethnic Identity as Related to Skin Color, Social Class, and Selected Variables," Ph.D. Dissertation, Temple University, Philadelphia, 1971.

[4] It is possible to move up quickly in status by marrying into a prestigious family, but mobility of this kind is not only infrequent but fortuitous.

another either by the offspring or by the family head himself, in which case it is termed as career or intragenerational mobility.

As Smelser and Lipset point out in Chapter 25, there are two general societal types of mobility, collective and individual, based on ascription and achievement, respectively. Technologically advanced societies generally exhibit some sort of mixture of the two types, particularly at the middle levels of the stratification structure. Individual movement from one status community to another will signify individual mobility, based on achievement. In addition, a given status community may become more highly valued and experience an increased demand for the skills and services of its members, thus experiencing *collective* upward mobility. An example of upward movement in status for entire occupational groups is seen in the recent rise of medical doctors, morticians, and rocket engineers. Such a status situation may represent a gain in all three dimensions of class, status, and political influence or merely a gain in one or two of Weberian dimensions.

One aspect of intergenerational mobility in a society is the rate of occupational inheritance. Recent mobility studies indicate that from one-half to two-thirds of the American males in the labor force are in the same occupational categories as their father or at immediately adjacent levels.[5] The degree of specificity of occupational inheritance is an indicator of the openness of a stratification system. From all appearances the rate of occupational inheritance in the United States implies a relatively open system.

The optimistic nature of the "American dream" of occupational and monetary success seems to have precluded much consideration of downward mobility. Yet, this is an important feature of the stratification system of the modern industrial state. One might describe the overall mobility processes of modern society as being similar to a coffee perculator; that is, there is a continuous movement over time from bottom to top *and* from top to bottom. Schumpeter refers to this phenomena in discussing the destiny of many families in society by reminding the reader how small the number of families is that remain important or known for long periods of time in the history of a country or locality.[6] A casual comparison of the richest and most prestigious families of the American revolutionary period, and at intervals since then, will provide insight into the variability of the composition of the top levels at various points in time. As referred to previously, there is evidence that those who occupy the levels close to either side of the white-collar blue-collar line tend to move back and forth, with a considerable number of the sons of white-collar workers dropping down to a blue-collar level.

[5] Form "Occupation and Careers," p. 251.

[6] Joseph Schumpeter, "Movement Across Class Lines," in Joseph Schumpeter, *Social Classes: Imperialism* (New York: Meridian Books, 1951), pp. 124-134.

25 *Neil J. Smelser and Seymour Martin Lipset*

SOCIAL STRUCTURE AND THE ANALYSIS OF MOBILITY

Three features of social structure are critical in determining the *forms* of social mobility in any society: ascription-achievement; level of differentiation of social structures; and locus of control of sanctions. We shall now discuss each of these briefly. . . .

1. Ascription-achievement

Societies vary considerably in the degree to which persons are assigned to roles (occupational, religious, political, etc.) on the basis of status ascribed at birth. The basis of ascription may be kinship, age, sex, race or ethnicity, or territorial location. So far as these criteria dominate, the society emphasizes ascription. So far as assignment to roles rests on some sort of behavioral performance, the society emphasizes achievement.

The implication of ascription-achievement for the form of social mobility is this: If ascription is firmly institutionalized, mobility tends to be collective; if achievement, mobility tends to be individual.[1]

To illustrate: Classical India displays a stratification system at the ascriptive extreme. Under ideal-typical conditions, virtually every aspect of an individual's future life was determined by his birth into a particular caste: his marriage choice, his occupation, his associational memberships, his ritual behavior, his type of funeral, and so on. Choices were determined at the instant of birth. In this way the caste system discouraged individual mobility from one caste or caste-associated role to another during his lifetime. What form did mobility take, then? According to Hutton's account, mobility manifested itself as the *collective* splitting off of subcastes, or what he calls the "fissiparous tendencies in Indian castes." Members of a caste were aggregated into a subcaste, which for a time accepted wives from other subcastes but simultaneously refused to give daughters to these subcastes. This established a claim to superiority, which was fortified by some change in occupational duties. The final step was to adopt a new caste name and deny all connection with the caste of origin. Thus, in Hutton's language, "by organization and propaganda a caste can change its name and in the course of time get a new one accepted, and by altering its canons of behavior in the matter of diet and marriage can increase the estimation in which

Reprinted from Neil J. Smelser and Seymour Martin Lipset, editors, *Social Structure and Mobility in Economic Development* (Chicago: Aldine Publishing Company, 1966); copyright ©1966, by Neil Smelser and Seymour Martin Lipset.

[1] This argument concerns only the movement of persons. Societies that institutionalize ascription also encourage the distribution of rewards to existing "estates" or "classes," whereas societies that institutionalize achievement encourage the movement of persons to rewards.

it is held."[2] This multiplication of castes over the centuries provides the clue to the distinctive form of social mobility in classical India.

American society possesses, ideally, a stratification system at the achievement extreme. An individual is able, in his lifetime, to move away from ascribed positions (based on region, ethnic background, even family of orientation) into new roles. In practice, of course, ascribed characteristics, especially racial ones, prevent the operation of this system in pure form.

One reason for the pronounced hostility toward "welfare" practices in the United States stems from this distinctive American emphasis on achievement. The introduction of welfare measures means bringing facilities and rewards to certain defined classes of persons, rather than having persons move to these facilities and rewards. One of the interesting justifications for introducing welfare measures in the United States–as opposed to continental European states, where state welfare is taken more for granted–is that such measures must presumably *facilitate* equality of opportunity for individuals in the society. If it can be argued that *not* to give welfare somehow impedes the life chances of a potentially mobile individual or class of individuals, then welfare measures are more likely to be accepted as legitimate.

Within the United States some interesting variations on the dominantly individual form of mobility are observable. When a person assumes an adult occupational role and reaches, say, age 30, his mobility as an individual is more or less completed, except perhaps within the same occupational category. Thus adult occupational status is in certain respects an ascribed position, though this ascription is not a matter of position at birth. Under these circumstances mobility tends to become collective. Whole occupational groups try to improve their standing or guard it from erosion. Collective mobility in the American system becomes legitimate, in short, when the battle for individual mobility is in effect closed for an individual, when he becomes lodged in an ascribed group.

Great Britain constitutes a system intermediate between extreme individual mobility and extreme collective mobility. Individual mobility is emphasized but individuals carry with them certain ascribed and semi-ascribed markings–accent, habits, manners, etc.–which reflect family and educational background and operate as important status symbols. Full mobility takes place only in the next generation, when mobile individuals can give their own children the appropriate cultivation and education. This case is intermediate because it is the family that moves collectively upward over two or more generations.[3]

2. Differentiation of social structures.

One point of contrast between simple and complex societies is the degree of differentiation of social structures. In an ideal-typical simple society, little differ-

[2] J. H. Hutton, *Caste in India* (Cambridge: The University Press, 1946), pp. 41-61, 97-100.

[3] This example is not meant to imply that several-generation mobility is absent in the United States. The contrast between Britain and the United States is a relative one.

entiation exists between a position in a kinship group (e.g., elderly men in a certain clan), political authority (since elderly men in this clan hold power as a matter of custom), religious authority (since political and religious authority are undifferentiated), and wealth (since tributes flow to this position). The social structures are undifferentiated, and an individual occupies a high or low position in all roles simultaneously . . .

In complex societies, by contrast, a position in the age structure does not necessarily entitle a person to membership in specific roles in the occupational structure,[4] a position of importance in the religious hierarchy does not necessarily give an individual access to control of wealth. Thus, though some individuals *may* simultaneously receive great amounts of different rewards–wealth, power, prestige–these rewards are often formally segregated in a highly differentiated social structure.

Many colonial societies of the late nineteenth and early twentieth centuries are intermediate between the simple and the complex. In these societies the social order broke more or less imperfectly into three groupings: first, the Western representatives who controlled economic enterprises and political administration, and who frequently were allied with large land-owners; second, natives–when drawn into the colonial economy–were tenant farmers, wage laborers, etc,; and third, a group of foreigners–Chinese, Indians, Syrians, Goans, Lebanese, etc.–who fit "between" the first two as traders, moneylenders, merchants, creditors, etc. This view is oversimplified, of course, but many colonial societies approximated this arrangement. The important structural feature of such systems is that economic, political, and racial-ethnic roles *coincide* with one another.

Two implications of the level of differentiation of social structure for the form of social mobility are: (1) The less differentiated the system, the more difficult it is for individuals to move with regard to a *single* role (e.g., through occupational success). The individual would have to move with regard to all roles–political, economic, ethnic, etc. This means that individual mobility is difficult, and that the distribution of rewards is effected not by movement of the individuals to positions so much as by collective competition among multifunctional groupings. In highly differentiated systems it is possible to move, for example, into a new occupational role thereby achieving economic success without simultaneously having to become a political leader, change one's ethnic identification, etc. Segmental mobility, in short, is conducive to individual mobility. (2) The highly differentiated system leaves room for status disequilibrium (being high in one role and low in another, as in the case of the [black] doctor). This phenomenon is rare in societies with coinciding social hierarchies.

[4] Very young and very old persons are generally *excluded* from occupational positions, however. The institutionalization of the seniority principle in industry and elsewhere also constitutes a qualification on the principle of separation of age and occupation.

3. The locus of control of sanctions

Where does the locus of power to apply sanctions reside in a society? Consider several different types of economic activity: In an ideal-typical paternalistic industrial setting, the industrial manager has at his own disposal both economic and political—and perhaps even moral—sanctions to recruit and control employees. In an ideal-typical free enterprise system, the industrial manager may utilize both economic and political sanctions, but for both he is held accountable to a central political source.

To compare and contrast political situations such as these, and to assess their implications for social mobility, two dimensions are particularly important: (1) Elitist-egalitarian, which refers to the locus of control over rewards and facilities in the stratification system itself. In the elitist case power to allocate sanctions is concentrated in the hands of a few; in the egalitarian case the origin of decisions to allocate is presumably dispersed, even though the implementation of these decisions may rest in the hands of a few. (2) The locus of power in territorial terms: just as the elitist-egalitarian dimension refers to the concentration of power in social space, the dimension of central-local refers to the same concentration in geographical space. (3) The degree to which the several concentrations of sanctions coincide. Are those classes with primary responsibility for decisions concerning economic sanctions the *same* classes that determine educational policy, religious doctrine, and so on? This last dimension, closely related to the concept of differentiation, refers to the relations among the distributions of several types of sanction.

DEVELOPMENT AND THE FORM OF SOCIAL MOBILITY

What are the typical consequences of rapid social and economic development in terms of these dimensions? In a general way the answer is that rapid development sets up tensions between ascription and achievement, between differentiated and undifferentiated structures, between egalitarian and hierarchical principles, and between central and local power. Let us examine each type of tension briefly:

1. As economic and social development proceeds, various criteria of achievement—attainment of wealth, attainment of political power, etc.—begin to intrude on ascribed memberships as bases for assigning persons to roles. Castes, ethnic groups, and traditional religious groupings do not necessarily decline in importance *in every respect* during periods of modernization. As political interest groups or reference groups for diffuse loyalties, they may even increase in salience. As the bases of role assignment and ranking, however, ascriptive standards begin to give way to economic, political, and other standards which gives rise in turn to tension between ascriptive and achievement standards for organizing roles and recruiting personnel to them.

2. Because of the widespread tendency for social structures to become

differentiated from one another during periods of rapid development,[5] individual mobility through occupational and other structural hierarchies tends to increase. This signifies the separation of the adult's roles from his point of origin. In addition, individual mobility is frequently substituted for collective mobility.[6] Individuals, not whole castes or tribes, compete for higher standing in society. This phenomenon of increasing individual mobility appears to be one of the universal consequences of industrialization.[7]

3. Most contemporary developing areas, emerging from colonial domination of one sort or another, are committed to egalitarian ideologies. Since most of these societies have traditional hierarchical social arrangements, yet another source of tension–between hierarchical and egalitarian principles–is introduced by rapid development.

4. Most contemporary underdeveloped countries have chosen a highly centralized approach to the management of their economy and social structure. This choice generates many tensions and conflicts, however, since most of the countries in question have strong local traditions of tribalism, community life, etc.

These several tensions frequently make their appearance in the relation between *demands* for mobility imposed by the exigencies of development on the one hand, and the *supply* of potentially mobile individuals and groups with appropriate motivations, attitudes, and skills on the other.

Issues that arise on the demand side of mobility in developing societies

For any society attempting to modernize we must ask which sectors of the social structure provide the developmental vanguard movement, and which lag behind? Under the influence of the classic British model of industrialization and lingering materialist assumptions as well, analysts have tended to assume that economic development leads the way, and that other sectors change in order to adjust. Parliaments are reformed, education is strengthened, etc., as a response to the exigencies imposed by economic change. This is not the only pattern of development, however. Although the *commitment* to economic change is pronounced in many African societies, for instance, these societies have moved much faster into the modern age in the political sphere (with universal suffrage, parliaments, parties, and administrative bureaucracies) than in the economic sphere. In these same societies, moreover, changes in the educational structure seem to be outdistancing actual economic accomplishments . . .

A related issue concerns the organizing principles employed in fostering development, and the ways in which such principles change the course of devel-

[5] Neil J. Smelser, "Mechanisms of Change and Adjustment to Change," in Bert F. Hoselitz and Wilbert E. Moore (eds.), *Industrialization and Society* (The Hague: Mouton, 1963).

[6] The degree to which this takes place depends also on the residue of ascription in industrial societies, as well as the locus of power with regard to the control of major social sanctions.

[7] Seymour Martin Lipset and Reinhard Bendix, *Social Mobility in Industrial Society* (Berkeley: University of California Press, 1959), pp. 13ff.

opment. By "organizing principles" we refer to the kinds of sanctions (rewards and deprivations) used to establish roles and to induce personnel to perform in them. The following organizing principles might be considered:

1. Reliance on monetary sanctions. This refers to the system of wages, salaries, and profits that can be employed to determine the role distribution in a society, the recruitment of individuals into these roles and the degree of effort elicited within them. Such sanctions may operate positively (e.g., the offer of high wages in industrial operations) or negatively (e.g., the "push" of agricultural wage laborers from the land into urban settings during periods of slack demand).

2. Reliance of political measures. These include physical coercion or the thread of coercion, influence, bargaining, persuasion, the promise of political power, etc. Again, these sanctions may be used to induce individuals into new roles or to force them from old ones, or both.

3. Integrative measures. One focus of integrative pressure is particularism, or membership in some ascriptive group. Membership in kinship grouping, for instance, not only may set up expectations with respect to roles that a given member may assume, but also may determine the conditions of entry and tenure in a role. Group membership may also be important for controlling a person once he has entered a role. The key feature of particularistic sanctions of this sort is that the sanctioner appeals to the integrative ties (memberships) of the actor in question. Other foci of particularism are caste membership, tribal affiliation, membership in ethnic groups, and so on. Such integrative measures, like the other sanctions, may operate positively (e.g., in the case of particularistic hiring in the Japanese case) or negatively (e.g., in the case of escaping burdens to extended family and tribe, as reported for some African societies).

4. Value-commitments. Commitment to fundamental principles can be used as a lever to induce individuals to enter roles and behave in certain ways, once in them. Specific areas in which fundamental values operate as sanctions are in religious doctrine, nationalism, anti-colonialism, socialism, and communism, or any combination of these. Again, in specific cases entry into a role may be as a result of the pull of a positive commitment to a "modern" value-system, or as a result of the push of alienation from some "traditional" value-system.

The *effectiveness* of these organizing principles refers in the first instance to the ability to stimulate the social mobility requisite for the society's developmental needs. In addition, however, reliance on a particular type of sanction has consequences other than merely stimulating mobility. For example, in some cases political sanctions may be the most effective means for establishing and filling roles necessary for economic production, though these same sanctions may not be the most effective means of allocating roles to foster changes in the educational sector. Furthermore, the wholesale application of political sanctions may set up inflexible political cleavages that paralyze a society, thus making these sanctions ineffective in the long run.

A final issue concerns the locus of power with respect to the organizing principles during periods of rapid development. In any empirical case a society relies on *several* of the organizing principles for development. Broadly speaking, the dominant principles of recruitment into economic roles in American society are: (a) reliance on the belief in fundamental values such as free enterprise, inculcated in potential incumbents of occupational roles during periods of early socialization and education; (b) reliance on monetary compensation, implemented through the market mechanism; (c) reliance on the outcome of political contests among interest groups, especially labor and management; (d) reliance on more centralized political machinery, usually when the second and third principles seem to be functioning inadequately. In general the political controls over these different organizing principles are dispersed in [American] society; a single political agency is *not* presumed to have direct control over the education of children in the basic values of society, the operation of the labor market, the settlement of industrial disputes, etc. In other societies–e.g., theocratic, totalitarian–the political centralization of control over organizing principles is much greater.

Social mobility may be viewed as a consequence of the organizing principles involved, the capacity of the society to maintain such organizing principles, and their effectiveness in achieving the ends for the society. Mobility in turn is an important variable in determining the rate and form of development, and development in its own turn may feed back to the organizing principles and patterns of mobility by occasioning shifts in the power balance of society, changes in the distribution of wealth, and so on.

Issues that arise on the supply side of mobility in developing areas

On this subject we may be briefer. The effectiveness of the organizing sanctions depends very much on the predisposition of the persons and groups in society to be moved by such sanctions. This depends in turn on their motivation, attitudes, and skills. The social structures that are critical in forming these characteristics are religion, education, community, and kinship, for these structures "specialize" in creating commitment and social outlook. Many of the problems that new nations face revolve around the attempt by those eager for development to undermine traditional familial, community and religious structures and establish new ones–especially in education–so as to modify the supply conditions for mobility.

Any historical case of individual or collective mobility resolves into the interplay of various demand and supply conditions for mobility. One familiar case of mobility involves immigrant groups in the United States during the past 150 years. Roughly speaking, migrants have filled the lowest economic rung–unskilled labor–upon arrival, only to be displaced "upward" by a new wave. Although most ethnic groups have remained at the very lowest level for only a short time, they have moved upward economically at different rates, and each wave leaves behind its dregs, who make up an important component of the "disreputable poor" . . . Four factors appear to determine the relative speed of ascent:

1. Economic conditions of demand. The rise of the [black] during World War II and the postwar prosperity has resulted in large part from increased economic opportunities throughout the occupational structure.

2. The degree to which the ethnic group is "held back" through discrimination by the majority group. Every ethnic minority has experienced some discrimination; but for the [black] this has been extreme. Hence [blacks] traditionally have been consigned to manual labor and servant work, and are underrepresented in professional, business, and clerical occupations. Discrimination may be direct, when employers resist employment of [blacks] because they are [blacks]; or indirect, when employers refuse to hire [blacks] because they are less technically qualified for employment (which usually means that they have experienced discrimination elsewhere in the system, especially in education).

3. The internal resources of the ethnic group itself, both financial and socio-cultural. Thus the Jews, Greeks, and Armenians, with a much more highly developed commercial tradition than the Polish, Irish or Italian peasants, possessed an initial advantage in terms of capital and commercial skills. Also the Irish pattern of kinship and community loyalties fit Irishmen particularly for American political-party life, in which the Irish have been notably successful.

4. The continuing strength of particularistic ties. Once an ethnic group makes an inroad on a new higher-level occupation, the successful few will allocate their new talent and resources to bring in people of their own kind to reap the advantages. This particularistic pressure applies in varying degree to every ethnic group.

A final issue arising on the supply side of mobility concerns not the *conditions* under which persons become mobile, but rather the psychological and social *consequences* of mobility once it has occurred. Two potentially disruptive consequences of mobility are: (1) The creation of individuals and groups who have moved upward rapidly according to one set of rewards, but whose advance is constricted in other spheres. The "unemployed intellectuals" so frequently found in the developing areas are an example. Sometimes groups of such persons do constitute a vocal portion of public opinion calling for changes in the pattern of development. In such a case the "supply" side of mobility begins to affect the nature of development itself and hence the "demand" side for mobility . . . (2) The creation of individuals and groups that are forced to move downward by virtue of the changes in the social structure. Examples are handicraft workers displaced by factory production, traditional chiefs displaced by the growth of centralized political structures, peasants displaced by programs of land reform, and so on. Both the irregularly upwardly mobile and the downwardly mobile groups in the developing societies provide many candidates for protest movements. The political stability of these societies depends in large part on the extent of this protest and on the ways in which the constituted authorities respond to such protest . . .

26 *Peter M. Blau*

SOCIAL MOBILITY AND INTERPERSONAL RELATIONS

Social life can be conceptualized as a series of dilemmas. Choices between alternatives that confront people typically require the sacrifice of some ends in the interest of others. In the course of solving one problem, new ones are created. This is not a new idea. It is at least as old as the Socratic method of argument and the Christian doctrine of original sin. It is fundamental to Hegel's and Marx's dialectical approach. . . . Parsons and Shils have made the concept of dilemma a central element in their theory of action,[1] and so has Bales (using the term "strain") in his interaction theory.[2] Merton's concept of dysfunction has similar implications.[3]

Occupational mobility, both upward and downward, poses special dilemmas for establishing interpersonal relations and becoming integrated in the community. Attributes and orientations associated with socio-economic status do not furnish unambiguous criteria of social acceptance for mobile persons. They are marginal men, in some respects out of tune with others both in their new and original strata in the occupational hierarchy. Difficult adaptions are necessary, whether they seek to cultivate friendships among the one group or the other. The upwardly mobile must choose between abandoning hope of translating his occupational success into social acceptance by a more prestigeful group and sacrificing valued social ties and customs in an effort to gain such acceptance. The downwardly mobile must choose between risking rejections for failure to meet social obligations that are beyond his financial resources and resigning himself to losing his affiliation with a more prestigeful group. These conditions are not conducive to the development of integrative social bonds. The central hypothesis of this paper is that the dilemmas faced by mobile individuals in their interpersonal relations inhibit social integration and are responsible for many aspects of their attitudes and conduct.

Reprinted from the *American Sociological Review*, volume 21, No. 3, June, 1956, pp. 290-295, by permission of the author and the American Sociological Association.

Paper read at the annual meeting of the American Sociological Society, August, 1955.

[1] Talcott Parsons and Edward A. Shils (eds.), *Toward a General Theory of Action* (Cambridge: Harvard University Press, 1951), pp. 53-109. See also Talcott Parsons, *The Social System* (New York: Free Press, 1951).

[2] Robert F. Bales, *Interaction Process Analysis* (Cambridge: Addison-Wesley Press, 1949), pp. 831-834, 153-157. See also his article in Talcott Parsons, (eds.), Robert F. Bales and Edward A. Shils, *Working Papers in the Theory of Action* (New York: Free Press, 1953), pp. 111-161.

[3] Robert K. Merton, *Social Theory and Social Structure* (New York: Free Press, 1949), pp. 49-55. See also Peter M. Blau, *The Dynamics of Bureaucracy* (Chicago, University of Chicago Press, 1955).

ACCULTURATION

If the occupational hierarchy is divided into two broad strata, four categories can be distinguished, two of persons who have remained in the stratum in which they originated, and two of those who have experienced occupational mobility: stationary highs, stationary lows, upwardly mobile, and downwardly mobile. Empirical data on the ways of acting and thinking of people in these four categories reveal several distinct patterns. In the first of these, behavior of both mobile groups is intermediate between that of the two non-mobile ones, so that the frequency distributions have the following rank order: stationary highs first, upwardly and downwardly mobile sharing second place, and stationary lows last. Restriction of family size manifests this pattern and so does political behavior. On the average, upwardly and downwardly mobile have fewer children than others in working-class occupations and more children than others in middle-class occupations.[4] Similarly, the upwardly mobile are more likely to vote Republican than people who have remained workers and less likely to do so than those who have originated in the middle class.[5] Finally, the downwardly mobile are less apt to join unions than workers whose parents were workers, too.[6]

This pattern, which may be called the pattern of acculturation, can be explained in terms of the hypothesis that mobile persons are not well integrated in either social class. Without extensive and intimate social contacts, they do not have sufficient opportunity for complete acculturation to the values and style of life of the one group, nor do they continue to experience the full impact of the social constraints of the other. But both groups exert some influence over mobile individuals, since they have, or have had, social contacts with members of both, being placed by economic circumstances amidst the one, while having been socialized among the other. Hence, their behavior is expected to be intermediate between that of the two non-mobile classes. Verification of this explanation of the observed differences would require evidence that the differences tend to disappear if extent of interpersonal relations is held constant.[7] Those mobile persons who have established extensive interpersonal relations with others in their new social class should not differ in their conduct from the rest of its members. Correspondingly, those non-mobile persons who are relatively isolated

4 See Jerzy Berent, "Fertility and Social Mobility," *Population Studies*, 5 (March, 1952), pp. 240-260.

5 See Bernard R. Berelson, Paul F. Lazarsfeld and William N. McPhee, *Voting* (Chicago: University of Chicago Press, 1954), pp. 90-91; and Patricia S. West, "Social Mobility among College Graduates," in Reinhard Bendix and Seymour M. Lipset (eds.), *Class, Status and Power* (New York: Free Press, 1953), p. 478.

6 See Seymour M. Lipset and Joan Gordon, "Mobility and Trade Union Membership," in Bendix and Lipset, *Class, Status, and Power* p. 492.

7 For the methodological principle involved, see Patricia L. Kendall and Paul F. Lazarsfeld, "Problems of Survey Analysis," in Robert K. Merton and Paul F. Lazarsfeld (eds.), *Continuities in Social Research* (New York: Free Press, 1950), pp. 113-196.

should also be prone to manifest deviating tendencies, for only this would show that lack of integration is indeed a main source of deviation. It is, therefore, among the malintegrated non-mobiles that we would expect to find the social striver, the individual who adopts the style of life of a more prestigeful class to which he does not belong, and the disenchanted member of the elite, the individual who adopts the political orientation of a less powerful class than his own.

SOCIAL INSECURITY

In a second pattern, the main contrast is between the mobile and the non-mobile with relatively little difference between socio-economic strata. The rank order of frequency distributions in this case is: downwardly and upwardly mobile sharing first place, stationary lows second, and stationary highs a close third. The extreme position of the mobile dramatically indicates that occupational mobility rather than occupational status is of primary significance here. Prejudice against minorities tends to assume this pattern. Specifically, mobile persons are more likely than non-mobile ones to feel that various minorities are getting too much power, and to stereotype Jews as dishonest and [blacks] as lazy and ignorant.[8] (In nine out of ten comparisons, a larger proportion of the mobile is prejudiced, an average difference of 9 percent.) Quite a different attitude reveals the same pattern, namely, that toward health. Mobile individuals, whatever the direction of their mobility, are more apt to be preoccupied with their health than non-mobile ones, whether in high or in low socio-economic positions.[9]

Feeling threatened by the power of such groups as [blacks] or foreigners and holding hostile stereotypes of them may be considered expressions of insecurity, and so may preoccupation with one's health.[10] If this inference is correct, the hypothesis used to account for the first pattern can also help to explain this second one, different as the two are. For if it is true that the mobile individual is poorly integrated, it follows not only that there is relatively little communication between him and others, but also that he does not receive much social support from them. In the absence of extensive communication, he cannot fully assimilate the system of life of the members of his new social class, with the result that his beliefs and practices are intermediate between theirs and those of the members of his class of origin. Simultaneously, lack of firm social support engenders feelings of insecurity, and this has the result that the mobile person tends to assume the extreme position, not the intermediate one, in respect to those attitudes that constitute expressions of insecurity.

8 See Joseph Greenblum and Leonard I. Pearlin, "Vertical Mobility and Prejudice," in Bendix and Lipset, *Class, Status, and Power* pp. 480-488.

9 See Eugene Litwak, "Conflicting Values and Decision Making," Ph.D. dissertation, Columbia University, 1956.

10 Indeed, Greenblum and Pearlin interpret their findings in this manner; *Class, Status, and Power* pp. 486, 491.

Two kinds of findings support this interpretation. First, relatively direct indications of insecurity–nervousness and mental disorders–reveal the same contrast: the upwardly as well as the downwardly mobile are more troubled by nervousness than the non-mobile,[11] and they are also more prone to become mentally ill.[12] Second, according to the hypothesis, among the non-mobile, too, those with less extensive interpersonal relations should experience greater insecurity. The working class is therefore expected to exhibit more insecurity, since its members have fewer close associates and belong to fewer voluntary associations than the members of the middle class.[13] Indeed, among the non-mobile, the lows are more likely to have prejudiced images of minorities than the highs.[14] Of course, such inferential evidence only makes the hypothesis more plausible. . . .

THE APPEARANCE OF OVERCONFORMITY

In a third pattern, the upwardly mobile and the stationary lows are at the opposite extremes, so that the rank order of frequency distributions is: upwardly mobile first, stationary highs and downwardly mobile sharing second place, and stationary lows last. For example, discrimination against [blacks] as neighbors, in contrast to having prejudiced ideas about them, is more pronounced among stationary highs than stationary lows. The downwardly mobile–persons who have moved from high to low–discriminate just as much as the stationary highs, and the upwardly mobile–those who have moved from low to high–discriminate most of all.[15] In other words, downward mobility seems to have no effect in this instance, while upward mobility has a considerable effect. This is also the case for identification with the conjugal family. Two thirds of the stationary highs are very interested in spending time with their families, compared with less than one half (45 percent) of the stationary lows. The downwardly mobile express such family identification in exactly the same proportion (66 percent) as the highs, and the upwardly mobile do so in greater numbers than any other group (75 percent).[16] Status consciousness, as indicated by a scale that measures concern with the impression made on others, reveals the same pattern.[17]

[11] Litwak, "Conflicting Values."

[12] See A. B. Hollingshead, R. Ellis, and E. Kirby, "Social Mobility and Mental Illness," *American Sociological Review*, 19 (October, 1954), pp. 577-584.

[13] Evidence from various sources on class differences in informal as well as formal social participation is summarized in Genevieve Knupfer "Portrait of the Underdog," *Public Opinion Quarterly*, 11 (Spring, 1947), pp. 103-114.

[14] Greenblum and Pearlin, *Class, Status, and Power.*

[15] Ibid.

[16] Litwak, "Conflicting Values." (Women are more identified with their families than men, but the same pattern of distribution is found among both sexes.)

[17] Ibid.

The combined influences of acculturation and insecurity seem to be responsible for this pattern. Since middle-class people are more inclined than working-class people to discriminate against minorities, to be concerned with social status, and to be identified with their conjugal family, the process of acculturation alone would place the upwardly and downwardly mobile in intermediate positions. But these three items of behavior are also affected by feelings of social insecurity, which often arise consequent to occupational mobility. Just as it engenders prejudicial beliefs about minorities, insecurity intensifies discriminatory tendencies against them. Without integrative social relations to define and support his standing in the community, the individual becomes anxiously concerned about his social status. And the less security a person derives from close relations with friends, colleagues, and neighbors, the more apt he is to turn to his conjugal family for emotional support.

For the downwardly mobile, social insecurity exerts pressures that increase discriminatory practices, status consciousness, and family identification, whereas the process of acculturation to the style of life of the lows exerts pressures in the opposite direction, since the lows discriminate less than the highs, are less status conscious, and identify less with their family. As these pressures in opposite directions neutralize one another, the behavior of the downwardly mobile remains the same as that of members of their class of origin (the highs). For the upwardly mobile, on the other hand, the pressures exerted by insecurity and acculturation to the style of life of the highs are in the same direction. Both kinds of pressure intensify discriminatory tendencies, concern with social status, and attachment to spouse and children. As a result, the upwardly mobile differ widely in these respects from members of their class of origin (the lows) and seem to overconform with the practices prevalent among their new social class (the highs). It may well be that the label of over-conformity often conceals, as it would here, the influences of more complex social forces.[18]

DIMENSIONS OF SOCIAL MOBILITY

So far, the discussion has dealt with detrimental consequences of occupational mobility for integrative social relationships. But a dilemma implies a choice between alternatives as well as impending difficulties. Occupational mobility increases the chances that an individual's social contact will include people who occupy a wide range of socio-economic positions. In the course of selecting from among occasional contacts persons with whom he enters into closer association, the mobile individual therefore chooses, more than the non-mobile does, between associates from different social classes. To be sure, this choice is not

[18] For quite a different example of apparent overconformity which analysis reveals to be the result of more complex sociopsychological processes, see Robert K. Merton and Alice Kitt, "Contributions to the Theory of Reference Group Behavior," in Merton and Lazarsfeld, *Continuities in Social Research*, pp. 70-77. See also Blau, *Dynamics of Bureaucracy* pp. 184-189.

entirely up to him; it also depends on the attitudes of others toward him. Neither members of his former socio-economic stratum nor those of his present one are prone to accept him readily, since his style of life differs in some respect from that which prevails in either group, and this is the very reason for his lesser social integration. Nevertheless, few mobile individuals remain completely isolated, and the effective choice they make by establishing friendly relations with people in one social position rather than another has important implications.

In examining the social status of the companions of the occupationally mobile, we are, in fact, looking at the relationship between two dimensions of social mobility, movement between occupational strata–socio-economic categories–and movement between social classes–prestige groups with distinct styles of life which restrict intimate social access. Persons upwardly mobile in the occupational hierarchy who continue to associate largely with working-class people, and downwardly mobile persons who continue to associate mostly with middle-class people, have changed their economic position but not their social affiliation. Their occupational status and social status do not coincide. Economic changes are transformed into shifts in social affiliation only by those occupationally mobile individuals most of whose friends are members of their terminal social stratum, the middle class in case of the upwardly mobile, the working class in case of the downwardly mobile.[19]

Changes in style of life are expected to be most evident among the latter groups, that is, the occupationally mobile who have shifted their social affiliation. The mobile individual is not likely to be accepted by members of a social class in which he did not originate unless he has started to adapt his behavior to their style of life. Moreover, it is only after he has established social ties with some of his new peers that they and their values can exert a profound influence over his beliefs and practices.

On the other hand, the psychological impact of the experience of occupational success or failure is apt to be most pronounced and persistent for those mobile persons who maintain friendly relations primarily with members of their class of origin and thus do not change their social affiliation. If the upwardly mobile still associates largely with members of his former, lower socio-economic stratum, his occupational success is recurrently called to his attention by contrast with their less fortunate position. But if he loses contact with them and finds his companions among middle-class people, he fails to be reminded of the ascent he has experienced. The same is true for the downwardly mobile, although it has the opposite significance for him. If most of his social life is spent with members of his former, higher stratum, his inability properly to repay social obligations in this circle keeps alive his feelings of deprivation and occupational failure. But if he ceases to associate with them and befriends instead people as poor as himself, he is socially permitted to forget how much more

[19] See W. Lloyd Warner and Paul S. Lunt, *The Social Life of a Modern Community* (New Haven: Yale University Press, 1941), esp. pp. 81-84, 222-224, and 350-355.

fortunate he could have been, and his occupation is not a sign of failure in this group.

In short, regardless of the direction of occupational mobility, interpersonal relations that do not involve a change in social affiliation reinforce the invidious significance of the mobility experience itself, whereas interpersonal relations that do involve a change in social affiliation reduce its significance as a symbol of achievement. His social companions play, therefore, different roles for the occupationally mobile individual before and after he moves into a new social class, although they constitute a point of reference in terms of which he orients his outlook in both situations. As long as he remains attached to his class of origin, the economic position of his friends differs from his present one, and social interaction serves as a continual reminder of his economic success or failure. Once he cultivates friendships with his new economic peers, regular social contacts no longer furnish a contrast of occupational achievement but now provide channels of communication and influence through which he is encouraged to adopt their style of life.

The dilemmas that confront the upwardly and the downwardly mobile in their interpersonal relations are, of course, not identical. Fundamentally, the one has to choose between two kinds of social gratification, the other, between two kinds of social deprivation. Besides, there is another difference that is no less important. If an upwardly mobile person is anxious to become affiliated with a more prestigeful social class, he must make difficult adaptations in his behavior and still is unlikely to attain a fully integrated position. But if he is willing to forego the advantages of a higher social status, he can remain an integrated member of his class of origin and simultaneously enjoy the respect his occupational achievement commands among his less successful associates. Hence, one of the alternatives available to the upwardly mobile preserves social integration. In contrast, both alternatives open to the downwardly mobile inhibit social integration. If he attempts to maintain his affiliation with his class of origin, social interaction with friends whose superior economic position continually revives his sense of frustration and failure undermines his security, his relations with these friends, and thus his integrated position as one of them. And if, to escape from such experiences, he seeks the companionship of members of the working class, differences between his values and theirs make it most difficult for him to accept them unequivocally and to become completely accepted among them. Few people reject an individual simply because he has been unsuccessful in his career, but the predicament of the downwardly mobile is that the social conditions of his existence make it nevertheless likely that he will find himself without close friends.

SUMMARY

To summarize, three implications of the hypothesis that occupational mobility creates special dilemmas for interpersonal relations have been explored. First, if the mobile person is neither well integrated among those whose similar economic position is of long standing, nor among those whose socio-economic status he once shared, his behavior can be expected to deviate from that prevalent in both groups. This expectation is borne out by the finding that many beliefs and practices of the upwardly and of the downwardly mobile are intermediate between those of the stationary highs and those of the stationary lows. Second, the lesser social integration of the mobile is expected to be manifest in stronger feelings of insecurity. Indeed, both categories of mobile persons are found to be more prone than either non-mobile group to express feelings of insecurity in various ways, such as hostility against minority groups. Third, the mobile person's choice of associates determines which of two functions, in addition to that of social support, interaction with regular companions has in his case. Social interaction with members of his class of origin serves to perpetuate the rewarding or threatening meaning of the experience of occupational success or failure, while social interaction with members of his terminal class serves to constrain him to change his style of life.

27 *Ely Chinoy*

THE CHRONOLOGY OF ASPIRATIONS

Despite the cultural admonition to pursue large ambitions, automobile workers focus their aspirations on a narrow range of alternatives. They do not aspire to the top levels of business and industry; they want to become skilled workers, to gain promotion to supervision, to engage in small-scale farming, to open a retail store or a small service establishment of some kind. Since even most of these alternatives entail serious difficulties, however, comparatively few workers persist in hope, remain strong in intention, or persevere in effort. But desire frequently survives.

The varied patterns of desire, intention, plan, and effort revealed by the workers interviewed in Autotown must be seen as only in part the reactions of workers with different personal and social characteristics to similar concrete circumstances. To some extent, these varied patterns of aspirations with regard to both advancement in the plant and out-of-the-shop goals constitute a series linked in time; the same worker may change from one pattern to another as he moves through his occupational career. Indeed, the following hypotheses which have already emerged from our analysis suggest the existence of a more or less typical chronology of aspirations among these workers in a mass-production industry.

1. Many young men who come to work in the factory define their jobs as temporary; they do not expect to remain in the ranks of factory labor.
2. Workers with the most clearly defined out-of-the shop goals are married men in their late twenties or early thirties who have not acquired substantial seniority.
3. Workers are most likely to develop or sustain hope for promotion to supervision if while still relatively young they gain some form of advancement as wage workers, that is, if they secure jobs at the top of the hierarchy of desirability or if they move from nonskilled to skilled work.
4. The longer workers remain in the plant, the less likely are they to muster the initiative to leave, even if they continually talk of doing so.
5. As their seniority increases, workers can look forward to the possibility of individual wage increases (however small they may be) and of transfer to more desirable jobs.
6. The weight of increasing or already heavy family responsibilities keeps men with long seniority from seriously considering out-of-the-shop goals.
7. Workers who do not gain promotion to supervision before the age of forty or thereabouts quickly lose hope because of management's preference for younger men.
8. After workers reach the low wage ceiling at the top of the hierarchy of desirability, they may be satisfied with what they have achieved or, alternatively, they may become bitter and frustrated because of their inability to go further.
9. Some workers, as they approach the age of retirement, may become interested in out-of-the-shop goals as sources of income for their remaining years.

Only a careful longitudinal study could test these hypotheses and expose in full detail the changing patterns of workers' aspirations. But we can, on the basis of our data, fill in the broad outlines of the chronology of aspirations suggested by these hypotheses.[1]

From these propositions it seems clear that workers' aspirations emerge from a process in which hope and desire come to terms with the realities of

[1] Our data consist primarily of retrospective accounts and of comparisons of workers of different ages, supplemented by the material from the dozen workers who were interviewed more than once. Both types of data must, of course, be used with caution, and their inadequacies for constructing a chronological pattern taken into account. Retrospective accounts are likely to contain some distortion of past events and attitudes; age comparisons suffer from the changing historical contexts in which men of different generations grow up and pursue their occupational careers.

working-class life. But this process is not one which seems simply the gradual dissolution of originally large expectations as obstacles to advancement become evident. Instead we find that workers must repeatedly accommodate new desires generated by fresh stimuli to the concrete circumstances they face at different stages of their occupational careers.

The changing patterns of workers' aspirations therefore bear little resemblance to the popular stereotype of single-minded striving toward ambitious goals. It may well be that the rational tradition in our culture has continually overplayed man's singleness of purpose, that, encouraged by the pioneer ethos of self-help, we have overstressed the power of individual effort against the press of circumstances. It is quite likely that finding oneself vocationally involves in most cases considerable floundering among available alternatives, that few men exhibit the terrible tenacity of Henry Ford or the elder Rockefeller. It seems altogether possible that for men on the level of wage labor, the period of floundering lasts longer, perhaps indefinitely, as they pitch such ambitions as they muster against the limited opportunities available to them.

The process of reconciling desire with reality begins early for industrial workers. In the public schools, if not at home, the working-class youth is repeatedly exposed to the values of success, the belief in the existence of opportunity for all, and the varied prescriptions for getting on in the world. "We were talking about Abe Lincoln in school and how he worked himself up," said the eighteen-year-old son of a machine-operator who had performed the same kind of work in the factory for eighteen years. "That shows that working yourself up depends on the person, not on the chances you have." But as soon as he leaves school, or even before, the working-class youth must come to terms with a world of limited opportunity where there are few chances. Lacking financial resources, he cannot look forward to the possibility of professional training, or even to four years of college which would widen his perspectives and increase his skills. He cannot step into a family business or acquire easily the funds with which to launch one of his own. As soon as his education ends, he must find some kind of job. And in Autotown even a large proportion of high-school graduates will probably become factory workers; a third of all employed persons in the city were engaged in factory labor of some kind, primarily in the four large automobile plants.

Many working-class boys therefore give up dreams of a rich and exciting occupational future—if they ever had such dreams—even before taking their first full-time job. In a questionnaire submitted to all boys about to graduate from Autotown's two high schools in June 1947 and June 1948, the question was asked: "If you could do what you wanted to what occupation would you choose?" Forty percent of all working-class boys (47 of 118) had no choice or chose occupations which carried comparatively little prestige and provided only limited rewards. (Occupations included in those with low prestige and low rewards were skilled work, clerical jobs, military service, and miscellaneous jobs which required no training. Those with high prestige and high rewards were the professions, technical and semiprofessional occupations, art and literature, scientific farming, and business.) Only 23 percent of the middle-class boys, on the other hand, were without a choice or chose low-prestige, low-reward occupations, indicating a statistically significant difference.[2] When asked about their actual intentions, 40 percent of the working-class boys said that they merely intended to "look for a job," without specifying any particular kind of job. Another 20 percent intended to learn a skilled trade, to apply for some definite manual job which did not require previous training, or to enlist in the armed services. These figures compare with 15 and 12 percent respectively for boys of middle-class origin.

Some working-class boys, particularly those without academic aptitudes or interest, may quit school as soon as they are able to secure a job since they feel that they will find themselves in the factory eventually, even if they do graduate from high school. They can no longer do as their parents might have done in the past, leave school in order to learn a trade, since admission to formal apprentice training for any trade now usually requires a high-school diploma. The jobs they find, therefore, promise little for the future.

Many working-class boys only come to grips with vocational reality when they finally graduate from high school. Stimulated to a high level of aspiration by the mass media, encouraged by parents and, sometimes, by teachers, they entertain inflated ambitions until the time when they must choose a definite course of action. For example, a third of the boys whose parents were manual workers reported that they intended to go to college. While some boys with requisite academic abilities do muster the necessary financial resources and enter college, most of them in fact find themselves looking for a job after they graduate from high school. According to high school officials, less than a third of all graduates from Autotown's two high schools go to college, most of them probably from middle-class families. An even smaller proportion even complete work for a degree. It is therefore highly probable that a very large proportion of those working-class boys who said that they intended to go to college did not do so.

The quick surrender by working-class youth to the difficulties they face is not necessarily forced or unwilling. Although they are encouraged to focus their aspirations into a long future and to make present sacrifices for the sake of eventual rewards, they are chiefly concerned with immediate gratifications. They may verbally profess to be concerned with occupational success and advancement (as did 14 working-class boys who were interviewed), but they are likely to be more interested in "having a good time" or "having fun." They want to "go

[2] A. B. Hollingshead reports similar findings in his discussion of class differences in the levels of aspiration among teen-age youth. See *Elmtown's Youth* (New York: Wiley, 1949), pp. 282-287. Most studies of job choice among high school students have stressed the generally inflated character of youthful aspirations and the inevitable comedown rather than noting the differences in the extent to which students from different classes respond to the American Dream. See, for example, D. S. Miller and W. H. Form, *Industrial Sociology* (New York: Harper & Row, 1951), pp. 589-592.

out," to have girl friends, to travel, to own a car or a motorcycle. When asked if "fun" would be given up in order to take a job which might lead to advancement in the future, an eighteen-year-old boy about to graduate from high school answered: "Do you want me to tell you the truth? I'd rather have fun."

The concern with immediate gratifications unrelated to one's occupation is encouraged by prevalent values in American society. The massed apparatus of commercial advertising incessantly stimulates the desire for things which are immediately available—on the installment plan, if necessary. Together with movies, television, radio, and magazines, advertising sets up attractive—and expensive—models of leisure and recreation. And these models have become increasingly important as American culture has shifted from a central concern with the values of production to the values of consumption.[3] In a long-range sense, the pecuniary animus of the culture backfires among working-class youth, for the desire for maximum income, when linked with an emphasis upon immediate satisfaction in the sphere of consumption, leads to decisions which virtually eliminate the possibility of a steadily increasing income in the future. "Sometimes I say to myself," said a thirty-year-old machine-operator who could have attended college but had instead gone to work in the factory, " . . . you could have been somebody . . . if you hadn't been so interested in the almighty dollar."

Since "fun" in this world of commercialized entertainment requires money, the immediate objective becomes a well-paid job, a goal most easily achieved by going to work in an automobile plant. Within a few months the son of an automobile worker who goes to work in the factory may be earning as much as his father, who may have been there for twenty years. Despite the low status of factory work and the hope frequently expressed by automobile workers that their sons will not follow in their steps, many boys head for factory personnel offices as soon as they are old enough or as soon as they finish high school. And others find themselves seeking factory employment after having tried other, less remunerative jobs.

Many of these young workers are aware of the dead-end character of most factory jobs. "You don't get advanced by going in the factory; there's no future there," said one high-school senior whose father had spent his entire adult life in the city's automobile factories. When they do go into the factory, they therefore define their jobs as temporary, particularly if they have earned a high-school diploma. They say that they intend to stay in the factory only until a promising opportunity comes along. In this fashion they can maintain the impression, both for themselves and for others, that they still intend to get ahead, that they are still ambitious.

Because the first job is frequently on the assembly line, these young workers

[3] See D. Riesman: *The Lonely Crowd* (New Haven: Yale University Press, 1950); and L. Lowenthal: "Biographies in Popular Magazines," in P. F. Lazarsfeld and F. Stanton (eds.), *Radio Research, 1942-1943* (New York: Duell, Sloan and Pearce, 1944), pp. 507-520.

do not quickly become satisfied. They soon seek ways of gaining a more desirable job in the factory. But beyond that limited goal they pay little attention to the possibilities of advancement. They are too young to expect promotion to supervision. They are unwilling to undertake apprentice training, in part because they would have to accept lower wages temporarily, in part because they may define factory work itself as temporary.

Even if these young workers say that they intend, eventually, to "go into business," they make no definite plans. Their main interest lies in the things they do in their leisure hours. For example, a twenty-two-year-old single worker in the plant cared little for his work, although he boasted that he had managed to secure a transfer from the assembly line to a job which consisted of driving completed cars off the end of the line. He had gained this transfer by threatening to quit in a period of acute labor shortage. (Since he had no family responsibilities, he probably would have quit and gone to work in some other factory if he had not been transferred.) He had not thought of the possibility of foremanship or of learning a trade. He insisted, however, that he would some day leave the factory—"I don't intend to stay here forever," he said—but he had no concrete objectives or plans. His chief interests were baseball, girls, and his car. He had recently bought a new A.B.C. car, but he wanted to replace it with the model which was scheduled to appear at the beginning of the following year. One reason for going to work in the A.B.C. plant rather than elsewhere was the fact that A.B.C. employees with more than six months' seniority were given a large discount if they bought a new car.

Several older workers gave retrospective accounts of similar behavior which had preceded their "settling down." A forty-year-old union officer commented:

> Most young fellows are just like I was, they can't see ahead of their noses. They just want to have a good time and the devil take the rest of it. If they can make more money that's where they'll go. They don't think about anything else . . .

"Before I got married," said a thirty-nine-year-old oiler (whose work consisted of oiling moving parts of large machines, a nonskilled job), "I was only interested in three things, getting paid on Saturday, getting drunk on Saturday night, and having a girl." Others are undoubtedly more sober and conservative in their interests, but their attitudes toward their work and their future are much the same: as long as the pay is good and the job not too demanding or difficult, they are content to go along from day to day seeking their pleasures in leisure hours, careless about the future.

It seems a tenable hypothesis that this pattern of youthful aspirations represents a model type which applies to a substantial proportion of working-class youth, as well as those lower-middle-class boys who become nonskilled factory workers. The chief deviation from this pattern is the youth who decides early to become a skilled worker, or who decides after a short tenure in the factory to apply for apprentice training. His ambitions do not focus on rich images of success, but on the promise of a reasonable income, a respected status in the community, and a job which provides interesting work.

These latter values conflict, however, with the immediate gratifications which can be gained by going to work in the factory as a nonskilled laborer. The teen-age working-class youth is not likely to make the sacrifice of present satisfaction unless his aspirations gain support from a personally significant model or are encouraged by persons whom he respects, admires, or loves. One thirty-one-year-old skilled worker whose father had also been a skilled worker commented:

> When I was an apprentice I was torn by two desires. One was to go to work on the line like the rest of my friends and make some money. But there's no future in that. The other was to stick to the apprenticeship in hopes of getting some place. Seeing the way my dad worked through—even if he had his troubles and lost his home—I felt that it paid my father dividends anyway.

It is noteworthy that 39 percent of all apprentices registered with the Autotown Technical School in 1947[4] (50 of 129) were sons of skilled workers; only 11 percent were the sons of nonskilled workers. The rest came from the urban lower-middle class or from farm families.

The typical attitudes of young nonskilled workers toward jobs, advancement, and the future persist until marriage or, perhaps, parenthood. With the assumption of family responsibilities, workers tend to become actively concerned about the possibilities of advancement. "When I got married," said the oiler quoted above, "I suddenly realized that I'd better do something or I was really going to be stuck." The immediate need for more money leads workers to consider seriously the alternatives open to them and the arrival of children generates a fresh interest in the future.

By the time these workers marry and have children, however, they have already made decisions which limit the alternatives open to them. Some left high school in order to take jobs which offer little prospect of advancement; others went willingly into an automobile plant after graduating. Now they find that they lack the training which is requisite for advancement in the corporate hierarchy. They have gained no skills which can be used outside the factory. They have not added to their scanty knowledge about the prerequisites and potentialities of alternative jobs. Nor, in their concern with buying a car or having a good time, have they tried to acquire the resources which might enable them to buy a profitable farm or start a successful business.

The responsibilities of marriage and the uncertainties facing the non-skilled worker tend to keep attention focusing on the present and to counterbalance the new stimuli to planning for the future. The pressure of the weekly grocery bill,

4 This includes all apprentices in the city except those in the A.B.C. apprentice program. The A.B.C. plant provided its own classroom instruction for apprentices; all other apprentices received their classroom instruction at the Autotown Technical School.

the rent or mortgage payment, installments on a refrigerator or a washing machine or vacuum cleaner, the need for a new pair of work pants or a pair of shoes for a child, the doctor's bill for a tonsillectomy, all keep life on a pay-day-to-pay-day basis. The future, for men in an industry known for irregular employment, bristles with threats. They are not usually well prepared to cope with unemployment or with sickness and accident, the normal hazards of life. And the future is still resonant with echoes of the depression of the 1930's; men were employed by the WPA in Autotown until the eve of war in 1941. Workers may conclude, therefore, that "it doesn't pay to think about the future," as a thirty-one-year-old line-tender put it.

As unmarried men without responsibility, these workers were careless about the future; now they are forced into taking a defensive stance toward the future despite the stimulus to aspiration and effort. There is no change, therefore, in the pattern of life to which they have been accustomed; life's rhythms of tension and release remain short, from week-end to week-end, from one good time to another. Life may occasionally be pointed toward a vacation a few months ahead, toward Christmas or Easter, toward a birthday or some other family celebration. But long-run desires and expectations are avoided as both past and future are minimized and life is compressed into the week's routine.

Lacking occupational skills and financial resources, most workers confine their aspirations to the limited array of alternatives we have already examined. Since they are unwilling or unable to plan for the long future, they see these goals as isolated small moves rather than as part of a long-range plan. Only one worker, a would-be businessman, talked of becoming rich. He was a twenty-nine-year-old toolmaker who was about to open his own tool-and-die shop. Only the two young workers who intended to go to college could see in their plans the beginning of a career. Unlike the professional or the salaried officeholder, the factory worker does not see his present job as part of a career pattern which channels his aspirations and sustains his hope. Unlike the businessman, he has no ever beckoning goal of increasing sales and expanding profits to stimulate his efforts.

Hope for one or another of the alternatives on which workers do focus their aspirations may, for a while, run high. Despite the obstacles in their path, some workers are determined and purposeful. The period shortly after marriage when workers become concerned with their future, when they are at or near their physical peak, when family responsibilities may still serve as a stimulant to ambition and effort rather than as a brake, is probably the time of maximum ambition and of greatest expectation, for skilled as well as nonskilled workers. . . . Four of the six workers who thought they might be chosen as foremen were about thirty years old and five of the eight who had taken positive steps toward out-of-the-shop goals were in their twenties or early thirties. (Two of these eight . . . were over sixty years of age and were chiefly concerned with gaining a secure income for their remaining years.)

But many workers see little reason for hope when they assay the possibilities of advancement in the factory and examine the problems and the risks inherent in business or farming. If they have not already gained some advancement on the level of wage labor, they are not likely to see any prospect of promotion to supervision. Indeed, if they have not had an opportunity to learn how to carry responsibility and exercise authority, they are not likely, even if offered promotion, to be willing to take on the problems which they know are inherent in the foreman's role. In order to start a business or buy a farm, one needs money; the family responsibilities which stimulate ambition also make it difficult to save. If they do manage to start a business or buy a farm, not only must they risk their savings, they must also surrender whatever security their seniority in the plant gives them. (One might therefore expect that workers most intent on leaving the factory would be those who, for one reason or another, have not been in the plant for very long. Five of the eight workers with definite out-of-the-shop plans had been there for less than a year.)

Workers who feel impelled to seek advancement despite the limited opportunities in the factory and the risks inherent in leaving tend to dilute their aspirations to a loose welter of hopes and a medley of alternative plans. And workers whose insistent hopes and positive efforts do not bear quick fruit give up their ambitions after a while and cast about as vaguely and uncertainly as the others. Without a "life-plan" which commits them to follow a series of more or less recognized steps,[5] workers simultaneously entertain alternative goals, or they continually shift their attention from one goal to another, usually without investing much hope or effort in any particular one.

While waiting for advancement in the factory which may not come and, in any case, is largely contingent upon forces over which they have little or no control, workers frequently consider the possibility of going into business or buying a farm, as twenty-three of the sixty-two workers interviewed were doing. Even those who are hopeful about advancement in the plant recognized the uncertainties involved and may therefore look elsewhere at the same time. Thus four of the six workers who felt that they would eventually become foremen had also thought of leaving the factory and said that they planned to "go into business" if they did not gain the desired promotion within some reasonable time. (None had been promoted and all were still in the plant in June 1951.)

Interest in out-of-the-shop goals usually represents the desire for escape from the factory rather than a positive search for success. Such interest is, therefore, particularly susceptible to changes in workers' job status and the conditions of work. These changes bear no positive relationship to the objective possibilities of success or failure in business or farming or to the nature of workers' resources or skills. Interest and, in some cases, action may therefore be stimulated—or inhibited—at the wrong time.

Thus business and farming ambitions are frequently whipsawed by changes

[5] See K. Mannheim: *Man and Society in an Age of Reconstruction* (New York: Harcourt Brace Jovanovich, 1944), p. 56, 104n.

in general business conditions. In the upward phase of the business cycle, when production is being maintained at a high level or is increasing and workers are regularly employed, the desire to leave the factory is at a minimum even though opportunities for small business may be at their best. When production falls off and temporary layoffs and short workweeks occur, interest in out-of-the-shop goals increases even though workers' resources are being rapidly drained away and the chances of business failure are especially high.

Interest in out-of-the-shop goals, as well as hope for advancement in the factory, may also fluctuate with variations in workers' feelings that occurs without reference to changes in their jobs. For example, a welder, when first interviewed, complained about the difficulties in his job and was anxious to leave the factory despite his lack of savings and the importance he attached to his twelve years of seniority. He had been working on the second shift (4:00 P.M. to 12:30 A.M.) when interviewed and was obviously tired and irritable. When interviewed again several weeks later, he was on the first shift (workers in most departments changed shifts every four weeks), rested, and in much better spirits. He no longer complained about his job, and though he still talked about leaving the factory "some day," he did so without force or urgency.

In a moment of hope, stimulated by some unexpected suggestion, workers may undertake a correspondence course in salesmanship, in automobile repairing, in accounting, in foremanship. (Four workers volunteered the information that they had once taken some kind of correspondence course; two others were doing so at the time they were interviewed.) In a moment of discouragement, the course is dropped, the money invested in it lost completely. The tentative and uncertain character of such efforts was evident in the case of one worker who quickly asked the interviewer if he thought there was much value in the correspondence course in foremanship and supervision he was taking at the cost of $120. Two months later he dropped the course because he was not "getting anything out of it." At a time when things in the factory seem to be at their worst, workers may look into farm prices, search for a small business of some kind, perhaps answer advertisements for salesmen or look for other factory jobs. But as their mood changes, the search is ended, negotiations that may have been begun are broken off, workers fail to follow up the steps they have already taken.

It seems likely that interest in out-of-the-shop goals may be endlessly renewed by the constant turnover among workers, some of whom do go into business, farming, or white-collar jobs. (The weekly newspaper published by the Autotown C.I.O. Council frequently featured stories about union members who had gone into business for themselves.) But interest, when unsupported by knowledge or resources, rarely remains focused on one particular objective for very long. Since many workers plan to do "something" "as soon as things get better," "if I can save up a few hundred dollars," or "when I get straightened out," they entertain in usually disorderly succession various out-of-the-shop goals which are critically scrutinized and rejected as impractical or are mulled over, dreamed about, vaguely examined, and eventually permitted to fade away. This pattern emerged clearly in the case of one worker who was interviewed three times. In the first interview he said that he was thinking of "buying some tourist property up north." When asked how much money he would need and how much he had, he admitted that he did not know how much he would need, had no savings, and did not expect to save any money within the near future. A month later he was talking of a turkey farm, again with little attention to the concrete problems he would face. A year later he said that he had been thinking of a "bee farm," but that he had finally given up any thought of leaving the plant.

The pattern of shifting goals and tentative plans may persist for the major part of a worker's occupational life. Occasionally plans congeal into positive action under the impact of a particularly strong stimulus or under the cumulative pressure of a series of events. Frequently these actions are abortive. Thus a thirty-one-year-old worker with twelve years of seniority who had been moved after the war from a job as a toolmaker-upgrader to an unskilled maintenance job to the paint line angrily left the factory in order to take a job in a small chemical plant in which his father worked, even though this move meant lower wages. Two years later he was back in the A.B.C. plant as a machine-operator, but now without the long seniority he had once had. A bitter disagreement with the foreman, an unresolved grievance, a job assignment to which he objects, these and many other specific occurrences can provoke a worker into quitting, even though he must start looking for another job without much likelihood of gaining any basic improvement. He may, as many have done, find himself back eventually at the same kind of work in the same plant.

The longer workers remain in the plant, the less seriously do they consider the possibility of leaving, even though they recognize that they are probably going to remain on the level of wage labor in the factory.Eventually they cease to entertain out-of-the-shop goals, accept the fact that they will remain in the factory, and confine their aspirations to a better job in the plant. This shift does not occur at any particular age; it may take place when a worker is thirty, it may not occur until he is fifty or even older. In some instances, of course, it may never occur. And a last burst of interest in business may appear as workers approach the age of retirement when, bedeviled by the economic problems of old age, they seek methods of supplementing whatever pension they are entitled to.

Workers give up their desire to leave the factory as they come to realize that they are not likely to be successful in business or farming and are not likely to gain much merely by changing jobs. At the same time they come to place a heavy stress upon the security provided by long seniority in the plant. This disappearance of ambition does not necessarily mean disappointment or frustration, however. Skilled workers, for example, may never consider any other alternative to their factory jobs, although many do in as amorphous a manner as do most nonskilled workers. They can count on a comparatively good income with a measure of security from a relatively interesting and satisfying job. The worker who manages to become skilled through some sort of upgrading program, formal or informal, may give up his out-of-the-shop goals and resign himself contentedly to what he has achieved. One worker, for example, was intent on buying a farm when he was interviewed in 1947. But in 1951, after he had been recalled to the electrician's job he had held as an upgrader during the war, he was no longer thinking of leaving the factory. Even nonskilled workers who manage to secure jobs at the top of the informal hierarchy of desirability may be reasonably satisfied, particularly if their ambitions were not set very high at the outset, if they have not felt pressure from their families to go into business or seek a better job elsewhere, or if they have not been stimulated by the example of friends or relatives who have done well economically.

Some workers, scarred by experience, resign themselves to a future in the factory without satisfaction, but without resentment. They no longer demand much of life except for some kind of job and some assurance that they can keep it. One fifty-two-year-old line-tender, for example, had not held a regular job from 1932 until 1941; he had tried subsistence farming, small businesses of various kinds, and had worked at a wide variety of manual jobs. Now he was grateful to have a job, although he did not like assembly-line work, and he was hoping to be permitted to remain in the factory without being disturbed or forced to look for work again.

But if workers come to feel that they must stay in the factory because there is no opportunity in business or farming, if they do not have desirable jobs in the plant, if they began their careers with large ambitions and high hopes, or if they have seen relatives or friends "get ahead in the world," then their acceptance of a future in the factory is accompanied by bitterness and resentment aimed at themselves, at others, or at the world in general.

AUTHOR INDEX

SUBJECT INDEX